ROMANTICISM AND TIME

Romanticism and Time

Literary Temporalities

Edited by
Sophie Laniel-Musitelli and Céline Sabiron

https://www.openbookpublishers.com

© 2021 Sophie Laniel-Musitelli and Céline Sabiron. Copyright of individual chapters is maintained by the chapter's author.

This work is licensed under a Creative Commons Attribution 4.0 International license (CC BY 4.0). This license allows you to share, copy, distribute and transmit the work; to adapt the work and to make commercial use of the work providing attribution is made to the authors (but not in any way that suggests that they endorse you or your use of the work). Attribution should include the following information:

Sophie Laniel-Musitelli and Céline Sabiron (eds), *Romanticism and Time*. Cambridge, UK: Open Book Publishers, 2021. https://doi.org/10.11647/OBP.0232

Copyright and permissions for the reuse of many of the images included in this publication differ from the above. This information is provided in the captions and in the list of illustrations.

In order to access detailed and updated information on the license, please visit https://doi.org/10.11647/OBP.0232#copyright. Further details about CC BY licenses are available at http://creativecommons.org/licenses/by/4.0/

All external links were active at the time of publication unless otherwise stated and have been archived via the Internet Archive Wayback Machine at https://archive.org/web

Digital material and resources associated with this volume are available at https://doi.org/10.11647/OBP.0232#resources

Every effort has been made to identify and contact copyright holders and any omission or error will be corrected if notification is made to the publisher.

This book has been published with the support of the Institut Universitaire de France. Univ. Lille, ULR 4074—CECILLE—Centre d'Études en Civilisations, Langues et Lettres Étrangères, F-59000 Lille, France.

ISBN Paperback: 978-1-80064-071-9
ISBN Hardback: 978-1-80064-072-6
ISBN Digital (PDF): 978-1-80064-073-3
ISBN Digital ebook (epub): 978-1-80064-074-0
ISBN Digital ebook (mobi): 978-1-80064-075-7
ISBN Digital (XML): 978-1-80064-076-4
DOI: 10.11647/OBP.0232

Cover Image: J.M.W Turner, *Ancient Italy—Ovid Banished from Rome* (1838). Wikimedia, https://commons.wikimedia.org/wiki/File:Turner_Ovid_Banished_from_Rome.jpg.
Cover Design by Anna Gatti.

Contents

Acknowledgements		vii
Introduction: The Times of Romanticism		ix
Sophie Laniel-Musitelli and Céline Sabiron		
Section I: Restoration, Revival, and Revolution across Romantic Europe		1
1.	'Future Restoration' Paul Hamilton	3
2.	'Anthropocene Temporalities and British Romantic Poetry' Evan Gottlieb	25
3.	'Beethoven: Revolutionary Transformations' Gregory Dart	49
Section II: Romantic Conceptions of Time		75
4.	'The Temporality of the Soul: Immanent Conceptions of Time in Wordsworth and Byron' Ralf Haekel	77
5.	'"Footing slow across a silent plain": Time and Walking in Keatsian Poetics' Oriane Monthéard	97
Section III: The Poetics of Time		119
6.	'Contracting Time: John Clare's *The Shepherd's Calendar*' Lily Dessau	121
7.	'Book-Time in Charles Lamb and Washington Irving' Matthew Redmond	145
8.	'"a disciple of Albertus Magnus [...] in the eighteenth century": Anachronism and Anachrony in *Frankenstein*' Anne Rouhette	163

Section IV: Persistence and Afterlives — 181

9. 'Heaps of Time in Beckett and Shelley' — 183
   Laura Quinney

10. '"Thy Wreck a Glory": Venice, Subjectivity, and Temporality in Byron and Shelley and the Post-Romantic Imagination' — 205
    Mark Sandy

Section V: Romanticism and Periodisation — 225

'Romanticism and Periodisation: A Roundtable' — 227
David Duff, Nicholas Halmi, Laurent Folliot, Martin Procházka, and Fiona Stafford

List of Contributors — 273

List of Figures — 279

Index — 281

Acknowledgements

This book originates from an international conference on 'Romanticism and Time' held at the Université de Lille in November 2018 and organised jointly by the French Society for the Study of British Romanticism (SERA) and the Universités de Lille and Lorraine. Our warm thanks go to the SERA, who set this project in motion, and to the scientific committee of the Romanticism and Time conference, Caroline Bertonèche, Mathieu Duplay, Thomas Dutoit, Jean-Marie Fournier, and Marc Porée, for their guidance. We are grateful to our institutions, the Université de Lille and the Université de Lorraine, and, in particular, to our research centres CÉCILLE[1] and IDEA[2], who supported the project from the start. We are particularly thankful to Marie-France Pilarski and Bruno Legrand (Université de Lille) for their invaluable help throughout the project and to Isabelle Gaudy-Campbell (Université de Lorraine) for welcoming this project, as well as for her trust and support.

We are also grateful to Nicholas Roe and Ann Winnicombe for granting us permission to reprint a revised version of section II from Mark Sandy's article in the *Romanticism* online issue on 'Light' (22. 3. 2016: https://doi.org/10.3366/rom.2016.0287). We would also like to thank Sarah Wootton for permission to reprint revised parts of Mark Sandy's chapter from *Venice and the Cultural Imagination* (Abingdon and New York: Pickering & Chatto, 2012) as well as Kostas Boyiopoulos and Michael Shallcross for permission to reprint revised sections of Mark Sandy's essay in *Aphoristic Modernity: 1880 to the Present* (Leiden and Boston: Brill, 2020). The research for Martin Procházka's contribution was supported by the European Regional Development Fund Project

---

1   Univ. Lille, ULR 4074 – CECILLE – Centre d'Études en Civilisations, Langues et Lettres Étrangères, F-59000 Lille, France.
2   Univ. Lorraine, UR 2338 – IDEA – Interdisciplinarité Dans les Études Anglophones, F-54000 Nancy, France.

'Creativity and Adaptability as Conditions of the Success of Europe in an Interrelated World' (No. CZ.02.1.01/0.0/0.0/16_019/ 0000734). We are deeply thankful to the Institut Universitaire de France who supported the Romanticism and Time conference and this publication.

Finally, we would like to express our sincerest thanks and gratitude to our contributors for committing their considerable talent, energy, and enthusiasm to this project.

Introduction:
The Times of Romanticism

Sophie Laniel-Musitelli[1] and Céline Sabiron[2]

'Eternity is in love with the productions of time'.[3]

In this volume, we have decided to take Blake's aphorism as an invitation to see Romantic writing as a 'production of time'; to look for the work of time within Romantic literature. One of the aims of this collection is to understand Romanticism as the product of its own time, in its ability to reflect history and in the emergence of its specific poetics through time. Blake's words can also be read as a meditation on poetics unfolding 'in time': on poetic form as the product of rhyme and rhythm. Yet, if we attend to the reversibility that characterises Blake's 'Proverbs of Hell', this aphorism also offers a vision of Romanticism as an active 'production of time', not only registering the passing of time but also shaping conceptions of time and making history. Romantic writing then also appears as an art of time, creating new representations of temporal phenomena and generating new modes of time-consciousness. The contributions in this collection, which includes a selection of revised papers from the 'Romanticism and Time' conference as well as specially

---

1   Université de Lille and Institut Universitaire de France. Univ. Lille, ULR 4074—CECILLE—Centre d'Études en Civilisations Langues et Lettres Etrangères, F-59000 Lille, France and Institut Universitaire de France (IUF).
2   Université de Lorraine. Univ. Lorraine, UR 2338—IDEA—Interdisciplinarité Dans les Études Anglophones, F-54000 Nancy.
3   William Blake, 'Proverbs of Hell', l. 10, in *The Complete Poetry & Prose of William Blake*, ed. by David Erdman (New York: Random House, 1988), p. 36.

commissioned essays,⁴ are thus held together by the common ambition to study Romantic writing as 'authentically temporal':⁵ as a process in time that displays a form of agency over time.

This collection explores the ways in which British Romantic literature creates its own sense of time, from the end of the eighteenth century to the mid-nineteenth century, from William Blake, William Wordsworth, John Keats, Lord Byron, and Percy Shelley, to John Clare and Samuel Rogers, raising the question of the evolution of the Romantic canon over time. The presence of poets such as Clare and Rogers, who eluded academia's field of vision for so long, exposes our own temporal locatedness as academics. It gestures towards the writers who still elude that field of vision and towards those who are surreptitiously drifting out of it. The essays are bound by a common approach to the creative relations Romanticism entertains with the notion of time, with an emphasis on poetry.⁶ It aims at offering a reflection on the role of poetic writing as a mode of perception of time. The Romantics explored the possibilities opened up by poetry as a form of time, as experiences of time were reflected but also took shape within poetic forms.

Nevertheless, the scope of this collection is not limited to the realm of poetry. The affinities between temporality and narrative, but also between temporality and the order of reason in essay-writing manifest themselves in the multiple temporalities of prose.⁷ This is why this volume also looks into the temporalities of Romantic novels and essays, from Mary Shelley to Charles Lamb and William Hazlitt. Furthermore, some of our contributors were particularly sensitive to the Romantics' eager exploration of other forms of artistic manipulation of time, and

---

4   The conference was held in November 2018 and organised jointly by the French Society for the Study of British Romanticism and by the Universités de Lille and Lorraine, with the support of the Institut Universitaire de France.
5   Paul De Man, *Blindness and Insight: Essays in the Rhetoric of Contemporary Criticism*, 2nd ed. (London: Routledge, 1983), p. 206.
6   For a wide-ranging, and yet very detailed, introduction to Romantic poetry analysed in its larger social, cultural, geographical and political contexts, see Fiona Stafford, *Reading Romantic Poetry* (Oxford: Wiley-Blackwell, 2012), https://onlinelibrary.wiley.com/doi/book/10.1002/9781118228104
7   See for instance Paul Ricœur, *Temps et récit, I. L'intrigue et le récit historique* (Paris: Seuil, 1983) and Jacques Rancière, *Les mots de l'histoire : Essai de poétique du savoir* (Paris: Seuil, 1992).

to their tropism towards music in particular, hence the place given to Beethoven's *Fidelio* in Section I.

Few have attempted to consider the various temporalities of Romanticism as a form of cross-fertilisation between nations, with the notable exception of Martin Procházka, Nicholas Halmi and Paul Hamilton,[8] also contributors to this volume. We share their ambition to study the Romantic poetics of history as a European phenomenon. As 'a literature that represents its own fluid conditions of becoming',[9] Romanticism is also a process in time, constructed by various generations of artists and critics in a complex dynamic of transience and persistence. With the aim of confronting British Romanticism with some of its later European counterparts, some chapters explore the dialogues between Byron and Nietzsche, and between Shelley and Beckett. Challenging the linearity of deterministic conceptions of influence, Romantic texts experiment with creative modes of intertextuality, inventing their origins and imagining their legacies. This volume thus offers a vision of Romanticism as a moment of 'obstinate questionings' of the temporalities of literature,[10] as its uncanny persistence into later literary movements generates turbulence in the course of traditional literary history.

In its various instantiations in time and across borders, Romanticism 'defines itself through a process of self-dissemination which leaves each moment of its instantiation characteristically fragmentary',[11] raising epistemological questions for the field of literary studies and its reliance on periodisation. The proceedings of the roundtable 'Romanticism and Periodisation', edited by David Duff, interrogate our critical practices,

---

8   See in particular Martin Procházka's 2005 comparative studies of European, American and Czech Romanticism in *Romantismus a romantismy* (Romanticism and Romanticisms), ed. by Martin Procházka and Zdeněk Hrbata (Nakladatel: Karolinum, 2005); Nicholas Halmi's *The Genealogy of the Romantic Symbol* (Oxford: Oxford University Press, 2007), https://doi.org/10.1093/acprof:oso/9780199212415.001.0001, in which he pointed at the interrelation between German philosophically-minded Romanticists and English poets like Wordsworth or Shelley in their wish to re-enchant the world; and Paul Hamilton, *Realpoetik: European Romanticism and Literary Politics* (Oxford: Oxford University Press, 2013), https://doi.org/10.1093/acprof:oso/9780199686179.001.0001

9   Christopher Miller, *The Invention of Evening: Perception and Time in Romantic Poetry* (Cambridge: Cambridge University Press, 2006), p. 3, https://doi.org/10.1017/cbo9780511720031

10 Percy Shelley, 'Alastor', l. 26, in *Shelley's Poetry and Prose*, ed. by Donald Reiman and Neil Fraistat, 2nd ed. (New York: Norton, 2002), p. 74.

11 Hamilton, *Realpoetik*, p. 7.

and fascination for Romantic presences, persistence, and legacies.[12] In its ability to bend the course of literary chronologies, Romanticism thus appears as essentially untimely.

This volume looks for Romanticism as a movement out of time: generated by and precipitating the acceleration of history. The close readings here trace the ways in which Romantic 'time disseminates itself'[13] into widely varying scales, paces, and planes, in an age of political, industrial, and epistemological revolutions. Such a 'vertiginous temporality'[14] manifests itself in scalar discrepancies, from the span of a lifetime to unfathomable geological and astronomical sequences, especially in the passage from the timeless and tabular representation of a Linnean nature to the more arrow-like conception of time in pre-evolutionist theories. The emergence of Romanticism corresponds to the moment when geological time and human time collide, 'as the Anthropocene simultaneously forces human and planetary timescales together and undoes our longstanding belief in the priority of the former over the latter' (Evan Gottlieb). The experience of time takes varying paces: from the time of agricultural labour embedded in the cycles of nature to the capitalist time of feverish production and constant consumption. The epistemology of time is fragmented into competing paradigms and fields of knowledge, between the poles of Kantian time as an a priori intuition and Newtonian time, with its undifferentiated flow and homogenous course.

The Romantic poetics of time reflects that dissemination. It bears witness to 'a disconnection and out-of-jointness' at work within

---

12   Several recent publications offer a vision of 'Romanticism as a mode rather than a genre of writing' (*The Legacies of Romanticism: Literature, Culture, Aesthetics*, ed. by Carmen Casaliggi and Paul March-Russell (New York: Routledge, 2012), p. 1, https://doi.org/10.4324/9780203110096), thus partly freeing Romanticism from periodisation. See also Michael O'Neill, *The All-Sustaining Air: Romantic Legacies and Renewals in British, American, and Irish Poetry since 1900* (Oxford: Oxford University Press, 2007), https://doi.org/10.1093/acprof:oso/9780199299287.001.0001, *Romantic Presences in the Twentieth Century*, ed. by Mark Sandy (Burlington: Ashgate, 2012), https://doi.org/10.4324/9781315606958, and *Romantic Echoes in the Victorian Era*, ed. by Andrew Radford and Mark Sandy (Aldershot: Ashgate, 2008), https://doi.org/10.4324/9781315243917

13   Georges Didi-Huberman, *Devant le temps: Histoire de l'art et anachronisme des images* (Paris: Éditions de Minuit, 2000), p. 43, our translation.

14   Joel Faflak, ed., *Marking Time: Romanticism and Evolution* (Toronto and Buffalo: University of Toronto Press, 2017), p. 14, https://doi.org/10.3138/9781442699595

chronological time.[15] Contained in Shelley's 'We look before and after, /And pine for what is not—'[16] is that sense of an elusive present caught in the constant tension between past and future, between the poles of anamnesis and prophecy. Romantic temporality thus lies in the 'co-existence of distinct timelines' (Anne Rouhette) upsetting what Rancière calls 'the self-coincidence of time'.[17] It emerges within the discrepancy between a 'transformational instant' (Gregory Dart) and the *longue durée* of history, within a 'multiplicity of temporal lines, [with] several senses of time experienced at the "same" time'.[18] This multilinear experience takes shape in the tension between the sense of time rooted in 'the manifold quirks and variations of lived experience' (Matthew Redmond) and the otherness of non-subjective temporalities. Romantic texts allow for embodied experiences of time to emerge: time fleshes itself out within the 'body as a temporal medium' (Oriane Monthéard). Poetic time encounters biological time: the opaque, often undecipherable temporality at work within the human body, its vital rhythms and its course towards ageing and death.

Blake's meditation, 'Eternity is in love with the productions of time', challenges the mutual exclusion of the transient and the timeless. Romantic literature has sometimes been seen as cultivating the belief 'that poetry by its nature can transcend the conflicts and transiences of this time and that place',[19] trying to avoid the wounds of time's arrow in a tropism towards timelessness. Yet, in the words of Giorgio Agamben, 'Those who are truly contemporary, who truly belong to their time, are those who neither perfectly coincide with it nor adjust themselves to its demands. [...] But precisely because of this condition, precisely through this disconnection and this anachronism, they are more capable than others of perceiving and grasping their own time'.[20] Romantic writers endeavour to bring about a new distribution of the

---

15 Giorgio Agamben, 'What is the Contemporary?', in *What is an Apparatus? and other Essays*, ed. and trans. by David Kishik and Stefan Pedatella (Stanford: Stanford University Press, 2009), pp. 39–54 (p. 40), https://doi.org/10.1515/9781503600041-004
16 Percy Shelley, 'To a Sky-Lark', lines 86–87, in *Poetry and Prose*, p. 306.
17 Jacques Rancière, 'Le concept d'anachronisme et la vérité de l'historien', *L'Inactuel*, 6 (Fall 1996), 53–68 (p. 67), our translation.
18 Ibid.
19 Jerome McGann, *The Romantic Ideology: A Critical Investigation* (Chicago and London: The University of Chicago Press, 1983), p. 69.
20 Agamben, 'What is the Contemporary?', p. 40.

transient and the timeless by conferring on poetry a temporality that sees beyond current events and that bears the responsibility of political change. This collection considers the Romantic poetics of time less as a drive towards atemporal transcendence than as the record of a 'falling into time' (Ralf Haekel).[21] It has chosen to look at Romanticism in time: embedded in time and reflecting on history. The close readings in this volume explore less the historiographical ambitions than the poetics of history in Romantic writing, 'envisioning anew the role that poetic forms and stylistic techniques play [...] in the way Romantic literature engages with history'.[22] Our aim is not to see Romantic poems as merely reactive to the course of events, but as creative engagements with history in the making. Romanticism was immersed in its own time, yet not passively so, inventing 'new modes of historical consciousness' and making history.[23]

Rather than investigating the Romantic poetics of history as a memorial art, this volume focuses on what 'permits the private space of the self entrance into those monumental moments recorded by, and for, history' (Mark Sandy). In the same way, the Romantic ambition to attend to the 'shadows which futurity casts upon the present'[24] is seen in this book as part of an endeavour to change the course of events. In the words of Ian Balfour, 'Prophecy is a call and a claim much more than it is a prediction, a call oriented toward a present that is not present'.[25] In the politics of Romanticism, prophecy is part of the will to shape the present: to liberate the efficacy of poetry and set the forces of history in motion.

That ability to envision futurity takes place in a moment of latency, as it awakens new political aspirations. According to Richard Eldridge, that moment, in between the promise of advent and indefinite deferral, is the temporality of political freedom: 'This sense of simultaneous direction toward and deferral of the achievement of freedom accounts for the

---

21 No page number is indicated for references to the chapters in this volume.
22 Emily Rohrbach, *Modernity's Mist: British Romanticism and the Poetics of Anticipation* (New York: Fordham University Press, 2016), p. 15, https://doi.org/10.2307/j.ctt175x2fs
23 Ernst Behler, *German Romantic Literary Theory* (Cambridge: Cambridge University Press, 1993), p. 4, https://doi.org/10.1017/cbo9780511519437
24 Percy Shelley, 'A Defence of Poetry', in *Poetry and Prose*, p. 535.
25 Ian Balfour, *The Rhetoric of Romantic Prophecy* (Stanford: Stanford University Press, 2002), p. 18.

predominance in Romantic writing of remembrance and anticipation rather than of present statement of the features of things',[26] revealing the political import of the Romantic poetics of time. The Romantics' conception of futurity involves their commitment to envision the future in a dark present. In the words of Paul Hamilton, Romantic writing reveals 'the interwoven quality of the future in past and present'.

The Romantic poetics of time thus transforms time from the inside, upsetting chronologies, introducing loops and detours, shaking the foundations of a 'temporal economy [...] of the sort implied in the concept of linear time' (Laura Quinney). Taking an active part in the 'essential dishomogeneity' of its times,[27] Romanticism refracts rather than merely reflects time. The Romantic poetics of time also redistributes origins and aftermaths when posterity becomes a driving force and a process of origination: 'For the Romantics, [...] posterity is not so much what comes after poetry as its necessary *prerequisite*—the judgement of future generations becomes the necessary condition of the act of writing itself'.[28] Romantic poetics thus open up various lines of time, disjointing and combining temporal layers within the play of literary language: 'dividing and interpolating time, [the poet] is capable of transforming it and putting it in relation with other times'.[29] In order to attend to time in the making in Romantic texts, this volume looks into their ability to interweave various lines of time.

Romanticism is sometimes seen as dismissive of a clockwork conception of time that divides the continuum of temporal experience into a series of discrete units. Romantic poetics consists less in the rejection of quantifiable and linear time than in the subversion of its homogeneity based on the return of identical units. The Romantic poetics of time introduces difference within patterns of repetition, when poetic rhythm creates other forms of periodicity. Hence the swirling movement guiding the breath of the Spirit of the Hour in *Prometheus Unbound*: 'Thou breathe into the many-folded Shell,/Loosening its

---

26 Richard Eldridge, *The Persistence of Romanticism, Essays in Philosophy and Literature* (Cambridge and New York: Cambridge University Press, 2001), p. 21.
27 Agamben, 'What is the Contemporary?', p. 52.
28 Andrew Bennett, *Romantic Poets and the Culture of Posterity* (Cambridge: Cambridge University Press, 1999), p. 4, https://doi.org/10.1017/cbo9780511484100
29 Agamben, 'What is the Contemporary?', p. 53.

mighty music'.[30] The breath of the Spirit of the Hour turns into a melody within the spiral structure of the conch. In Shelley's spiral vision of time, poetry emerges at the exact same time as the advent of a swerve or swirl, as the emergence of an open circular movement within the shell. That spiral motion manifests itself as a strain between reminiscence and prophecy:

PROMETHEUS [...]

[*Turning to the* Spirit of the Hour.]

For thee, fair Spirit, one toil remains. Ione,

Give her that curved shell, which Proteus old

Made Asia's nuptial boon, breathing within it

A voice to be accomplished, and which thou

Didst hide in grass under the hollow rock.[31]

The shell, given long ago by 'Proteus old', is a convoluted form bearing within itself the depths of time. The trochaic inversions at the onsets of the segments 'Give her that curved shell' and 'breathing within it' seem to invert the stress pattern for a spell of time before the iambic rhythm reasserts itself. They introduce a form of reversibility within the flow, offering a synthesis of linear and circular lines of time, a movement embodied by the motif of the spiral. As a remembrance and a promise intricately weaved into the rhythms of poetry, the voice contained within the shell points to the Romantic art of subverting the course of representation. It tells of the way Romantic poetics complicates the temporality of mimesis, in which the model is supposed to come before the work. In Shelley's temporal spiral, poetry is mimetic of the future it envisions.

Poetry comes first, and intimates the advent of what it longs for: the anticipation contained within a distant memory. In the Romantic poetics of intimation, the future is contained within the past and the past will blossom in the future. Romantic poetics reveals its apprehension of

---

30   Shelley, 'Prometheus Unbound', Act III, scene iii, lines 80–81, in *Poetry and Prose*, p. 261.
31   Ibid.

the delicate fabric of time in transformative moments. Indeed, these involutes[32] can be traced in the political concepts of revolution and restoration which, in the words of Paul Hamilton, offer 'this future-rich understanding of the past in the present'. The collision of several temporalities 'compose rhythms whose *tempi* are out of joint'.[33] It consists in an act of composition in the musical sense. The Romantic poetics of time introduces a swerve in the structure of time, generating ripples and lapses. It derives its specific rhythm from the constant disjointing and interweaving of several temporal threads. The Romantic art of incipience, when the shell is about to 'loos[en] its mighty music', reawakens the force of the potential. It gestures toward that inchoate moment when the pen is about to touch the page. That moment of temporisation is an act of composition that interweaves actuality and potentiality. At that instant, textual potentialities—all the poems that might have been—dissolve before the poem that emerges. And yet, they somehow survive the moment of writing, vibrating in the background of the actual poem, generating alternative strata of time, embracing all its pasts, presents and futures.

Section I, 'Restoration, Revival, and Revolution across Romantic Europe', studies the way Romanticism developed at different moments and within different cultures in Europe. Paul Hamilton's chapter, 'Future Restoration', lays the stress on the crucial importance of 'restoration', rather than 'revolution' (and its French historical representation, which has already been the subject of many a critical study), for English Romantics, in particular Blake and Wordsworth. They resorted to it creatively in their quest for a continuum between past, present and future, and through their grasp of both temporality and literature across Europe. The Romantics' skill at unearthing a political imagery matching their perception of time is further developed in Evan Gottlieb's essay on 'Anthropocene Temporalities and British Romantic Poetry'. In the Romantic era, this sense of a human temporal continuity—partly based on the impression of a permanent imperishable natural world on which humanity relies and as conveyed by Wordsworth's poetry—is yet

---

32 This is a reference to De Quincey's 'involutes' in *Suspiria de Profundis*, in Lindop, Grevel, ed., *Thomas De Quincey: Confessions of an English-Opium Eater and Other Writings* (Oxford: Oxford University Press, 1996), p. 104.
33 Didi-Huberman, *Devant le temps*, p. 39, our translation.

questioned by the rapid technological and industrial transformations and the geopolitical disturbances induced by the Napoleonic Wars. Wordsworth's younger British contemporaries, especially Keats, P.B. Shelley and Byron, thus came up with alternative temporalities, four of which are traced back in the chapter. The Romantics' self-reflexivity on their own historicity is eventually examined through a close-up on lyrical art and the way classical music, and particularly Beethoven's operatic paean to freedom, *Fidelio,* interacts with and has an impact on the history of the period. Gregory Dart's piece reflects on the various versions of the opera as 'instances of a shifting political-historical consciousness' and as a string of distinct but related "spots of time", an allegory of history. He shows how music is gradually subjected to the pressures of real and historical times, and how timing becomes the political virtue of the future. The first section, dealing with the way poetry and the arts, especially music, are progressively shaped by historical events in the Romantic period, leads to a more subjective and intimate approach to time.

Section II focuses on the 'Romantic Conceptions of Time' as it is felt and experienced. Taking his cue from Walter Benjamin's philosophy of time as developed in his *Theses on the Philosophy of History,* Ralf Haekel investigates the temporality of the soul in William Wordsworth's 'Ode. Intimations of Immortality' and Lord Byron's *Childe Harold's Pilgrimage.* To him they both convey a much bleaker vision and even disillusioned picture of the nature of time and history than is usually agreed upon by critics like Helen Vendler, Michael O'Neill, James Chandler, and Jerome McGann, to quote but a few recent examples. Longing for an eternity that seems forever gone, the poets yet depict time as fleeting and transient. This perception of time coincides with the shift from an essentially eternal conception to a temporal and thereby finite concept of human nature. Byron's epic, mirroring the hero's walking in a disenchanted world echoes Keats's perception of time as discussed by Oriane Monthéard in the following chapter. Taking a walking tour of Scotland in the summer of 1818, the poet got the chance to harmoniously connect with temporality. Wishing to break away from the constraints of the ordinary measurement of time, as he recorded in his letters, Keats ended up experiencing a fictionalised temporality through picturesque tourism when he visited the landscape with a literary gaze, thus following the tracks of other poets. Past and present merged through the poet's physical act of walking on a ground pervaded with memories, while he also felt much more anchored in his own time. This redefinition of a more personal take on time needs studying and theorising; hence the following section dedicated to the poetics of time.

Section III, entitled 'The Poetics of Time', considers the work of time and the uneasy tension, in Lily Dessau's chapter, between natural- and man-made time (the mechanical church clock), simultaneously tracked across the cyclical recurring of seasons and the daily schedule of a farm labourer busy with various agricultural tasks in John Clare's extended work *The Shepherd's Calendar* (1827). Dessau contrasts these temporal variations and progressions with what happens in the 'May' poem in which, she says, 'Clare keeps us perpetually trapped in the present, denying access to the narrated past of custom and tradition'. Through a close-reading analysis of the poem, she underlines the cuts in the published version when compared to the manuscript, thus metafictionally questioning the role played by both editors and patrons in these compressions and contractions. The acceleration of time, as also enabled by the development of print and the accompanying industrialisation, is further discussed by Matthew Henry Redmond in his chapter on two landmark essayists, the British Charles Lamb and the American Washington Irving, presented as combative antiquarians in a world of machines and breakneck speed. They both advocate reading as a way to exercise one's critical judgment and to escape from their age's most pressing and irrational controversies. If promoting reading and antiquarianism may at first sound anachronistic in the Romantic era, so do Victor's alchemical pursuits in *Frankenstein*. In her chapter dedicated to Mary Shelley's novel, Anne Rouhette shows how the book brings forward at least two approaches to time: historical and mythical. Yet, instead of contrasting them, it tries to superimpose or even merge them through the precarious, uneasy cohabitation of the linear and the cyclical, thereby demonstrating that chronological disorder and anachronism can be used to poetical ends. This creative handling of time in literature and its effect on both the diegesis and the reader raises questions pertaining to the field of reception studies.

Section IV, 'Persistence and Afterlives' turns to Romantic legacies and the way Romantics, like Shelley and his last poem 'The Triumph of

Life', have paradoxically served as a source of inspiration for twentieth-century authors like Beckett, as demonstrated by Laura Quinney in her comparative study of the two writers. Her chapter, entitled 'Heaps of Time in Beckett and Shelley', undoes the difference between speed—as seemingly conceptualised in Shelley's poem that stages the Chariot of Life hurtling forward on its destructive course and figuring the overwhelming momentum of time—and vacancy, as embodied by Beckett's characters who feel entrapped in a time that never runs out, but perpetually runs on and in slow motion, up to the point when it becomes static, as if they had become prisoners of a purgatorial temporality. Mark Sandy eventually spirits the readers of this volume away to Venice, a place presented as both real, through its distinctive architecture and key historical sites, all rooted in time, but also mythical, thanks to the juxtaposition of several timelines and the creative intertwining of personal memories. This fanciful and yet genuine Italian cityscape is central to the poetics of atemporality in Byron and Shelley. It seems to be a welcome and just allegory of the way Romantic writing creates its own sense of time, in its own terms. Like the city that is a perpetually charmed spot and broken spell for Byron and Shelley, the movement appears as essentially untimely through its ability to bend the course of time and to persist beyond the so-called Romantic period.

Co-written by David Duff, Nicholas Halmi, Fiona Stafford, Martin Procházka, and Laurent Folliot, the closing section, entitled 'Romanticism and Periodisation: A Roundtable', explores the problem of literary periodisation in Romanticism. It is a vast, and yet little-studied issue in the literary field that becomes the specific focus of this forum, whose formal difference results from its dynamic interplay of voices and standpoints. It offers a qualified overview of the various attempts at defining the period by both contemporaries and later generations, and stresses the main characteristics of Romanticism in terms of keywords, timelines and perspectives, whose differences are induced by a new historical awareness at the turn of the eighteenth century. While it reopens the methodological issue of periodisation in literary history, it also broadens it by subtly highlighting cross-border differences, be they regional or transnational, with a reference to European or even Transatlantic Romanticism. This concluding debate, edited by David Duff, questions the effectiveness of the concept of the 'Romantic period' to approach literary history, and its aptness to reflect the multiple distinctions and nuances within Romantic literature.

Works Cited

Agamben, Giorgio, 'What is the Contemporary?', in *What is an Apparatus? and other Essays*, ed. and trans. by David Kishik and Stefan Pedatella (Stanford: Stanford University Press, 2009), pp. 39–54, https://doi.org/10.1515/9781503600041-004

Balfour, Ian, *The Rhetoric of Romantic Prophecy* (Stanford: Stanford University Press, 2002), https://doi.org/10.7202/009264ar

Behler, Ernst, *German Romantic Literary Theory* (Cambridge: Cambridge University Press, 1993), https://doi.org/10.1017/cbo9780511519437

Bennett, Andrew, *Romantic Poets and the Culture of Posterity* (Cambridge: Cambridge University Press, 1999), https://doi.org/10.1017/CBO9780511484100

Casaliggi, Carmen and Paul March-Russell, eds, *The Legacies of Romanticism: Literature, Culture, Aesthetics* (New York and London: Routledge, 2013), https://doi.org/10.4324/9780203110096

Chandler, James, 'Wordsworth's Great Ode: Romanticism and the Progress of Poetry', in *The Cambridge Companion to British Romantic Poetry*, ed. by James Chandler and Maureen N. McLane (Cambridge: Cambridge University Press, 2008), pp. 136–54, https://doi.org/10.1017/ccol9780521862356.008

De Man, Paul, *Blindness and Insight: Essays in the Rhetoric of Contemporary Criticism*, 2nd ed. (London: Routledge, 1983), https://doi.org/10.4324/9780203713716

Didi-Huberman, Georges, *Devant le temps: Histoire de l'art et anachronisme des images* (Paris: Éditions de Minuit, 2000).

Eldridge, Richard, *The Persistence of Romanticism, Essays in Philosophy and Literature* (Cambridge and New York: Cambridge University Press, 2001).

Erdman, David, ed., *The Complete Poetry & Prose of William Blake* (New York: Random House, 1988).

Faflak, Joel, ed., *Marking Time: Romanticism and Evolution* (Toronto and Buffalo: University of Toronto Press, 2017), https://doi.org/10.1007/s40656-018-0237-7

Halmi, Nicholas, *The Genealogy of the Romantic Symbol* (Oxford: Oxford University Press, 2007), https://doi.org/10.1093/acprof:oso/9780199212415.001.0001

Hamilton, Paul, *Realpoetik: European Romanticism and Literary Politics* (Oxford: Oxford University Press, 2013), https://doi.org/10.1093/acprof:oso/9780199686179.001.0001

Lindop, Grevel, ed., *Thomas De Quincey: Confessions of an English-Opium Eater and Other Writings* (Oxford: Oxford University Press, 1996).

McGann, Jerome, *The Romantic Ideology: A Critical Investigation* (Chicago and London: The University of Chicago Press, 1983).

Miller, Christopher, *The Invention of Evening: Perception and Time in Romantic Poetry* (Cambridge: Cambridge University Press, 2006), https://doi.org/10.1017/CBO9780511720031

O'Neill, Michael, *The All-Sustaining Air: Romantic Legacies and Renewals in British, American, and Irish Poetry since 1900* (Oxford: Oxford University Press, 2012), https://doi.org/10.1093/acprof:oso/9780199299287.001.0001

——, *Romanticism and the Self-Conscious Poem* (Oxford: Clarendon Press, 1997), https://doi.org/10.1093/acprof:oso/9780198122852.001.0001

Procházka, Martin and Zdeněk Hrbata, eds, *Romantismus a romantismy: Pojmy, proudy, kontexty* (Romanticism and Romanticisms) (Nakladatel: Karolinum, 2005).

Rancière, Jacques, 'Le concept d'anachronisme et la vérité de l'historien', *L'Inactuel*, 6 (Fall 1996), 53–68.

——, *Les mots de l'histoire : Essai de poétique du savoir* (Paris: Seuil, 1992).

Reiman, Donald and Neil Fraistat, ed., *Shelley's Poetry and Prose*, 2nd ed. (New York: Norton, 2002).

Ricœur, Paul, *Temps et récit, I. L'intrigue et le récit historique* (Paris: Seuil, 1983).

Rohrbach, Emily, *Modernity's Mist: British Romanticism and the Poetics of Anticipation* (New York: Fordham University Press, 2016), https://doi.org/10.2307/j.ctt175x2fs

Sandy, Mark, ed., *Romantic Presences in the Twentieth Century* (Burlington: Ashgate, 2012), https://doi.org/10.4324/9781315606958

Sandy, Mark and Andrew Radford, eds, *Romantic Echoes in the Victorian Era* (Aldershot: Ashgate, 2008), https://doi.org/10.4324/9781315243917

Stafford, Fiona, *Reading Romantic Poetry* (Oxford: Wiley-Blackwell, 2012), https://doi.org/10.1002/9781118228104

Vendler, Helen, 'Lionel Trilling and the Immortality Ode', *Salmagundi*, 41 (Spring 1978), 65–85.

SECTION I

RESTORATION, REVIVAL, AND REVOLUTION ACROSS ROMANTIC EUROPE

1. Future Restoration

Paul Hamilton

> *For the Romantics, the idea of Restoration could signify simultaneously historical events and moments of consciousness. Historically, Restoration during the Romantic period followed the French Revolution and the ensuing Napoleonic imperium. What was restored at the Congress of Vienna and its successors was the sovereignty of European nations, although of course what was to count as a nation was in the gift of the ruling powers—especially England, Austria, Russia and Prussia. Literature written at the same time, though, questioned and experimented with what could count as a restorative experience. This paper examines current images of a restored Europe running counter to the official political outcome of the Congresses. These drew on the Romantic interest in the way in which future and past could be interrelated in a creative way, so that the restoration of lost values could be as radically revisionary as any model of revolution, with conflicting opportunities for imagining new forms of integration or confusion.*

Time restored, *le temps retrouvé*, is a topic that lends itself both to philosophical and to historical treatments: we can either consider it as raising questions about time, and what time is; or it can make us wonder about differences in the way time was experienced at a particular period of history. Proust does both. Romanticism, constantly investigating interiority alongside our consciousness of things, was preoccupied with the extent to which one could be mapped on to the other, the inner on to the outer, the flow of consciousness on to history. Romantic writers and thinkers tried to find common structures in what Reinhart Kosellek neatly calls 'history in the singular and histories in the plural'.[1]

---

1 Reinhart Koselleck, *Futures Past: On the Semantics of Historical Time* (Cambridge, MA: MIT Press, 1985), p. 94.

I am defined by my history, you by yours; but our different trajectories inhabit a common temporal dimension sharing a single chronology. Time appeared to Kant to be the framework in which we experienced ourselves, the 'form of inner sense'. Nevertheless, the vocabulary of this *durée*, as Bergson called it, or inner time, was often spatial. Past events appeared to inhabit greater or lesser distances from us. Sometimes time passed quickly, sometimes slowly, as the future approached us at different rates of acceleration. Time could drag, or fly. The future could be imminent or far away. And, less obviously, the future could be visible in the past, located embryonically, a secret code to be deciphered. Returning the compliment, the future could fulfil the past, or just repeat it. For Wordsworth, famously, to discover the presence of the past in the present meant that the future was always potentially restorative. The inherence of the future in the past meant that to think of the past now could deliver an experience

> Felt in the blood, and felt along the heart;
>
> And passing even into my purer mind
>
> With tranquil restoration...[2]

Such restoration, though, also meant that only now could we understand the true significance of the past—that is what it prefigured, what it is doing to me now, its sometime future. This interaction of past and future defining history could be fraught; we might, like *The Prelude*'s narrator, overinvest in the future with damaging consequences. But the remedy is still the restoration of Books 11 and 12: 'Imagination: How impaired and restored'.[3]

The imagining of the future in the Romantic period in Europe lays claim to two epochal moments. The first cataclysm was the French Revolution, no surprises there; but, secondly, came the Congress of Vienna and its successors which together composed the European Restoration. The Revolution immediately appears more conducive to the exercise of imagination. The Revolutionary calendar of the

---

2 William Wordsworth, 'Lines written a few miles above Tintern Abbey', lines 29–31, in *William Wordsworth* (The Oxford Authors), ed. by Stephen Gill (Oxford: Oxford University Press, 1984), p. 132.

3 Ibid., p. 559.

Jacobins even re-invented time – or how we record it. Its re-naming of the months captured the *durée* of the seasons: Germinal, Floréal, Prairial, Messidor, Fructidor and so on. Restoration is a less obvious candidate as the bearer of imagination. But the shuttling back and forth in time required to understand it is more akin to the displacements and over-determinations of internal events that so gripped Romantic introspection. The immanent dynamic of memory and desire suggested to Romantics that the future was not to be apprehended independently of its prophetic character; 'the mind overflowed the intellect', as Bergson put it.[4] The future was to be found inscribed in the past and realised in the present. Marx's genuine revolution, as he tells us in *The Eighteenth Brumaire of Louis Bonaparte*, would produce 'a new language [...] without reference to the old'.[5] Failing that, however, all conjurations of the future are inherently literary, restorative of old meanings in new forms, metaphorical, deplorably so for a revolutionary purist but encouragingly so for radicals who, falling short of Marx's standards, still considered themselves revolutionary, and for whom, as Percy Shelley put it, poets were 'mirrors of the gigantic shadows which futurity casts upon the present'. Or in Friedrich Schlegel's even more involved formulation, the historian is 'a prophet looking backwards', and so a bardic figure who destabilises the self-sufficiency of any time-period, making each—past, present and future—dependent on the other.[6] The present makes us reinterpret the past, but in a way so as to produce the prophecy of what might happen, the future, which at present is hard to see. Kierkegaard attacks Romanticism for envisaging a repetition of the past in which nothing is restored: one lives the same life but as if born again, as if for the first time. Comparably, Nietzsche, in his idea of the eternal return of the same, pointedly criticises Romanticism by

---

4 Henri Bergson, *Creative Evolution*, trans. by Arthur Mitchell (London: Macmillan, 1964).

5 Karl Marx, 'The Eighteenth Brumaire of Louis Bonaparte', in *Surveys from Exile: Political Writings*, ed. by David Fernbach, trans. by Ben Fowkes (Harmondsworth: Penguin, 1973), p. 147.

6 Percy Shelley, 'A Defence of Poetry', in *Shelley's Poetry and Prose*, ed. by Donald H. Reiman and Sharon B. Powers (New York and London: Norton, 1977), p. 508; Friedrich Schlegel, 'Athenaeum Fragment', no. 80, in *Philosophical Fragments*, trans. by Peter Firchow (Minnesota: University of Minnesota Press, 1991), p. 27.

accepting a fate unproductive of change. Romanticism becomes what it is, 'a self-realizing ideal'.[7]

To what degree was Europe reinvented after Napoleon? The Congress of Vienna, you will remember, followed the first conclusive defeat of Napoleon and was convened in 1814. When Napoleon's defeat turned out to be premature, and Napoleon enjoyed his hundred days after escaping Elba in March 1815, the Congress was suspended in some embarrassment, to be re-convened after Waterloo. Subsequently, a 'congress system' was set up. The Congress of Vienna was based on earlier dealings at the Treaties of Chaumont and Paris, but was also coloured by a host of less well-known assemblies whose goings-on were far from transparent to all concerned with the later Congress. The most notorious of those precursors was the Treaty of Kallisch of February 1813 in which Russia and Prussia agreed on a carve-up: Russia could have Poland, and Prussia Saxony. This deal would have been anathema to other main players like Britain and Austria, who, respectively, feared too much territorial influence going to the unpredictable and ambitious Czar Alexander I's Russia and to Frederick William III's Prussia.

All such agreements simultaneously take up positions towards the Ottoman Empire, and therefore towards the possibility of a free Greece, which might create a buffer-zone between Turkey, Russia and the more Western countries. Also at issue are the political principles on which the new Europe would be constructed, and these could range from the 'Legitimacy' formulated by Talleyrand, trying to do his best for a defeated France, and the strange political Christianity concocted by Alexander and the Baroness von Krüdener, consecrated in the Holy Alliance, momentarily echoing earlier religious imaginings by Chateaubriand and Novalis of an ultra-generous political communion and anticipating those to come, like that of Lamennais. The dominant idea, though, apart from the 'Legitimacy' or conservative theodicy into which the Holy Alliance would collapse by the 1820 Congress of Troppau, was the 'balance of power' pragmatically espoused by Britain's Lord Castlereagh, which perhaps most consistently guided the collective actions of the Congress. The Congress, then, had a complicated pre-history but also an extended afterlife in a 'system' of congresses

---

7   Friedrich Nietzsche, *The Will to Power*, trans. by Walter Kaufmann and R.J. Hollingdale (New York: Random House, 1968), sec. 253, p. 147.

held subsequent to Vienna at Aix-La-Chapelle, Troppau, Laibach (Ljubljana), Verona and St Petersburg. The 'balance of power', as soon as one begins to describe it, becomes a thing of infinite intricacy and convoluted selfishness. Castlereagh famously opposed the slave trade at the Congress, and got a sub-committee to devote its time to it. While he no doubt felt the pressure of the ethical arguments of British abolitionists (Thomas Clarkson, William Wilberforce and many others), negotiations actually come down to an economic argument: Britain has *already* done so well out of the slave trade it should pay strategic compensation in cash or colonies to Spain, Portugal and the Dutch; countries supposed to be understandably reluctant to give up the slave trade until they had gained economic parity with British profits from past slavery. The liberal political imagination here balances powers by book-keeping in putative human lives. Like Gogol's dead souls, the reparation costs are a trafficking in imaginary slaves. Contemporary critiques of Castlereagh's language, his 'set trash or phrase', as Byron called it, responds to this kind of moral incoherence with poetic performances whose contrasting articulacy and clarity must automatically gain oppositional political force.[8]

My point is that the usual conclusion—that if this was the Restoration of Europe after Napoleon's imperium, you can see how Restoration got a bad name in liberal circles—needs to be supplemented by the recognition that Restoration implies an imaginative opportunity for political change more comparable with Revolution than we usually acknowledge. Other writers grabbed that opportunity, and their indignation with the Congress was that it spoiled the chance of a better future. In fact, the idea of a proper Restoration, as opposed to a reactionary settlement, is often embedded in the idea of Revolution. Maybe restoration can be revolution by other means, and maybe it should be? Schlegel thought that the French Revolution was a 'tendency' (*Tendenz*) rather than an achieved event. Even the Tory Thomas De Quincey called it a 'legacy' answering to some basic human discontent. Mary Wollstonecraft believed that

---

8   See Nikolai Gogol, *Dead Souls*, trans. by David Magarshack (Harmondsworth: Penguin, 1961); *Don Juan*, 'Dedication', in Lord Byron, *The Complete Poetical Works*, ed. by Jerome J. McGann (Oxford: Clarendon Press, 1986), vol. V, p. 7.

revolution might better begin at home, in the home in fact.[9] Certainly when one looks more closely at British polemics written against the Congress of Vienna one finds that what is primarily deplored is a failure to use the political imagination. What we do not find are arguments more familiar recently, miming Marx's polemic in *The German Ideology* (four years after *Dead Souls*, in 1846): that to introduce imagination into the political sphere is bound to sublimate or disguise the fact that any imaginary resolutions are simply ways of giving up on finding real political solutions. Literary resolutions are substituted for ones in the actual, historical world of practical politics. These large, redemptive schemes, which M.H. Abrams thought described the Romantic project of imagination in *Natural Supernaturalism*, were the defining target for new historicist criticism.

Historicism can cut both ways, and throw up all sorts of alternatives to binaries we often use to navigate cultural history. So, the French Revolution can scarcely be understood if we only contrast it to the preceding *ancien régime*. The Girondin liberal period was followed by the extraordinary Jacobin freedoms, then a contradictory safeguarding of the Revolution by the Committees of Public Safety, the Terror, makeshift stages like the Directory and eventually Napoleonic dictatorship. Far from being discredited as an idea, though, revolution continued to be reconceived and reconstructed, sometimes still as revolution, sometimes as a strategic revisionism, and sometimes maybe as Restoration. Metternich's Congress of Vienna certainly could appear as a reactionary counter to all this creative re-shaping of Revolution. Ruled by Legitimacy, it used the hereditary principle to guarantee authority, and so settled into a defence of Church and State and King. But the strange Holy Alliance, initiated by Czar Alexander at Aix-La-Chapelle and strategically espoused by Austria and Prussia, once more echoes Romantic ideas of a recovery of Christendom in order to be able to think a more effective European franchise, the sort of hope we find guiding Burke, Chateaubriand, Novalis and Friedrich Schlegel. That it declines into the Troppau Protocol, even more in hock to Legitimacy than its competitor, the Quadruple Alliance, cannot erase this initial, embarrassing continuum with all sorts of counter-images of a restored

---

9   Schlegel, 'Athenaeum Fragment', no. 216, in *Philosophical Fragments*, trans. by Peter Firchow, p. 46.

Europe, prevalent at the time and surprisingly prominent once one begins to search for them. I would like to look at how Restoration might figure in a British Romantic-period sensibility extremely interested in the future shape of a new Europe.

Byron, again in the 'Dedication' to *Don Juan*, saw that 'Europe' could be 'sung' in various ways: according to the hymn sheet offered by the 'congress' or 'conspiracy' of Vienna, or to another tune. The point to be taken now is less the one of who was on which side, and more the need to realise that after the French Revolution the rules of politics were transvalued. Although itself a reactionary settlement, the 'Restoration' following the final defeat of Napoleon could not hide the fact that it, too, was in the business of unearthing a political imaginary. Writers, even conservative writers like Novalis and Chateaubriand, had earlier bought into this political extension of imaginative authority. With their political visions, we can aptly compare Burke's 'glory of Europe' in the end obscured, as he sees it, by the bad modernity of the French Revolution. The 'anarchy' Shelley attributes to the reactionary violence of post-Napoleonic England is similarly opposed to a contrastingly coherent *internationale*, 'a volcano heard afar' (like the Indonesian one of four years before which had darkened European skies in the summer of 1816, 'the year without a summer').[10] The boundaries of the political collaboration Shelley wanted his poetry to contribute to were always primarily European rather than British, historically as well as geographically, as evidenced in the history he gives to poetry in his *Defence* of it. As long as they remain unestablished, these images of international unity in need of restoration survive poetically—Burkean chivalry, Novalis's Christianity or Europe, Chateaubriand's genius of Christianity, or the wandering spirit of inspired liberty in Blake, Shelley and Anna Barbauld. This is poetry in Shelley's 'unrestricted' sense, according to which, in *A Defence of Poetry*, the poetry of Rome could lie in its 'institutions' as much as in Virgil, Horace or Ovid. Unrestricted poetry is like German *Poesie*, the idea of a general, improving creativity inspiring ideas of human progress, an idea going back explicitly to Diotima's speech in Plato's *Symposium*, celebrating the act of making

---

10   Shelley, 'The Mask of Anarchy', l. 363, *Poetry and Prose*, p. 310.

visible a core creativity in *all* human activity if we only have the *poetic* wit to isolate and prize its edifying impulse.[11]

Romantic futures are optimistic, I am suggesting, the more explicitly they are engaged in producing a counter-image to those proffered by the Napoleonic empire and then by the post-Napoleonic settlement of the Congress of Vienna. Germaine de Staël, both in the Europe described by her journey in exile from Napoleon's France, and in her writings, is the most combative. She addressed the culture of other countries as unified entities she could then challenge to produce credentials for joining the Europe of nations she, unlike Burke, envisaged as a reality recoverable in modern form. Her book on Germany recorded that country's successful reply to her direct questioning on her visit. Her intervention in the controversy over Romanticism in Italy through her article on translation in *Biblioteca Italiana* of 1816 provoked the young Giacomo Leopardi, who would become Italy's second poet after Dante, to clarify his ideas about how to recover a new cultural poise in Italy, one owing nothing to imitations of Byron and others.[12] In the same year, Felicia Hemans published her poem *The Restoration of the Works of Art to Italy*, calling on Italy to 'rouse once more the daring soul of song', but in conclusion generalising the value of this as 'a heightened consciousness', not envisaging a new Italian identity but an aesthetic delight, as Diego Saglia says, generated by 'a fervid transnational imagination', contrasting with 'the futility of imperial self-renovations'.[13] But maybe the heightened consciousness of the past empowers Italians to recover or restore Italy in an alternative political form?

---

11 Such creative foundationalism is very different from the historicist school, which, from Hegel and Friedrich Karl von Savigny onwards, opposed Kantian and Jacobin rationalism but was eventually accused of the same degree of constriction by Nietzsche—who nevertheless had no time for Romantic irony.

12 See Anna Luisa Staël Holstein, 'Sulla maniera e l'utilità dell traduzioni', in Giacomo Leopardi, *Discorso di un Italiano intorno alla poesia romantica*, ed. by Rosita Copioli (Milano: Biblioteca Univerzale Rizzoli, 1997), pp. 391–99.

13 'The Restoration of the Works of Art to Italy: A Poem' (1816), ll. 25, 512, in *Felicia Hemans: Selected Poems, Letters, Reception Materials*, ed. by Susan J. Wolfson (Princeton and Oxford: Princeton University Press, 2000), pp. 18–34. Diego Saglia, *European Literatures in Britain, 1815–32: Romantic Translations* (Cambridge: Cambridge University Press, 2019), pp. 220–21, https://doi.org/10.1017/9781108669900; 'British Romanticism and the Post-Napoleonic South: Writing Restoration Transnationally', *Essays in Romanticism*, 24.2 (2017), 105–24, https://doi.org/10.3828/eir.2017.24.2.2

Leopardi, after all, was a poet who could conjure restoration from almost nothing. The fiercely convincing poetic integrity he constructed out of the incoherent misery of his life was almost immediately read as proto-Risorgimento—that is, as modelling how to summon into existence a future Italy out of its current fragmentary state. Staël provoked even those who outwardly opposed her, like Leopardi, to make common cause with her by modelling, in poetic restorations of the integrity of a disintegrating individual, the national unity Italian patriots desired for their fragmented country. As they departed from this embattled engagement, their vision of the future tended to blur, and pessimism set in. After all, the French Revolution was only the precursor to a spate of nineteenth-century revolutions, none of which achieved their aims— 1820, 1830, 1848, to name the major ones.

This cycle of repeatedly raised hopes and diminishing political gains had a corrosive effect. In the wake of the July Revolution of 1830, the *trois glorieuses*, Balzac wrote an entire novel about life defeated in proportion to the ambitiousness of its desire, *La peau de chagrin*. Comparably, Delacroix's great painting '28th of July 1830, *la liberté guidant le people*', surely superimposes an earlier, republican adventure on to the establishing of the constitutional monarchy of Louis Philippe? Delacroix himself referred to it simply as 'barricade', and the catalogue to the big Paris exhibition of his paintings in 2018 described a hugely over-determined painting as 'haunted by the promises of the future' and so 'transforming itself quickly into a tomb', Balzac's logic exactly.[14] The haunting, though, registered in the expressions of her awestruck companions, is by Marianne, a spectral figure from 1789, but spectral also through her statuesque, solid physiognomy, in this paradoxical way recognizable as the ghost of substantial revolution. Delacroix scrambles temporalities: the figure of revolution now recovers her once robust form (Michelangelo-like to most critics), but only in a sculpted perfection. Let me give one more example of this law of diminishing returns from Alfred de Musset.

If Leopardi's powers of imagining his own restoration, making something out of nothing, *il nulla*, are limitless, Alfred de Musset's capability for self-loathing in his 1836 epochal *Confession of a Child of*

---

14 Sébastien Allard and Côme Fabre, *Delacroix: L'art et la matière* (Paris: Louvre éditions: Hazan, 2018), pp. 104–05.

our Time (my cheeky translation of *La Confession d'un enfant du siècle*), of reducing something to nothing, shows the reverse. Musset's story of an age whose politics has ruined its culture, creating a *mal de siècle* responsible for every personal misfortune is compulsive, hugely ambitious and knowingly self-serving. You do not believe a word of it at the same time as you admire the literary opportunism of an indefensible stance. It has been justly celebrated for its spectacularly historical articulation of the individuality open to Musset's generation, one that 'filled its lungs with the air Napoleon had breathed'.[15] In *La Confession* the lovers finally know each other so 'profoundly' that relationship is impossible. 'Another', he says to her, 'will offer you a worthier, more reliable, fitting ('dignement') love, but none as profound a love' (288).

At the personal level, the sense of always being discontented in Musset's confessional text makes for a kind of inertia, the consequence of forever imagining new, more satisfying dispensations. Musset is the opposite of the politically active love of his life, George Sand, here. And there is a kind of pointlessness in this superiority to what is available, which we tend to call decadent. In his 1842 poem on Leopardi, 'Après une lecture', Musset sees that Leopardi writes 'without complaining about fate', but adds that 'he savoured the charm of death', that he was the 'gloomy lover of death, poor Leopardi'. It is in opposition to this false interpretation, I am suggesting, that the obscure Leopardi has been increasingly prized for his restorative poetic power.

What do British and Irish ideas about Restoration look like against this European background? When Wordsworth famously writes in the 1805 *Prelude*, just after the description of the 'spots of time' that 'I would enshrine the spirit of the past/For future restoration', his words fit into the tradition of creative restorations which, I have argued, will be taken to extremes in Leopardi and discounted in Musset's decadent alternative.[16] To the English ear, though, Wordsworth immediately echoes the Milton who, within a few lines of the start of *Paradise Lost*, sees our human condition as directed 'till one greater man/Restore

---

15   Maurice Allem and Paul-Courant, eds, *Œuvres Complètes en Prose d'Alfred de Musset* (Bibliothèque de la Pléiade, 1960), p. 65.
16   *The* Prelude, XI. 341–43, in Gill, *William Wordsworth*, p. 567.

us and regain the blissful seat'.[17] We can be pretty sure that Milton's apparent 'mortalism' here—a greater *man* not God redeems us—or the belief that salvation is temporal and limited, pointedly does not envisage Charles II as a candidate for the role of 'greater man'. *Paradise Lost* was published in 1667, well into the Restoration period, a Restoration to which, like European writers 150 years later, he wants to imagine an alternative. Placed even earlier than the first lines, his prefatory note on 'THE VERSE', in the fourth issue of the first edition of 1668, describes a stylistic restoration he wants us to hear in his poem, 'the first in English, of ancient liberty recovered to heroic poem from the troublesome and modern bondage of rhyming' (39).

New ways of thinking restoration are not bound to the Caroline travesty of restoration Milton deplores. New ideas of restoration are at issue here, rather than simply an unhappiness with rhyme, as is evident from what happens to Milton's subsequent writing. He writes a *rhyming* tragedy against slavery, *Samson Agonistes*, arguably transvaluing the tragic genre just as he had claimed to have done the epic in *Paradise Lost*. And the dramatic humanism of *Paradise Regained*, where Jesus preserves the freedom of his mind as sufficient resistance against a supernatural opponent, departs further from hereditary literary machinery.

When Wordsworth, at the end of 'Home at Grasmere' and the start of the 'Prospectus' to *The Excursion*, passes by Milton's own machinery to take up lodging in 'the mind of Man,/My haunt and the main region of my song', he, too, is continuing the work of Miltonic restoration, recasting the poetic conventions of his predecessors, this time by psychologizing inherited religious discourse.[18] In effect, he is connecting with Milton through his own mortalism, or acceptance, as in *The Prelude*, that this is 'the place in which, in the end/We find our happiness or not at all'(X. 726–7). A new contract, a new grasp of the 'fit' between mind and nature is proposed. Here we usually cannot help hearing Blake's objections to fitting and fitted, '& please you Lordship', and remembering that, for Blake, psychologism rather uncovered a 'mental fight', ideological conflict. But Wordsworth's conceit is more futuristic than prescriptive,

---

17   John Milton, *Paradise Lost*, ed. by Alastair Fowler (Hong Kong: Longman, 1976), pp. 40–41.
18   Gill, *William Wordsworth*, p. 198.

'the image of a better time'.[19] It is on the side of the fittingness to which Musset would oppose his unfortunate profundity.

Blake's prophetic books, too, have their restorative logic. In successive drafts, the virtue of Wordsworth's 'spots of time' is first 'fructifying', then 'vivifying' and finally 'renovating', which is closest to 'restoration'. Blake's 'moment in each day which Satan cannot find' in his Prophetic Book, *Milton*, also 'renovates every moment of the day if rightly placed'. Without forcing the meaning, his key tropes in *Jerusalem* of 'awakening' and 'redeeming' also let us see the work's project of restoring potential, recovering the 'four-fold' being we all should enjoy.[20] Blake's renovating moment, then, is not a sequence, but an ever present potential, something which, if we keep it in mind, 'if rightly placed', can transform any other instant into something significant, rather than an item in the parade of 'empty, homogeneous time'. And this transformation comes about, I'd suggest, by seeing the contemporaneous quality of past, present and future, what the Bard sees, after all, at the beginning of *Songs of Innocence and Experience*—

Hear the voice of the bard,

Who present, past, and future sees –

Whose ears have heard

The Holy Word

That walked among the ancient trees... ('Introduction')[21]

The transformation may sound 'messianic', but if so, it is 'messianic' in Walter Benjamin's 'weak' sense. What makes for revelation is not the inculcation of dogmatic belief in some millennium to come: such convictions would be numbered for Blake among the fundamentalist heresies of those he calls 'the Elect' and 'the Reprobate'. Rather, revelation is of the interwoven quality of the future in past and present; so, what is revealed is our task, if we are to belong to 'the Redeemed',

---

19 William Blake, *Complete Writings*, ed. by Geoffrey Keynes (London: Oxford University Press, 1969), p. 784; 'Home at Grasmere', later 'Prospectus', in Gill, *William Wordsworth*, p. 199.
20 William Blake, *The Complete Poems*, ed. by W. H. Stevenson and D. V. Erdman (Hong Kong: Longman, 1972); *Milton*, Second Book, Plate 35; *Jerusalem*, Plate 15.
21 Ibid., p. 209.

to take responsibility for the future—a torment of doubt rather than acquiescence in dogma. (First Book, Plate 26). The historical Milton is restored for Blake by future possibility, a potential only discovered by revisiting, driven by present need, the Milton of the past and re-reading him radically against the grain. A once-and-for-all meaning of Milton dies. Milton, Blake writes, goes to 'eternal death', which is also his release into the active meanings of eternity, the creative mutuality of past, present and future. In comparison with this lively historical interaction, it is Milton's confinement to a single historical meaning then that looks 'spectral' and not of this world. The perception of what Milton, despite his intentions, really meant is inseparable from the realization of what we need him to be! This maybe is what Blake means near the end of *Jerusalem* by 'speaking the words of Eternity in human forms' (Plate 95). Or what he meant earlier in *The Marriage of Heaven and Hell* by saying that 'Eternity is in love with the productions of time'.[22] Again, the two categories are dialectically interdependent. To be human is to have this future-rich understanding of the past in the present, and time is just our characteristically simultaneous deployment of the different tenses. *Durée*, how we experience time imaginatively, is our access to the concept of eternity.

John Wilson Croker was never one to miss the chance of doing a good literary woman down. He was satirised by Thomas Love Peacock as Mr Killthedead in *Melincourt*. When, however, he called his fellow Irishwoman, Sydney Owenson (Lady Morgan), 'the great Corinna of the Radicals', he actually paid her a huge compliment not far off the mark.[23] Morgan's two guides, *France* (1817) and *Italy* (1821) move out of the genres of travelogue or memoir into that kind of politicised cultural commentary Staël—a model again—had really created in *De l'Allemagne* and prepared for in her famous novel *Corinne ou l'Italie*. Like Byron, Morgan twinned Italian and Irish subjugation and thought of them interactively. She even has a triple indictment of Castlereagh in a footnote to *Italy*. Castlereagh helps perpetrate the Act of Union and its brutal policing against the United Irishmen; having ruined Ireland, he

---

22 Blake, *The Marriage of Heaven and Hell*, Plate 7, ibid., p. 108.
23 See the very useful discussion by Donatella Abbate Badin of Morgan's mixed genres, reception and use of Staël, *Lady Morgan's Italy: Anglo-Irish Sensitivities and Italian Realities* (Bethseda: Academica Press, 2007), pp. 2, 72.

sets to work on Britain; and then, at the Congress, Europe is in the firing line.

> When Count Confalonieri, one of the deputies from Milan, in reply to Lord Castlereagh's question of 'what they wanted?' said, 'a Constitution like that of England!' the minister, we were assured, significantly replied, *Ce n'est pas ce que nous avons de mieux!* (That is not the best thing we have!) If any man in England was justified in uttering this blasphemous sarcasm, it was that Minister, who having destroyed the liberties of his *own* country, has laboured so hard to annihilate those of the nation, by which he has been adopted.[24]

Morgan wrote four appendices to her book, *France*, the fourth one of which was 'On the State of Political Opinion in France'. There she describes in patriotic, constitutional terms what has been, in her view, betrayed by the deal struck at the Congress of Vienna. Like the last quotation, her remarks are not very far from Wordsworth's. Both recall the wording of Wordsworth's political sonnets a decade and a half before, extolling Milton, Algernon Sidney, Marvell, Harrington and Vane as writers who 'Taught us how rightfully a nation shone/In splendour', linking them all as patriots. But she also believes that some thinking outside the binary of revolution and counter-revolution is necessary: revolution, in other words, is to be thought of as something productive not just of reaction but of other versions of itself.

> To consider the revolution then as at an end, and to imagine that the allied sovereigns have conquered the absolute possession of despotic power, either for themselves or for the French monarchs, would be the excess of folly. The dislocation of society has been too complete, and the shock given to prejudices and opinions too violent, to admit of a quiet resumption of old habits and ideas... A complete counter-revolution is impossible; and any despotism which can be substituted for it, must be composed of such jarring and ill-assorted materials, as never can dovetail and consolidate into harmony and stability.[25]

Well, what would be a proper political unity for Morgan in contrast to what she calls 'the European republic thus disjointed' (clxxx)? She

---

24 Lady Morgan [Sydney Owenson], *Italy*, 3rd ed., 3 vols. (London: Henry Colburn, 1821), I, p. 266n.
25 Lady Morgan [Sydney Owenson], *France*, 2 vols. (London: Henry Colburn, 1817), p. clxvii.

finishes her account of Lombardy, the first area that will be annexed and activated later during the Piedmont-led Risorgimento, with an interesting mix of materialist analysis and hortatory idealism:

> Against the liberties of Italy are the sovereigns of Europe, their armies, and their treasures: but armies are no longer to be trusted; and treasures, thanks to the thoughtless profusion of modern exchequers, are no longer to be commanded. In their favour are the kindling illumination of the age, the sympathy of the whole population of the civilized world; and all the force that belongs, in the eternal nature of things, to justice and to right.[26]

Affinities with the near-contemporary *Prometheus Unbound* mingle with a very realistic reference to the composite armies that had to replace national standing armies in the fight against Napoleon to secure victories like that of 1813 at Leipzig (*der Völkerschlacht*), never mind Waterloo. Along with this goes an awareness of the growing circulation of capital and the global dimension Marx was going to attribute to it. Like Hazlitt, Morgan thinks that the French Revolution has given mankind a 'sensible shock' connected with an inexorably approaching modernity. Most important will be decisions about what we want to preserve in the new dispensation, and whether we can imagine older values in a viably restored form. Can there be a European republic which is *not* hopelessly 'disjointed'?

The most grotesque contemporaneous satire on being so 'disjointed' comes, unsurprisingly, from the Irish poet Tom Moore—liberal Irish patriot and friend of Byron. In 'Letter Nine' of *The Fudge Family in Paris* (1818), a hilarious account of the Parisian tourism (made possible by the post-Waterloo peace) of an Irish/English family, he has that avid admirer of Castlereagh, Mr. Phil. Fudge, write to the great man about his visit to a madman who had fantasised a Restoration to their owners of the heads of all those guillotined in the Revolution.[27] Only some did not quite return to the right ones. In his own case, the lunatic was convinced, he had got the wrong head. Fudge finds food for thought here, and innocently imagines the inter-changeability of the heads of Sidmouth, the Prince Regent and other luminaries with satirically apt

---

26   Lady Morgan, *Italy*, I, p. 277–78.
27   Thomas Moore, *The Fudge Family in Paris, Edited by Thomas Brown the Younger, Author of the Twopenny Post-bag*, 4th ed. (London: Longman et al., 1818).

recipients; pickpockets, tailors and other disreputables. Eventually, though, the apotheosis is reached when he pleasurably imagines putting on Castlereagh's own head:

At last I tried your Lordship's on,

And then I grew completely addled—

Forgot all other heads, od rot 'em!

And slept, and dreamt that I was—BOTTOM. (Letter IX, pp. 100–4)

The top is the bottom, and the viscount is in the right company, that of another master of malapropism, Shakespeare's Bottom. (I don't know if Castlereagh's political cant was exceptional in comparison with what we hear nowadays. He talked of 'men turning their backs upon themselves', which is certainly a contortion difficult to imagine. He incorrectly used 'joining issue' as an opposite of 'taking issue', which was one of Moore's favourites). To take issue with his policies, though, it is clear that, for liberals like Moore and Byron, convincing Restoration will not be achieved by the invasion of France by the British proxy, Louis XVIII. Some accounts have the Bourbon getting a send-off from Britain to France comparable to the welcome accorded to the returning Charles II 150 years before. Moore is aware of this and fully exploits the irony right at the start of *The Fudge Family*. In Letter I, Miss Biddy is talking of her father, in slightly comical anapaests—da da dum, the poetic 'foot' more worthy of the shoddy monarch than heroic dactyls—dum da da, the dominant foot of Greek and Latin epic, anapaest turned the other way—ἄνδρα μοι ἔννεπε, ... Arma virumque cano... and so on. So, contrast:

By the by, though, at Calais, Papa *had* a touch

Of romance on the pier, which affected me much.

At the sight of that spot, where our darling DIX HUIT

Set the first of his own dear legitimate feet*

(Modell'd out so exactly, and – God bless the mark!

'Tis a foot, Dolly, worthy so *Grand* a *Monarque*)

He exclaimed 'Oh mon Roi!' and with tear-dropping eye,

>Stood to gaze on the spot – while some Jacobin, nigh,
>
>Mutter'd out with a shrug (what an insolent thing!)
>
>'Ma foi, he be right – 'tis de Englishmen's King
>
>And dat *gros pied de cochon* – begar, me vil say
>
>Dat de foot look mosh better, if turn'd toder way.'
>
>*To commemorate the landing of Louis le Desiré from England, the impression of his foot is marked out on the pier, and a pillar with an inscription raised opposite to the spot. (Letter I, pp. 3–4)

I cannot help hearing a caricature of Irish in 'begar'—the anapaest asks for the accent on 'gar', so it sounds less like 'beggar' and more like 'begorrah' shortened—which would fit the mixed critical idiom Castlereagh provoked, the Anglo-Irish abuser of Ireland, England and now Europe—as the French become the new Irish.

In his *Political Essays* of 1819, Hazlitt argued that, through the settlements imposed by the Congress of Vienna, Britain seemed intent on inflicting on the rest of Europe a hereditary monarchy. But in its own case, it prided itself enormously on having replaced hereditary legitimacy with something much more like a Miltonic magistracy— 'when the monarch still felt what he owed to himself and the people, and in the opposite claims which were set up to it, saw the real tenure on which he held his crown'.[28] For Hazlitt, this real tenure of Kings and Magistrates defines itself against 'the cant of legitimacy' (p. xi). His Milton, nevertheless, returns him to 1688, rather than 1649, restoring the spirit of a constitutional monarchy rather than a revolution succeeded by a republic. William Cobbett, too, in a surprisingly supportive letter to Chateaubriand around the time of the Congress of Verona, resents the way that post-Napoleonic France is kept weak, in his eyes, by not being allowed the same degree of political democracy as England. A Bourbon dependency is established at a time that, as Lady Morgan put it, 'an individual sentiment of patriotism, an entire conviction of the equality of rights among all orders of the state, and an attachment to the basis of the constitution, pervade private conversations, and give a very general tone to French society' (*France*, p. clxvi). Elsewhere, in 'Fables

---

28 William Hazlitt, *Political Essays* (London: William Hone, 1819), p. xi.

for the Holy Alliance', Moore implies that Sir Robert Filmer, apologist for monarchy from Biblical precedent (in *Patriarca, or the Natural Power of Kings*, 1680), is the guru of the Congress, with Algernon Sidney, one of Wordsworth's Commonwealth Men, as the opponent favoured by Moore.[29] By contrast, in *The Fudge Family*, Phelim Connor's straight, enraged polemic, addressed to Castlereagh, grasps, as did Hazlitt, at what Napoleon had promised: that unlike monarchs, or *'vulgar* Kings', he had 'rais'd the hopes of men', although only before dashing them— 'All this I own—but still...'[30] This aposiopesis ends the Letter, which a footnote tells us has been censored because 'so full of unsafe matter-of fact'.

In conclusion, it is helpful to think about Byron in the light of what I have been talking about. Byron laughs at Castlereagh's language as much as Moore does. They both think he cannot speak English. Sometimes Byron is unable to contain his contempt, as in the 'Dedication' to *Don Juan*.[31] His disgust for Castlereagh's 'language of Mrs Malaprop', keeps re-surfacing. Castlereagh, he says callously, committed 'sentimental suicide', he was 'the Werther of politics' (Preface to Canto VI). In any case, Byron was a frequently passionate advocate of the political importance of the proper use of one's language. Dullness is what especially appears to rouse Byron—as it had done his hero Alexander Pope—a fault in which all others can be poetically dissolved. The connection between language and political action is taken as given. In 1817, in the final Canto Four of *Childe Harold's Pilgrimage*, the hero, Childe Harold, had virtually vanished; according even to the Preface to Cantos One and Two he had been present only 'for the sake of giving some connection to the piece'.[32] The real hero, as some commentators have pointed out, becomes the Spenserian stanza, which Byron manipulates expertly and updates from the start, following James Beattie in claiming in the same Preface that it 'admits of every variety'. Here, like Milton, he 'recovers ancient liberty', but to the genre of romance, modernising and restoring it to political efficacy in the process. By the time he writes the letter to John

---

29 Thomas Moore, 'Fable IV' of 'Fables for the Holy Alliance', *The Poetical Works of Thomas Moore*, ed. by A.D. Godfrey (London: Oxford University Press, 1910), pp. 497–98.
30 Moore, 'The Fudge Family in Paris', Letter XI, *The Poetical Works*, p. 488.
31 McGann, *Lord Byron, The Complete Poetical Works*, vol. V, pp. 1–8.
32 *Childe Harold's Pilgrimage*, in ibid., vol. II, p. 4.

Cam Hobhouse at the start of Canto 4 of *Childe Harold*—Hobhouse in collaboration with Foscolo wrote the notes on Italian literature to Canto 4—this political edge has become still more obvious and pointed.[33] Again in the Dedication to *Don Juan*, Castlereagh is described as someone who 'mends old chains'. In contrast to the contemporary Congress system, Byron writes there as elsewhere in the service of the new Italy he wants to see established, the imaginary character with which he has replaced Harold, the 'child of imagination'.

The letter to Hobhouse does appear to want us to keep the parallel with what he calls 'the late transfer of nations' in mind. Towards its end, Byron recalls the lament sung by Roman workmen—'Roma! Roma! Roma! Roma! non è più com' era prima'—and contrasts it with the yells of those pleased with the dismemberment of Italy approved by the Congress of Vienna. But to resign oneself to this melancholy would be the equivalent of Samuel Rogers's pretty lament in his *Italy: A Poem* of 1822—lamenting nostalgically, 'Wouldst thou hadst less, or wert as once thou wast'.[34] By contrast, Byron's letter is up to date with the cultural furore in Italy over Madame de Staël's aforementioned essay on translation, which urged Italian literary practice to be less indebted to Italy's classical past in order to press more effectively her claims as a modern nation. Byron's intervention in this debate is a bit like Leopardi's. He stresses the capabilities of the Italian language. Writing in Italian, he advocates a pluralism, calling for an Italian poetry diversified by the different aesthetic stances open to it, feeding like Schlegel's *Poesie* a general Italian genius. He reels off a list of miscellaneous contemporary Italian luminaries qualifying Italy for serious consideration as a major European nation, concluding that in sculpture 'Europe—the World—has but one Canova'.

Ugo Foscolo was one of the poets he commended, and Foscolo had in 1812 written his own poem on Canova, *Le Grazie* (*The Graces*), his *Carme* or lyrical hymn to Canova celebrating an earlier version of the statue of the three Graces just commissioned by the Duke of Bedford. Foscolo had also published his most famous poem, *Dei Sepolcri* (*On Tombs*), in 1807, all about how new Napoleonic requirements that burials take place outside

---

33   Ibid., pp. 120–24.
34   Samuel Rogers, *Italy: A Poem* (London: Longman et al., 1822), p. 62.

city walls interfered with the idea of the restorative presence of the great dead in inspirational form at the heart of the current community.

The restoration of Italy, when it came, would see itself as the resurgent restoration of ancient *virtù* desired by Foscolo and Leopardi, anticipated surely by the famous *assunta* of Venice in the opening stanzas of Canto 4 of *Child Harold*:

She seems like a sea Cybele, fresh from ocean,

Rising with her tiara of proud towers

At airy distance, with majestic motion,

A ruler of the waters and their powers:

And such she was;—her daughters had their dowers

From spoils of nations, and the exhaustless East

Pour'd in her lap all gems in sparkling showers.

In purple was she robed, and of her feast

Monarchs partook, and deemed their dignity increased. (IV, lines 10–18)

Venice appears as that sometime republic inspiring English republican polemic of the greatest kind, like James Harrington's *The Commonwealth of Oceana*—'immortal Venice' and her 'incomparable commonwealth'.[35] Harrington was not against restoration as such, of course, he just wanted to restore a republic, not a monarchy; and in dedicating his work to Cromwell, the 'The Lord Protector of the Commonwealth', he was reminding him of what he should ideally be protecting. Venice is the source too of Byron's recovery of tragedy in *The Two Foscari* and *Marino Faliero*, as well as being exemplary for him of that openness to the East that drove his own Turkish Tales. Ultimately Venice stands for a political authority which, far from deferring to monarchy, might let its own legitimacy rub off on monarchs a little if they were lucky, 'their dignity increased'. The restorative interactions here are complex and rewarding. Venice's 'assumption', 'rising with her tiara of proud towers', is not into Heaven but into the *Realpolitik* of the day. Byron's sheer delight in

---

35 James Harrington, *The Commonwealth of Oceana* and *A System of Politics*, ed. by J.G.A. Pocock (Cambridge: Cambridge University Press, 1992), p. 99.

what Venice has been—'The revel of the earth, the masque of Italy!'—is turned into a historical reproach to the current treatment of Italy, and an incentive to realise something 'brighter', 'more beloved', something which 'replaces what we hate', 'with a fresher growth replenishing the void'. In Canto 4, Venice finally leads Byron to the ocean, 'the image of eternity' (p. CLXXXIII). For Harrington, 'The sea giveth law unto the growth of Venice, but the growth [of his ideal republic] Oceana giveth law unto the sea' (p. 7). Byron's ocean too makes 'monarchs tremble in their capitals', an element become as much a creature of imagination as the Childe had been. On this political warhorse the poet once 'laid my hand upon thy mane as I do here', literally as a swimmer, but now figuratively as a political poet mounted on a sublime power more powerful than any tyranny.[36] To this figure, the poem's conclusion entrusts the idea of the restoration of political justice.

Works Cited

Allard, Sébastien and Côme Fabre, *Delacroix: L'art et la matière* (Paris: Louvre éditions: Hazan, 2018).

Allem, Maurice and Paul Courant, eds, *Œuvres Complètes en Prose d'Alfred de Musset* (Paris: Bibliothèque de la Pléiade, 1960).

Badin, Donatella Abbat, *Lady Morgan's Italy: Anglo-Irish Sensitivities and Italian Realities* (Bethseda: Academica Press, 2007).

Bergson, Henri, *Creative Evolution*, trans. by Arthur Mitchell (London: Macmillan, 1964), https://doi.org/10.5962/bhl.title.17594

Keynes, Geoffrey, ed., *William Blake Complete writings* (London: Oxford University Press, 1969).

Gill, Stephen, ed., *The Oxford Authors William Wordsworth* (Oxford: Oxford University Press, 1984), https://doi.org/10.1093/notesj/33.2.248

Godfrey, A.D., ed., *The Poetical Works of Thomas Moore* (London: Oxford University Press, 1910).

Gogol, Nikolai, *Dead Souls*, trans. by David Magarshack (Harmondsworth: Penguin, 1961).

Hazlitt, William, *Political Essays* (London: William Hone, 1819).

---

36   Ibid., p. 7; McGann, *Lord Byron, Complete Poetical Works*, vol. II, p. 186 (stanza 184).

Harrington, James, *The Commonwealth of Oceana* and *A System of Politics*, ed. by J.G.A. Pocock (Cambridge: Cambridge University Press, 1992), https://doi.org/10.1017/cbo9781139137126.005

Koselleck, Reinhart, *Futures Past: On the Semantics of Historical Time* (Cambridge, MA: MIT Press, 1985).

Leopardi, Giacomo, *Discorso di un Italiano intorno alla poesia romantica*, ed. by Rosita Copioli (Milano: Biblioteca Univerzale Rizzoli, 1997).

McGann, Jerome J. ed., *Lord Byron, The Complete Poetical Works*, vol. II and V (Oxford: Clarendon Press, 1980, 86), https://doi.org/10.1093/actrade/9780198127543.book.1, https://doi.org/10.1093/actrade/9780198127574.book.1

Marx, Karl, 'The Eighteenth Brumaire of Louis Bonaparte', in *Surveys from Exile: Political Writings*, ed. by David Fernbach, trans. by Ben Fowkes (Harmondsworth: Penguin, 1973).

Milton, John, *Paradise Lost*, ed. by Alastair Fowler (Hong Kong: Longman, 1976), https://doi.org/10.4324/9781315834726

Moore, Thomas, *The Fudge Family in Paris, Edited by Thomas Brown the Younger, Author of the Twopenny Post-bag*, 4th ed. (London: Longman et al., 1818).

Morgan, Lady [Sydney Owenson], *Italy*, 3rd ed., 3 vols. (London: Henry Colburn, 1821).

——, *France*, 2 vols. (London: Henry Colburn, 1817).

Nietzsche, Friedrich, *The Will to Power*, trans. Walter Kaufmann and R.J. Hollingdale (New York: Random House, 1968).

Reiman, Donald H., and Sharon B. Powers, eds, *Shelley's Poetry and Prose* (New York and London: Norton, 1977).

Rogers, Samuel, *Italy: A Poem* (London: Longman et al., 1822).

Saglia, Diego, *European Literatures in Britain, 1815–32* (Cambridge: Cambridge University Press, 2019), https://doi.org/10.1017/9781108669900

——, 'British Romanticism and the Post-Napoleonic South: Writing Restoration Transnationally', *Essays in Romanticism*, 24.2 (2017), 105–24, https://doi.org/10.3828/eir.2017.24.2.2

Schlegel, Friedrich, 'Athenaeum Fragment', no. 80, in *Philosophical Fragments*, trans. by Peter Firchow (Minnesota: University of Minnesota Press, 1991).

Stevenson, W.H. and D. V. Erdman, eds, *Blake: The Complete Poems* (Hong Kong: Longman, 1972).

Wolfson, Susan J., ed., *Felicia Hemans: Selected Poems, Letters, Reception, Materials* (Princeton and Oxford: Princeton University Press, 2000), https://doi.org/10.2307/3737958

2. Anthropocene Temporalities and British Romantic Poetry

Evan Gottlieb

As Dipesh Chakrabarty has argued, the dawning of the Anthropocene has created not only tangible environmental and political effects, but also has threatened to alter our traditionally anthropocentric sense of time, which (following Quentin Meillassoux) I dub "correlationist time." Although these alterations feel novel, however, evidence of temporality's malleability can be traced back at least to the British Romantics, who like us were navigating uncharted waters, politically as well as ecologically. After outlining the modern Western consolidation of "correlationist time" and locating its representational epitome in some early poetry of William Wordsworth, I sketch four alternatives to "correlationist time" limned by other British Romantics poets: deep time (Charlotte Smith, Percy Shelley); slow time (Keats), revolutionary time (Shelley again), and hyper-Chaotic time (Byron).

According to Reinhart Koselleck's influential formulation, the defining experience of modernity has been acceleration. Combined with what he calls a new sense of an 'open future', Koselleck argues that this privileging of progress and novelty has been the reigning temporality since the late eighteenth century.[1] Although this thesis clearly takes its cues from the Industrial Revolution's speeding up of socio-political and economic processes, it neglects to consider the environmental impacts that have today become (nearly) impossible to ignore.[2] This oversight

---

1   Reinhart Koselleck, 'The Eighteenth Century as the Beginning of Modernity', in *The Practice of Conceptual History: Timing History, Spacing Concepts*, trans. by Todd Samuel Presner and others (Stanford: Stanford University Press, 2002), p. 165.
2   I say '(nearly) impossible to ignore' because some governments, political parties, industries, corporations, and other entities remain all too eager to deny, downplay,

is symptomatic not just of Koselleck's scholarly milieu but also of the fact that the transition from older (feudal) modes of historical thinking to newer, modern ones nevertheless retained a basic assumption: that human temporalities are largely divorced from planetary ones.[3] Indeed, the carry-over from earlier eras, which generally held nature to be at best a passive backdrop for human activity, and at worst a stubborn obstacle to be overcome by human ingenuity and industry, arguably lies behind capitalist modernity's penchant for treating the natural world primarily as a resource to be exploited.

But in the time of the Anthropocene, this pretence is now untenable, at least for those of us who, following Bruno Latour, are ready to admit that 'we [have] shifted from a mere ecological crisis into what should instead be called *a profound mutation in our relation to the world*'.[4] This mutation takes many forms, to be sure, and Dipesh Chakrabarty identifies its temporal dimension in his formative 2009 article, 'The Climate of History: Four Theses', where he observes that 'anthropogenic explanations of climate change spell the collapse of the age-old humanist distinction between natural history and human history [...]. A fundamental assumption of Western (and now universal) political thought has come undone in this crisis'.[5] The assumption to which Chakrabarty alludes, moreover, is as basic as it is increasingly uncertain: 'that our past, present, and future are connected by a certain continuity of human experience'.[6] Such continuity seemed to be guaranteed both by the supposed distinction (retained by Koselleck's accelerated modernity) between human and planetary history, and modernity's imagined triumph of the former over the latter: precisely the two postulates that the Anthropocene threatens to disprove with increasing violence, as Chakrabarty demonstrated more than a decade ago.

---

or otherwise distract from the realities of global warming.

3   This is not to deny that strands of philosophical thinking have long proposed various connections between our sense of time and our geophysical situatedness as upright bipedals; for a fascinating meditation on such theories, see Thomas Moynihan, *Spinal Catastrophism: A Secret History* (Windsor Quarry, Falmouth: Urbanomic, 2019).

4   Bruno Latour, *Facing Gaia: Eight Lectures on the New Climatic Regime*, trans. by Catherine Porter (Cambridge: Polity, 2017), p. 8.

5   Dipesh Chakrabarty, 'The Climate of History: Four Theses', *Critical Inquiry* 35 (Winter 2009), 197–222 (pp. 201, 207), https://doi.org/10.1086/596640

6   Ibid.

Chakrabarty posits this development as new because, like many historians, he largely sees the Anthropocene itself as a relatively new affair. But there are good reasons to recognise anthropocenic effects beginning much earlier than 'the Great Acceleration' of the post-World-War-II period or even the Industrial Revolution; humans have been systematically altering our environments, after all, since the dawn of agriculture in the Fertile Crescent some 10,000 years ago. Moreover—and more to the point in this chapter, which will argue for William Wordsworth's poetry as the norm of Romantic-era constructions of anthropocentric temporality, before outlining a number of his contemporaries' alternatives—the idea of the earth as primarily dead or at least inert matter (and thus merely waiting to be exploited by us) was already being challenged in the later nineteenth century, not least by the *naturphilosophie* of Friedrich Schelling. As Iain Hamilton Grant, Ben Woodard, and others have demonstrated, for Schelling (in his early works at least) nature must be understood in its properly active modality, not just as 'the ground' (both literal and metaphorical) of all human thought and being, but as an active force in its own right, replete with a 'fundamental productivity' that takes place on timescales far in excess of the human.[7] Schelling's *naturphilosophie*, moreover, was in line with roughly contemporary work in the budding discipline of geology, or 'natural philosophy' as it was still known, which was challenging Biblical accounts of the Earth's formation and history with evidence drawn first from the fossil record and then, more compellingly, from contemporary lithic evidence. In France, the Comte de Buffon and his rival Georges Cuvier had already put forth competing theories of geological change; in Britain, James Hutton was observing Scottish rock formations, concluding that their visible strata represented successive cycles of lithic uplift and erosion that could only be accounted for via an 'abyss of time' that makes 'the mind see[m] to grow giddy', in the words of his friend and populariser James Playfair.[8] As Jeffrey J. Cohen

---

[7] Ben Woodard, 'Inverted Astronomy: Ungrounded Ethics, Volcanic Copernicanism, and the Ecological Decentering of the Human', *Polygraph* 22 (2010), 79–93 (p. 81). See also Iain Hamilton Grant, *Philosophies of Nature after Schelling* (London and New York: Continuum, 2006), https://doi.org/10.5040/9781472547279; Woodard, *Schelling's Naturalism: Motion, Space, and the Volition of Thought* (Edinburgh: Edinburgh University Press, 2019).

[8] Quoted in 'James Hutton', Wikipedia. https://en.wikipedia.org/wiki/James_Hutton

remarks, by recognizing that the igneous expanses of Edinburgh's Arthur's Seat—the remains of a once-active volcano—had thrust through younger sedimentary stone, Hutton essentially 'discerned the opening of deep time, [of] the earth's slow liveliness'.[9] Despite the ever-increasing evidence of the planet's titanic age and inhuman productivity, however, the existence of God could still guarantee that the natural world was— and by implication would remain—conducive to human flourishing. Charles Lyell makes this plain in the final chapter of his *Principles of Geology* (1830–33), which first states that geologists can safely conclude 'it is not only the present condition of the globe that has been suited to the accommodation of myriads of living creatures, but that many former states also have been equally adapted to the organization and habits of prior races of beings', before reiterating the need for 'a just estimate of the relations which subsist between the finite powers of man and the attributes of an Infinite and Eternal Being'.[10] Although the immediate context of Lyell's final call for scientific humility is the admission that scientists may never attain a complete understanding of planetary history, the implication is that the mismatch between human and divine temporalities need not trouble us so long as our faith in the benevolence of God and His creation—the Earth itself—remains unshaken.

As Noah Heringman and others have persuasively argued, these developments in geology did not go unnoticed by the Romantic poets of the day.[11] In this vein, a sense of human flourishing as both predicated on and guaranteed by the natural world's durability is perhaps best expressed by William Wordsworth's well-known lines: 'My heart leaps up when I behold/A Rainbow in the sky:/So was it when my life began;/So is it now I am a Man;/So be it when I shall grow old,/Or let me die!'[12] Although God is nowhere mentioned here, Wordsworth's choice of a rainbow as his central image seems overdetermined by its symbolic status in the Judeo-Christian tradition, where it appears most

---

9   Jeffrey J. Cohen, *Stone: An Ecology of the Inhuman* (Minneapolis and London: University of Minnesota Press, 2015), pp. 188–89.
10   Charles Lyell, *Principles of Geology*, ed. by James A. Secord (London and New York: Penguin, 1997), pp. 437–38.
11   Noah Heringman, *Romantic Rocks, Aesthetic Geology* (Ithaca and London: Cornell University Press, 2004), pp. 1, 5.
12   William Wordsworth, 'My heart leaps up', in *Wordsworth's Poetry and Prose*, ed. by Nicholas Halmi (New York and London: Norton, 2014), pp. 417–18, lines 1–6. Subsequent citations refer to this edition.

prominently in Genesis as a sign of God's 'postdiluvian covenant with all living creatures not to destroy the earth [again]'.[13] Wordsworth's shrewd incorporation of the rainbow into his poem, then, subtly reminds readers that, whatever geology might be discovering about the earth's unpredictable productivity, its ultimate stability could still be counted on as the basis of human life and, by extension, morality. Just as '[t]he Child is Father of the Man', Wordsworth reassures us that, come what may, our environment will sustain us, spiritually as well as physically, just as the speaker's days, ideally, will be 'Bound each to each by natural piety'.[14]

To be sure, many of Wordsworth's other poems are populated with more uncanny earthly phenomena: the 'sounding cataract' that 'haunt[s]' the 'boyish' Wordsworth 'like a passion' in 'Lines Written a Few Miles above Tintern Abbey' (74–78), for example, or the inexplicable, isolated 'huge Stone' that serves as an extended simile in 'Resolution and Independence' (399).[15] Even in these examples, however, what remains certain is Wordsworth's conviction that the natural world fundamentally exists in harmony with the human one, if only we can learn to see it rightly. Elsewhere, I have written about this 'tendency [of Wordsworth] to correlate things to their human significances', drawing on Quentin Meillassoux's influential diagnosis of 'correlationism' as the mode of modern thought, inherited most directly from Immanuel Kant, which claims we can never perceive, know, or even think about the world on its own terms, but rather only in terms of its relation to us (and vice versa).[16] Hence we have access only to what 'correlates' between us and 'the great outdoors', as Meillassoux terms it. Understood in this light, it makes perfect sense that 'My heart leaps up' should appear in the 'Moods of my Own Mind' section of Wordsworth's *Poems, in Two Volumes*. Indeed, the apparent redundancy in that title—*my own mind*—emphasises precisely Wordsworth's commitment to correlationism:

---

13   Ibid., p. 417, n1.
14   Wordsworth, 'My heart leaps up', lines 7–9.
15   For more on the appearance of these and similar natural objects in Wordsworth and certain of his inheritors, see, e.g. Mary Jacobus, *Romantic Things: A Tree, a Rock, a Cloud* (Chicago and London: University of Chicago Press, 2012).
16   Evan Gottlieb, *Romantic Realities: Speculative Realism and British Romanticism* (Edinburgh: Edinburgh University Press, 2016), p. 36.

the world is knowable, not to mention meaningful, only insofar as it correlates to Wordsworth's mental experience of it.

We can see such correlationism everywhere in Wordsworth, but for reasons of space, another poem published in the same 1807 volume will have to suffice as our lone second example. Here are the opening stanzas and closing stanzas of 'To the Daisy':

In youth from rock to rock I went,

From hill to hill, in discontent,

Of pleasure high and turbulent.

    Most pleas'd when most uneasy:

But now my own delights I make

My thirst at every rill can slake,

And gladly Nature's love partake,

    Of thee, sweet Daisy!

When soothed a while by milder airs,

Thee Winter in the garland wears,

That thinly shades his few grey hairs;

    Spring cannot shun thee;

Whole summer fields are thine by right;

And Autumn, melancholy Wight!

Doth in thy crimson head delight,

    When rains are on thee.

* * * *

And all day long I number yet,

All seasons through, another debt,

Which I wherever thou art met,

    To thee am owing;

An instinct call it, a blind sense;

A happy, genial influence,

Coming one knows not how nor whence,

    Nor whither going.

Child of the Year! That round dost run

Thy course, bold lover of the sun,

And cheerful when the day's begun

    As morning Leveret,

Thou long the Poet's praise shall gain;

Thou wilt be more belov'd by men

In times to come; thou not in vain

    Art Nature's Favorite.[17]

Notwithstanding Wordsworth's apparently high estimation of this poem—he placed it at the opening of the first book of *Poems, in Two Volumes*—its jaunty meter and repeating octaves deny it the high seriousness of much of Wordsworth's better-known early verse. Nevertheless, its opening contrast between the speaker's supposed prior heedlessness and his current, hard-earned maturity shares the narrative DNA of many of Wordsworth's more acclaimed poems, especially 'Lines Written a few Miles above Tintern Abbey'. Like that poem, too, 'To the Daisy' credits nature's benevolent influence with the speaker's transformation from febrile boy to cool-headed man. Unlike 'Tintern Abbey' and the later *The Prelude*, however, here that sense of psychological and philosophical progress is uncomplicated by any narrative recursion or fascination with semi-traumatic 'spots of time'. Instead, the speaker establishes his mature sense of self by aligning it with the various but predictable appearances of the titular flower, which in turn reflect the regular cycles of the seasons in the first stanza and the solar year in the final stanza. This calibration of human and planetary

---

17 Wordsworth, 'To the Daisy', pp. 384–86, lines 1–16, 65–80.

rhythms thus provides the 'genial influence' whose appearance and destination Wordsworth rather disingenuously claims not to know in lines 70–71. His penultimate declaration that the daisy 'wilt be more belov'd by men/In times to come', however, is clearly beholden to precisely this certainty, since Wordsworth's confident prediction of human continuity and even improvement ('*more* belov'd'; my italics) is implicitly underwritten by the poem's preceding delineations of a regular, predictable, earthly temporality—'all day long [...]/all seasons through'—which governs all.

Following Meillassoux, I propose to call the temporality Wordsworth limns here as 'correlationist time'. By this I don't mean a radically subjective sense of time, but rather one that connects natural history to human history in a reassuringly correlationist manner, such that the expectation of human continuity is underwritten by an ultimately anthropocentric faith in humanity's connection with a natural world perceived by us as metastable and enduring. Although the once-common assumption that, after the Flood, the Earth existed in a homeostatic, generally unchanging state had been thrown into doubt by the new earth sciences, Wordsworth's poetry helps (re-)establish the basic coordinates of a correlationist time in which human history and natural history are gently 'bound each to each'. Chakrabarty's thesis that human history and natural history were perceived as divergent by modernity prior to the Anthropocene thus needs amending in light of Wordsworth's influential promotion of correlationist time as an antidote to modern malaise. Nevertheless, it is worth considering that correlationist time, in its quiet support of a 'world for us' mindset, ironically chimes with extractive capitalism's treatment of the natural world as a resource to be exploited and a dumping-ground for 'external costs' like waste water.

Yet even as this Wordsworthian attitude toward both nature (as what sustains humanity) and history (as progress toward a more-or-less predictable future) became more widespread, a number of alternatives to the paradigm of correlationist time began to appear in other British Romantic poetry. For reasons of space, I can only gesture here toward some of the social, political, and economic factors that may have contributed to this fracturing: the massive political upheavals set off by the French Revolution and then partially globalised by the Napoleonic Wars; the subsequent rehabilitation of much of Europe's old order following the Congress of Vienna; and the dramatic, post-1815 downturn in the British economy, which in turn was worsened by a variety of factors including the heavy national debt incurred during wartime; the repatriation of thousands of British troops; a devastating series of bad harvests; and an increasingly displaced agricultural workforce.[18] Parliamentary reform, long promised, still seemed a distant dream—one that was literally trampled on by the infamous Peterloo Massacre of August 1819. This is not an exhaustive list by any means, and as we will see below, alternatives to correlationist time were beginning to appear prior to at least some these events. Nevertheless, when considered alongside many younger Romantics' disillusionment with Wordsworth's increasing conservatism—exemplified in Percy Shelley's sonnet 'To Wordsworth' and Mary Shelley's scathing judgment after hearing parts of Wordsworth's *Excursion*: 'He is a slave'[19]—it becomes clear that the break between so-called first- and second-generation Romantics remains pertinent to any consideration of poetic as well as political transformation during the era. At the risk of schematism, then, I propose we can see in the work of Wordsworth's peers and inheritors at least four alternatives to correlationist time, which I will briefly outline and exemplify in what follows.

1. Deep Time

As discussed above, the burgeoning discipline of geology made it increasingly evident that planetary history demands to be understood on timescales that dwarf not only individual human lives but also humanity as a whole. As Heringman puts it, even when Hutton, Lyell and others made incorrect or vague conjectures about the origins and processes that created the rock formations they observed, their accounts cumulatively painted a picture of a 'geological past [...] so remote that its vestiges can be read only as signs of obscure, titanic processes'.[20] These processes clearly preceded human life and presumably would

---

18 'History of the British national debt', *Wikipedia*. https://en.wikipedia.org/wiki/History_of_the_British_national_debt
19 The dismissal is from Mary Shelley's journal entry of September 14, 1814, *Shelley's Poetry and Prose*, ed. by Donald H. Reiman and Neil Fraistat, p. 92, n1.
20 Heringman, *Romantic Rocks, Aesthetic Geology*, p. 4.

continue without it; barring the insertion of an all-seeing and benevolent God into the picture, the clear implication was that 'correlationist time' simply cannot account for the majority of Earth's history. As it happens, this insight forms the basis of Quentin Meillassoux's opening gambit in his book *After Finitude*, whose first chapters outline the problems caused for correlationists by the existence of what Meillassoux calls the 'arche-fossil': artefactual evidence of material existence that clearly preceded conscious life, or indeed any life at all.[21]

Not coincidentally, such fossils find their way into much Romantic poetry, where they likewise frequently serve as reminders of the incommensurability of 'deep time' with an anthropocentric or correlationist view of the world. Charlotte Smith's 'Beachy Head' (1807), although written too early to be considered a 'true' second-generation Romantic poem, has recently returned to the forefront of the Romantic poetic canon in no small part because of its attention to the fossilised shells whose presence stirs Smith's curiosity as she walks at some distance inland from the Sussex coastline:

Ah hills! so early loved! in fancy still

I breathe your pure keen airs; and still behold

Those widely spreading views, mocking alike

The Poet and the Painter's utmost art.

And still, observing objects more minute,

Wondering remark the strange and foreign forms

Of sea shells; with the pale calcareous soil

Mingled, and seeming of resembling substance.

Tho' surely the blue Ocean (from the heights

Where the downs westward trend, but dimly seen)

Here never roll'd its surge. Does Nature then

Mimic, in wanton mood, fantastic shapes

---

[21] Quentin Meillassoux, *After Finitude: An Essay on the Necessity of Contingency*, trans. by Ray Brassier (London and New York: Continuum, 2008), pp. 1–27.

> Of bivalves, and inwreathed volutes, that cling
>
> To the dark sea-rock of the wat'ry world?
>
> Or did this range of chalky mountains, once
>
> Form a vast basin, where the Ocean waves
>
> Swell'd fathomless? What time these fossil shells,
>
> Buoy'd on their native element, were thrown
>
> Among the imbedding calx: when the huge hill
>
> Its giant bulk heaved, and in strange ferment
>
> Grew up a guardian barrier, 'twixt the sea
>
> And the green level of the sylvan weald.[22]

As Kevis Goodman notes, in this passage Smith takes readers through a quick tour of the various geological theories of her day, including the idea that such apparent abnormalities as inland ocean fossils might represent nothing more than '*lusus naturae* (sports or tricks of nature)'.[23] Given that Smith spends much more time considering more scientific possibilities, however, Goodman plausibly concludes that 'for Smith, meditating on the fossil shells far from the sea, spatial displacement encodes historical difference'. In *Beachy Head*, human history is thoroughly mixed up with the vestiges of a primordially productive earth; but the presence of fossilised shells far from the sea also highlights the disjunction between human history and the deep, planetary time that Smith can only guess and wonder at in these lines. Certainly, Smith's verse suggests that, *contra* Wordsworth, human and planetary temporalities cannot be unproblematically aligned.

This suggestion is taken up even more emphatically in Percy Shelley's alpine meditation, 'Mont Blanc' (1817). When Mary and Percy toured the Chamonix Valley in the summer of 1816 and gazed up at the

---

22 Charlotte Smith, *Beachy Head*, in *Charlotte Smith: Major Poetic Works*, ed. by Claire Knowles and Ingrid Horrocks (Peterborough, ON: Broadview Press, 2017), lines 368–89.

23 Kevis Goodman, 'Conjectures on Beachy Head: Charlotte Smith's Geological Poetics and the Grounds of the Present', *ELH*, 81.3 (Fall 2014), 983–1006 (p. 991), https://doi.org/10.1353/elh.2014.0033

cloud-obscured peaks of Mont Blanc from a bridge over the Arve river, they were hardly the first British tourists to do so; indeed, although 'Mont Blanc' has long been interpreted as Shelley's philosophical riposte to Wordsworth's 'Tintern Abbey', it more directly responds to S.T. Coleridge's explicitly theocratic 'Hymn before Sun-Rise, in the Vale of Chamouni' (1802). 'Mont Blanc' has recently become a touchstone poem for literary critics, including me, interested in applying Speculative Realist principles to Romantic poetry (and vice versa).[24] Here, then, it will be enough to note how the poem is filled with allusions to the literally inhuman spans of time over which, Shelley correctly assumes, the mountain and its surrounding vales were formed. One passage, drawn from the fourth section, can stand for the whole in this regard:

> All things that move and breathe with toil and sound
>
> Are born and die; revolve, subside and swell.
>
> Power dwells apart in its tranquility
>
> Remote, serene, and inaccessible:
>
> And *this*, the naked countenance of earth,
>
> On which I gaze, even these primaeval mountains
>
> Teach the adverting mind.[25]

The contrast between the temporality of a human life-cycle—or, for that matter, the life-cycle of any living thing—and that of the monumental lithic formation with which Shelley is confronted, could not be clearer; Wordsworth's daisy wilts by comparison. Even as Shelley's imagination is drawn to the mountain's peak—his mind 'advert[s]' to it, implying

---

24 See, e.g., Greg Ellermann, 'Speculative Romanticism', *SubStance*, 44.1 (2015), 154–74, https://doi.org/10.1353/sub.2015.0008; Gottlieb, *Romantic Realities*, pp. 161–67; Anne C. McCarthy, 'The Aesthetics of Contingency in the Shelleyan "Universe of Things," or 'Mont Blanc' without Mont Blanc"', *Studies in Romanticism*, 54.3 (2015), 355–75, https://doi.org/10.1353/srm.2015.0012; Steven Shaviro, *The Universe of Things: On Speculative Realism* (Minneapolis and London: University of Minnesota Press, 2014), pp. 57–59, https://doi.org/10.5749/minnesota/9780816689248.001.0001; Chris Washington, *Romantic Revelations: Visions of Post-Apocalyptic Life and Hope in the Anthropocene* (Toronto, Buffalo, and London: University of Toronto Press, 2019), pp. 44–54, https://doi.org/10.3138/9781487530310

25 Percy Shelley, 'Mont Blanc', in *Shelley's Poetry and Prose*, p. 99, lines 94–100.

an involuntary absorption or fascination—the disparity between mind and matter makes clear that they may inhabit the same space, the same 'universe of things' (to quote the poem's opening line), but not the same temporality. In this light, Shelley's famous final question to the mountain—'And what were thou, and earth, and stars, and sea,/If to the human mind's imaginings/Silence and solitude were vacancy?'[26]—is anything but rhetorical; whatever else we might make of it, the deep time of Mont Blanc precedes, exceeds, and recedes from us.

2. Slow Time

In *The Poetics of Decline in British Romanticism*, Jonathan Sachs makes a compelling case for 'slow time' as an alternative temporality of the Romantic era, one that is 'not simply a reaction to [the] acceleration' of modern commercial life, but also 'reveals the development of new kinds of literary experience'.[27] While Sachs' interest is largely in slow time as an experiential category, I think it also appears as an alternative Romantic temporality in a more objective sense. I am primarily thinking here, of course, of John Keats's use of this phrase in his opening address to the object of antiquity he calls a Grecian Urn: 'Thou still unravish'd bride of quietness,/Thou foster-child of silence and slow time […]'.[28] As a product of human labour, the artefact in question obviously differs in kind from the geological features that populate the previous section's deep time. The questions that the urn raises for Keats, however, in some respects differ only in degree from those that the fossils raise for Smith, or that Mont Blanc raises for Shelley. What is the meaning of this non-human thing, of indeterminate age, that confronts humans with evidence of our own relative insignificance in the historical record prior to the Anthropocene? Is it desirable—or even possible—to strike up an imaginative relation with it, or is that simply an act of hubris, at best a compensatory cognitive movement designed to forestall recognition of our historical ephemerality? The fact that Keats' poem, like Shelley's,

---

26 Ibid., lines 141–43.
27 Jonathan Sachs, *The Poetics of Decline in British Romanticism* (Cambridge and New York: Cambridge University Press, 2018), p. 7, https://doi.org/10.1017/9781108333115
28 John Keats, 'Ode on a Grecian Urn', in *The Works of John Keats* (Ware, Hertfordshire: Wordsworth Editions, 1994), p. 233, lines 1–2.

ends on a famously ambiguous note—are we really supposed to believe that the neo-classical platitude, 'Beauty is truth, truth beauty',[29] provides genuine salvation for suffering, mortal humans?—seems far from coincidental when seen in this light; these are not questions we will answer in our lifetime, or any lifetime.

Yet thanks precisely to its clearly human origins, the urn offers something that neither fossils nor mountains can: evidence of the potential endurance of material artefacts far beyond the original intentions, lifespans, and even civilizational contexts of their makers. The urn that Keats likely saw in the British Museum was probably not originally designed merely to be displayed and admired, but rather to be used—quite possibly as a funereal vessel. Notably, however, Keats shows no interest whatsoever in the urn's original usage, nor in the manner in which it eventually arrived at the British Museum for exhibition; instead, he remains almost entirely focused on its exterior scenes.[30] Keats' silence on these questions, then, implies his intuitive recognition that the urn's history, first as a useful implement and later as a token of Britain's increasing dominance on the world stage, is literally neither here nor there; rather, the urn's spatial presence in front of Keats (and its virtual presence in front of us, Keats' readers) stands in contrast to its temporal dislocation as an object 'out of time', existing neither in its original context nor unproblematically in the present moment (whether representational or experiential). The urn thus materially embodies Ian Hodder's anthropological observation that 'things and humans live in different temporalities', despite their inevitable entanglement.[31]

Not all things exist in the 'slow time' of Keats' urn, of course—many things, by contrast, exist at temporalities so minuscule (from a human perspective, at least) that we are hardly aware of them. But as a survivor of an ancient civilization brought into Keats' modern world of 1817, the urn's existence in a 'slow time' continuum exemplifies Hodder's thesis that 'There is more to history than a linear account of sequences of events; there is also the material history, the heritage of

---

29 Ibid., p. 234, line 49.
30 On Keats' relation to museum culture see, e.g., Christopher Rovee, 'Trashing Keats', *ELH*, 75.4 (Winter 2008), 993–1022, https://doi.org/10.1353/elh.0.0022
31 Ian Hodder, *Entangled: An Archaeology of the Relationships between Humans and Things* (Malden, MA and Oxford: Wiley-Blackwell, 2007), p. 98.

past acts, the detritus of past millennia that bumps up against us in a non-linear way'.[32] This insight, in turn, lends further piquancy to Keats' half-playful admonishment of the urn: 'Thou, silent form, dost tease us out of thought/As doth eternity. Cold Pastoral!' (44–45).

3. Revolutionary Time

Among the canonical Romantic poets, Percy Shelley kept the fires of revolutionary hope burning most strongly in the poetry of the post-Waterloo era. Shelley, then, becomes the primary keeper of what, again following Sachs, we can call 'revolutionary time': 'the possibility of change [that] is both instantaneous and radically transformative because it produces a rupture between past and present'.[33] Although such thinking might seem born of desperation, there was natural philosophical precedent for it in geological theories of 'catastrophism', which hypothesised that the earth's history was generally homeostatic except for moments of major (usually disastrous) alteration that could not be predicted. (The Biblical Flood was the first and ultimate precedent here.) Thanks to newer work by the likes of Hutton and Lyell, catastrophism was less in favour by the turn of the nineteenth century than the gradualist theories of slow, accretional change that correspond to the temporalities already discussed; sudden catastrophes like the 1755 Lisbon earthquake, however, provided vivid evidence of the potential for massive, unheralded alterations in the social fabric. In the political realm, moreover, the original French revolutionaries remained a major inspiration for British radicals, not only because they represented (again, in Sachs' words) 'a rupture, a break in secular time and a separation from the past', but also because they self-consciously tried to re-start the political clock, for example by instituting the first day of 'Year One' immediately after their monarchy's abolition.[34]

Revolutionary time thus offered a stark and, for Shelley and his peers, attractive alternative not just to correlationist time but also to the 'deep' and 'slow' temporalities outlined above. For any given moment to become visible or at least thinkable as containing the potential

---

32 Ibid., p. 101.
33 Jonathan Sachs, *The Poetics of Decline in British Romanticism*, p. 146.
34 Ibid., p. 147.

for a sudden, even unforeseen transformation, the present must be apprehended in both its historical and synchronic dimensions—an apprehension that writing is especially well positioned to accomplish, as (to revert to Derridean terms) the play of signification is always a matter of spacing as well as timing. This is precisely the burden of Shelley's sonnet 'England in 1819', which was far too radical to be publishable in Shelley's lifetime:

> An old, mad, blind, despised, and dying King;
>
> Princes, the dregs of their dull race, who flow
>
> Through public scorn,—mud from a muddy spring;
>
> Rulers who neither see nor feel nor know,
>
> But leechlike to their fainting country cling
>
> Till they drop, blind in blood, without a blow.
>
> A people starved and stabbed in th' untilled field;
>
> An army, whom liberticide and prey
>
> Makes as a two-edged sword to all who wield;
>
> Golden and sanguine laws which tempt and slay;
>
> Religion Christless, Godless—a book sealed;
>
> A senate, Time's worst statute, unrepealed—
>
> Are graves from which a glorious Phantom may
>
> Burst, to illumine our tempestuous day.

Notably, the entire sonnet is composed of two sentences, each of which piles sub-clause on sub-clause until, like Walter Benjamin's remediation of Paul Klee's *Angelus Novus*, it seems that all we can do is bear witness to the disastrous reign of George III, the depredations of his minions, and the suffering of the British people. But as James Chandler observes in his still-unparalleled reading of this poem,

> the terms of the times in Shelley's catalogue—the conditions of his tempestuous day—are not simple evils and are not simply overcome by the arrival of an enlightening "deus ex machina". Rather [...] the

conditions of his day become the occasion for the kind of illumination that the final couplet anticipates.[35]

Translated into revolutionary temporality, in other words, Shelley uses the resources of the sonnet to spread out and display conditions that, experienced in 'normal' time, are a welter of simultaneous confusion—and it is this arrangement, in turn, that allows the illumination and saturation of the revolutionary spirit.

Significantly, like deep and slow time, and unlike correlationist time, revolutionary time is at least theoretically divorced from human action or even intention. Although Shelley became a hero to the nineteenth-century Chartists thanks to lyrics like 'Men of England' ('Men of England, wherefore plough/For the lords who lay ye low?/Wherefore weave with toil and care/The rich robes your tyrants wear?'), which celebrate the power of the combined masses, many of his most striking depictions of actual revolutionary moments do not involve human actors. Instead, like the Phantom that bursts from the graves of the dead at the end of 'England in 1819', or like the figure of Hope in 'The Mask of Anarchy' (also unpublishable in Shelley's lifetime due to its radicalism), Shelley's revolutionary moment—the instant when past and present coincide, temporality is converted to spatiality, and new arrangements of both time and space can therefore be imagined—frequently invoke abstractions or personifications as their prime movers. Regardless of whether this testifies to Shelley's idealism or desperation, it strongly suggests that Romantic revolutionary time, in its contingency and unpredictability, has more in common with what Alain Badiou calls 'an event'—which, in lieu of a full explanation here, we can simply define via Christopher Norris' helpful gloss as 'that which occurs unpredictably, has the potential to effect a momentous change in some given situation, state of knowledge, or state of affairs, and—above all—has consequences such as require an unswerving fidelity or a fixed resolve to carry them through'[36]—than with what Chandler, writing in

---

35 James Chandler, *England in 1819: The Politics of Literary Culture and the Case of Romantic Historicism* (Chicago and London: Chicago University Press, 1998), pp. 30–31.
36 Christopher Norris, 'Event', in *The Badiou Dictionary*, ed. by Steve Corcoran (Edinburgh: Edinburgh University Press, 2015), pp. 115–16.

the late 1990s, interprets as evidence of a still vaguely humanist new historicism.[37]

4. Hyper-Chaotic Time

Questions of contingency and unpredictability lead to my final proposed alternative Romantic temporality: the time of hyper-chaos. I borrow this term, like correlationism itself, from Meillassoux. In *After Finitude*, Meillassoux deploys the principle of non-contradiction, the mathematical non-totalisability of reality, and correlationism's own insistence that we can give no account of the world-without-us (only the world *for* us), to establish that there is only one metaphysical necessity: 'only the contingency of what is, is not itself contingent'.[38] (Hence the book's full title: *After Finitude: An Essay on the Necessity of Contingency*). In Meillassoux's rigorous (although by no means uncontroversial) account, the fact that reality appears to be governed be a stable set of 'natural laws', for example, is literally merely a fact—a temporary state of affairs, theoretically subject to change at any moment, whose stability and permanence only appear as such to us because of the foreshortened timescales (and logical shortcuts) by which we tend to think about such things. To think the universe as it truly is, says Meillassoux, is to recognise that the only absolute we can truly think 'is nothing other an extreme form of chaos, a *hyper-Chaos*, for which nothing is or would seem to be impossible, not even the unthinkable'.[39]

For Meillassoux, the temporality of hyper-Chaos—what he calls, elsewhere, 'Time without Becoming'—is not a bad thing despite its formidable name; on the contrary, in his account, it offers philosophy a route out of the Kantian cul-de-sac and back to 'the great outdoors' where it belongs. More, it allows Meillassoux to conceive of the coming of a new 'World of justice'; this is the frame in which, in *Romantic Realities*, I use Meillassoux's most ambitious ideas regarding apocalyptic revelations to read Shelley's *Prometheus Unbound*, which likewise imagines the possibilities for earthly renewal when the seeming

---

37 I borrow the outlines of this argument from Austin Webster, 'An Evental Romanticism' (MA thesis, Oregon State University, May 2019).
38 Meillassoux, *After Finitude*, p. 80.
39 Ibid., p. 64.

predictability of what happens to exist gives way to the 'reality' of pure contingency—a process in which we may find ourselves in an altogether different temporality, as Chris Washington observes in his neo-post-apocalyptic reading of *Prometheus Unbound*.[40]

If we turn away from this quasi-messianic face of hyper-Chaos, however, we can see its more nihilistic side playing out in Byron's nightmarish poem, 'Darkness', whose 82 lines of hard-nosed blank verse set out an unstinting picture of utter destruction.[41] Here are some 'highlights' of Byron's vision:

I had a dream, which was not all a dream.

The bright sun was extinguish'd, and the stars

Did wander darkling in the eternal space,

Rayless, and pathless, and the icy earth

Swung blind and blackening in the moonless air; [...]

A fearful hope was all the world contain'd;

Forests were set on fire—but hour by hour

They fell and faded—and the crackling trunks

Extinguish'd with a crash—and all was black. [...]

               The world was void,

The populous and the powerful—was a lump,

Seasonless, herbless, treeless, manless, lifeless—

A lump of death—a chaos of hard clay. [...]

The waves were dead; the tides were in their grave,

The moon, their mistress, had expir'd before;

The winds were wither'd in the stagnant air,

And the clouds perish'd; Darkness had no need

---

40 See Washington, *Romantic Revelations*, pp. 28–65.
41 Lord Byron, *The Major Works*, ed. by Jerome J. McGann (Oxford and New York: Oxford University Press, 2000), pp. 272–73.

Of aid from them—She was the universe. (1–5, 18–21, 69–72, 78–82)

The poem is not entirely free from melodrama and sentimentality, to be sure, but it almost entirely lacks Byron's well-known fondness for self-pity, the absence of which makes the cosmic impersonality of 'Darkness' all the more formidable. Its immediate context was the 'Year without a Summer' of 1816, in which unusually cloudy conditions and frigid temperatures persisted through the summer months in Europe. Around the world, harvests failed, famines claimed millions of lives, and outbreaks of cholera and other deadly diseases took many more; in Britain, the already unsettled conditions of post-Waterloo society deteriorated further, leading more-or-less directly to the Peterloo Massacre. We know now what caused the 1810s to be the coldest decade on record: a series of volcanic explosions that spewed millions of tons of ash into the atmosphere, culminating in the massive eruption of Indonesia's Mount Tambora in April of 1815, with a magnitude roughly double that of the much more celebrated Krakatau eruption of 1883.[42] But of course Britons, on the other side of the world, had no knowledge of this event—only of the permanently overcast skies, failing harvests, and unseasonable temperatures from which there would be little relief until 1819 (celebrated in Keats' 'To Autumn' of that year, with its 'mellow fruitfulness').[43] It is no coincidence, then, that Byron's poem begins with a flat description of an apocalyptic event—'The bright sun was extinguish'd' (2)—shorn of either prelude or causation; in line with Meillassoux's assertion that 'there is no reason for anything to be or to remain the way it is',[44] the world-for-us in Byron's poem simply and suddenly ends, succeeded by a world-in-itself hostile to all life. The frailty of human civilization, whose collapse Byron mercilessly describes over the course of the poem, is such that it leaves behind not even a trace of itself.

Byron's vision of hyper-Chaotic time may be extreme and, in its melodramatic touches, inherently anthropocentric. More, its nightmarish

---

42 Gillen D'Arcy Wood, *Tambora: The Eruption that Changed the World* (Princeton, NJ and Oxford: Princeton University Press, 2014), pp. 36–40. See also David Higgins, *British Romanticism, Climate Change, and the Anthropocene: Writing Tambora* (London: Palgrave Macmillan, 2017).
43 D'Arcy Wood, *Tambora*, p. 39.
44 Meillassoux, *After Finitude*, p. 60.

vision of a world extinguished by frozen temperatures would, in the main, appear at odds with our present, greenhouse-oriented future. But in its depiction of an unprecedented environmental disaster that renders the planet inhospitable, it returns us to the timeliness of the Romantics' navigation of such questions in the context of our own precarious eco-situation. The subversion of the Wordsworthian certainty regarding the beneficent relationship between humanity and the natural world—a subversion whose initial expression I have traced in this chapter, primarily via the explosion of alternatives to standard 'correlationist temporality'—now seems more pressing than ever, as the Anthropocene simultaneously forces human and planetary timescales together and undoes our longstanding belief in the priority of the former over the latter. In this light, British Romanticism's deep time, slow time, revolutionary time, and even hyper-Chaotic time may retroactively appear as harbingers of the 'deep contradiction and confusion' (to quote Chakrabarty again) that the Anthropocene has introduced into our contemporary historical situation.[45] Whether they afford us enough insight and imagination to respond decisively, creatively, and humanely to the challenges that confront us remains unknown. As what Percy Shelley famously called 'the mirrors of the gigantic shadows which futurity casts upon the present',[46] however, we can at least say that the Romantic poets have given us the opportunity to reflect critically on their imaginative responses to the changing world they encountered. Whether we manage to translate those reflections into productive and collective action with regard to the accelerated environmental changes that increasingly define our Anthropocene era, of course, remains to be seen—as does the question (not necessarily the most important one, to be clear) of whether there will be anyone left to reflect on our reflections.[47]

---

45 Chakrabarty, 'The Climate of History', p. 198.
46 Shelley, 'A Defence of Poetry', in *Shelley's Poetry and Prose*, p. 535.
47 I wish to express my appreciation to Ridvan Askin for inviting me to present an early version of this chapter to the Department of Languages and Literatures at the University of Basel.

Works Cited

Byron, Lord George Gordon, *The Major Works*, ed. by Jerome J. McGann (Oxford and New York: Oxford University Press, 2000).

Chakrabarty, Dipesh, 'The Climate of History: Four Theses', *Critical Inquiry*, 35.2 (2009), 197–222, https://doi.org/10.1086/596640

Chandler, James, *England in 1819: The Politics of Literary Culture and the Case of Romantic Historicism* (Chicago and London: University of Chicago Press, 1998).

Cohen, Jeffrey J., *Stone: An Ecology of the Inhuman* (Minneapolis and London: University of Minnesota Press, 2015), https://doi.org/10.5749/minnesota/9780816692576.001.0001

Ellermann, Greg, 'Speculative Romanticism', *SubStance*, 44.1 (2015), 154–74, https://doi.org/10.1353/sub.2015.0008

Goodman, Kevis, 'Conjectures on Beachy Head: Charlotte Smith's Geological Poetics and the Grounds of the Present', *ELH*, 81.3 (2014), 983–1006, https://doi.org/10.1353/elh.2014.0033

Gottlieb, Evan, *Romantic Realities: Speculative Realism and British Romanticism* (Edinburgh: Edinburgh University Press, 2016).

Grant, Iain Hamilton. *Philosophies of Nature after Schelling* (London and New York: Continuum, 2006), https://doi.org/10.5040/9781472547279

Halmi, Nicholas, ed., *Wordsworth's Poetry and Prose* (New York and London: Norton, 2014).

Heringman, Noah, *Romantic Rocks, Aesthetic Geology* (Ithaca and London: Cornell University Press, 2004).

Higgins, David, *British Romanticism, Climate Change, and the Anthropocene: Writing Tambora* (London: Palgrave Macmillan, 2017), https://doi.org/10.1007/978-3-319-67894-8

Hodder, Ian, *Entangled: An Archaeology of the Relationships between Humans and Things* (Malden, MA and Oxford: Wiley-Blackwell, 2007), https://doi.org/10.1002/9781118241912

Jacobus, Mary, *Romantic Things: A Tree, a Rock, a Cloud* (Chicago and London: University of Chicago Press, 2012), https://doi.org/10.7208/chicago/9780226390680.001.0001

Keats, John. *The Works of John Keats* (Ware, Hertfordshire: Wordsworth Editions, 1994).

Knowles, Claire and Ingrid Horrocks, eds, *Charlotte Smith: Major Poetic Works* (Peterborough, ON: Broadview Press, 2017).

Koselleck, Reinhart, 'The Eighteenth Century as the Beginning of Modernity', in *The Practice of Conceptual History: Timing History, Spacing Concepts*, trans. by

Todd Samuel Presner and others (Stanford: Stanford University Press, 2002), pp. 154–69.

Latour, Bruno, *Facing Gaia: Eight Lectures on the New Climatic Regime*, trans. by Catherine Porter (Cambridge: Polity Press, 2017).

Lyell, Charles, *Principles of Geology*, ed. by James A. Secord (London and New York: Penguin, 1997).

McCarthy, Anne C., 'The Aesthetics of Contingency in the Shelleyan "Universe of Things, or 'Mont Blanc' without Mont Blanc"', *Studies in Romanticism*, 54.3 (2015), 355–75, https://doi.org/10.1353/srm.2015.0012

Meillassoux, Quentin, *After Finitude: An Essay on the Necessity of Contingency*, trans. by Ray Brassier (London and New York: Continuum, 2008).

Moynihan, Thomas, *Spinal Catastrophism: A Secret History* (Windsor Quarry, Falmouth: Urbanomic, 2019).

Norris, Christopher, 'Event', in *The Badiou Dictionary*, ed. by Steve Corcoran (Edinburgh: Edinburgh University Press, 2015), pp. 115–20.

Reiman Donald H. and Neil Fraistat, eds, *Shelley's Poetry and Prose*, 2nd ed. (New York: Norton, 2002).

Rovee, Christopher, 'Trashing Keats', *ELH*, 75.4 (2008), 993–1022, https://doi.org/10.1353/elh.0.0022

Sachs, Jonathan, *The Poetics of Decline in British Romanticism* (Cambridge and New York: Cambridge University Press, 2018), https://doi.org/10.1017/9781108333115

Shaviro, Steven, *The Universe of Things: On Speculative Realism* (Minneapolis and London: University of Minnesota Press, 2014), https://doi.org/10.5749/minnesota/9780816689248.001.0001

Washington, Chris, *Romantic Revelations: Visions of Post-Apocalyptic Life and Hope in the Anthropocene* (Toronto, Buffalo, and London: University of Toronto Press, 2019), https://doi.org/10.3138/9781487530310

Webster, Austin. *An Evental Romanticism*, MA thesis, Oregon State University, 2019, https://ir.library.oregonstate.edu/concern/graduate_thesis_or_dissertations/0c483r01m

Wood, Gillen D'Arcy, *Tambora: The Eruption that Changed the World* (Princeton, NJ and Oxford: Princeton University Press, 2014), https://doi.org/10.1515/9781400851409

Woodard, Ben, 'Inverted Astronomy: Ungrounded Ethics, Volcanic Copernicanism, and the Ecological Decentering of the Human', *Polygraph*, 22 (2010), 79–93

——, *Schelling's Naturalism: Motion, Space, and the Volition of Thought* (Edinburgh: Edinburgh University Press, 2019).

3. Beethoven: Revolutionary Transformations

Gregory Dart

This chapter investigates Fidelio's relation to the French Revolution by looking at it as the last of a series of revisitings of a revolutionary 'spot of time'. First laid out by Bouilly and Gaveaux's 1798 rescue opera, Léonore, ou L'Amour Conjugal (1798), *which was supposedly based on a true story of the Jacobin Terror, this 'spot' was then returned to, and reworked, by several European composers of the early nineteenth century, who produced operas with the same plot, most notably Beethoven, whose* Leonores *of 1805 and 1806, and* Fidelio *of 1814 betray a subtly unstable perspective on recent revolutionary history. Lastly, this chapter looks at the role of melodrama in Beethoven's opera, not only as a curious technical innovation, but also as a new means of conceiving of, and dramatising, historical action, and argues that one way of seeing the dénouement of 1814 is as an essentially conservative attempt to bury the traumatic vision of history—of history as sforzando—that its earlier incarnations had opened up.*

GEFANGENE	PRISONERS
O welche Lust! In freyer Luft	Oh what joy! In the open air!
Den Athem leicht zu heben, nur hier,	Lift your breath slightly, only here,
nur hier ist Leben.	Only here is Life!

Chor der Gefangenen, Chorus of Prisoners, *Fidelio* Act I.[1]

That Beethoven's operatic paean to freedom *Fidelio* has an intimate relationship with the French Revolution is well known. But what the

---

1 Ludwig van Beethoven, *Fidelio: Oper in Zwei Aufzugen* (Bonn: Simroch, n. d. [1815]). The English translations of the 1814 libretto, and of the words in the 1805 score, are my own.

work's precise attitude to the history of the period, or indeed to the idea of history more generally, might be, is less easy to determine, not least because of the way in which that relationship might be deemed to have changed over time, as the opera underwent significant revision between 1805 and 1814. *Fidelio*, the canonical form of the opera, was the final revised version, unveiled in the summer of 1814, shortly after the first fall of Napoleon, and only a few months before the Congress of Vienna. But the opera had first seen the light of day nearly ten years earlier, as *Leonore, or the Triumph of Conjugal Love*. That this work failed badly at its first attempt in November 1805 was hardly surprising, given the circumstances surrounding its premiere. Napoleon's army had entered Vienna only a few days earlier, and most of the city's population had retreated to the country.[2] On the night of the first and only performance the stall seats were mainly filled by French soldiers; although there was a certain strange fittingness in this, given the provenance of the plot. Six months later—in 1806—*Leonore* was put on again in Vienna, this time in revised form. Convinced that the initial failure had been for dramatic rather than musical reasons, Beethoven's supporters had persuaded him to cut the three acts down to two, and to rearrange and shorten some of the numbers.[3] These changes were, however, very minor in comparison with the more significant refashioning that took place in 1814. Often, when assessing the various versions of the opera, critics have focused on purely aesthetic questions, debating which of the three works they consider to be the best musically, or to be the most effective on stage.[4] In this chapter, however, I want to look at these versions as instances of a shifting political-historical consciousness, changing perspectives on a 'spot of time'.

---

[2] Edgar Istel and Theodore Baker, 'Beethoven's "Leonore" and "Fidelio"', *Musical Quarterly*, 7.2 (April 1921), 226–51 (p. 231).

[3] See Winton Dean, 'Beethoven and Opera', in *Fidelio: Cambridge Opera Handbooks*, ed. by Paul Robinson (Cambridge: Cambridge University Press, 1996), pp. 40–42. Hereafter this volume is cited as *Fidelio: COH*.

[4] Dean, for example, thinks that the version of 1814 is *musically* a great improvement on the two previous versions, but *dramatically* weaker (Ibid., esp. pp. 44–45, 49–50).

I

On the front page of Jean Nicholas Bouilly's *Léonore, ou L'Amour Conjugal* (1798), the original French opera upon which Beethoven's was based, there was a striking assertion, set forth in big capital letters, just below the title: FAIT HISTORIQUE (TRUE STORY).[5] Before embarking on a career as a dramatist, Bouilly had been a government administrator in Tours during the Revolutionary Terror of 1793–94, and in his memoirs of 1837 he claimed that the character of Leonore was based on a real acquaintance, a woman who had disguised herself as a turnkey's assistant in order to free her husband, unjustly imprisoned in a Jacobin gaol.[6] Whether or not this story had a genuine historical basis, all trace of its original context was effaced from the ensuing libretto. Like its later Beethovenian incarnations, Bouilly and Pierre Gaveaux's opera has a deliberately vague Spanish Renaissance setting, with a king on the throne and a villain named Pizarro, presumably in honour of the sixteenth-century conquistador. Not that any of this would have fooled the first-night audience of the Theatre Feydeau in Paris, where the opera was first produced in February 1798. No sooner would Leonore's covert search for her imprisoned husband have been presented to them, than the contemporary nature of the story would have become clear. Recent history would have furnished forth countless parallels—from personal experience, from the daily papers, from printed memoirs, and from gossip. Somewhat surprisingly, perhaps, given *Fidelio*'s reputation as a revolutionary or liberationist opera, the original emphasis of *Leonore* was pretty clearly counter-Revolutionary, or, at least, anti-Terrorist in nature: its victims were aristocrats and its perpetrator a rogue official, acting in a recognisably Jacobin manner.[7]

Leonore is a 'rescue' opera, a sub-genre that enjoyed a considerable vogue in the 1790s and early 1800s. One of the first to be staged successfully during the Revolution itself was Luigi Cherubini's *Lodoïska* (1791), a *'comédie héroïque'* based on a romantic episode in J-B Louvet's

---

5 *Léonore, ou L'Amour Conjugal, Fait Historique, en deux actes et en prose mêlée de chants. Paroles de J.N. Bouilly, Musique de P. Gaveaux* (Paris: Barba, An Septième [1799]).

6 *Mes Récapitulations* (Paris, 1836–37). See also Istel and Baker, 'Beethoven's "Leonore" and "Fidelio"', pp. 227–28.

7 On the Théatre Feydeau's strong links with royalism in this period, see David Charlton, 'The French Theatrical Origins of *Fidelio*', in *Fidelio: COH*, pp. 61–63.

Amours de Faublas (1787–90) which ends with the eponymous heroine being delivered from a Polish castle in a spectacular cavalcade of guns and horses.[8] Cherubini composed another 'rescue' drama after the Terror, but this time the plot and characters were considerably less chivalric. *Le Porteur d'eau, ou Les Deux Journées* (1800) is the story of a lowly Parisian water-carrier who saves an unjustly proscribed politician by smuggling him out of the gates of the city in one of his barrels.[9] Like *Leonore*, this libretto was by Bouilly, and although set in the time of Cardinal Mazarin, actually based on another real incident from the 1790s. The 'rescue' opera, as a genre, had considerable international appeal in this period, an appeal that was concomitant with the new fashion for melodrama. This is evident when we look at the rapidity with which examples were smuggled over and adapted in England. In 1794 John Philip Kemble produced a version of *Lodoïska* at Drury Lane.[10] More tellingly still, in October 1802 Thomas Holcroft adapted *Les Deux Journées* as *The Water Carrier*, commissioning new music for the drama from Thomas Dibdin.[11]

Beethoven admired Cherubini's music for *Les Deux Journées* enormously,[12] having the score at his elbow when he composed *Leonore*, and one of the things that must have struck him about both stories was their interest in how ordinary lives are transformed when they get embroiled in politics and political history. When opera critics criticise Beethoven's opera they often take issue with its generic and stylistic hybridity, complaining about the mismatch between the comic first act—which is very much in the spirit of Mozartian romantic

---

8   Interestingly, Pierre Gaveaux, the future composer of *Léonore*, played Floreski in the first Paris production of *Lodoïska*. In 1802 *Lodoïska* reached Vienna, being put on at Schikaneder's 'Theater an der Wien' in March of that year.

9   *Les Deux Journées, Comédie Lyrique en trois actes, paroles de J.N. Bouilly, membre de la Société Philotechnique, Musique du Citoyen Chérubini* (Paris: André, [An Huitième], 1800).

10 On his *Account of the English Stage* John Genest notes its first night at Drury Lane, 9 June 1794: 'This musical Romance in 3 acts was very successful—it was translated from the French by Kemble—it is a pretty good piece for the sort of thing—much better calculated for representation than perusal' (vii, pp. 151–52).

11 'The Escapes, or, The Water Carrier', a Musical Entertainment in Two Acts, first performed at Covent Garden on October 14, 1801. Genest's comment is: 'this musical Entertainment, in 3 parts, was acted 12 times—but is not printed—it is a tolerable piece' (vii, pp. 548–49).

12 Like *Lodoïska* it came to Vienna in 1802, in a version translated by G.F. Trietschke, the future librettist of Beethoven's own *Leonore*.

comedy—and the tense and heroic second.[13] But what such criticism fails to acknowledge is just how much this combination was a conscious and deliberate feature of the post-Revolutionary 'rescue' genre within which Beethoven was working. There are many innovatory things about the dramatic spectacle that Cherubini creates in *Lodoïska*, but essentially the Revolutionary action is imagined in heroic, aristocratic terms. In Bouilly's post-Terror libretti, *Léonore* and *Les Deux Journées*, however, most of the leading characters are resolutely, relatably ordinary—figures out of a comic milieu who are forced to rise to the challenge of history.

One of the main organising ideas in Beethoven's opera—in all its versions—is the notion of the *'Augenblick'*—the eye-blink, or window of opportunity.[14] This is a political conception, a reflection on the micro-level of that high French sense of the revolutionary *'journée'*, the intense, spontaneous, decisive moment of action. The second of the two days that make up Bouilly and Cherubini's *Deux Journées* contains just such a moment. But the *'Augenblick'* is also, at the same time, a religious moment, having links with the conversion experience, and with the advent of the Last Judgement. In *Leonore/Fidelio* Beethoven presents us with the paradigm of the *'augenblick'* first of all in *negative* terms. News has arrived that the Minister is coming to investigate the prisons, having been informed that they contain several victims of arbitrary power. Pizarro, the governor of one particular gaol, has thus only a few hours to get rid of Florestan, the young aristocrat who had threatened to reveal him as a tyrant two years previously, and has been kept in secret and solitary confinement ever since. Pizarro is slenderly characterised in Bouilly and Gaveaux's opera. He only has a speaking part, and there is nothing explicit in the libretto linking him to the excesses of the revolution. That said, I don't think any French audience of the period would have had any difficulty identifying him with the many unprincipled usurpers of public authority that had flourished during and after the Terror. He is, to this

---

13 Paul Robinson runs through this argument in his '*Fidelio* and the French Revolution', *Fidelio: COH*, p. 69: 'The whole, for many critics, is dangerously contradictory—an opera whose conclusion explodes its musical and dramatic premises'.

14 Beethoven's 'Augenblicke' in *Fidelio* and elsewhere have been discussed by several critics, most notably Joseph Kerman in 'Augenblicke in Fidelio', *Fidelio: COH*, pp. 132–44. Nicholas Mathew writes about the static, spectacular nature of Beethoven's stretched-out moments in *Fidelio* in 'Beethoven's Moments', *Political Beethoven* (Cambridge: Cambridge University Press, 2013), p. 59, https://doi.org/10.1017/cbo9780511794483

extent, very much a villain of the *Directory*, a popular bugbear of 1798. In Sonnleithner and Beethoven's hands the implicit connection between Pizarro and revolutionary terrorism is, if anything, even stronger. One of the first and most important things that Pizarro gives to *Fidelio*, in that extraordinary opening aria of his 'Welch ein Augenblick!', is a powerful sense of—indeed an overriding commitment to—the moment, the '*Augenblick*', the transformational instant that will change everything forever. Like one of the *Septembriseurs* of 1792, he reads the imminent return of the old established order as an invitation to consummate his revenge upon a captive enemy. Fate has, he believes, effectively forced his hand, and is *impelling* him to triumph.

> PIZARRO
> Ha! ha! Ha! Welch' ein Augenblick!   Ha! What a moment!
> Die Rache werd' ich kühlen!   I shall cool my vengeance!
> Dich rufet dein Geschick!   Your fate calls you!
> In seinem Herzen wühlen,   To plunge in his heart,
> O Wonne! großes Glück!   O bliss, great joy!
> Schon war ich nah', im Staube   Once I was nearly in the dust,
> Dem lauten Spot zum Raube,   A prey to open mockery,
> Dahin gestreckt zu sein.   To be laid low;
> Nun ist es mir geworden   Now it is my turn
> Den Mörder selbst zu morden...   To murder the murderer myself...

Pizarro, 'Ah! Welch ein Augenblick!' *Fidelio* (1814)

At the opposite pole to this is the moment at the end of the opera, when the returning Minister Don Fernando pays tribute to Leonore's heroic rescue of her husband by giving her the key to release him from his shackles.

> LEONORE, FLORESTAN
> O Gott! O welch' ein Augenblick!   O God! O What a moment!
> O unaussprechlich süsses Glück!   O inexpressibly sweet happiness!
> 'O Gott' *Fidelio* (1814)

The expansive, yearning melody Beethoven deploys here is, it turns out, a piece of direct self-quotation, being lifted directly from his early *Funeral Cantata on the Death of Joseph II* (1790), specifically his setting of the words 'Then did men climb into the light, then the earth spun more joyfully around the sun, and the sun warmed it with the heaven's light'. It was because of this connection that Alfred Heuss saw fit to dub it Beethoven's *Humanitätsmelodie*.¹⁵ In *Fidelio* its emergence arguably carries at least three layers of musical-dramatic meaning. It is a religious moment—a moment of awe and thanksgiving; it is a humanitarian moment—a moment of peace and reconciliation, and last but not least it is a moment that celebrates the power of the moment. As in Pizarro's first aria, this is music in praise of the transformational instant; the difference is that in this case it glows with utopian promise.

This dramatisation of the power of the revolutionary moment is brilliantly handled by Beethoven, and sings out most clearly in the final, revised version of the opera. 'Post a trumpeter on the roof!' Pizarro had said in Act I, on hearing of the Minister's intended visit, 'and as soon as you see a coach, have the signal sounded *immediately*'. But nothing could be further from the audience's mind in the middle of the Act II dungeon scene, when Leonore throws herself between her husband and Pizarro, pistol in hand, before shouting out: 'One more sound and you are dead!' The utopian theorist Ernest Bloch has written of the liturgical paradigm underlying this moment. As in a Requiem Mass, he says, the *Dies Irae* of Leonore and Pizarro's confrontation is suddenly and unexpectedly interrupted by a *Tuba Mirum*—the trumpet signal heralding the last judgment.¹⁶ It is a sound that we have not yet heard but are nevertheless absolutely prepared for. What had been intended by Pizarro as a warning for him, a merely literal herald of the Minister's arrival, is transformed by Beethoven into a moment of universal deliverance.

PIZARRO	
Geteilt hast du mit ihm das Leben	You have shared life with him,
So theile nun den Tod mit ihm.	Now share death with him.
LEONORE	
Der Tod sei der geschworen,	Death I have sworn you,
Durchboren mußt du erste diesen Brust!	first you must stab this heart!
Ihm schnell eine Pistole vorhaltend	*Suddenly brandishing a pistol at him...*

---

15 Alfred Heuss, Die *Humanitätsmelodie* im 'Fidelio', *Neue Zeitung fur Musik*, 91 (1924), 545–52.

16 Ernest Bloch, *Essays on the Philosophy of Music* (Cambridge: Cambridge University Press, 1985), pp. 241–43.

Noch einen Laut – und du bist tot!	One more sound—and you are dead!
Trombe auf dem Theater	[*The trumpet sounds from the tower.*]
Ach! Du bist gerettet! Großer Gott!	Ah! You are saved! Almighty God!
FLORESTAN	
Ach! Ich bin gerettet! Großer Gott!	Ah! I am saved! Almighty God!
PIZARRO	
Ha! Der Minister!	Ha! The Minister!
Höll und Tod!	Death and damnation!
ROCCO	
O! Was is das? Gerechter Gott!	Oh! What is that? Righteous God!

Pizarro and Rocco stand dumbfounded. Florestan and Leonore embrace. The trumpet sounds again, but louder. Jaquino, with two officers, and soldiers bearing torches, appear at the uppermost opening on the staircase.

Trumpet Signal, *Fidelio* (1814)

In the 1814 version, no sooner is the trumpet heard than everyone on stage knows exactly what it means. It means the Minister has arrived; it means Pizarro's tyranny is over, it means Florestan and Leonore are saved. Rocco the jailer, hitherto a sleepy moral accomplice to Pizarro, races out of the dungeon after him, but not before making his virtuous intentions clear to Leonore and Florestan. Heartened, the two lovers throw themselves immediately into their breathless duet 'O namenlose Freude!' ('O unspeakable joy!). The act closes, the scene changes, and the next time we see them Leonore and Florestan have been moved from the dungeon to the parade ground, and from the darkness to the light. Together, and with every other member of the *dramatis personae,* Rocco and Marzelline, prisoners and populace, in attendance, they receive the Minister of Prisons, Don Fernando, and the opera turns into a ceremonial cantata of public joy. 'Hail the Day, hail the hour' sing the Chorus. Brotherhood and amity abound; not only Don Florestan but also all the other captives of the prison are freed.

This is what happens in 1814. But in 1805 and 1806, events had played out very differently. Following the original French libretto much more closely, the narrative in the first versions of Beethoven's opera moves forward much more anxiously and uncertainly. As in *Fidelio,* the trumpet call in *Leonore* No. 1 and No. 2 brings hope of deliverance, but almost immediately this is thrown into doubt when Rocco the jailer seizes Leonore's pistol and rushes out without a word. In these incarnations, which are very much in the spirit of Bouilly and Gaveaux, the lovers' duet 'O namenlose Freude' is sung in the full expectation that Pizarro will soon return to kill them. So their joy is the joy of being reunited, with no expectation of being freed. What is more, in this version, the duet is prefaced by a long recitative, in which the fragile air of hope, which is strongly identified with the oboe in this opera, repeatedly blooms and dies (Figure 1). Thought to slow down the action unnecessarily, all such anticipatory yearnings were cut in 1814.

Fig. 1 Ludwig van Beethoven, Recitative und Duett 'O namenlose Freude', *Leonore* (1805 version) (Leipzig: Breitkopf and Härtel, 1905), p. 221. Public domain.

After this duet, in both the 1805 and 1806 versions, Leonore and Floresten hear the prison echo with calls for Revenge—*Rache*—which they interpret (wrongly) to be directed at them. In actual fact they are directed at Pizarro, and indicate a powerful retributive energy on the part of the prisoners, which now sound like a burgeoning Revolutionary mob.

CHOR/CHORUS	
Zur Rache! Zur Rache!	Revenge! Revenge!
Die Unschuld werde befreit!	The innocent will be released!
Gott schutzet die gerechte	God protects the righteous
Sache und straft die Grausamkeit!	And punishes cruelty!

'Zur Rache' from *Leonore* (1805, 1806)

Beethoven may have had Cherubini's early rescue opera *Lodoïska* (1791) in mind when he composed this, because there is a 'Revenge' chorus at the climax of that opera, based on a similar musical motif. 'Notre fureur est légitime!' the crowd sing in Cherubini: 'Engloutissez ces lieux affreux!'.[17] Crucially, no change of scene takes place before the Finale in 1805 or 1806. In these versions Don Fernando, Father Rocco, Jaquino, Marzelline, Pizarro and the Chorus of Prisoners all enter Florestan and Leonore's dungeon, and it is there that Florestan is released from his chains. Both musically and dramatically, there is something infinitely more spontaneous about the glorious '*Augenblick*' in these incarnations. In 1805 Don Fernando hands Leonore the keys; 'O Gott' she sings, alone, before having her thought completed by the rest of the cast, 'O Gott, Welch ein Augenblick' (Figure 2).

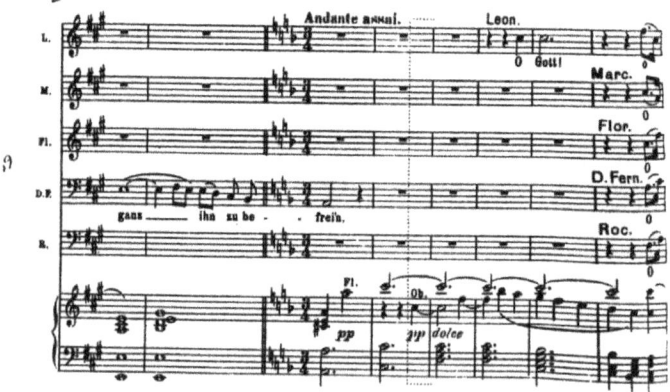

---

17 *Lodoïska, Comédie Héroïque, en trois actes, mise en musique* by le Citoyen Cherubini (Paris: Naderman, 1791), pp. 424–25.

Fig. 2 Ludwig van Beethoven, 'O Gott, Welch ein Augenblick', *Leonore* (1805 version) (Leipzig: Breitkopf and Härtel, 1905), pp. 246–47. Public domain.

In 1806 Beethoven was persuaded to cut this sublime number—the true climax of the opera in 1805—from 97 bars to 53, and also, intriguingly, to give the first line of it to the Chorus, the very same Chorus that had been clamouring for Revenge a few bars earlier, with the soloists, including Leonore and Florestan, only joining in afterwards.

But if we move on to the final version of 1814, the adjustments are far more profound. The melody, the spirit, are essentially the same, but this time they emerge after a scene change. Now everyone has been assembled on the parade ground, and in the conscious light of day. Arguably, what we have here is no longer the moment—the *augenblick*—itself but the formal commemoration of it; not the winning of the race but the presentation of the medals.[18] Leonore begins by singing the first

---

18 As Joseph Kerman describes it, 'the entire last scene in the prison courtyard is ceremonial rather than dramatic', '*Augenblicke* in *Fidelio*', in *Fidelio: COH*, p. 153.

line of the *Humanitätsmelodie*, Florestan supplies the second. Then Don Fernando joins in, followed by Rocco and Marzelline, and only in the fullness of time do we hear the Chorus. Notwithstanding the fact that Beethoven and Trietschke are less explicit about Florestan and Leonore's aristocratic status than Bouilly and Gaveaux, the musical arrangement of 'O Gott' in 1814 does make a point of calling everybody forward in order of socio-dramatic precedence: Leonore sings the first line, and is then joined by Florestan, who sings the next with her. There then follows Don Fernando, and only after that Rocco and Marzellina. Gone is the spontaneous, disorderly concussion of private and public feeling that had been such a feature of both 1805 and 1806.

So how do we account for these differences between the three Beethoven *Leonores*? The composer was working with a different librettist in each case. Sonnleithner, his original librettist of 1805, was responsible for the work's initial obsession with *'augenblicks'*; Stefan von Breuning, his 1806 collaborator, was mainly looking to cut supposed *longueurs*.[19] Joseph von Trietschke's interventions in 1814 were of a more ambitious nature than von Breuning's—and served to redirect the dramatic and one might almost say the political impact of the piece. But from a certain perspective it could be argued that, finally, the differences between these versions have less to do with the biases of the individual librettists, as writers, or even with Beethoven's own changing musical inspirations, than with the historical moments in which these acts of revision took place—as landing-places in history.

1813–14, which saw the first fall of Napoleon, was a patriotic moment for many across Europe. In 1813 von Treitschke wrote a Cantata celebrating the Allied Forces entering Paris, to which Beethoven contributed a final Chorus 'Germania'. Shortly after completing *Fidelio* the composer also wrote a cantata entitled 'Die Glorreiche Augenblick' ('The Glorious Moment') to celebrate Vienna's hosting of the peace congress that was convened in November 1814. Unquestionably, this new conception of the *Augenblick* as a moment of awakening national consciousness had an influence upon Beethoven and von Treitschke's final revisions to *Fidelio*, encouraging them to make the climax of the opera more patriotic in nature. In the original French libretto Don Fernand had been almost

---

19 See Istel and Baker, 'Beethoven's "Leonore" and "Fidelio"', p. 234.

apologetic when he arrived late to rescue Florestan, only too aware of the extent to which his sufferings exposed a failure of public authority: 'Let us try to efface the memory of this sad crime' he says, 'through a return to truth and justice'. In Beethoven's first version of 1805, however, a different emphasis is made. As in Bouilly's libretto, Don Fernando responds to the Chorus's demands for revenge by condemning Pizarro to life imprisonment, while Leonore and Florestan appeal for mercy. But it is at this point that Sonnleithner makes a clear attempt to go beyond the spirit of Thermidorean revenge in his French source. Responding to the lovers' wishes, his Don Fernando pulls back, promising to refer Pizarro's fate to the monarch instead:

Don Fernando
Der König wird sein Richter sein;
kommt, Freunde, laßt zu ihm uns eilen,
er wird mit mir die Wonne theilen,
verfolgte Unschuld zu befrei'n.

The king will be his judge;
come, friends, let us hurry to him,
he will share the bliss with me,
to rescue persecuted innocence.

Don Fernando, only in *Leonore* (1805)

This is a clear attempt on Sonnleithner's part to dispel the atmosphere of political critique that was present in the French original, but even it can't help raising certain questions about the wisdom and authority of those in power. Will the king side with Don Fernando and the people's demand for just punishment? Or will he share the generosity of the two lovers? It is going to be difficult for him to satisfy both.[20] In 1806 Stefan von Breuning, who perhaps felt that there was something rather embarrassing—and exposing—about leaving it up to the king to make all these odds even, had simply cut this passage entirely, reducing Don Fernando's judgment on Pizarro to 'Away with this villain!'. In 1814, however, von Trietschke—and Beethoven—had returned to this moment with greater confidence, resolving the matter more fully into compliance with the master key.

---

20 See the more extended discussion of this problem in Martin Nedbal, 'How Moral Is "Fidelio"? Didacticism in the Finales of Beethoven's "Leonore" Operas', *The Musical Quarterly*, 95.2/3 (Summer-Fall 2012), 396–449 (pp. 420–21), https://doi.org/10.1093/musqtl/gds025

Don Fernando

Der besten Königs Wink und Wille	Our best of kings' will and pleasure
Führt mich zu euch, ihr Armen, her,	Leads me here to you, poor people
Dass ich her Frevel Nacht enthülle	That I may uncover the night of crime,
Die All'umfangen, schwarz und schwer.	Which black and heavy encompassed all.
Nicht länger kniet sklavisch nieder,	No longer kneel down like slaves.
Tirannenstrenge sey mir fern,	Stern tyranny be far from me!
Es sucht der Bruder seine Brüder,	A brother seeks his brothers,
Und kann er helfen, hilfet er gern.	And gladly helps, if help he can.

The clear implication is that, even though (as far as we know) Florestan seems to be the only political prisoner in this particular gaol, *all* the inmates are going to be freed. After this intervention, it is difficult not to see the final version of *Fidelio* as an allegory for the liberation of Austria from the rule of the Napoleonic 'tyrant', a meaning that it singularly did not carry in 1805 or 1806.

But it is not simply a matter of the political message of the opera becoming more patriotic and conservative in 1814—there is also a transformation in the conception of the *'Augenblick'*—the revolutionary moment. In the final scene of *Fidelio* there is a chorus of public celebration—'Heil sei dem Tag! Heil sei der Stunde!' ('Hail the Day! Hail the Hour!')—which sets the cantata atmosphere, and introduces 'O Gott, Welch ein Augenblick'. But in 1805, as has already been mentioned, 'O Gott' had arisen spontaneously, with no formal introduction, and had been almost twice as long as in later versions. It is in this first *Leonore* that we find the greatest investment in the miraculous, unaccountable, even providential power of the moment—the moment as a virgin birth from the blind womb of history, quite outside of the 'Wink und Will' of power. But there is also, in 1805, a far greater interest in the various anxious steps leading up to that moment, and in the modern individual's increasingly uncertain relation to heroic action.

II

In every version of Beethoven's opera, the final act begins with Florestan in his dungeon, lamenting his abandonment, keeping hope alive by picturing his wife's fair image. Thereafter the proper action of the second half begins: Rocco and Leonore (disguised as Fidelio) enter the dungeon, Pizarro having told them to make a grave ready for the only prisoner in it. 'How cold it is in this vault!' Leonore says, as they descend: 'That is only natural', replies Rocco, 'It's so deep'. 'There's the man'. 'Where?' 'There—on the stones'. 'He seems not to move at all'. 'Perhaps he is dead'. 'You think so?' 'No, no—he is sleeping'. In 1805 this exchange was part of a short episode marked '*Melodram*'. 'Melodrama' was a technical term in the operatic language of the period—referring to a scene which combined the use of music and spoken dialogue. New in standard drama, this was also a novelty in opera, occupying a position somewhere between the sung dialogue or recitativo that bridged the musical numbers in Italian opera, and the unaccompanied prose speech characteristic of German *singspiel*. The '*Melodram*' that Beethoven wrote for the first performance of *Leonore* in 1805 is short, but evocative; sufficiently inessential that it could be cut completely in 1806, and yet sufficiently suggestive that it could be reinstated in 1814 (see Figure 3). What is important about this '*Melodram*', one could argue, is not so much what it is *in itself* as a musical number, but the tone that it sets for the rest of the act, an atmosphere of naturalistic suspense.[21]

---

21   Istel and Baker, 'Beethoven's "Leonore" and "Fidelio"', p. 247. Winton Dean queries whether the short '*Melodram*' that has come down to us is precisely the one that was performed in 1805 ('Beethoven and Opera', *Fidelio: COH*, p. 37).

Fig. 3 Ludwig van Beethoven, Melodram (No. 14), *Leonore* (1805 version) (Leipzig: Breitkopf and Härtel, 1905), pp. 188–89. Public domain.

LEONORE.
Es ist unmöglich, seine Züge zu unterschneiden.
Gott steh mir bei, wenn er es ist (Andante con moto).
ROCCO.

It is so dark, I cannot distinguish his features,
Oh, God help me, if it is my husband!

Hier unter diesen Trümmern ist die Cisterne,	Somewhere under these ruins is the old well
Von der ich dir gesagt habe.	That I told you about.
Wir brauchen nicht viel zu graben,	We shall not need to dig far,
um an die Öffnung zu kommen	To get to the opening.
Hole mir eine Haue und stelle dich hieber.	Give me the pickaxe and come here.
Mir scheint, du zitterst?	It seems to me you are trembling.
Fürchtest du dich?	Are you afraid?
(Allegro).	
LEONORE.	
O, nein—es ist nur so kalt!	No, I'm only cold.
ROCCO.	
So mach fort!—	Well then, set to work;
Im Arbeiten wird dir schon warm werden.	That'll soon make you warm.

At a similar juncture in the Second Act of *Les Deux Journées* Cherubini had interposed a more obviously melodramatic *mélodrame* as the soldiers began to interrogate Constance, the wife of the proscribed politician Armand, who was trying to pass herself off as Antonio's sister:

(Allegro)	
Le deuxième COMMANDANT	
Regarde-moi (plus brusquement encore). Regarde-moi donc.	Look at me (more roughly still) Look at me.
CONSTANCE, *full of emotion*.	
Vos regards sont si terribles!	Your looks are so terrible!
Le deuxième COMMANDANT	
Ce tremblement, tout annonce...	This trembling says everything.
ANTONIO.	
Dam, vous l'intimidez aussi.	False! you are intimidating her.
Le deuxième COMMANDANT	
Allons, allons, au corps-de-garde!	Come, come to the guard-house!
(Plusieurs soldats saissisent Constance),	(Several soldiers seizing Constance),
Dialogue en Chant.	
COMMANDANT	
O mon frère! je t'en supplie!	O my brother! I beg of you!
Antonio, ne m'abandonne pas.	Antonio, don't abandon me.

ANTONIO, *l'arrachent des mains des gardes*	*tearing her out of the guards' hands.*
Il faut que l'on m'ôte la vie,	They'll have to kill me
Avant d't'arracher de mes bras	Before tearing you from my arms.
Le deuxième COMMANDANT	
Que fais-tu, jeune téméraire?	What are you doing, you rash young man?
Oser ainsi te révolter!	Daring to revolt!

And in the Trio that followed there is a good example of what Beethoven most admired and sought to emulate in Cherubini's musical style: its tense, spare urgency, its earnest, half-smothered passion.

As Beethoven's corresponding '*Melodram*' slips into an A minor Duet, Leonore's disguise also begins to slip. This scene, and the action in it, is heavily emblematic. Rocco knows that his master is planning to murder the prisoner, but has apparently decided not to step out of line. Leonore, while continually seeking to get a better glimpse (an *augenblick*) of the poor man in the corner, and find out whether it is indeed her husband, continues to help Rocco with the digging. In the corresponding moment in the French original the instruction is for the Duet between Roc and Leonore to be sung 'à demi-*voix*', and there is a similar naturalism in Beethoven's version, a latent tension:

ROCCO.	
Nur hurtig fort, nur frisch gegraben,	Come, set to work, for time is pressing;
es währt nicht lang er kommt herein.	We have not long to dig the grave.
LEONORE	
Ihr sollt ja nicht zu klagen haben,	With all my strength I'm here to help you.
ihr sollt gewiß zufrieden sein.	No fault to find with me you'll have.
ROCCO	
Komm, hilf, komm hilf	Then come, help, come help,
doch diesen Stein mit heben,	Stand by and help me lift the stone up;
hab acht, hab acht, er hat Gewicht!	Take care and hold it fast.
LEONORE	
Ich helfe schon,	I'm already helping

sorgt euch nicht,	Don't worry
ich will mir alle Mühe geben.	I want to do my best.
ROCCO	
Ein wenig noch!	A little more!
LEONORE	
Geduld!	Patience!
ROCCO	
Er weicht!	It's moving!
LEONORE	
Nur etwas noch!	Just a little more!
ROCCO	
Es ist nicht leicht!	It's not light!
LEONORE	
Laßt mich nur wieder Kräfte haben,	Just let me get my strength back,
wir werden bald zu Ende sein.	We'll be finished soon.
Wer du auch seist,	That man, whoe'er you are,
ich will dich retten,	I'll save you!
bei Gott, bei Gott,	by God, by God! I swear, I will not let him die;
du sollst kein Opfer sein,	You shouldn't be a victim,
gewiß, gewiß,	certainly, certainly
ich löse deine Ketten ich	I'll loosen your chains, you poor man,
will du Armer, dich befrein!	and set you free!
ROCCO	
Was zauderst du	Why do you hesitate
in deiner Pflicht?	In your duty?
LEONORE	
Mein Vater, nein, ich zauderst nicht!	My father, no, I'm not hesitating!
Ihr sollt ja nicht zu klagen haben,	You shouldn't have to complain,
laßt mich nur wieder Kräfte haben,	Just let me get my strength back,
denn mir wird keine Arbeit schwer.	Because no work is difficult for me.

This duet between a sleeping and an awakening conscience Beethoven dramatises with music that is, like Cherubini's, full of fear and suspense. Far less well known than Leonore's famous 'Hope' Aria, or the Prisoner's Chorus, it is nevertheless at the core of what is most original about the opera. Muted tremolando violins and a rasping trombone provide a strong sense of threat, while below that, low in the bass, the bassoons and cellos keep their heads down and get on with their work. Only the clarinet and then the oboe attempt to lift a lantern in the gloom (Figure 4).

Fig. 4 Ludwig van Beethoven, Duet (No. 14), *Leonore* (1805 version) (Leipzig: Breitkopf and Härtel, 1905), pp. 189–90. Public domain.

In the score Beethoven left an indication that this Duet was to be played 'very quietly with the *sforzandos and fortissimos* not being emphasised too much'. The *sforzando* marking, which tells the performers to put strong accents on certain, often unexpected, notes, was one of the key elements of his middle-period style. Here what he is seeking to achieve is a series of minor shocks to the system, recurrent pulses of mild panic. In atmosphere this duet is very well suited to the plot's dark nature and gothic setting; but it is also appropriate in a broader, deeper sense, because of the way in which it encourages us to experience the passage of time. As a musical dramatist in the commonly accepted sense, Beethoven cannot compete with Mozart: he is no match for him as a storyteller, nor as a painter of character. But where he is exceptional, as an instrumental composer, is in his ability to conjure drama out of the movement of the music itself. So keenly are we made to feel the various forces that go into its making, and so palpably do we feel its progress as a kind of struggle, that at certain points we cannot help experiencing its forward development as a string of actions, a sequence of causes and effects, an allegory of history. This quality is everywhere present in Beethoven's non-vocal works—in the 'Eroica' symphony of 1803 for instance—but only briefly in his opera. Indeed, arguably, it is only really a feature of the music that runs from the *'Melodram'* to the trumpet signal in Act II.

Though the comic opera of the period—*opera buffa*—had proved itself capable of catching human emotions developing and changing in real time, *opera seria*, the heroic aristocratic form, had always retained a temporal etiquette all of its own. Conventionally, real time stopped dead during the performance of its arias. When it came to the expression of princely virtue, the clock never appeared to be ticking. One way of interpreting the invention of melodrama in the late eighteenth century is to see it not simply in its technical aspect, as a new way of combining music and drama, but as an attempt to subject serious music, that is, music attempting to convey a heroic message, to the larger pressures of what might be called 'real' or 'historical' time. Indeed, it might be thought of as being one of the unconscious motives of melodrama, as a genre born in the Revolutionary decade, to investigate and expose something that was only just beginning to be apprehended about modern history—namely, its status as a force above and beyond the control of mere individuals, latent with meanings yet to be revealed.

What Beethoven's Duet helps dramatise, one could argue, is the *sforzando* of post-Revolutionary history, with each successive accent representing another tentative footstep in the dark. How appropriate it is, then, that when Leonore comes to the universal moral realization that, in fact, she is going to try to save the prisoner, *whoever he is*—she does so *in the very midst of this music*.[22] She catches this insight, in other words, as the moment offers it to her; she weaves it out of the strands of what has gone before. Leonore is slow to action, preferring to lie low and bide her time. But so too is Rocco, for he too (or so it turns out) is waiting for the proper moment to make a difference—a loophole of agency. Where in another context we might have been tempted to interpret Leonore's patience as a product of her feminine marginality— her status as a victim, not an agent, of history—the circumstances of the dungeon scene are such that we cannot but experience it as archetypally modern, an illustration that the political virtue of the future will be all about timing.

Strictly speaking, of course, Beethoven's *Leonore* of 1805 is not a melodrama, but what is only too clear is the extent to which its second act has been influenced by this rapidly expanding new genre, in general spirit as well as in particular facets. For melodrama was a genre that, as Jeffrey N. Cox has recently argued, brought a new kind of 'sensational realism' to the theatre, 'a poetics and politics of speed'.[23] In neither of the other two contemporary versions of *Leonore* is there anything comparable to the effects that are created in Beethoven's A minor Duet, for example. In Ferdinando Paer's *Leonore* (1804) the corresponding number comes straight out of *opera buffa*, with Leonore giving a performance of general bluff good cheer, interspersed by occasional anxious asides. In Simon Mayr's *L'Amor Conjugal* (1805) this Duet is replaced by a tender folk-like '*Romanza*'—the story of a wretched wife whose husband was taken

---

22 'It is a significant assertion for our understanding of Leonore', Paul Robinson writes, 'because in it she announces her adherence to the humane principles for which her husband has been imprisoned. She is motivated, in other words, not simply by wifely devotion but also by a more impersonal and categorical imperative' ('*Fidelio* and the French Revolution', p. 79). See also Irving Singer, 'Beethoven: The Passion in *Fidelio*', in *Mozart and Beethoven: The Concept of Love in their Operas* (Cambridge, MA: MIT Press, 2010), p. 132.

23 'Melodramatic realism worked on its audiences the way our powerfully sensationalist movies work on us: we come away having had a "real" experience, having "really" felt something while we were in the theatre [...] music is an important part of this rousing of the passions, but music, a strongly temporal, forward-moving art, also increases the speed of the experience, with the structure of the plot being another important contributor to what Holcroft calls "anxious and impatient suspense", that is, a desire to get to the end of play so as to resolve the tension of the storyline', Jeffrey N. Cox, *Romanticism in the Shadow of War* (Cambridge: Cambridge University Press, 2014), p. 51, https://doi.org/10.1017/CBO9781107786165

away—which Leonore sings while digging.[24] Only in Beethoven is there a full dramatisation of the strange mixture of latency and emergency in the situation in which she finds herself, 'a music of preparation and awakening suspense'.[25]

This feeling was at its most expansive in the *Leonore* of 1805, but was progressively curtailed in 1806 and 1814. Where in *Leonore* No. 1 private anxiety—and private virtue—had taken centre stage, over and above the backdrop of contemporary politics, in *Fidelio* Beethoven and Trietschke had seen an opportunity to celebrate the final end of Revolutionary turmoil and the return of benevolent patriarchy.[26] Tempting as it might be to think of the three incarnations of Beethoven's opera as amounting to three distinct works, with different emphases and different meanings, I think a better way would be to consider it as a series of revisitings of Bouilly and Gaveaux's *Leonore*, its original 'spot of time'. These returns, like those of Wordsworth to his vale of 'visionary dreariness' in Book XI of *The Prelude*, are to a particular scene of historical trauma, a scene that is at one and the same time a rich mine and an open wound.

What is palpable is that with each revision, Beethoven and his collaborators took the *Leonore* story further and further away from the spirit of 1798, a spirit that had been, to coin a Wordsworthian phrase, 'interrupted by uneasy bursts of exaltation'.[27] But what is equally clear is that with each successive smoothing of the dramatic structure, the

---

24 'In place of the grave-digging duet Leonore sings a popular strophic song in popular French style, hoping that Florestan will recognise her voice', Dean, 'Beethoven and Opera', p. 34.

25 The quotation is from Thomas De Quincey's description of one of his dreams of historical conflict in the *Confessions of an English Opium-Eater* (*London Magazine*, October, 1821, 377): 'The dream commenced with a music which I now often heard in dreams—a music of preparation and awakening suspense; a music like the opening of the Coronation Anthem, and which, like *that*, gave the feeling of a vast march—of infinite cavalcades filing off—and the tread of innumerable armies.'

26 'The *Fidelio* of 1814 is now generally regarded as a glorification of contemporary political authority at a time when the balance of power was palpably shifting toward the restoration of the monarchies', Louis Lockwood, 'Opera and Republican Virtue: Beethoven's *Fidelio*', *Journal of Interdisciplinary History*, 36.3, *Opera and Society: Part I* (Winter, 2006), 473–82 (p. 474), https://doi.org/10.1162/002219506774929827

27 In Book XI of *The Prelude* (1805) Wordsworth described how, after hearing news of Robespierre's death while walking on Leven Sands in the Lake District, he had 'forth-breathed' a 'Hymn of Triumph' and 'Thus, interrupted by uneasy bursts/Of exultation' pursued his way 'Along that very shore which I had skimmed/In former times' (XI, lines 560–63).

opera took on an ever more utopian aspect. Restored to the old parade ground of history, the final reconciliation of 1814 is, oddly enough, more thoroughly imbued with the abstract principles of liberty and fraternity than any of its predecessors. Never before had reminiscences of the patriotic amnesty celebrated at the first Bastille Day *Fédération* of 1790 been stronger. But if *Fidelio* is, to a measurable degree, more certain than any of its earlier versions about what it wants to *take* from the French Revolution, it is also more remote from it, as a source of power. In 1814 Leonore and Florestan deliver 'O namenlose Freude' in triumph—they know they have been saved. Back in 1805, however, their rendition had been, like that of the proscribed Girondins singing the *Marseillaise* in prison on the night before their execution, framed by doubt and despair. Melodramatic 'spaces of irresolution'[28] that were awkwardly, thrillingly open in the first versions of the opera, had, by the time of the final revision, been narrowed.

> The days gone by
>
> Come back upon me from the dawn almost
>
> Of life; the hiding-places of my power
>
> Seem open, I approach, and then they close;
>
> I see by glimpses now, when age comes on,
>
> May scarcely see at all; and I would give
>
> While yet we may, as far as words can give,
>
> A substance and a life to what I feel:
>
> I would enshrine the spirit of the past
>
> For future restoration. (Wordsworth, *The Prelude* (1805) XI, 334–43)

Arguably, Florestan's dungeon is just such a 'hiding-place' of power—it is the wound that *Fidelio*, at the third attempt, has finally succeeded in healing, in an act of public enshrinement, or 'restoration', that must also involve, almost by definition, a semi-effacement of the past. 'Our best of

---

28   Jonathan Goldberg talks of the Duet in Act II in particular as a melodramatic 'space of irresolution' in '*Fidelio*: Melodramas of Agency and Identity' *Criticism*, 55.4 (Fall 2013), pp. 547–65 (pp. 547–48), https://doi.org/10.1353/crt.2013.0033

kings' will and pleasure/Leads me here to you, poor people', sings Don Fernando during the final scene in 1814, 'That I may uncover the night of crime'. The 'spirit of the past' that *Fidelio* restores *is* a French Revolutionary spirit, but it is one that has been shorn of its democratic aspirations and uncertainties. It is the Revolution as National Liberation—with all the old aristocratic ideas of history and agency surreptitiously repaired.

Works Cited

Beethoven, Ludwig van, *Fidelio: Oper in Zwei Aufzugen* (Bonn: Simroch, n. d. [1815]).

——, *Leonore, Oper in Drei Acten* [1805 version] (Leipzig: Breitkopf and Härtel, 1905), p. 221.

Bouilly, Jean-Nicolas, *Léonore, ou L'Amour Conjugal, Fait Historique, en deux actes et en prose mêlée de chants. Paroles de J.N. Bouilly, Musique de P. Gaveaux* (Paris: Barba, An Septième [1799]).

——, *Les Deux Journées, Comédie Lyrique en trois actes, paroles de J.N. Bouilly, membre de la Société Philotechnique, Musique du Citoyen Chérubini* (Paris: André, [An Huitième], 1800).

——, *Mes Récapitulations* (Paris, 1836–37).

Bloch, Ernst, *Essays on the Philosophy of Music* (Cambridge: Cambridge University Press, 1985).

Charlton, David, 'The French Theatrical Origins of *Fidelio*', in *Fidelio: Cambridge Opera Handbooks*, ed. by Paul Robinson (Cambridge: Cambridge University Press, 1996), pp. 51–67.

Cherubini, Luigi, *Lodoïska, Comédie Héroïque, en trois actes* (Paris: Naderman, 1791).

Cox, Jeffrey N., *Romanticism in the Shadow of War* (Cambridge: Cambridge University Press, 2014), https://doi.org/10.1017/cbo9781107786165

Dean, Winton, 'Beethoven and Opera', in *Fidelio: Cambridge Opera Handbooks*, ed. by Paul Robinson (Cambridge: Cambridge University Press, 1996), pp. 22–50.

Genest, John, *Some Account of the English Stage*, 10 vols. (London and Bath: 1832).

Heuss, Alfred, 'Die *Humanitätsmelodie* im "Fidelio"', *Neue Zeitung fur Musik*, 91 (1924), 545–52.

Gill, Stephen, ed., *William Wordsworth: 21st Century Oxford Authors* (Oxford: Oxford University Press, 2010).

Goldberg, Jonathan, '*Fidelio*: Melodramas of Agency and Identity', *Criticism*, 55.4 (Fall 2013), 547–65, https://doi.org/10.13110/criticism.55.4.0547

Istel, Edgar and Theodore Baker, 'Beethoven's "Leonore" and "Fidelio"', *Musical Quarterly*, 7.2 (April 1921), 226–51.

Kerman, Joseph, '*Augenblicke* in *Fidelio*', in *Fidelio: Cambridge Opera Handbooks*, ed. by Paul Robinson (Cambridge: Cambridge University Press, 1996), pp. 132–44.

Lockwood, Louis, 'Opera and Republican Virtue: Beethoven's *Fidelio*', *Journal of Interdisciplinary History*, 36.3, *Opera and Society: Part I* (Winter, 2006), 473–82, https://doi.org/10.1162/002219506774929827

Mathew, Nicholas, *Political Beethoven* (Cambridge: Cambridge University Press, 2013), https://doi.org/10.1017/cbo9780511794483

Nedbal, Martin, 'How Moral Is "Fidelio"? Didacticism in the Finales of Beethoven's "Leonore" Operas', *The Musical Quarterly*, 95.2/3 (Summer-Fall 2012), 396–449, https://doi.org/10.1093/musqtl/gds025

Singer, Irving, *Mozart and Beethoven: The Concept of Love in their Operas* (Cambridge, MA: MIT Press, 2010).

Robinson, Paul, '*Fidelio* and the French Revolution', in *Fidelio: Cambridge Opera Handbooks*, ed. by Paul Robinson (Cambridge: Cambridge University Press, 1996), pp. 68–100.

SECTION II

ROMANTIC CONCEPTIONS OF TIME

4. The Temporality of the Soul: Immanent Conceptions of Time in Wordsworth and Byron

Ralf Haekel

This chapter investigates the temporality of the soul in the Romantic period. Just like traditional concepts of the soul, time oscillates between immanence and transcendence: an immanent transient temporality, on the one hand, and transcendent notions of eternity, on the other. Whereas the latter are often associated with religion, theology, and philosophy, the former is connected to history and historicism. Taking its cue from the similarities and differences of the concepts of time and history in the writings of Walter Benjamin and Benedict Anderson, the chapter argues that Romantic poetry is likewise characterised by this tension between immanence and transcendence expressed by these two twentieth-century authors. This is particularly the case in poems in which the soul is the main trope and symbol. The chapter concludes with an analysis of two poems shaped by the conflicting conception of time: William Wordsworth's Ode: Intimations of Immortality *and Lord Byron's* Childe Harold's Pilgrimage. *Both poems, the chapter argues, are ultimately characterised by an immanence that borders on pessimism—even Wordsworth's poem, which is usually read in a much more optimistic and positive manner.*

In a famous passage of *Imagined Communities*, Benedict Anderson, quoting from Walter Benjamin's 'Theses on the Philosophy of History' (*Über den Begriff der Geschichte*), distinguishes two different concepts of time:

> Our own conception of simultaneity has been a long time in the making, and its emergence is certainly connected, in ways that have yet to be well studied, with the development of the secular sciences. But it is

a conception of such fundamental importance that, without taking it fully into account, we will find it difficult to probe the obscure genesis of nationalism. What has come to take the place of the mediaeval conception of simultaneity-along-time is, to borrow again from Benjamin, an idea of 'homogeneous, empty time', in which simultaneity is, as it were, transverse, cross-time, marked not by prefiguring and fulfilment, but by temporal coincidence, and measured by clock and calendar.[1]

In order to develop his well-known theory of nationalism, Anderson juxtaposes a religious medieval 'messianic' concept of time and the empty, homogeneous time of secularised modernity. Whereas the former comprises the present moment in time as part of an eschatological idea of history—a 'simultaneity of past and future in an instantaneous present'[2]—the latter is characterised by a post-Enlightenment approach that conceives of history merely in terms of the natural sciences and exists without a concept of transcendence—be that a Judaeo-Christian heaven or a philosophical realm of ideas.

This dichotomy of two distinct conceptions of time suggested by Anderson, however, hardly does Benjamin's 'Theses on the Philosophy of History' justice.[3] In his late work—the *Geschichtsphilosophische Thesen* were written in 1939, a year before he committed suicide in Portbou whilst fleeing from the Nazis—Benjamin does not contrast two concepts of time but rather two different philosophies of history; he does indeed describe a dichotomy, but one between historicism and historical materialism. Historicism, in this context, has to be understood against the German background, as a term denoting *Historismus*, the nineteenth-century German theory of historiography as the positivist assembling of historical facts.[4] Whilst this form of historicism aims at describing the past 'the way it really was', historical materialism in Benjamin's sense, on the other hand, tries to seize the past in the present moment in order to inspire hope for the future. According

---

1 Benedict Anderson, *Imagined Communities: Reflections on the Origins and Spread of Nationalism* (London and New York: Verso, 1991), p. 24.
2 Ibid., p. 12.
3 Walter Benjamin, 'Theses on the Philosophy of History', in *Illuminations*, trans. by Harry Zohn, ed. by Hannah Arendt (New York: Schocken, 1969), pp. 253–64.
4 See for an overview the article on 'Historismus, Historizismus', in *Historisches Wörterbuch der Philosophie*, ed. by Joachim Ritter, Karlfried Gründer and Gottfried Gabriel (Darmstadt: Wissenschaftliche Buchgesellschaft, 1971–2007), https://doi.org/10.24894/hwph.1554

to Benjamin's understanding, the past is not fixed and given, hence objectively describable, but dependent on the historian's perspective and thus also prone to change. In Benjamin's idiosyncratic reading of classical Marxism, historical materialism is fundamentally shaped by theology:

> The kind of happiness that could arouse envy in us exists only in the air we have breathed, among people we could have talked to, women who could have given themselves to us. In other words, our image of happiness is indissolubly bound up with the image of redemption. The same applies to our view of the past, which is the concern of history. The past carries with it a temporal index by which it is referred to redemption. There is a secret agreement between past generations and the present one. Our coming was expected on earth. Like every generation that preceded us, we have been endowed with a *weak* Messianic power, a power to which the past has a claim. That claim cannot be settled cheaply. Historical materialists are aware of that.[5]

Hence, Walter Benjamin does not, as Benedict Anderson's passage suggests, contrast a medieval Christian concept of time with the modern secular notion of time structured by clock and calendar. Benjamin's criticism of German historicism rather needs to be understood from the position of a theologically infused historical materialism that focuses on the present moment as that point in time in which past and future meet in an intimation of eternity. Benjamin emphasises this notion in an appendix to his 'Theses on the Philosophy of History':

> Historicism contents itself with establishing a causal connection between various moments in history. But no fact that is a cause is for that very reason historical. It became historical posthumously, as it were, through events that may be separated from it by thousands of years. A historian who takes this as his point of departure stops telling the sequence of events like the beads of a rosary. Instead, he grasps the constellation which his own era has formed with a definite earlier one. Thus he establishes a conception of the present as the 'time of the now' which is shot through with chips of Messianic time.[6]

In the following, I wish to argue that the way Benjamin conceptualises and problematises history and time in his historico-philosophical theses of 1939 bears striking resemblance to the Romantic period—although

---

5 Benjamin, 'Theses', p. 254.
6 Ibid., p. 263.

I am aware of the anachronism. Just as in Benjamin's conception, the Romantic concept of time betrays a sometimes bewildering co-existence of transcendence and secularism. This resemblance may not be a coincidence, however, as Benjamin, having written his doctoral dissertation on the concept of criticism in German Romanticism, was an expert in Romantic philosophy and aesthetics.

In ways that differ fundamentally from each other, William Wordsworth and Lord Byron also refer to transcendence and eternity in poems that are ultimately entirely secular in their outlook—*Ode: Intimations of Immortality* and *Childe Harold's Pilgrimage*. In order to stress the similarities as well as the striking differences regarding temporality in both poems, I want to investigate a topic that is peculiarly situated between materiality and immateriality, time and eternity, history and messianic time: the concept of the soul. I argue that both poets represent the transition from a religiously infused to a worldly concept of mind that betrays the dawning of the modern historical worldview that both Anderson and Benjamin have in mind. In their treatment of the past, both Romantic poets are remarkably close to Benjamin's vision: Wordsworth calls up a Platonic notion of eternity, whilst Byron's bleak view of history seems already wholly immanent; only in its melancholy does it betray a longing for change that has transcendental overtones. In order to contextualise my readings of both poems I will first outline the change in the concept of time as well as the temporality of the soul in the Romantic period.

Falling into Time: The Temporality of the Soul

The conception of time around 1800 is fundamentally shaped by transformations occurring in the preceding age of Enlightenment. During the long eighteenth century—the period of the Enlightenment and Romanticism—the concept of time underwent a fundamental change. One key aspect is the development of a 'dual structure of Enlightenment time',[7] i.e. the separation of absolute time, on the one hand, and subjective time, on the other. The former concept conceives of time as something objective and scientifically measurable. Perhaps

---

7   Russel West-Pavlov, *Temporalities* (London and New York: Routledge, 2013), p. 48, https://doi.org/10.4324/9780203106877

the most famous definition is provided by Isaac Newton in his *Principia Mathematica* of 1687: 'Absolute, true, and mathematical time, of itself and from its own nature, flows uniformly, without regard to anything external'.[8] Opposed to this is the conception of time as subjective and conditional on personal experience.

One hundred years after Newton's definition, the concept of absolute time was first contested in the critical philosophy of Immanuel Kant. West-Pavlov describes Kant's treatment of time as 'a subjective factor integral to perception itself'. He states:

> In other words, time was a condition of possibility of perception of the world, and only because it framed perception could it mistakenly be ascribed to the external world itself. To this extent, Kant was the forerunner of modern phenomenological theories of temporality.[9]

During the Romantic period, time is further treated as highly idiosyncratic and individual, for instance in William Wordsworth's notion of memory as particular 'spots of time' which constitute a co-existence of two states of temporal consciousness: of remembered past and lived presence. Jonathan Wordsworth explains this concept as follows:

> The 'forms' (images) stamped upon the mind yet (still, at the time of writing) exist, with their independent life, achieving within the mind a permanence comparable to that of their 'archetypes' (the landscapes, natural forms, from which they derive). [...] it is clear that we should expect the 'spots of time' to be not just memories where time stands still, but images, pictures in the mind, imprinted as the result of more than usually important emotional experience.[10]

This subjective conception of time based on personal experience finds its pinnacle later in nineteenth-century philosophy with Henri Bergson who distinguishes between time as 'a homogeneous medium in which our conscious states are ranged alongside one another as in space' and 'pure duration',[11] which he conceives of as a solely psychological state.

---

8   Isaac Newton, quoted in West-Pavlov, *Temporalities*, p. 36.
9   West-Pavlov, *Temporalities*, p. 42.
10 Jonathan Wordsworth, 'William Wordsworth: *The Prelude*', in *A Companion to Romanticism*, ed. by Duncan Wu (Oxford: Blackwell, 1998), pp. 183–84.
11 Henri Bergson, *Time and Free Will: An Essay on the Immediate Data of Consciousness* (London and New York: Routledge, 2013), p. 90, https://doi.org/10.4324/9781315830254

The Romantic period, situated right in the middle of this development, is characterised by a tension of time as externally measurable and as subjectively experienced. It negotiates a modern secular conception of time as shaped by science and Enlightenment reason and the Romantic insight that a human being is, to quote Shelley's fragment 'On Life', 'incapable of imagining to himself annihilation, existing but in the future and the past, being, not what he is, but what he has been and shall be'.[12] This focus on the present betrays a desire typical of many Romantic authors to reconcile scientific progress with a more universal approach to life and being that transcends the conception of time as merely homogeneous and empty. It is, in other words, an attempt to bring together time and eternity by means of what Benjamin might describe as a '*weak* Messianic power'.

The soul is of particular importance here, even as it further complicates the matter. Traditionally a philosophical *and* religious entity, the soul encapsulates both *eternity* associated with transcendence and *temporality* associated with immanence. In a scientific age, the soul is therefore per se characterised by this double tension between eternity and time, as well as subjective time and objective scientific time.

I will begin, however, by very briefly delineating the transformation of the concept of the soul around 1800.[13] During the Romantic period, the soul was part of a larger revolution of the scientific understanding of the human—and of the scientific system in general—encompassing the entire eighteenth and nineteenth centuries. The history of the soul is therefore part of the fundamental scientific change concerning the theory of the human from Early Modern natural philosophy to the Modern scientific system. In the course of this transformation of the human sciences, the traditional Aristotelian tripartite soul—nutritive, sensitive, and rational—makes way for the modern scientific notion based on an organic and nervous conception of a human being and human consciousness. The change in the conception of the human soul, together with the scientific system and the shape of cultural knowledge, had not only an immediate impact on the field of science

---

12 Percy Bysshe Shelley, 'On Life', in *Shelley's Poetry and Prose*, ed. by Donald H. Reiman and Neil Fraistat (New York and London: Norton, 2002), pp. 506–07.
13 The following historical survey as well as the interpretation of Wordsworth's *Ode* are based on my study *The Soul in British Romanticism: Negotiating Human Nature in Philosophy, Science and Poetry* (Trier: WVT, 2014).

but also on the medium of literature in which these concepts were expressed.

In the context of literature and the Romantic history of ideas in general, Platonic and Neoplatonic philosophy is particularly relevant. In Plato and Neoplatonists such as Plotinus, the soul mediates between the world of ideas or the One, on the one side, and the immanent and transient world in which we live, on the other. The soul is part of the human, but its own nature is closer to the divine, as Socrates states in Plato's dialogue *Phaedo*: 'The soul is most like the divine and immortal and intellectual and uniform and indissoluble and ever unchanging, and the body, on the contrary, most like the human and mortal and multiform and unintellectual and dissoluble and ever changing'.[14]

Many of the Romantic poets use Neoplatonic ideas to tackle the paradoxes they experience in poetry and art. Samuel Taylor Coleridge's famous definition of beauty as 'Multëity in Unity', according to which a poem tries to reconcile transcendence with immanence in order to capture the one in the manifold (and vice versa), is exemplary in this context. Time, in this Neoplatonic approach, therefore exists in two forms: as *eternity* in the realm of ideas, i.e. the unchanging and transcendent intelligible world, and as *time* within the physical sensory world. Andrew Smith describes the problem of time and soul in Plotinus's *Enneads* as follows:

> Moreover, since we are ourselves time-bound to a large extent and particularly in our reasoning it makes sense to have as full an understanding as we can of our human situation. Despite the fact that the real self may be located at the level of Intellect and eternity, the empirical self, the self which philosophizes discursively, is vested in the reasoning powers of the soul (V.3.3.35–6) whose life is time. To this extent the transcendent world may be, if not illuminated by, at least indicated from the time realm of reason. Hence the importance of time as well as eternity.[15]

Mediating between immanence and transcendence, the soul, in a way, encompasses both eternity and transient immanent time. For the

---

14 Plato, *Euthyphro. Apology. Crito. Phaedo. Phaedrus*, trans. Harold North Fowler (Cambridge, MA: Harvard University Press, 1977), 80b, https://doi.org/10.4159/dlcl.plato_philosopher-phaedo.1914

15 Andrew Smith, 'Eternity and Time', in *The Cambridge Companion to Plotinus*, ed. by Lloyd P. Gerson (Cambridge: Cambridge University Press, 1996), p. 205, https://doi.org/10.1017/ccol0521470935.009

Neoplatonic concept of the soul, the process of being born is not only a transition from transcendence to immanence but literally a falling into time.

What happened to the concept of soul in the Romantic period can be described as a paradox. By losing its status as a scientific and philosophical truth defining life and cognition, the soul, particularly if it appeared in the medium of literature and especially in the genre of poetry, became a metaphor of transcendence, eternity, and immortality. Yet, by pointing to these aspects that are decidedly otherworldly, the topic of the soul reflects the fact that *any* kind of poetry—or art in general—is necessarily immanent and may thus only anticipate an ideal it can never reach. As the second generation of Romantic poets became increasingly frustrated with the transcendental aspects of their own aesthetic theory the focus shifted back to the linguistic material of poetry. This led to a characteristic form of self-reflexivity in poems on the soul, which thus, paradoxically, highlighted the poems' mediality and materiality: the very fact that the soul denotes transcendence highlights the immanence of the poem in which it does so.

Looking at the topic of the temporality of the soul in Romantic poetry, one can discern the tendency to reconcile modern scientific progress with a desire for transcendence and eternity. Due to its self-reflexive tendency, the soul in poetry has fundamental implications for the formal arrangement of a literary work of art. In what follows, I discuss two poetic ways to approach the temporality of the soul: a circular concept and a progressive one, William Wordsworth's *Ode* and Lord Byron's *Childe Harold*.

William Wordsworth, *Ode: Intimations of Immortality*

In William Wordsworth's *Ode: Intimations of Immortality from Recollections of Early Childhood*, time is, as the title unmistakably indicates, linked to notions of immortality, particularly the Platonic concept of the immortality of the soul.[16] The speaker describes the beginning of life and the awakening of the mind as a fall from eternity into time:

---

16 The 'Ode' was written in two stages. The first four stanzas were composed in 1802, and Coleridge wrote his 'Dejection. An Ode' in answer to the feelings of loss expressed in this first part—but he comes to a significantly different conclusion. The latter part of the 'Ode' was written in 1804 and the complete poem was first

> Our birth is but a sleep and a forgetting:
>
> The Soul that rises with us, our life's Star,
>
>> Hath had elsewhere its setting,
>>
>>> And cometh from afar:
>>
>> Not in entire forgetfulness,
>>
>> And not in utter nakedness,
>
> But trailing clouds of glory do we come
>
>> From God, who is our home:
>
> Heaven lies about us in our infancy! (58–66)[17]

With the moment of birth, a gradual process of forgetting sets in, and eventually all access to the pre-natal state is barred for the adult speaker. The concept of the soul in Wordsworth's *Immortality Ode*, arguably the most famous Romantic poem on the topic, is complex and problematic; it embraces many of the multifaceted and sometimes contradictory elements that characterise the concept of the soul around 1800. The *Ode* is, hence, a poem about the immortality of the transcendental soul and simultaneously a poem about the immanent secular mind.

Referring to the Platonic notion of *anamnesis*, the poem juxtaposes eternity and time, but, surprisingly perhaps, it does not end up glorifying transcendence. The *Ode*'s first stanzas are concerned with a severe crisis: the speaker's initial experience of loss—the loss of an original insight that is still accessible in early childhood:

> There was a time when meadow, grove, and stream,
>
> The earth, and every common sight,
>
>> To me did seem

---

    published in his *Poems in Two Volumes* of 1807. The proximity between Coleridge's and Wordsworth's poems has long been noted and examined as early as 1930 by Herbert Hartman, albeit with an awkward focus on Coleridge's son Hartley (see Herbert Hartman, 'The "Intimations" of Wordsworth's *Ode*', *The Review of English Studies* 6 (1930), 129–48), https://doi.org/10.1093/res/os-vi.22.129

17 William Wordsworth, 'Ode. Intimations of Immortality from Recollections of Early Childhood', in *The Poetical Works*, vol. 4, ed. by Ernest de Selincourt and Helen Darbishire (Oxford: Clarendon Press, 1963–66), pp. 279–85.

> Apparelled in celestial light,
>
> The glory and the freshness of a dream.
>
> It is not now as it hath been of yore; –
>
> Turn wheresoe'er I may,
>
> By night or day,
>
> The things which I have seen I now can see no more. (1–9)

According to Plato, any human knowledge is a form of memory that recalls knowledge of the immortal and eternal soul before it entered the body: to learn means to remember what we once knew before we were born and what was lost at the moment of birth. Hence, the soul still has limited access to the realm of ideas through learning—which is at the same time an act of remembrance. Whilst in Plato learning is remembering, in Wordsworth, on the contrary, the boy moves further and further away from this form of innocent wisdom as he grows older, matures, and gains worldly knowledge. This sense of loss, however, is, and this is the gist of the poem, gradually replaced by an enhancement of the immanent mind and the faculty of the imagination—linked to time and not to eternity. Wordsworth's poem thus proposes an epistemology that consists of a strange mixture between both the Platonic model and the dominant Lockean empiricist theory according to which the mind of a child is a *tabula rasa* at birth—and yet the poem is at the same time opposed to both of them. For the growing child, who originally had access to the realm of ideas, the process of learning is a form of forgetting. The more experienced the boy becomes, the further he moves away from the original state of the soul.

As the poem proceeds, it becomes clear that it is not the care for an afterlife or the soul's salvation that is at its heart. Instead, the speaker's concern is with the human mind in *this* life and especially with the creative mind of the poet-speaker himself. The main theme of the *Ode* is, therefore, the crisis of the imagination, and this crisis is also the *volta* of the poem. Although the adult speaker does not have immediate access to the realm of ideas, he still has the ability to remember his own childhood:

> Hence in a season of calm weather
>
> Though inland far we be,

> Our souls have sight of that immortal sea
>
> > Which brought us hither,
> >
> > Can in a moment travel thither,
> >
> > And see the children sport upon the shore,
> >
> > And hear the mighty waters rolling evermore. (164–70)

The mind can remember remembering. This act of memory, however, is also a poetic act, and therefore it is identical with Wordsworth's famous notion that poetry 'takes its origins from emotion recollected in tranquillity'[18] and also with his notion of the 'spots of time'—the coexistence of 'two consciousnesses' he describes in *The Prelude*. It is not the eternal realm of ideas but actually their *loss* that gives rise to the creative process, and only in the act of remembering are there 'intimations of immortality'—not in the ideas as such. In other words, the idiosyncratic reinterpretation of the Platonic concept of anamnesis in the *Ode* contains Wordsworth's entire poetic theory of the imagination in a nutshell.

It thus becomes clear that Wordsworth's concept of the soul betrays a focus on the immanent mind and not on some otherworldly ideal. By referencing Plato's *Phaedo*, the poem evokes the entire classical discourse on the soul, yet it never fully accepts the religious and mythological dimensions of this discourse. The allusion to Platonic idealism is therefore not made to evoke the immortality of the soul; rather, these classical pre-texts are invoked in order to describe poetry as a philosophical act and thus to elevate the dignity of the poet's imagination.

This turn from transcendence to immanence is also visible in the poem's formal features. The *Ode* is arranged in a circular manner and consequently often described as a prime example of an organic work of art hinting at the realms of transcendence and eternity. Therefore, it has been analysed time and again as a poem that leads from crisis and scepticism to closure and harmony[19] and, hence, it has been seen to be

---

18 William Wordsworth and Samuel Taylor Coleridge, *Lyrical Ballads*, ed. by R.L. Brett and A.R. Jones (London and New York: Routledge, 1991), p. 266.

19 See for instance M.H. Abrams, 'Structure and Style in the Greater Romantic Lyric', in *From Sensibility to Romanticism: Essays Presented to Frederick W. Pottle*, ed. by Frederick W. Hilles and Harold Bloom (New Haven: Yale University Press, 1965), pp. 527–60; Helen Vendler, 'Lionel Trilling and the Immortality Ode', in *Salmagundi*, 41 (Spring 1978), 65–85; Michael O'Neill, *Romanticism and the*

a prime example of the Romantic ideology in Jerome McGann's sense.[20] But a closer look reveals that the *Ode* undermines, rather than fulfils, the harmony promised by the organic work of art. The joy that the speaker feels is fragile and fleeting. The immortal world soul—another Neoplatonic concept evoked in Wordsworth's poem—is a mere point of reference for the poet speaker's imagination. Due to this problematic crisis and pseudo-resolution, there is a constant tension involved in the acts of the imagination—the fear that it may utterly fail again in the future is always present. The imagery is fraught with tension and the vocabulary used in the *Ode's* final stanza is highly ambiguous and sceptical, and thus it is doubtful whether the poem really has, to quote Matthew Arnold, 'Wordsworth's healing power'.[21] The many connotations and puns make it clear that the form of the poem undermines the speaker's positive resolution.[22]

I will try to demonstrate this in a close reading of the poem's closing stanza:

> And O, ye Fountains, Meadows, Hills, and Groves,
>
> Forebode not any severing of our loves!
>
> Yet in my heart of hearts I feel your might;
>
> I only have relinquished one delight
>
> To live beneath your more habitual sway. (187–91)

At first glance, the final stanza seems to be closing the poem on a positive note, directly turning the negative emotions of the poem's beginning

---

Self-Conscious Poem (Oxford: Clarendon Press, 1997), https://doi.org/10.1093/acprof:oso/9780198122852.001.0001; James Chandler, 'Wordsworth's Great Ode: Romanticism and the Progress of Poetry', in *The Cambridge Companion to British Romantic Poetry*, ed. by James Chandler and Maureen N. McLane (Cambridge: Cambridge University Press, 2008), pp. 136–54, https://doi.org/10.1017/ccol9780521862356.008. For a more critical reading of the 'Ode' that also takes the negative tendencies into account see Peter Simonsen, 'Reading Wordsworth after McGann: Moments of Negativity in "Tintern Abbey" and the Immortality Ode', *Nordic Journal of English Studies* 4 (2005), 79–99, https://doi.org/10.35360/njes.174

20 See Jerome McGann, *The Romantic Ideology: A Critical Investigation* (Chicago: University of Chicago Press, 1983).

21 Matthew Arnold, 'Memorial Verses', in *Norton Anthology of English Literature*, 8th edition, ed. by Stephen Greenblatt et al. (New York: Norton, 2006), p. 63.

22 I wish to thank Bill Bell for pointing out the possibility of reading the poem in a more ambiguous if not negative manner.

into a positive mood at its close as a result of the speaker's introspective development. This reading, however, disregards the ambiguities that characterise almost each of the final seventeen lines. One may claim that the speaker finds his strength 'In the soothing thoughts that spring/Out of human suffering' (183–84); yet, the overall impression is that joy does not eventually conquer fear but, on the contrary, that the impression of loss prevails. The line 'And O, ye Fountains, Meadows, Hills, and Groves', with which this final stanza opens, consciously repeats and reflects the opening line of the entire poem, suggesting a positive development, but also, by remembering the initial crisis, hinting at the fact that this is only momentary and therefore transient and brittle. The very next line is an expression of fear, because this invocation of nature can be read not only as a statement but as the speaker's pleading: 'Forebode not any severing of our loves!' The 'habitual sway' of line 191 refers, on a literal level, to the swaying groves, but ultimately, on a symbolical level, it self-reflexively refers to the speaker's mood swings, the comings and goings of poetic inspiration.

The seemingly innocent description of nature is highly ambiguous as well:

I love the Brooks which down their channels fret,

Even more than when I tripped lightly as they;

The innocent brightness of a new-born Day

    Is lovely yet;

The Clouds that gather round the setting sun

Do take a sober colouring from an eye

That hath kept watch o'er man's mortality (192–98)

The brook does not simply flow but it frets, a word that also connotes anxiety and worry; furthermore, the speaker trips, which indicates that even in a light-hearted and innocent mood, danger is lurking underneath. Furthermore, the simple word 'yet' is doubly stressed and therefore deserves attention. First, the line is the only one in this stanza that does not conform to the iambic pentameter, and, second, it rhymes with the ambiguous term 'fret'. Considering that the genre of the ode is closely linked with the religious hymn and, hence, takes its origin in an oral setting, a different stress in pronouncing the line gives it a totally different, more negative, connotation: 'The innocent brightness of a new-born Day/Is lovely *yet;*/The Clouds'. In an oral recitation, the readers could make a break between 'lovely' and 'yet', thus stressing the latter term. Furthermore, in a purely acoustic rendering 'yet' could thus move much closer to 'the clouds' as if in an enjambment. In this reading, 'yet' becomes part of an enjambment, and the menacing clouds would be emphasised in a way that was hidden before. Thus, if the orator should choose to pronounce the word as if belonging to the following line, the stress is put on darkness rather than on light. The clouds take on a double meaning as well. On the one hand, they are the symbol of a medium between the eternal One, symbolised by the sun, and the immanent world. On the other hand, the clouds obviously darken the light and hide the sun from view. Quite tellingly, the notion of immortality is now turned into 'man's mortality'—hence, the transition from the transcendental soul to the immanent mind is complete. The final lines nevertheless seem to emphasise a positive turn right before the poem's close:

> Thanks to the human heart by which we live,
>
> Thanks to its tenderness, its joys, and fears,
>
> To me the meanest flower that blows can give
>
> Thoughts that do often lie too deep for tears. (203–06)

I would claim, however, that the *Ode* retains the pessimism and negativity that characterise its first stanzas. The most obvious instance of this inclination towards the negative can be found in the very last word 'tears', which tellingly rhymes with 'fears'. But also the flower in the penultimate line is not just simple, it is 'mean'. And all of these ambiguities refer not to the world or to humankind in general but 'to me'—hinting at the solipsism responsible for the initial crisis.

The *Immortality Ode* thus turns out to be an example of an extreme form of solipsism, and furthermore, one that the text—through its ambiguities—, but not the speaker, is aware of. The temporality of the soul that lies at the heart of the poem seems to promise a resolution and closure, and the movement from transcendental immortality to mortal immanence has its origin in a severe crisis, which is seemingly resolved in a coming-to-terms with the poetic self. The vocabulary, however, undermines this and hints at a fundamental crisis that returns regularly. Thus, the poem does not present a resolution typical of an organic artefact. Rather, the catastrophe of the opening stanzas remains looming in the background. The ambivalence characterising the final stanza and thus ultimately the entire *Ode* is part of the transition of the soul from immortality and transcendence to secular imagination and immanent mind, from eternity to time.

Lord Byron, *Childe Harold's Pilgrimage*

An even bleaker vision can be found in Lord Byron's *Childe Harold's Pilgrimage*. Whilst Wordsworth's *Ode* hides its anxiety and scepticism underneath a layer of optimism, Lord Byron's *Childe Harold* presents an openly disillusioned picture of the nature of time and history. *Childe Harold's Pilgrimage. A Romaunt*, published in four cantos between 1812 and 1818, made its author, as Byron himself claimed, famous overnight. The long poem is written in Spenserian stanzas and based on Byron's own travels through Europe during—in Cantos I and II—and after—in Cantos III and IV—the Napoleonic Wars.[23] The term 'pilgrimage' in the title is slightly misleading as the poem can hardly be called a spiritual work; neither is it based on a tour with religious intentions and a clearly definable destination. More accurately, it is a poem that takes account of Europe from a radically sceptical and even negative point of view. Childe Harold is, most of the time, not actively involved in the ongoing plot but rather a passive onlooker who becomes almost invisible and at times drifts out of view entirely. The reference to the protagonist in the title therefore also leads readers astray, as it is sometimes difficult to say whether the traveller is really at the centre of attention, as the poem's point of view frequently changes between the narrator and the eponymous hero Harold, who both are implicitly rather than explicitly identified with Lord Byron himself.

The first two cantos were begun in Albania in 1809, mainly written in Greece, and finished in Turkey. This first part of the poem was influenced by the experiences Byron had on his Grand Tour from 1809 to 1811, and it reflects key issues of this journey and the places Byron visited. Cantos III and IV were composed much later, after the Congress

---

23 For the biographical background see Caroline Franklin, *Byron* (London and New York: Routledge, 2007).

of Vienna and Napoleon's defeat in the Battle of Waterloo on 18 June 1815. They recount two further journeys Byron undertook, the first from Waterloo up the Rhine River, and the second and final from Venice to Rome. Although the entire poem gives an account of three journeys, it is apt to say that the first two and the latter two Cantos each form a unit and the whole makes up one coherent poem: whilst Cantos I and II paint a picture of the Napoleonic Wars, Cantos III and IV are a disillusioned account of Europe after Waterloo and an ongoing reflection on history, civilization, culture, and art. The poem furthermore features the first of Byron's 'Byronic heroes', Childe Harold, who is anything but a chivalric hero but rather a gloomy and melancholy character. Furthermore, the speaker-narrator, who at times can hardly be distinguished from Harold, may be read as such a Byronic hero as well.

The poem gives a negative, even nihilistic, account of contemporary European history in a semi-fictitious manner. The outlook on time and history is an ostensibly pessimistic one, and Europe is described as decaying or already lying in ruins. Time, which in *Childe Harold's Pilgrimage* thus features primarily as the necessary condition of a historical situation characterised by disintegration, decay, and decline, is presented as immanent time towards death, and the soul is symptomatically described as mortal and subject to an empty, homogeneous time.

In the second Canto, the hero travels from Portugal and Spain to Greece, a country that automatically, for a Romantic traveller at least, calls up history and classical art. Yet, Byron's is a Greece that is plundered by other nations, especially Britain; and even art loses its quality to outlast time. Invoking the goddess Athena as his muse, the speaker contrasts a glorious past with a desolate present: 'Ancient of days! august Athena! where,/Where are thy men of might? thy grand in soul?/Gone – glimmering through the dream of things that were'.[24]

Right at the beginning of the canto, the speaker describes the corpse of an imaginary Ajax whose dead body metaphorically signifies the decline from ancient glory. The sense of misery connected with the present as opposed to the past becomes clear in the description of the hero's cranium that even the worms shun: 'Remove yon skull from out

---

24 George Gordon Byron, *Childe Harold's Pilgrimage*, in *The Complete Poetical Works*, vol. 2, ed. by Jerome J. McGann (Oxford: Clarendon Press, 1980), II.2.

the scattered heaps:/Is that a Temple where a God may dwell?/Why ev'n the Worm at last disdains her shattered cell!' (II.5).

In the next stanza, the skull is described as the seat of the soul, which is then immediately connected with the topics of time and history:

> Look on its broken arch, its ruined wall,
>
> Its chambers desolate, and portals foul:
>
> Yes, this was once Ambition's airy hall,
>
> The Dome of Thought, the Palace of the Soul:
>
> Behold through each lack-lustre, eyeless hole,
>
> The gay recess of Wisdom and of Wit
>
> And Passion's host, that never brooked control:
>
> Can all Saint, Sage, or Sophist ever writ,
>
> People this lonely tower, this tenement refit? (II.6)

The skull is the classic symbol of *memento mori*- and the *vanity*-topoi, and these immediately conjure up a link with mortality and hence the immanence of time. This is indeed a conception of time that is homogeneous and empty—the soul no longer promises an access to transcendence and eternity. Byron's poem describes even the most traditional concepts that hint at eternity—religion and the ancient gods—as immanent concepts prone to passing and vanishing:

> Even Gods must yield – Religions take their turn:
>
> 'Twas Jove's – 'tis Mahomet's – and other Creeds
>
> Will rise with other years, till Man shall learn
>
> Vainly his incense soars, his victim bleeds (II.3)

Religion, the gods, the glories of ancient art—all these topics referencing the past evoked in the poem eventually only refer to time's transience. This all-encompassing notion of decline and decay is also emphasised in Stanza 53 of Canto II:

> What valley echoed the response of Jove?
>
> What trace remaineth of the Thunderer's shrine?

> All, all forgotten – and shall Man repine
>
> That his frail bonds to fleeting life are broke?
>
> Cease, Fool! the fate of Gods may well be thine:
>
> Wouldst thou survive the marble or the oak?
>
> When nations, tongues, and worlds must sink beneath the stroke! (II.53)

Notions of eternity and transcendence are only called up to stress the poem's bleak view on Napoleonic Europe—and time and history in general. It seems therefore only fitting that the nineteenth century would also engender the theory and practice of historicism so fiercely attacked by Benjamin in his 'Theses on the Philosophy of History'.

The form of Byron's text, however, I argue in conclusion of this chapter, critically reflects this immanent comprehension of time. *Childe Harold's Pilgrimage* is an epic poem, yet, both in its conception and for its readership, it functions as a piece of travel writing. Although it is termed a pilgrimage, it is not clear where that pilgrimage is supposed to lead or what its purpose is—certainly not a religious one. The melancholy Byronic hero is travelling an empty and forlorn world mirroring his own emptiness inside. There is no salvation anywhere, which is also why the text's temporality is immanent. As a travel book, it maps out the secular world, and its empty and homogeneous time is mirrored in the progressive and repetitive form of the poem: the Spenserian structure could go on endlessly, repeating stanza after stanza like clockwork.

The poem's very melancholy stance, however, betrays a yearning for a different temporality, characterised by intimations of immortality and eternity. Regarding its philosophy of time, this poem is, in a manner, the reversal of the *Immortality Ode*. Whereas Wordsworth's poem ends with a reconciliation of immanent time and transcendent eternity that betrays its anxiety in the negativity and ambiguity of its final stanza, *Childe Harold's* concept of time is, at first glance, wholly immanent and subject to a history of decline and decay. Only the melancholy point of view of its protagonist as well as its narrator shows a longing for a concept of time that transcends the secular world and the perspective of a persona 'incapable of imagining to himself annihilation'.

I began this chapter with an anachronistic reference to Benedict Anderson and Walter Benjamin. Anderson's strict opposition of messianic time characterised by the simultaneity of past, present, and future, on the one hand, and empty, homogeneous time, on the other, serves him to construct a teleology starting from a religious medieval worldview to a secular modern one. The text he quotes, however, Benjamin's 'Theses on the Philosophy of History', undermines this strict contrast. Benjamin's own conception of a theologically informed historical materialism constructs the present as a conception of time as *weakly* messianic—characterised both by an immanent conception of time, but with a longing or at least a hope for change and transcendence. Benjamin's blending of eternity and time, I claim, finds an equivalent in the tension between eternity and time of the Romantic period.

The two different texts—Wordsworth's and Byron's—are both immanent poems that refer to the soul—a topic traditionally mediating between eternity and time, transcendence and immanence. They focus both on time as fleeting and transient, but both, in ways almost diametrically opposed to one another, long to transcend the immanent and secular world. Whilst Wordsworth's poem constructs time as circular, hinting at eternity in its very form, Byron's epic is progressive, mirroring the hero's walking in a disenchanted world, whilst his melancholy expresses a longing for an eternity that seems forever lost.

Works Cited

Abrams, M.H., 'Structure and Style in the Greater Romantic Lyric', in *From Sensibility to Romanticism: Essays Presented to Frederick W. Pottle*, ed. by Frederick W. Hilles and Harold Bloom (New Haven: Yale University Press, 1965), pp. 527–60.

Anderson, Benedict, *Imagined Communities: Reflections on the Origins and Spread of Nationalism* (London and New York: Verso, 1991).

Arnold, Matthew, 'Memorial Verses', in *Norton Anthology of English Literature*, 8th edition, ed. by Stephen Greenblatt et al. (New York: Norton, 2006), p. 63.

Benjamin, Walter, *Illuminations*, trans. by Harry Zohn, ed. by Hannah Arendt (New York: Schocken, 1969), pp. 253–64.

Bergson, Henri, *Time and Free Will: An Essay on the Immediate Data of Consciousness* (London and New York: Routledge, 2013), https://doi.org/10.4324/9781315830254

Chandler, James, 'Wordsworth's Great Ode: Romanticism and the Progress of Poetry', in *The Cambridge Companion to British Romantic Poetry*, ed. by James Chandler and Maureen N. McLane (Cambridge: Cambridge University Press, 2008), pp. 136–54, https://doi.org/10.1017/CCOL9780521862356.008

De Selincourt, Ernest and Helen Darbishire, eds, *William Wordsworth, The Poetical Works* (Oxford: Clarendon Press, 1963–66).

Franklin, Caroline, *Byron* (London and New York: Routledge, 2007), https://doi.org/10.4324/9780203968000

Haekel, Ralf, *The Soul in British Romanticism: Negotiating Human Nature in Philosophy, Science and Poetry* (Trier: WVT, 2014).

Hartman, Herbert, 'The "Intimations" of Wordsworth's *Ode*', *The Review of English Studies*, 6 (1930), pp. 129–48, https://doi.org/10.1093/res/os-vi.22.129

McGann, Jerome J. ed., *Lord Byron: The Complete Poetical Works* (Oxford: Clarendon Press, 1980), https://doi.org/10.1093/actrade/9780198127543.book.1

McGann, Jerome J., *The Romantic Ideology: A Critical Investigation* (Chicago: University of Chicago Press, 1983).

O'Neill, Michael, *Romanticism and the Self-Conscious Poem* (Oxford: Clarendon Press, 1997), https://doi.org/10.1093/acprof:oso/9780198122852.001.0001

Plato, *Euthyphro. Apology. Crito. Phaedo. Phaedrus*, trans. Harold North Fowler (Cambridge, MA: Harvard University Press, 1977), https://doi.org/10.4159/dlcl.plato_philosopher-phaedo.1914

Reiman Donald H. and Neil Fraistat eds, *Shelley's Poetry and Prose* (New York and London: Norton, 2002).

Scholtz, Gunter, 'Historismus, Historizismus', *Historisches Wörterbuch der Philosophie*, ed. by Joachim Ritter, Karlfried Gründer and Gottfried Gabriel (Darmstadt: Wissenschaftliche Buchgesellschaft, 1971–2007), https://doi.org/10.24894/hwph.1554

Simonsen, Peter, 'Reading Wordsworth after McGann: Moments of Negativity in "Tintern Abbey" and the Immortality Ode', *Nordic Journal of English Studies* 4 (2005), pp. 79–99, https://doi.org/10.35360/njes.174

Smith, Andrew, 'Eternity and Time', in *The Cambridge Companion to Plotinus*, ed. by Lloyd P. Gerson (Cambridge: Cambridge University Press, 1996), pp. 196–216, https://doi.org/10.1017/ccol0521470935.009

Vendler, Helen, 'Lionel Trilling and the Immortality Ode', in *Salmagundi*, 41 (Spring 1978), pp. 65–85.

West-Pavlov, Russel, *Temporalities* (London and New York: Routledge, 2013), https://doi.org/10.4324/9780203106877

Wordsworth, Jonathan, 'William Wordsworth: *The Prelude*', in *A Companion to Romanticism*, ed. by Duncan Wu (Oxford: Blackwell, 1998), pp. 179–90, https://doi.org/10.1002/9781405165396.ch16

Wordsworth, William, and Samuel Taylor Coleridge, *Lyrical Ballads*, ed. by R.L. Brett and A.R. Jones (London and New York: Routledge, 1991), https://doi.org/10.4324/9780203413876

5. 'Footing slow across a silent plain': Time and Walking in Keatsian Poetics

Oriane Monthéard

Critics have extensively analysed Keats's work from the perspective of historical time, often by considering his integration into the cultural and literary community of his time. Yet his perception of time may also be envisioned through his experience of walking and travelling. Indeed, his summer 1818 walking tour in Scotland, that had social and literary implications and then created a specific relation to time, may be viewed as an opportunity for the poet to better adjust to temporality. In undertaking his tour, and as recorded in his letters, Keats first sought to break away from the constraints of the ordinary measurement of time. But roaming the Highlands also led him to take up the recently established habit of picturesque tourism and to relate both to a literary past and to more contemporary voices: following the tracks of other poets meant revisiting the landscape and experiencing a fictionalised temporality. Finally, Keats's poems and letters relate the physical act of walking and the experience of immediacy it entails. In several poems, feet and steps stage the contact between the poet's body and the ground loaded with memory. Thus, walking was for Keats a means to experience the past and to bridge past and present voices, which redefined his inscription in his own time.

Critics have extensively analysed John Keats's work from the perspective of temporality to discuss how his attitude towards historical time and periodicity shaped his writing. Among other things, the poet's sometimes uneasy relationship with his time, his struggle with feelings of social and temporal inadequacy have been pointed out, first through his attempts to be fully integrated into the early nineteenth-century cultural and literary community, but also because of his wish to address a potentially more receptive posthumous audience, as Andrew Bennett has argued.[1] Read as out-of-step in its time, his work brought about a sense of inappropriateness, or, in more positive terms, displayed an ability to be disruptive. Finally, towards the end of his life, the awareness of his impending death inevitably darkened Keats's vision of temporal cycles. His poetic constructions of temporality somehow echo these issues, as, for instance, his efforts to historicise his own career in narratives of progress and expectation, or his strategies to disturb the course of poetic time by working against narrative progression in his long poems.

But Keats's perception of time may also be appraised from another angle, narrower and yet revealing—namely his practice and his representation of walking and touring. In several poems, the role of walking or wandering is either structural or metaphorical: Endymion is the hero who surveys the world, gets lost and wastes his time chasing a goddess across nature, in a poem that extends narrative time in a never-ending digressive process. In a famous passage, *The Fall of Hyperion*'s speaker strives 'to gain the lowest steps' (l. 129) of the temple he is urged to reach in 'a slow, heavy, deadly' pace (l. 130). In these poems—and others—walking enacts the process of a quest, which may be measured out in narrative time and rhythm. Now Keats's 1818 expedition in the North of England and Scotland from 22 June to 8 August casts another light on the subject. Keats's letters, as a primary source, provide us with a very valuable, almost day-to-day testimony of the tour, and they also account for the writing experience of the walk. Along with the speculations on various subjects, the 'descriptive sketches' and the factual details of the walk—recording climate variations, distances and encounters—give evidence of the poet's vision of the landscape and of his aesthetic emotions, in the form of an impressionistic, stylistically heterogeneous and often humorous logbook. A few poems written during the tour or shortly

---

1 See Andrew Bennett, *Keats, Narrative and Audience: The Posthumous Life of Writing* (Cambridge: Cambridge University Press, 1994).

after were clearly derived from both the travel itself and its epistolary account.

Roaming the Highlands with his friend Charles Brown led Keats, as a poet and a letter writer, to reflect on his own relationship to time and space, as progression and rhythm were imposed by alternating motion, pauses, contemplation, and reflection. For any walker in the nineteenth century, touring was also endowed with social, cultural and literary implications that created a strong relationship to tradition. Thus, Keats's involvement in this activity may be viewed as an attempt to experience temporality differently, if not to better adjust to it. Walking in his letters and in some of his poems is indeed represented as a reconciling attitude, as a physical and intellectual act connecting literature and life, the body and the landscape, past voices and present perception. In this chapter, I would like to explore how the emotional, intellectual and physical dimension of the walk affected Keats's perception and representation of temporality. My intent is to show how Keats's approach to the tour led him to redefine the writing 'I' and forge a poetic and epistolary 'walking subject' involved in a specific temporality. To do so I will draw on the letters and on several poems, as well as on the values associated with walking in general and more particularly in the nineteenth century. I will first analyse how Keats's tour led him to step out of social and historical temporality, then I will focus on walking as an attempt to return to literary paths, and I will conclude on the role of the walking body as a temporal medium.

From Historical Time to Poetic Temporality

For Keats, the tour provided the perfect conditions to turn away from historical time and to perceive time more subjectively, as contemplation threw him into a suspended temporality that affected his sense of duration. In the first letter of the tour addressed to his brother Tom, Keats introduces his trip as a marginal episode and makes it clear that the first day of the tour ushers in a temporal parenthesis: 'Here beginneth my journal, this Thursday, the 25th of June, Anno Domini 1818'.[2] Though the formality of the statement may serve humorous purposes, there is

---

2   *The Letters of John Keats*, ed. by Hyder Edward Rollins, 2 vols. (London: Cambridge University Press, 1958), I, p. 298.

also something stylistically solemn about this epistolary introduction, announcing both the beginning of the journey (even though it actually started on 22 June) and the outset of its epistolary translation. As such, it points to Keats's need to single out the moment in his own personal timeline. Keats's experience of departing as a temporal disruption is soon confirmed, when he contemplates the lake and the mountains of Winander and is struck by the beauty of the place: 'I merely put *pro forma*, for there is no such thing as time and space, which by the way came forcibly upon me on seeing for the first hour the Lake and Mountains of Winander'.[3] While Keats fails to elaborate his thought here, the declaration nevertheless reveals how, in his mind, contemplation leads the observer to break away from an ordinary perception of temporality and to ponder on the very idea of time and space. To the young poet, the exceptional character of the walk and the temporary isolation from society it entailed would give him the chance to focus on his own perception of time in its relation to space and motion.

In addition, Keats was aware that his tour was opposed to ordinary walking in the sense that it turned a mundane act and a prosaic use of the body into a meaningful practice to which values and purposes may be attached. Keats's discourse on the journey to come, inevitably inscribed in the temporality of prediction, reveals high expectations; much more than providing temporary relief from society, his walk was to be the starting point of an authentic poet's life:

> I purpose within a Month to put my knapsack at my back and make a pedestrian tour through the North of England, and part of Scotland—to make a sort of Prologue to the Life I intend to pursue—that is to write, to study and to see all Europe at the lowest expence [sic]. I will clamber through the Clouds and exist. I will get such an accumulation of stupendous recollolections [sic] that as I walk through the suburbs of London I may not see them—I will stand upon Mount Blanc and remember this coming summer when I intend to straddle ben Lomond—with my Soul![4]

The disruptive quality of the moment to come is then expressed in a distorted perception of temporality that superimposes anticipation and remembrance: to Keats, the tour was sure to feed his imaginative

---

3   Ibid., p. 298.
4   Ibid., p. 264.

mind with overwhelming memories that might 'surpass'—a verb which is repeatedly used in his travel letters—any future vision. And the vividness of the memories would be such that they were to erase present experience and operate an alteration of temporal perception resulting in a form of time confusion.

Fig. 1 Francis Towne, *Windermere at Sunset* (1786). Watercolor and brown ink over graphite on medium moderately textured cream laid paper, Yale Center for British Art, Paul Mellon Collection, B1975.4.1759. Public domain.

Keats's first aesthetic emotions during the tour also seem to prevail over the unfolding of events, as they go together with a leap into timelessness. In the first letter of the tour, Keats explains how his perception of nature disturbs temporal vision: the contemplative mode and the aesthetic emotion it generates reshape his apprehension of time and urge him to inscribe temporality into the environment. When admiring Lake Windermere, the intensity of the vision (to borrow from the notion Keats discussed a few months earlier), as the poet soon realises, is aroused from the sense of eternity that the observer may feel:

> [The] two views we have had of [the lake] are of the most noble tenderness—they can never fade away—they make one forget the divisions of life; age, youth, poverty and riches; and refine one's sensual

vision into a sort of north star which can never cease to be open lidded and stedfast over the wonders of the great Power.[5]

In *Romantic Writing and Pedestrian Travel*, Robin Jarvis shows that touring 'brings a readjusted sense of proportion between humanity and the wider natural environment'.[6] As Keats seemingly expresses here, this rearranged perception in terms of proportion rather applies to time.[7] To him, as the walker becomes aware of the persistence of natural elements, he may put into perspective the human lifespan and the notion of permanence: mountains, rocks and the horizon have no age and their stability is equated to an eternal presence, which is also suggested in the sonnet addressed to Ailsa Rock, in which the mountain's life is said to be 'but two dead eternities' (l. 10). In another famous passage from the same letter, Keats analyses how the beauty of the Ambleside waterfall acts on him. Here again the sublimity of the vision is expressed in temporal terms, as it seems to prevent the process of both anticipation and memory. This ecstatic moment may exist only in the distorted temporality of a stretched and suspended present, the pure present of perception, during which the spiritual character of the emotion is transposed to the perceived objects. The contemplative mode induced by the walk takes the observer to a poetic temporality in which the experience of the sublime seems to freeze images in time:

> What astonishes me more than any thing is the tone, the coloring, the slate, the stone, the moss, the rock-weed; or, if I may so say, the intellect, the countenance of such places. The space, the magnitude of mountains and waterfalls are well imagined before one sees them; but this countenance or intellectual tone must surpass every imagination and defy any remembrance.[8]

As the transformation process described here is akin to the poetic process Keats discusses later in the same letter,[9] perception explicitly

---

5   Ibid., p. 299.
6   Robin Jarvis, *Romantic Writing and Pedestrian Travel* (London: Palgrave Macmillan, 1997), p. 69, https://doi.org/10.1057/9780230371361
7   See 'I cannot think with Hazlitt that these scenes make man appear little', *The Letters of John Keats*, I, p. 301.
8   Ibid.
9   The passage is famous: 'I shall learn poetry here and shall henceforth write more than ever, for the abstract endeavour of being able to add a mite to that mass of

becomes both a poetic and temporal experience, and the temporality of the walk, as worded in these passages, reproduces poetic temporality.

Finally, touring meant freedom from an ordinary measurement of time: wandering freely, as Wordsworth claimed to do, meant choosing and inventing the schedule, the rhythm and conditions of the walk. Improvisation was also part of Keats's tour, as any tour, not to mention the possibility of losing one's path—which happened to him from time to time. For Keats, wasting time by digressing from the planned itinerary could turn out to be a sought-for temporal and contemplative experience, not unlike his indulging in the idea of 'productive leisure', such as the unnecessary but fertile time of intellectual indolence that eventually stimulates imagination: 'We, I may say, fortunately missed the direct path, and after wandering a little, found out [the water fall] by the noise—for, mark you, it is buried in trees, in the bottom of the valley—[...]'.[10]

Fig. 2 Thomas Hearne, *View from Skiddaw over Derwentwater* (between 1772 and 1782). Watercolor and graphite on moderately thick, slightly textured, cream wove paper mounted on moderately thick, slightly textured, cream laid paper, Yale Center for British Art, Paul Mellon Collection, B1977.14.4685. Public domain.

Of course, a tour in the nineteenth century was not devoid of constraints and did submit walkers to logistical difficulties related to the

---

beauty which is harvested from these grand materials, by the finest spirits, and put into etherial [sic] existence for the relish of one's fellows', Ibid.

10   Ibid., p. 300.

arrangement of the travel. It can't be denied that Keats devotes a large part of his account to organisational issues, and as he keeps complaining of tiredness or of the monotony of the Scottish meals, he presents the travel as a form of voluntary servitude. Yet, this servitude was chosen and worked out of the social regulation of time founded on obligation. To Robin Jarvis, the first Romantic travellers' tours were 'a clear assertion of autonomy: they travelled in a way they did not have to and in a way they could not be suspected of having to adopt from necessity'.[11] This was probably true for Keats and Brown.

Beside independence from necessity, what Keats and his contemporary walkers might have longed for was the opportunity to reinvent one's self and thus to experience 'freedom [...] from a culturally defined and circumscribed self',[12] an idea which may be found in Keats's words when he anticipates the tour, and states: 'I will clamber through the Clouds and exist'.[13] By connecting touring to a deeper, richer and more authentic mode of being, Keats's vision recalls Hazlitt's declaration in 'On going in a Journey', which discusses how a pedestrian traveller tends to 'lose [his] importunate, tormenting, everlasting personal identity, and become a creature of the moment, clear of all ties'.[14] Hazlitt's argument is that freedom in walking opens up the prospect of losing one's identity, because the walking self, focused both on the aesthetic perception of the environment and on the needs of the body, which are submitted to a cyclical temporal pattern, differs from the social self and has no historical mooring. These reflections recall Keats's experience and the way he accounts for it in his epistolary narrative, insofar as the walking and writing 'I' that emerges, letter after letter, defines a very subjective relationship to time. In *A Philosophy of Walking*, Frédéric Gros goes even further and asserts that '[b]y walking, you escape from the very idea of identity, the temptation to be someone, to have a name and a history. [...] The freedom in walking lies in not being anyone; for the walking body has no history, it is just an eddy in the stream

---

11   Jarvis, *Romantic Writing*, p. 28. More generally, Robin Jarvis shows that '[w]alking affirmed a desired freedom from context, however partial, temporary or illusory that freedom might be: freedom from the context of parental expectations and class etiquette, the context of a hierarchical and segregated society'.
12   Ibid., p. 28.
13   *The Letters of John Keats*, I, p. 264.
14   Quoted by Jarvis in *Romantic Writing*, p. 192.

of immemorial life'[15]. While the statement sounds very close to Keats's notion of the poetic subject that has no identity and thus no inscription in historical time, it also confirms the idea that the tour probably created the perfect conditions for Keats to see the world poetically. Yet, if a tour offered him the possibility of slamming the world's door, he also chose to walk on existing poetic paths.

Returning to Poetic Nature: Walking in a Fictionalised Landscape

By walking on well-trodden paths and in the invisible footsteps of other walkers before him, Keats's experience in his tour was coloured by his pre-conceived ideas and his literary representations of touring and the landscape, turning what should have been a discovery into a metaphorical return. To follow the tracks of learned tourists, radical walkers or pedestrian poets was a way for him to assert his belonging to that community of the past and of the present,[16] and thus to better inscribe himself into the cultural history of touring. Keats was certainly not a conqueror of virgin territory and sought instead to imitate other tours, notably the Lake District tours. Scotland was another usual destination, associated with foreignness and picturesque sceneries that naturally attracted the young poet.[17] For second-generation Romantics, undertaking a tour was a way to embrace a recently established habit that had emerged at the end of the eighteenth century. Experiencing the landscape had indeed become a cultural, social and possibly political experience, and then a necessary component of education, as the perception and practice of hiking had shifted from a lower-class and

---

15 Frédéric Gros, *A Philosophy of Walking* (London: Verso, 2014), p. 7. In his short essay, Frédéric Gros explores the intellectual and physical implications of walking in the twenty-first century but also the value of walking for eighteenth- to nineteenth-century poets and thinkers, such as Nietzsche, Rousseau, Thoreau, Nerval, Kant and Hölderlin.

16 Keats's wish to experience mountaineering and walking was stimulated by the example set by major writers including Ann Radcliffe, Dorothy and William Wordsworth, John Thelwall, Samuel Taylor Coleridge, Percy Bysshe Shelley, Lord Byron and Walter Scott.

17 On the cultural phenomenon of tourism in the Highlands, see Nigel Leask, *Stepping Westward: Writing the Highland Tour c. 1720–1830* (Oxford: Oxford University Press, 2020), https://doi.org/10.1093/oso/9780198850021.001.0001

ordinary event to a culturally privileged upper-class activity providing intellectual pleasure and aesthetic emotions. There was also, especially for the first-generation Romantics, a transgressive dimension to the temporary self-exclusion from society involved in touring. This evolution in the significance of touring certainly shaped Keats's vision of his tour, even though the value he pre-ascribed to his travel was also that of a didactic experience to be drawn from contemplation and encounters with local folklore.[18]

Yet his enterprise was not only about social and cultural inclusion, it was also a literary time travel, by which fictional temporality was superimposed on the present temporality of perceiving and walking. For Keats, a tour necessarily had literary implications, since in the touring tradition the emotions of contemplation were acknowledged as deeply related to poetic production and writing in general. As mentioned before, Keats had anticipated his tour before setting out on his journey, and the epistolary narrative confirms it is about validating—or not—his expectations on the landscape. This landscape he wandered in was then a literary one that had been aestheticised by literary representation and that, to him, bore the signs of literary concepts such as the sublime and the gothic—even though, as several epistolary passages and parodic poems indicate, Keats also mocked the Romantic posture of the poet who marvels at the sublimity of nature. Moreover, just as his epistolary writing often expresses facts of his everyday life using quotations from various authors, he probably had in mind the models of canonical literature of the epic, the pastoral and travel literature, of which his tour may be seen as a form of fulfilment, and his letters an autobiographical transposition.[19] Mr Abbey, the Keats family trustee, compared Brown and Keats to Don Quixotes, a remark that Keats gladly reported in one of his letters, as it matched his vision of the tour as a literary itinerary.[20]

---

18   See Keats's statements quoted above, "I shall learn poetry here and shall henceforth write more than ever [...]" (*The Letters of John Keats*, I, p. 301).
19   Yet Keats doesn't consider his travel account as a proper travel narrative, as he admits: 'I shall endeavour that you may follow our steps in this walk—it would be uninteresting in a Book of Travels—it can not be interest{ing} but by my having gone through it—' (Ibid., I, p. 329).
20   Ibid., I, p. 311.

5. Time and Walking in Keatsian Poetics

Fig. 3 Thomas Hearne, *The Ruins of the College of Lincluden, near Dumfries* (ca. 1806). Gray wash over graphite on moderately thick, moderately textured, cream laid paper, Yale Center for British Art, Paul Mellon Collection, B1975.4.509. Public domain.

If walking linked him to the literary tradition of the wandering poet looking for inspiration in natural beauty, it more particularly referred to the Lake poets and their walking practice. Landscapes that other walkers and poets had already seen, described or represented, and that therefore Keats had already imagined, determined the fictional temporal mode of his tour, which was not only about visiting the countryside, but also paradoxically about revisiting it. From this perspective, Keats's tour was about reading the traces and imprints of other poets as they were inscribed in the landscape by the observer's interpretation. Wordsworth's image, first, haunts his epistolary account, especially at the beginning of the trip, as he walked across the land of his poetry. Not that Wordsworth's and Keats's walking practices may really be compared: while Wordsworth was an avid walker, who invented walking and mountain-climbing as a poetic attitude, Keats's tour was an exceptional moment in his life. However, the way Wordsworth perceived and used the landscape surely inspired Keats and accompanied him in his own excursion. As Keats marvelled at the landscape which he knew had been observed by Wordsworth before him, he tried to share his vision of the landscape. After all, as Keats wrote to Reynolds on 3 May 1818, a few weeks before the tour, 'we read fine—things but never feel them to thee

[sic] full until we have gone the same steps as the Author',[21] a metaphor that was then turned into real experience.

Though Keats's plan of meeting Wordsworth during the tour was not fulfilled,[22] another encounter took place, as Keats walked in his steps, which generated a process of identification through perception. Keats clearly endeavours to see through Wordsworth's eyes when he imagines the viewpoint he must have had from one of his windows: 'Wordsworth's house is situated just on the rise of the foot of mount Rydall, his parlor window looks directly down Winandermere'.[23] Several times, perception seems to be guided by the memory of Wordsworth's poetry, as the presence of his texts is deciphered by Keats in the landscape: when he admires the Windermere lake, and writes that the two views of the place 'refine one's sensual vision into a sort of north star that can never cease to be open lidded and stedfast',[24] the poetic representation is reminiscent of *The Excursion*[25] and the immediacy of perception is blended with the memory of the text. In a letter to George and Georgiana Keats, the process of reading Wordsworth's text in the landscape is even more explicit, with a quotation from 'To Joanna': 'I have seen Kirkstone, Loughrigg and Silver How—and discovered without a hint 'that ancient woman seated on Helm Craig'.[26] Brown expresses the same idea in his journal: 'Mr. Wordsworth formerly had a house there. His line—"That ancient woman seated on Helm Craig" was brought to remembrance as the object itself came in sight'.[27] Thus, Keats turns his walk into enacted reading, involving the subject in space

---

21   Ibid., I, p. 279.
22   The missed encounter with Wordsworth led Keats to bitter disappointment. From people he met on his way to Wordsworth's house, Keats learned Wordsworth had come to support a Tory candidate, which he naturally saw as a betrayal of his early convictions, see ibid., I, p. 299.
23   Ibid., I, p. 307.
24   Ibid., I, p. 299.
25   See '[Chaldean Shepherds] Looked on the polar star, as on a guide/And guardian of their course, that never closed/His stedfast eye' (*The Excursion*, IV, lines 697–99). The similarity is pointed out by Florence Gaillet-de Chezelles in 'Voyage et initiation poétique: l'aventure de Keats en 1818', *E-rea* 3.1 (2005), https://doi.org/10.4000/erea.527
26   *The Letters of John Keats*, I, p. 303.
27   Carol Kyros Walker, *Walking North with Keats* (New Haven and London: Yale University Press, 1992), p. 231.

both intellectually and physically and bringing his own temporality into collision with that of Wordsworth's poems.

Fig. 4 Unknown artist, *Burns's Mausoleum at Dumfries* (with text); page 52 (Volume One), Yale Center for British Art, Paul Mellon Collection, B1974.12.860. Public domain.

In the case of Burns, to whose image and legacy Keats turns shortly after, the tour almost becomes a remembrance tour. The presence of Burns in Keats's trip, in his letters and in the sonnet paying tribute to him, takes the form of a pilgrimage, in which places of memory are not viewed in a collective sense, but from a very individual perspective, since visiting the places associated with the poet deeply affects the subject: 'One of the pleasantest means of annulling self is approaching such a shrine as the Cottage of Burns—we need not think of his misery—that is all gone—bad luck to it'.[28] The statement may be related to Keats's tendency to empathy and identification with the objects he perceives. Regarding Burns, it is also a form of 'temporal empathy', as suggested in the sonnet 'On Visiting the Tomb of Burns', which stages a poetic subject

---

28   *The Letters of John Keats*, I, p. 323.

whose present is already taken to the past, since discovering the place is depicted as both a present experience and a recollection: 'as in a dream I dreamed long ago', on lines 3 and 4, may even include a sense of *déjà vu*.

Keats's emotional, temporal and literary experience when visiting Burns's tomb and other places related to him calls to mind passages from Dorothy Wordsworth's account in her *Recollections of a Tour Made in Scotland*, in which she documents her emotions and those of her travelling companions when exploring the same places fifteen years before Keats. Keats's disillusionment when he discovered Burns's poor living conditions, which he expressed in 'His Misery is a dead weight upon the nimbleness of one's quill',[29] recalls Dorothy Wordsworth's statements: 'We could think of little else but poor Burns, and his moving about on that unpoetic ground' and 'but there is no thought surviving in connexion with Burns's daily life that is not heart-depressing'.[30] Moreover, Dorothy Wordsworth's perception of the places associated to Burns also takes the form of a temporal experience:

> [...] we talked of Burns, and of the prospect he must have had, perhaps from his own door, of Skiddaw and his companions, indulging ourselves in the fancy that we might have been personally known to each other, and he have looked upon those objects with more pleasure for our sakes.[31]

Keats probably did not have these statements in mind when taking his tour, but he knew of William and Dorothy Wordsworth's touring habits. In a broad sense, Keats's pilgrimage is a tribute to Burns but also to other travellers, including Coleridge, Dorothy and William Wordsworth, his itinerary being directed by Burns's texts and experience and by his contemporaries' tours in a more recent past.

---

29   Ibid., I, p. 325.
30   Dorothy Wordsworth, *Recollections of a Tour Made in Scotland*, ed. by Carol Kyros Walker (London: Yale University Press, 1997), p. 41, https://doi.org/10.2307/j.ctt1ww3v9z
31   Ibid., p. 44.

Fig. 5 David Octavius Hill, *Burns's Cottage* (1880), The Miriam and Ira D. Wallach Division of Art, Prints and Photographs: Print Collection, The New York Public Library. The New York Public Library Digital Collections. Fair use, https://digitalcollections.nypl.org/items/510d47da-f8f0-a3d9-e040-e00a18064a99

Keats's steps on his walk are undoubtedly guided by his wish to see what these other poets had seen. The temporality and topography of the walk is then partly determined by a time projection, as Keats strove to walk in other poets' elusive footsteps,[32] so as to revive the text and experience it in the landscape and in the time of perception. What is established then is a form of time coincidence between the memory of the text, its inscription in space and the poet-walker's involvement in the landscape, a process Keats performs by using his imagination, his eyes and his walking body.

The Body as a Temporal Medium[33]

In the letters written during the tour, Keats offers his addressees a narrative on the walking body and the physical experience of immediacy

---

32 Keats also follows Scott's footsteps during his tour, which fuelled his inspiration and led him to write several poems, among which was 'Old Meg she was a gipsy'. Yet in Keats's travel account, Scott seems to be far less important than Burns and Wordsworth.

33 On the issue of walking as an embodied experience involving feet, legs, hands and lungs, see Simon Bainbridge, *Mountaineering and British Romanticism: The Literary Cultures of Climbing* 1770–1836 (Oxford: Oxford University Press, 2020), https://doi.org/10.1093/oso/9780198857891.001.0001

and, as his journal-letters particularly testify, the tour gives him the opportunity to write about the body faced with daily physical exertion. This account, relating what may be called 'the physiology of the walk', includes a sub-discourse on exhaustion, physical pain, soreness, hunger, cold and discomfort caused by failing equipment:[34] all these troubles affecting Keats and Brown are carefully documented and they anchor both walkers to the present, with bodily sensations acting as constant reminders of the ongoing physical activity. For a poet who was particularly attentive to senses in general, strenuous effort was probably very instructive and productive, as it allowed him to witness how walking directly affected his impressions. This focus on the body goes together with a reduction of the viewpoint, confirmed in Keats's famous epistolary declaration 'I live in the eye and my imagination, surpassed, is at rest', suggesting a deeper awareness of physical sensations and an attraction to the immediacy of perception.[35] Just as bodily responses to the walk created unusual conditions to relate to the world, the perception of temporality seemed to be altered by the travelling rhythm: the aching, or at least moving body in which the walker and letter-writer was absorbed was then the perfect medium for an enhanced presence in the world and an enhanced attention to the moment.[36]

This unusual feeling of immediacy is conveyed in the physical sensations that sometimes arise unexpectedly in the epistolary discourse, which is originally devoted to aesthetic reflections, sociological commentaries or any other concern. The following passage, though written in a pastiche Swiftian mode, illustrates how the discourse on the walking body collides with the descriptive vein in the letters, mixing

---

34 These factual details are sometimes treated in a comic mode, so that they may remain entertaining: 'My dear Fanny I am ashamed of writing you such stuff, nor would I if it were not for being tired after my days walking, and ready to tumble int{o bed} so fatigued that when I am asleep you might sew my nose to my great toe and trundle me round the town like a Hoop without waking me—Then I get so hungry—a Ham goes but a very little way and fowls are like Larks to me—' (*The Letters of John Keats*, I, pp. 315–16).

35 Ibid., I, p. 301.

36 See Frédéric Gros: 'You are nobody to the hills or the thick boughs heavy with greenery. You are no longer a role, or a status, not even an individual, but a body, a body that feels sharp stones on the paths, the caress of long grass and the freshness of the wind. When you walk, the world has neither present nor future: nothing but the cycle of mornings and evenings' (Gros, *A Philosophy of Walking*, p. 4).

literary references and the sudden appearance of the walker's most trivial troubles as though these could not be escaped:

> I'll not run over the Ground we have passed. That would be merely as bad as telling a dream—unless perhaps I do it in the manner of the Laputan printing press—that is I put down Mountains, Rivers, Lakes, dells, glens, Rocks, and Clouds, with beautiful enchanting, gothic picturesque fine, delightful, enchancting [sic], Grand, sublime—a few Blisters &—and now you have our journey thus far.[37]

This interest in physical immediacy goes further, as Keatsian poetics establish a connection between feet and the ground to bridge past and present and stage poetic memory. In the letters recording the tour, and in several poems (written during the tour, but not only), frequent references to feet and steps may be noticed. Written the year before the tour, 'I stood tip-toe upon a little hill' opens on the image of the speaker's body bent forward and points to the feet as a de-centred agent of perception, since toes that support the whole body favour an enlarged perception. The Scottish girls' bare feet, mentioned two or three times in several of the travel letters, seemed to fascinate Keats, not only as signs of their destitution but also because they suited 'the scenery about them', by which he might have meant these girls had a more direct relation with nature.[38] The playful 'There was a naughty boy' written during the walk, ends on the motionless child standing in his shoes: as the walk is halted, the song is silenced, while the boy's hopping and bouncing his way to the North has shaped the poetic voice and rhythm all along. In 'This mortal body of a thousand days', this 'flat sonnet' written in Burns's cottage, as Keats complains, the power of the perceiving eye is superseded by the ability of the speaker's feet to relate to the dead poet:

> My eyes are wandering, and I cannot see,
>
> Fancy is dead and drunken at its goal;
>
> Yet can I stamp my foot upon thy floor,
>
> Yet can I ope thy window-sash to find
>
> The meadow thou hast tramped o'er and o'er [...] (lines 7–11).

---

37   *The Letters of John Keats*, I, p. 322.
38   Ibid., I, p. 318.

While the eye is commonly the organ representing perception, inner vision and imagination, feet provide here a more down-to-earth physical medium that is closer to the soil, where touch replaces sight. Feet, then, guarantee travel in both space and time.

In these examples, the act of walking embodies a poetic thought unfolding in time and space and based on the connection between the ground and the mind. If 'On visiting the tomb of Burns' indirectly evokes the poetic subject relating to the poet's memory through contact with the ground, this is what 'There is a joy in footing slow across a silent plain' expresses more explicitly. In this poem, the walk is the physical means to represent a journey through space and time where past and present are connected. This poem even seems to crystallise the main aspects of Keats's experience in his tour: first the inscription of the landscape in literature and history, then communion with nature in immediacy, and finally an involvement of the subject in a cultural legacy through interaction with the ground:

> There is a joy in footing slow across a silent plain,
>
> Where patriot battle has been fought, where glory had the gain;
>
> There is a pleasure on the heath where Druids old have been,
>
> Where mantles grey have rustled by and swept the nettles green:
>
> There is a joy in every spot made known by times of old,
>
> New to the feet, though each tale a hundred times be told:
>
> There is a deeper joy than all, more solemn in the heart,
>
> More parching to the tongue than all, of more divine a smart,
>
> When weary steps forget themselves upon a pleasant turf,
>
> Upon hot sand, or flinty road, or sea-shore iron scurf,
>
> Toward the castle or the cot where long ago was born
>
> One who was great through mortal days and died of fame unshorn.
>
> Light heather-bells may tremble then, but they are far away;
>
> Wood-lark may sing from sandy fern,—the Sun may hear his lay;

Runnels may kiss the grass on shelves and shallows clear,

But their low voices are not heard, though come on travels drear;

Blood-red the sun may set behind the black mountain peaks;

Blue tides may sluice and drench their time in caves and weedy creeks;

Eagles may seem to sleep wing-side upon the air;

Ring doves may fly convuls'd across to some high-cedar'd lair;

But the forgotten eye is still fast wedded to the ground—

As palmer's, that with weariness mid-desert shrine hath found.

At such a time the soul's a child, in childhood is the brain;

Forgotten is the worldly heart—alone, it beats in vain. (lines 1–24)

Memory, first, flows through the ground and the poets' body. Here again, the journey in space also involves time travel, and walking enacts this link between feet and the earth, between a physical movement unfurled in the poetic present and in the invisible footsteps of past figures. The speaker repeatedly evokes the different versions of this soil ('silent plain', l.1, 'nettles green', l. 4, 'pleasant turf', l. 9, 'hot sand and flinty road', l. 10, etc.) where the memory of 'the glories of old' is buried and received by the walking poet. In the poem, feet are a synecdoche of the physical presence of the poet, but also an indirect synesthetic image, in which feet may almost listen to old tales, as suggested by 'new to the feet, although the tales a hundred times be told' (l. 6). This communion, performed by inscribing one's footprint where others have done the same, is soothing (as the speaker feels joy and pleasure) and is performed slowly, so as to be savoured. This slow pace corresponds to the poetic rhythm that ensures the connection with the imaginary past, since feet also evoke the measurement unit of a poem. As expected, the tempo of the poem founded on rhyming couplets deprived of run-on-lines and with a comma or strong punctuation at the end of each line recreates the monotonous pace of a walk, in which steps are predictably followed by other steps. The poem, by equating walking in nature and the tempo of the text, confirms that wandering on a silent plain is a poetic action or even the enactment of the poetic process.

The other facet of the text which seems essential here is the role of the body in its relation to the subject's identity and his inscription in time. In the second part of the poem, steps, time and imagination are linked to discuss the dangers of self-absorption in poetic vision and poetic memory, or when 'weary steps forget themselves upon a pleasant turf' (l. 9). We should remember that this idea of self-absorption in contemplation and meditation may be related, according to Robin Jarvis, to 'the regular, alternating rhythm of right leg, left leg [that] can induce a hypnotically self-absorbed state (if the conditions of the ground are not such as to demand constant vigilance)'.[39] The state of weariness the speaking 'I' insists upon in the poem might pertain to that feeling. Moreover, the representation of the subject shifts from these forgetting steps to the 'forgotten eye' (l. 21), which 'is still fast wedded to the ground' (l. 21), a displacement confirming that feet are perceiving organs in an earthlier, incarnated version of perception that anchors the poetic body to the earth. The shift from 'forgetting' to 'forgotten' reinforces the absorption of the self that seems to pass into oblivion. Then, the ultimate transformation of the locus of imaginative memory occurs in 'Forgotten is the worldy heart' (l. 24), which achieves a full embodiment. Just as the ground that contains images and songs is revived by perception and imagination, the walking body bears the marks of time.

When reading Keats's travel letters and some of his poems, it becomes clear that he used his feet and legs in the service of poetic thought and expression. What he seemed to experience in his tour is even a sort of creative walking, in which perception is an active process involving the participation of the wanderer: 'We walked 20 miles [...] every 10 steps creating a new and beautiful picture'.[40] Walking was for him, as for other Romantic writers, not only a means to gaze upon the landscape, but also a literary and temporal event, if not an art of time, in the sense that the poet-walker may invent his own pace and his own relationship to the present circumstance. Keats's epistolary and poetic production during his tour certainly benefited from this interaction between motion and a constructed temporality. The multiple temporalities induced by the walk—immediacy, allegiance to the past, timelessness and fictional

---

39 Jarvis, *Romantic Writing*, p. 68.
40 *The Letters of John Keats*, I, p. 264.

temporality—shaped a walking and writing subject influenced by a strong anchorage of the poetic body in its environment, both inward-looking and particularly ready to receive aesthetic emotions. As several poems written during the trip are either satiric works or fugitive poems, this mobility in space and time also allowed for a liberated, irreverent, and sometimes even regressive poetic subject to emerge.

Works Cited

Bainbridge, Simon, *Mountaineering and British Romanticism: The Literary Cultures of Climbing 1770–1836* (Oxford: Oxford University Press, 2020), https://doi.org/10.1093/oso/9780198857891.001.0001

Bertonèche, Caroline, 'On Walking in Burns's "Great Shadow": Keats's Scottish Heritage', *Études écossaises*, 15 (2012), 29–38, https://doi.org/10.4000/etudesecossaises.542

Crinquand, Sylvie, '"An English poet in Scotland": John Keats's Letter to his Brother Tom', *Annals of the University of Craiova*, Year VI, n°1 (2005), 54–67.

Gaillet-de Chezelles, Florence, 'Voyage et initiation poétique : l'aventure de Keats en 1818', *E-rea* 3.1 (2005), https://doi.org/10.4000/erea.527

——, *Wordsworth et la marche: parcours poétique et esthétique* (Grenoble: ELLUG, 2007).

Gros, Frédéric, *A Philosophy of Walking* (London: Verso, 2014).

Jarvis, Robin, *Romantic Writing and Pedestrian Travel* (Basingstoke: Palgrave Macmillan, 1997), https://doi.org/10.1057/9780230371361

Leask, Nigel. *Stepping Westward: Writing the Highland Tour c. 1720–1830* (Oxford: Oxford University Press, 2020), https://doi.org/10.1093/oso/9780198850021.001.0001

Rejack, Brian, 'Keats Lives in the eye', *The Keats Letter Project* (2018), http://keatslettersproject.com/correspondence/keats-lives-in-the-eye/

Rollins, Hyder Edward, ed., *The Letters of John Keats*, 2 vols. (London: Cambridge University Press, 1958).

Wordsworth, Dorothy, *Recollections of a Tour Made in Scotland*, ed. by Carol Kyros Walker (London: Yale University Press, 1997), https://doi.org/10.2307/j.ctt1ww3v9z

Stillinger, Jack, ed., *Keats: Complete Poems* (Cambridge: The Belknap Press, 1982).

Thompson, Carl, ed., *The Routledge Companion to Travel Writing* (Oxford: Routledge, 2016), https://doi.org/10.4324/9780203366127

Wallace, Anne D, *Walking, Literature and English Culture: The Origins and Uses of Peripatetic in the Nineteenth Century* (Oxford: Clarendon Press, 1993), https://doi.org/10.1093/acprof:oso/9780198183280.001.0001

Walker, Carol Kyros, *Walking North with Keats* (New Haven and London: Yale University Press, 1992).

SECTION III

THE POETICS OF TIME

6. Contracting Time: John Clare's *The Shepherd's Calendar*

Lily Dessau

This chapter considers the work of time in the extended work of poetry The Shepherd's Calendar *by Northamptonshire poet of labour, John Clare. Divided into twelve months, each of which assumes a different verse-form in the style of Edmund Spenser, Clare's* Calendar *is a real-time engagement with the uneasy tension between natural- and man-made time, simultaneously tracked across the seasons and the working day. Drawing on E. P. Thompson's study of time- and class-consciousness, this chapter considers the active role of the church clock in 'May' to antagonise the agricultural workers, both human and non-human. It also addresses how the speaker's adoption of the simple present shapes the verse into anti-memorial and builds on existing criticism of pre- and post-enclosure time in Clare's earlier work. This focus of this chapter is on how these tensions play out in the manuscript version of 'May' but does conclude with a turn to the question of how time is contracted and compressed through the editorial interventions of Clare's editors John Taylor and James Hessey in preparation for publication of* The Shepherd's Calendar *in 1827.*

Calendars, Almanacs, and Clocks

Any poem might be the meeting point of multiple temporalities, but it is difficult to avoid thinking about time in a work called *The Shepherd's Calendar*, a book of twelve poems that simultaneously laments and resists the passage of time. Moreover, John Clare's *The Shepherd's Calendar* is a sequence of twelve poems that engages with the acceleration of time in the form of new technologies. The invocation of the church clock is asserted in the opening of 'May', and the poem tracks a tension between this and other modes of temporality, between the symbolic command of the clock and the syntactical resistance to linear time. Clare's poetic engagement with the spatial and temporal organisation of space around the clock tower destabilises a reading of clock-time as either an authentic measure, or a legitimate force in the poem, and as such performs a resistance to the antagonism of the clock that I argue is figured in the sequence. Perhaps, for Clare, this instability is a more authentic rendering of time, closer to that of nature than the alienating time of industry that is structured and informed by the clock.[1]

There is an emphasis on time in Clare's formal arrangement of *The Shepherd's Calendar* (published in 1827), following Edmund Spenser's *Shepheardes Calendar* (1579). Organising the poems according to the twelve months, throughout the sequence Clare adopts different scales, tenses and measures, allowing them to overlap and intermingle in one richly time-conscious piece of work. Carefully shaped into twelve formally distinct parts, *The Shepherd's Calendar* is attentive to the measured time of verse-form and metre, and to the function of cadence and rhythm in moving the reader onwards, in place of narrative or succession.[2] He portions his poem into months, his months into days, and often his days stand as a record of the day from morn to eve, even though little *happens*. The action of the poem is built out of comings and goings with little space marked out for labour, or we instead trace the space and time *in-between*. Nevertheless, labour is the framing device, regulated by the clock. Clare looks back through time, mourning

---

[1] This instability speaks to John Goodridge's reading of the openness of Clare's verse form in the 'enclosure elegies', which he describes as 'more uncertain [than Oliver Goldsmith], but also more involving and exploratory.' In *John Clare and Community* (Cambridge: Cambridge University Press, 2013), p. 110, https://doi.org/10.1017/CBO9781139047197

[2] Clare appeals to the long literary heritage from Virgil through to Spenser of poetic forms, and with John Taylor's editorial support he self-consciously engages with this literary tradition, though not without complication. *The Shepherd's Calendar* is a child of the eclogue as well as the georgic—the former through Spenser's work of the same name, and the latter through James Thomson's *Seasons* and Clare's inheritance of the pastoral tradition. In addition to Thomson's formative influence on Clare, combined with Taylor's encouragement to write in the tradition of Spenser, we might also include John Gay's *Shepherd's Week* as another important text in informing the structure of Clare's *Calendar*. Clare's interest in Spenser is evident elsewhere; notably the epigraph in Clare's second publication *The Village Minstrel* (1821) comes from Spenser's 'June' eclogue.

lost customs in 'May', and celebrating harvest days and holidays in 'September' and 'December'. We cannot set aside how Clare's own time has been divided by industry and capital, and how *The Shepherd's Calendar*, along with some of his other verse, performs the sense of a pre- and post-enclosure time as well as space. On the subject of Clare's representation of rural leisure in 'The Village Minstrel' Theresa Adams argues that there is an almost lapsarian effect of enclosure on Clare and his poetics, marking that 'after enclosure, popular culture is no longer a lived experience, but something to be remembered'. In reading a shift in the end of 'The Village Minstrel' into 'an elegiac meditation on time and memory', which is coupled with a break from the georgic model of cyclical nature, Adams maintains that 'Clare's nostalgia [is] itself a form of protest'.[3]

In *The Shepherd's Calendar*, and in particular the month of 'May' that is the focus of this chapter, there is a pull away from the past worked into Clare's temporal structure of 'May' (in manuscript), which I argue is a self-conscious exploitation through inversion of the elegiac form as a mode of resistance. With an almost pedantic use of the present tense, Clare withholds from his speaker, and readers, the space or time to lament. As I will expand on in the conclusion, in the manuscript version of 'May' Clare turns from the simple present continuous to the construction of a 'now' that is 'no more' (l. 435), that works to resist the elegiac mode, and the temporality of nostalgia in its etymological root of returning home. It is in response to the effects of enclosure that I read Clare's grammatical and syntactical resistance to succession or a progression through time in the manuscript version of *The Shepherd's Calendar*. Instead, Clare's parataxis stands in deliberate opposition to industrial 'progress' that is demarcated and measured out in 'clock-time' (an opposition that I will show as cruelly erased in the 1827 published version of the text).

The *Calendar* opens with a scene in which one labourer is reading an almanac. Hardly have we opened a collection of poems titled *The Shepherd's Calendar*, turning to the first poem 'January', before we are being drawn into an entirely different system for measuring time. Clare's quiet revolt against the mechanical operation of time imposed

---

3   Theresa Adams, 'Representing Rural Leisure: John Clare and the Politics of Popular Culture', *Studies in Romanticism*, 47.3 (2008), 371–92 (p. 391).

by both the clock and the calendar, a revolt against the mechanisms of industry and capital, is apparent from the start. The almanac stands as an invocation of natural time given its historical usage in agrarian practices, but is also significant within the period given its revival in France, as the Republicans make a revolutionary return to this more ecologically-driven form of time-keeping.[4] The almanac is afforded such significance in *The Shepherd's Calendar* as Clare sneaks it onto the same line, and in the same breath, as the Bible in this first, 'January', scene: 'All wonders are with faith supplyd/Bible at once & weather guide'.[5] Here, Clare exposes an ecological tension between natural and industrial, or man-made, time and opens a dialogue between the two by invoking and then returning to the almanac throughout 'January'. John Goodridge similarly considers the 'competing narrative forms' of Bible and almanac, in reading their close quarters in another *Middle Period* poem, 'The Sorrows of Love Or the Broken Heart A Tale', wherein 'the Bible "lay wi penny storys rustling near/ & almanacks prese[r]vd for many a year"'.[6] This return to the almanac, placed in the opening of the *Calendar*, marks Clare's time as ecological, offering an alternative to the

---

4   The Roman etymology of 'calendar' marks it as driven by religion and capital (listen out for the 'cal' 'ends'), 'almanac' comes from the Middle French and post-classical Latin for an astronomical calendar. Interestingly, there is speculation that 'almanac' also derives from the classical Arabic *munāḵ*. This is the verbal noun of *'anāḵa* to make (a camel) kneel; it functions as a noun of action (i.e. 'halt at the end of a day›s travel') and a noun of place (i.e. 'stopping place'). The assumed semantic development from the classical Arabic senses of the verbal noun to the sense 'calendar' has a parallel in the semantic development of *climate* in Arabic; in fact, *munāḵ*, or *manāḵ* is the standard Modern Arabic word for 'climate' (OED). See also Matthew Shaw, *Time and the French Revolution* (Woodbridge: The Boydell Press, 2011) for a robust study into the origins and consequences of the intervention into the measurement of *time* during the Revolution. French coins of the period naturally used this calendar, with many showing the year in Arabic numbers, although Roman numerals were used in some cases. I read the use of Arabic as an aligning with the semantic roots of almanac that link place, time and climate. Furthermore, the replacement of saints for aspects of nature, each day as 'Germinal' and celebrating a new natural thing, along with the names of the months returning to correspond with the seasons, all build towards this sensical reading of a 'tool' driven by natural time.
5   John Clare, 'January' (MS), *The Shepherd's Calendar*, ed. by Tim Chilcott (Manchester: Carcanet, 2006), lines 21–22. Of note to the temporality of *The Shepherd's Calendar*, this '&' becomes 'or' in the printed edition. I turn to the shifts from the manuscript version to the printed edition in the final section of this chapter.
6   Goodridge, *John Clare and Community*, p. 183.

mechanical arrangement of time as measured by the calendar or, as it is invoked in the poem 'May', by the clock.

'Jealous Eyes' and Nostalgic Ears

Clare's 'May' is perhaps the most fraught of all the month poems in confronting the industrial-agrarian capitalist division of time between labour and leisure through the invocation of the May Day holiday. This explicit tension between past and present, and the loss of customs through the enclosure of the commons, plays out in what I figure as real-time, or perhaps the antagonistic 'now-time' of the clock, to borrow anachronistically from Walter Benjamin.[7] The clock figures its presence through sight—first spied through the eyes of the village children 'Viewing with jealous eyes the clock' (l. 22; MS)—and sound—echoing through the 'now' of 'Each morning now the weeders meet' (l. 147; MS), antagonising the workers as it instructs and drives them on. But in sounding the present, it also serves to drown out the sounds of the past, and with it the customs of May Day. The 'no' and 'no more' rings out to mark the lost rituals in the final passage of this poem as it appears in manuscript, across lines such as:

No flowers are pluckt to hail the[e] now

Nor cotter seeks a single bough

The maids no more on thy sweet morn

Awake their thresholds to adorn

Wi dewey flowers –[8]

---

7   Walter Benjamin, 'On the Concept of History', in *Walter Benjamin: Selected Writings*, ed. by Howard Eiland and Michael W. Jennings, trans. by Harry Zohn (Cambridge, MT: Belknap Press, 2006), IV, pp. 389–400 (p. 395). See also E. P. Thompson's chapter on 'Custom Law and Common Right', which makes reference to Clare's representation of customs, and in particular describes how 'his poems *are* the evidence of a tormented customary consciousness', in *Customs in Common* (London: Merlin Press, 1991), p. 181; the poems encode the tension, unease, and antagonism brought out in the labourers in this changing moment of their relationship to work and land.

8   John Clare, 'May' (MS), in *The Shepherd's Calendar*, ed. by Tim Chilcott (Manchester: Carcanet, 2006), lines 433–37.

The echoes of 'no', 'nor' and 'no more' chime as a funeral toll, marking the loss of such customs. One might consider this drowning out with reference to nostalgia, the sirens, and the 'call' to return home that I have mentioned above. Thinking on the work of the 'swathy bees' with which we begin in the 'May' poem, perhaps in reading the clock as both an imposition and as a monument to *nostalgia*, one might recall in Homer's *Odyssey* the application of beeswax to the ears, to counter the song of the sirens.⁹ Elsewhere, bees perform an undersong, 'humming' through Clare's verse, but they are at the same time the source of the material that drowns out the sound of the sirens. The poem begins with 'humming joys' (l. 11; MS), underpinning an ecological poetics of sound and time that are then challenged by the 'church clocks hum' (l. 97; MS); Clare plays with sound to reproduce the antagonistic, but all the while interrelated relationship between industry and nature, under the rule of time as it is organised according to labour.

To foreground the importance of the Church Clock, and its bells, in 'May', I want to step outside the time of the poem and draw on a more recent reading of time that marks the power of the Clock. Displacement and dispossession continue to have an antagonistic, and profound, relationship to mechanical time and synchronicity well into our own contemporary moment, which is explored through a process of return in W.G. Sebald's *Austerlitz* (2011). There are many reasons to draw together Clare and Sebald; for one, both are writers grounded—or perhaps more accurately, ungrounded—in their own significant historical moment of upheaval and displacement, and as such both have literary projects that afford both space and time to itinerancy. In *Austerlitz*, Sebald offers an explicit confrontation to the colonial ministry of the clock, having a hand in coercing persons and things between places; I draw on this text as a point of comparison with Clare's own rendering of the Church spire and Clock as an earlier iteration of the antagonistic subject-object relation between time and persons. The figure of the Clock is central to the political and economic subjectivity of both Sebald's protagonist and Clare's villagers. When Sebald recounts his protagonist's suspicion of time, from inside Antwerp Station, we overhear:

---

9   Homer, *The Odyssey*, trans. by Emily Wilson (New York: W. W. Norton & Company, 2017), Book 12.

> [...] time, said Austerlitz, represented by the hands and dial of the clock, *reigns supreme* among these emblems. The clock is placed some twenty metres *above* the only baroque element in the entire ensemble [...] as the governor of a *new omnipotence* [....] The movement of all travellers could be *surveyed* from the central position occupied by the clock in Antwerp Station, and conversely all travellers had to *look up* at the clock and were *obliged to adjust* their activities to its *demands*.[10]

'Time, said Austerlitz', recounts the narrator Sebald, 'represented by the hands and dial of the clock, *reigns supreme*' (my emphasis). Here the mechanism for measuring time, placed high above all other emblems of power, shifts from that which represents, to that which now governs. I draw on this passage from a much later text for how it exposes the tension that is captured in thinking of time as active, or passive, or both simultaneously, but also for how time is governed spatially, as it emphasises this height from which the clock oversees. From its vantage point, time has become an active, shaping force over its domain, forcing its subjects to 'adjust'. But nonetheless, in the face of the clock, time still exists as number, measured and guaranteed, against which the movements of the subjects are recorded, especially when it comes to labour.

Tracing the history of how time is announced by the bells, from a solemn ringer, through to the mechanical intervention of time constituted and regulated by the clock, by the 1900s we can be confident that the Church Clock, and implicitly its bells, do offer a regulated measure of time.[11] By the time we are in Antwerp station, the synchronisation of the clocks across Europe has faded into memory, and timepieces are widely and privately owned; time, as for Austerlitz, reigns supreme. Moreover, this reign of time is articulated spatially, from above. Even when we return to Clare, prior to this synchronisation, we understand time

---

10   W.G. Sebald, *Austerlitz*, trans. by Anthea Bell (London: Penguin, 2011), pp. 141–44. My emphasis.

11   Compared with earlier invocations of time ringing out hourly—but perhaps not technically hours apart. As is described by clock-maker to the King, B.L. Vulliamy, in a short pamphlet *Some Considerations on the Subject of Public Clocks Particularly Church Clocks: with Hints for their Improvement* (London: McMillan, Bow Street, 1828), p. 2: 'I select that of St Paul's as a standard, not on account of the accuracy with which it measures time, but from its *local situation*' (my emphasis).

through space.¹² In 'May', this spatial rendering of time is parochial. It is shaped by the sound of bells, which conform to the clock-time that is shown at the base of the Church's prominent spire. The real spire, that of St Benedict's Church, Glinton, transforms the space of Clare's poetics into place, but it also situates this place in time through the permeating sound of the bells.

Critics have emphasised the significance of Glinton spire in Clare's autobiographical and poetical writings.¹³ The spire does not lose its religious function in 'May'. It stands as 'a mark to urge him [the schoolboy we began with] right' (l. 49; MS and 'guide' l. 43; print). But perhaps the tension that the looming presence of the clock tower invokes—in its dual role both as religious symbol and marker of time—plays out in this transition from the verb' urg[ing]' in the manuscript to 'guid[ing]' in the printed edition; the antagonism that can be read in the manuscript is diluted in print, as is the sense of time's control.¹⁴ There is an oft-quoted passage from Clare's *Autobiographical Fragments*, commonly used to foreground or underline Clare's acute sensitivity to place, in which he recalls how:

> I had imagind that the worlds end was at the edge of the orison and that *a days journey* was able to find it [...] I eagerly wanderd on and rambled

---

12 Borrowing in part from Henri Bergson on Church bells in *Time and Free Will*, trans. by F. L. Pogson (Mineola, NY: Dover Publications, 2001), p. 87: 'Perhaps [when] some people count the successive strokes of a distant bell [...] their imagination pictures the bell coming and going; this spatial sort of image is sufficient for the first two units, and the others follow naturally'; Vulliamy (above) also theorises the bell in relation to space, given that the function of the bell is to inform a particular, 'local', place. That both Vulliamy and Bergson present a spatial imagining of time through the successive rings of a bell, draws me towards such a reading in Clare's poetic response to time, as it relates to his own parochialism, too.

13 I am recalling, here, the less scholarly and more anecdotal significance of Clare's attention to the spire. In 2004, Clare's poem 'Glinton Spire' was said to be instrumental in defending the village against the building of a telephone mast by British Telecom. See Ian Herbert, 'Poetic justice: villagers defeat phone mast threat by quoting their local bard', *Independent*, 14 December 2004, https://www.independent.co.uk/news/uk/this-britain/poetic-justice-villagers-defeat-phone-mast-threat-by-quoting-their-local-bard-688497.html

14 I expand on the issue of reading the manuscript and printed edition in parallel, given that we cannot identify the changes as Taylor's or Clare's definitively, but in tracing the temporal patterns in the text—and how it is arrested throughout in the manuscript before unfolding as a series of events in the printed edition—I want to hazard that the latter ordering of time, and the structuring of succession or *narrative* to speak in literary terms, is the work of Taylor in preparing the text for publication.

among the furze the whole day till I got out of my knowledge [...] I was finding new wonders every minute and was walking in a new world often wondering to my self that I had not found the end of the old one [...].¹⁵

Describing his return to the bounds of Helpston(e), 'everything seemd so different the church peeping over the woods coud hardly reconcile me'.¹⁶ Much has been made of Glinton spire in marking the bounds of place, and as a shaping force in Clare's poetic identity, but of equal importance to understanding Clare's spatial imaginary is the lesser emphasised moment from just earlier in this same fragment, where Clare foregrounds the importance of the church spire in demarcating the bounds of his 'knowledge':

> *we heard the bells chime but the fields was our church* and we seemd to feel a religious feeling in our haunts on the sabbath while some old shepherd sat on a mole hill reading aloud some favour[i]te chapter from an old fragment of a Bible which he carried in his pocket for the day a family relic which possesd on its covers and title pages in rude scrawls geneoligys of the third and fourth Generations when aunts uncles and grandmothers dyd and when cousins etc were marri[e]d and brothers and sisters born occupying all the blank leaves in the book and the title pages bhorders which leaves were prese[r]ved with a sacred veneration tho half the contents had been sufferd to drop out and be lost [.]¹⁷

For Clare, in this fragment, the bells do not 'urge' him as they do the characters in 'May'. The function of the bells, in reading Clare, is highly dependent on context, both spatial and temporal. To the labourers, the bells might well mark time, but in recounting his own memories of childhood in leisure time, Clare acknowledges and formulates a poetic response to how they demarcate the parameters of the common and the Parish as a whole, and in particular his own place of worship in the fields.¹⁸

---

15 John Clare, *By Himself*, ed. by Eric Robinson and David Powell (Manchester: Carcanet, 2002), p. 87. My emphasis.
16 Ibid., p. 88.
17 Ibid., p. 86. My emphasis.
18 My reading of the church spire (and its bells) as at the topographical centre of the poem echoes Franco Moretti's reading of space in Clare, which in turn leans heavily on John Barrell, who writes, 'for those of its inhabitants [...] the parish itself was so to speak at the centre of the landscape'. In this chapter I am pushing this reading further, to argue that for *The Shepherd's Calendar*, it is time at the centre, structuring

Arresting Development, or the Lyric Present

The tension playing out across 'May', between past and present, tradition and innovation, best materialises in the face of the clock. Clock-time and the looming threat of productivity as measured through time, establishes itself from the first few lines.[19] In 'May', the speaker gives us a scene teeming with the sounds of natural activity, the noisy insects and animals joined together by the metronomically sounding 'and' of the ampersand.[20] But quickly there is an interruption to this abundant description, a foreign sound to those of nature: that of a regulated, mechanical time (that is, the present tense 'now-time' of the clock). Measured and inscribed, the repetition of 'every' in this line draws out the repetitive nature of time measured in ticks and tocks, but perhaps of more importance is how it conjures the reflexive mode of time that is *kept*. This 'every' invokes the pernicious notion that someone is watching the clock, quantifying or recording the 'every' time. In the poem we find:

& swathy bees about the grass

That stops with every bloom they pass

& every minute every hour

Keep teazing weeds that wear a flower (lines 7–10; MS)

The work of the bees is reduced to an elliptical, almost mechanical, measure, that of quantifiable time. Clare's syntax exaggerates this effect, as 'every' carries over from space (the flowerbed) into time (minutes,

---

space. Barrell, quoted in Franco Moretti, *Graphs, Maps, Trees* (London: Verso, 2007), p. 38.

19   Marx, in *The Poverty of Philosophy*, clearly sets out the creeping emphasis on productivity within the labour-time relationship, in *Marx & Engels Collected Works*, trans. by Frida Knight (Electronic Book: Lawrence & Wishart, 2010), VI, p. 127. This is also drawn out by E.P. Thompson in his work on time and work-discipline, which I expand on below. The opening of Clare's 'May' chimes with Benjamin's 'On the Concept of History', and the tensions between man and the mechanical forms of time are announced when 'the dials on clocktowers were being fired at simultaneously and independently from several locations in Paris', in Benjamin, 'On the Concept of History', p. 395.

20   See Simon Kövesi, 'John Clare & ... & ... & ... Deleuze and Guattari's Rhizome', in *Ecology and the Literature of the British Left*, ed. by John Rignall (Farnham: Ashgate, 2012), pp. 75–88, https://doi.org/10.4324/9781315578675, for an important consideration of Clare's use of the ampersand through an ecocritical perspective.

hours). Here, too, the ampersand flattens the temporal scale, as we, with the bees are 'ke[pt]' in the perpetual present. But while the movement of the bees repeats from flower to flower, we are – thanks to the Clare's temporally-resistant poetics—afforded the time to linger over and elongate the repeated sound /i:/ in 'K<u>ee</u>p t<u>ea</u>zing w<u>ee</u>ds'.

Time crops up again as provocateur soon after the bees clock in their hours.[21] Turning to the 'village children', the speaker describes 'In school times leisure ever short' (l. 14; MS), the ambiguous pluralising of 'times' opening the possibility that here *time* might be both at once under the dictate of 'school' and itself the agent of 'leisure'. Merely gestured to, the Church spire casts a shadow over this opening scene, towering above all that surrounds it, ready to distribute time across 'May'. Franco Moretti draws out of John Barrell's study of Clare's idiosyncratic approach to space in verse, an 'omnipresent, half-submerged culture of daily routines—positions of the fields, local paths, perceptions of distances, horizon—which historians tend to call *mentalité*, and which is often entwined with the performance of material labour'.[22] Whether 'half-submerged' or casting a shadow, the sense of the spire as looming is also felt through the antagonism with which the children are:

> Oft racing round the nookey church
>
> Or calling ecchos in the porch
>
> & jelting oer the weather cock
>
> *Viewing* wi jealous eyes the clock
>
> Oft leaping grave stones leaning hights
>
> Uncheckt wi melancholy sights (lines 19–24; MS; my emphasis)

This imperative 'viewing' is from ambiguous and undefined standpoints scattered throughout the churchyard; the clock is set above eye-level, but beneath the weathercock (in verse and in life) as a single unifying point in the scene. This is an active 'viewing', continuous and ever-renewed

---

21 The pun is anachronistic; Thompson cites 1885 as the first instance of a mechanical time-stamping system being used in industry, although non-mechanical, human timekeepers were employed well before this date. In Thompson, *Customs in Common*, p. 186.

22 Moretti, *Graphs, Maps, Trees*, p. 42.

by each pair of eyes that are 'fired' much like Walter Benjamin's armed revolutionaries fire at the Clock, simultaneously and independently.[23] But, in the churchyard, the speaker then reflects 'That time shall come when they shall lye' (l. 28; MS), unflinchingly looking towards a time when these young children shall be 'As lonely & as still as they' (l. 29; MS). Despite the nod towards death, the time to lament lapses, as this picture is one of renewal: 'other boys' quickly step in to repeat the scene. This speaker keeps to the present, the active verb on each line working like an unstoppable refrain ('calling', 'jelting', 'viewing', 'leaping'), governing an uncanny sense of almost timeless continuity, as the urgent reconstruction of the present takes place in the poem.

Later in 'May', the Church Clock announces itself again, as it overlooks one schoolboy's truancy, here:

He often ventures thro the day

At truant now & then to play

Rambling about the field & plain

Seeking larks nests in the grain

& picking flowers & boughs of may

To hurd awhile & throw away

Lurking neath bushes from the sight

Of tell tale eyes till schools noon night

Listning each hour for church clocks hum

To know the hour to wander home

That parents may not think him long

Nor dream of his rude doing wrong (lines 89–100; MS; my emphasis)

I am fascinated by the rhyme between 'hum' and 'home'.[24] A 'hum' for Clare is often implicitly vocal, whether that of a human- or non-human

---

23 Benjamin, 'On the Concept of History', p. 395.
24 Clare's patterning of rhyme both in this poem 'May', and other of his poems both in the sequence, and elsewhere, is fascinating yet perplexing to trace. There is not a decisive picture as to what the given pronuncation is—the question of pronunciation and rhyme in relation to both poetic tradition and dialect continue

animal. As the speaker describes in 'April', 'all Nature finds a voice, / And hums a waking song.' (lines 115–16; MS). And this personified—almost judgemental—character of the Church Clock, watching over and 'humming' disapprovingly at the boy stealing school time, tells of the uneasy tension experienced by the villagers under time's watch throughout 'May'. This diegetic sound of the clock interrupts the speaker's control over the metre and rhyme scheme with a warning to the schoolboy. The (potential) half rhyme with 'home' is striking, as it draws us back into the sound of the previous line, but this time through the boy's ear. Though the clock may 'hum' disapprovingly, to the ear of the labourers the sounds of Church bells chime with 'home'.

I want to labour on this point of subjective hearing, in how the sounds of the Church Clock are reproduced in the poem, and how they translate as heard by the figures in the text. I think it is important to underline this, both because this is part of a larger question I am asking of the production and reception of sounds in Clare's poetics, but also because I think it lends itself to a critique of the clock as such. What I am trying to emphasise is that the sounds that the church bells produce in this poem do regulate and oppress, but that through the act of listening performed in the poem, the sounds are redeemed as a comforting call for home, echoing the month's own 'welcome call' (l. 425; MS). I stress the particulars of the time, place, and lyric conditions under which the bells are sounded, because they operate entirely differently in Clare's later poem 'The Chiming Bells'.[25] Without diverting too much from my reading of 'May', this is nevertheless a good point of comparison to read the significance of context in how the bells sound, as the speaker moves through describing 'How peaceful sound the chiming bells' (l. 1), as 'Calmly they reach the Shepherd's ear' (l. 5), but crucially through this poem, the sounds always 'chime' with the day, 'sabbath chimes'

---

to circle above readings of Clare—and yet, whatever we take the rhyme to be (full, slant, non-existent) the point remains that here, there is something in the sound, or its asymmetry, that returns us to the previous line, making a jump back in time, forcing us into a process of engagement and adjustment. Nothing is fixed in the poem; everything shifts both towards the past, and into the future, of the poem and yet remains stubbornly in the simple present.

25 John Clare, 'The Chiming Bells', in *The Later Poems of John Clare, 1837–1864*, ed. by Eric Robinson and David Powell (Oxford: Clarendon Press, 1984), II, p. 1036. The poem is taken from the Knight Manuscripts, dated c. 1842–1864, for which there is scant detail.

and 'Sabbath bells' for a Sunday in Summer.[26] Similarly, in the sonnet 'Glinton Spire' we find little tension between the dominating spire and the speaker; no 'jealous eyes' are cast upon it here.[27] Instead there is a pure reverence, but nevertheless we still find the dominion of the 'taper spire':

> [...] making common things
>
> Around it glow with beautys not their own
>
> Thus all around—the earth superior springs
>
> Those strangling trees though lonely seem not lone
>
> But in thy presence wear superior power (lines 6–10)

Clare's verses often find themselves acting out a negotiation or tracing a resistance; as poet of the peripheries (read: hedgerows), his speaker cannot sit comfortably in any one spot. Even in a scene of comfort and security, there must be a self-conscious reconsideration of the scene; here in 'Glinton Spire', 'almost' and 'seem' draw out the anxiety often found in Clare's verse on the limitations of the imagination.

But back in 'May', Clare's grammar and syntax resist the regulation and onward thrust, albeit towards 'home', that come with the sound of time passing. Anne-Lise François initiates a turn to the poem in our present moment of ecological crisis, to 'consider anew the problem of lyric time', an invitation I want to take up here.[28] François describes lyric as a 'technique of presencing, intensification, and condensation [...] of linguistic utterance into a single verbal image on the page'.[29] The lyric time is rendered visible by grammatical measures rather than narrative sequence. I depart from François's productive reading of time and the

---

26 See further:
    How beautiful from yon old tower
    The chimes their story tells
    Theres little in the summer hour
    So sweet as chiming bells (lines 21–24)
27 John Clare, 'Glinton Spire', in *Poems of the Middle Period, 1822–1837*, ed. by Eric Robinson, David Powell and P.M.S Dawson (Oxford: Clarendon Press, 1998), IV, pp. 252–53.
28 Anne-Lise François, 'Ungiving Time', in *Anthropocene Reading*, ed. by Tobias Menely and Jesse Oak Taylor (Pennsylvania, PA: Pennsylvania State University Press, 2017), pp. 239–58 (p. 243).
29 Ibid., p. 248.

lyric in the shadow of the Anthropocene and deep time, because (as is habit with Clare) I want to take a microscopic look at how time operates in the sequence, and here stress the mechanical form of time that imposes itself upon the scene, through the ringing out of the Church bells in 'May'. These grammatical and syntactical measures destabilise time, working against the clock.[30] Clare's engagement with time is inextricable from his engagement with labour. I read the characters in 'May', given by names that are dictated by their labour, in light of Marx's note on the clock, in which 'Time is everything, man is nothing; he is, at the most, time's carcase':

> Does not this reduction of days of compound labour to days of simple labour suppose that simple labour is itself taken as a measure of value? If the mere quantity of labour functions as a measure of value regardless of quality, it presupposes that simple labour has become the pivot of industry. It presupposes that labour has been equalised by the subordination of man to the machine or by the extreme division of labour; that men are effaced by their labour; that the pendulum of the clock has become as accurate a measure of the relative activity of two workers as it is of the speed of two locomotives. Therefore, we should not say that one man's hour is worth another man's hour, but rather that one man during an hour is worth just as much as another man during an hour. Time is everything, man is nothing; he is, at the most, time's carcase. Quality no longer matters. Quantity alone decides every-thing; hour for hour, day for day[.][31]

Capturing this shift towards measuring value through 'simple labour', Marx situates man in time. By emphasising duration (see: 'during'), the relationship between man and time has been inverted; what once might have been man's possession, becomes that which possesses him. The hour remains the same, only the man changes. Clare's 'every minute every hour' chimes with Marx's similar utterance: 'hour for hour, day for day'. Clare's resistance to succession, through the paratactical joinder of the ampersand and the repetitive use of the simple present creating a lively simultaneity, work to protect his figures from being dragged along

---

30 I hope it is understood, and goes without saying, that this chapter is strongly influenced by E. P. Thompson's robust history of the clock, and time, in relation to labour and class-consciousness in the period, 'Time, Work-Discipline, and Industrial Capitalism' published in *Past & Present*, 38.1 (December 1967), 56–97, and reprinted in *Customs in Common* in 1991.
31 Marx, *The Poverty of Philosophy*, p. 127. My emphasis.

the current of time; instead they remain in the perpetual present tense of the lyric.

'&', 'Now', and 'No More'

Clare's paratactical stitching together of lines traces through 'May' an a-temporal—almost universal—present through the deictic 'now'. The refusal of coordination between lines stands as a resistance to narrative and temporal succession: that time of the clock, industry, and progress. Jonathan Culler describes this a-temporal, maybe universal, present as the 'lyric present', and notes how the ballad 'orchestrates' between the past and present tense, using the latter to 'enrich their ritualistic dimension, pulling themselves out of a narrated past and into a present of enunciation'.[32] But crucially this is not what happens in 'May'. Instead, Clare keeps us perpetually trapped in the present, denying access to the narrated past of custom and tradition; instead the May pole is reduced to a mere 'stump of old time' (l. 420, MS).[33] Moreover, Clare's present is complicated by its encoded absence. The temporal paradox of a 'no more' serves to clear a space for the trace of a past in the present.[34] This is a trace of both a former presence, and of the poetic past, because to me 'no more' has to be from Milton's 'Lycidas': 'Weep no more, woful Shepherds, weep no more [...] Now, *Lycidas* the Shepherds weep no more;'.[35] That said, it might also be drawn from Gray's 'Elegy' in which 'no more' marks the departure of figures from the scene, through a

---

32 Jonathan Culler, *Theory of the Lyric* (Cambridge, MT: Harvard University Press, 2015), pp. 283–84.

33 Echoes of this in the invocation of an inaccessible 'past' appear in the long poem 'Childhood' (c. 1830), where 'The treasures most preferred/Have left the honours of their place/Locked in that silent word' (lines 22–24). In 'Childhood', in *Poems of the Middle Period*, ed. by Eric Robinson, David Powell and P.M.S Dawson (Oxford: Clarendon Press, 1998), III, pp. 229–52.

34 See also in the repetition of 'no more' in 'May'.

35 We know Clare owned at least one copy of *Paradise Lost* by the 1820s (there are two listed in the record of his library collection at Northamptonshire), and given his reverence for Milton, it might not be unreasonable to hear the closing lines of 'Lycidas' in the invocation 'no more' ('May', l. 435, MS). John Milton, 'Lycidas', in *Complete Shorter Poems*, ed. by Stella P. Revard (Chichester: Wiley-Blackwell, 2009), pp. 74–80.

lapse in time.[36] Whereas Milton's speaker cries for his fellow shepherds to recover from their loss, Clare's 'no more' is closer to Gray's, no longer marking the departed figures in the scene. Moreover, through Clare's 'no more' ring the 'syllabled sounds' of mourn(ing), intensifying this inversion of a redemptive 'no more' (Milton's) to one that marks out a space for absence by negating the entire May Day that it anticipates.[37]

The active role of the ampersand in shaping (and suspending) time in the poem informs my reading of a quiet resistance against successive, or progressive, clock-time. The time of the poem is 'filled up', as Clare's editor John Taylor suggested he do, but not only through the ampersand. I want to draw you to another discrepancy between the manuscript and the published version of the poem to labour this reading of time, and to the resistance of the accumulative work heroic couplets do to perform a sense of progress in the poem. Going back to 'January', we find:

The schoolboy still in dithering joys

Pastime in leisure hours employs (lines 101–02; MS)

The schoolboy still, with dithering joys,

In pastime leisure hours employs (lines 29–30)

Similar to 'In school times leisure ever short' in 'May' (l. 14; MS), the verb 'employs' demarcates leisure time apart from, but still implicit in, the working day. This tension between time and labour, strained by the new means to measure one against the other in the shift from what I like to figure as 'loom-time' demarcated by the rotation and rhythm of the loom, or the worker's ownership of their own time, towards this 'working day' in which the time of work is defined by the employer, is invoked just before this moment, when the speaker recounts a 'soodling boy'

---

36   John Goodridge weaves together the important influence of both John Milton and Thomas Gray on Clare's own 'pastoral [elegies]', making particular note of a 'Miltonic scales of time and space' in the opening movement of one middle-period enclosure elegy, 'The Mores', in *John Clare and Community*, p. 125.

37   John Clare, *Natural History Prose Writings*, ed. by Margaret Grainger (Oxford: Clarendon Press, 1983), p. 312.

who 'stealing time he often stands' (l. 99; MS).[38] But here, comparing the schoolboy 'still in' of the manuscript to the later 'still, with' 'dithering joys', it is the repetition of 'in' from the first part of the couplet to the second that performs this stasis in time. Nothing happens. But in the printed edition, this stand against onward motion is edited out, and it is the accumulation of the dithering joys that moves the schoolboy to 'employ' these leisure hours in passing the time. Picturing the boy in the manuscript we see him embedded in concentric circles: the first circle being joy, and the second being time. Although the edited version does sustain the sense of being 'in' time, the picture is one of linear, onward movement through which the boy first acquires this 'joy' before being 'in pastime'. I wonder, too, if the sense of simultaneity makes itself all the more present here by its absence. Placing these two quotations side by side produces one more striking difference: what does happen in the 70-odd lines that have been taken out of the manuscript? For the sake of onward movement, nothing. But for the sake of Clare's teeming network of human and non-human beings, a lot. It just happens all at once, and supposedly we lose nothing by contracting the sequence of events.

Contracting Time: An Afterword on John Taylor's Interventions

Eric Robinson, in his introduction to the Oxford edition of *The Shepherd's Calendar* (1964 and 2014) cites the 1 August 1823 letter from John Taylor to the poet as this point from which we can chart the development of the poem as it came to be in its 1827 iteration. But we might also look back to the earlier communications between Clare, Taylor, and Taylor's publishing partner James Hessey, for its origins.[39] In the 21 January 1820

---

38   Eileen M. Willis, 'The Invention of purgatory: Contributions to Abstract Time in Capitalism', *Journal of Sociology of the Australian Sociological Association*, 44.3 (2008), 249–64, https://doi.org/10.1177/1440783308092883 She draws on both Marx and the Marxist historian Moishe Postone's work on time and labour, with reference also to Postone on 'abstract time' in *Time, Labor and Social Domination: A Reinterpretation of Marx's Critical Theory* (Cambridge: Cambridge University Press, 1993; 2003), https://doi.org/10.1017/CBO9780511570926

39   Tim Chilcott (to whom I give special thanks in the preparation of this chapter), in his introduction to the 2006 edition that places in parallel the manuscript and published version, gestures to the earlier invocation of a poem of this sort. See 'Introduction', in *The Shepherd's Calendar*, ed. by Tim Chilcott (Manchester: Carcanet,

letter from Taylor to Clare we see the productive role that the editor plays in shaping this poem cycle. Here we see his resistance to intervening prematurely, along with the sharp eye he casts across much of Clare's work, and the care he takes to tease out the poet's more substantial (perhaps marketable) ideas. Taylor encourages Clare to expand on a manuscript fragment, the 'Week in a Village', offering:

> [...] *that you should divide the Week's Employment* into the 7 Days, selecting such for each as might more particularly apply to that Day, which is the Case with some of the Occupations;—that the remaining time which might be pursued on any Day should be allotted *so as to fill up the Time*;—that the Sports, & Amusements should in like manner be apportioned out into the 7 Days;—and that one little appropriate Story should be involved in each Day's Description.—*A different Metre might sometimes be introduced*; for instance in the Tale, if it were supposed to be related by one of the Characters of the Piece;[40] or, otherwise the various Days might be marked by a varied Measure: but this would be as you thought best & found most agreeable to you.—I mentioned it *then*, & now again, because I thought it would allow of that part of your 'Peasant Boy', which you had written, being incorporated with the rest of the Plan, under the Head of 'Sunday'; as well as because I think that a varied Structure of Verse in a long Poem suits your Genius best.[41]

Even before considering the specific market conditions for publishing in the years leading up to the 1827 publication of *The Shepherd's Calendar*, we can infer the significance of any work's title to its publisher. Here it is shown by how productive the title of a manuscript fragment, this 'Week in a Village', proved to Taylor's editorial guidance. The overall form of *The Shepherd's Calendar* is evidently on Taylor's advice, which in turn informs a reading of the poem in dialogue with its georgic and

---

2006). In his introduction Robinson, too, explores the implication of Clare's earlier works in building towards *The Shepherd's Calendar*, emphasising the impression left on Clare of Gay's *Shepherd's Week* (1714), along with Clare's (sometimes fulfilled) ambition to contribute to one of the many popular almanacs of the day.

40 Given that this is the follow-up letter to Clare having received Chaucer's *Tales* alongside his personal copies of *Poems Descriptive*, is it out of the question to consider the form of the *Tales* as another source for Clare's eventual long poem, perhaps as an invitation to read the role of the lyric subject in each month.

41 John Clare, *The Letters of John Clare*, ed. by Mark Storey (Oxford: Clarendon Press, 1985), pp. 27–28.

bucolic predecessors.[42] Clare's debt to the georgic is noted by critics, but Taylor's invocation of Edmund Spenser is clear in the use of an overall temporally defined structure, portioned into poems of 'varied Measure', even before the 1 August letter urging him to adopt the same title.[43]

But the scene of the truanting schoolboy in 'May' does not appear in the published version. Of course, given the difficulty in defining who is responsible for each editorial decision made for Clare's manuscript, I cannot say for sure this is Taylor, as much as I might be inclined. But as the speaker simultaneously invokes, and resists the fulfilment of, a lament for the post-enclosure loss of the customs bound up in the May-day holiday, Clare's post-enclosure persona can be heard loud and clear in the fuller manuscript version. Indeed, it echoes the protesting voice of the 'enclosure elegies'. John Goodridge, on one such poem 'The Mores', reads Clare as 'clashing the past discordantly against the present, as it were, in order to emphasise the change that has occurred'.[44] And yet, it is difficult to give such a reading of *The Shepherd's Calendar* as it appears in its 'final' form. For it is during this period that interventions are made into the content of his verse, and the language through which it is shaped; such changes have been traced by, among others, Goodridge.[45] With *The Shepherd's Calendar*, Taylor abandons the glossary that accompanied his two earlier volumes, *Poems Descriptive of Rural Life and Scenery* (1820) and *The Village Minstrel* (1821), and instead approaches Clare's manuscripts with an eye to eliminate the need for a gloss from within. Tim Chilcott in

---

42   Spenser's *Calendar* (1579); but perhaps also Virgil, or Theocritus. In the aforementioned epigraph from Spenser, and its allusion to Mount Parnassus, Mina Gorji infers an 'ambitious genealogy, which Clare recognised', in *John Clare and the Place of Poetry* (Liverpool: Liverpool University Press, 2008), p. 77.
43   The *Catalogue of the John Clare Collection in the Northampton Public Library* (County Borough of Northampton: Public Libraries Museums and Art Galleries Committee, 1964) shows that Clare owned an 1819 edition of Spenser's *The Faery Queene*, but I am inclined to think this is taken from the 1819 edition *The Poetical Works of Edmund Spenser*, published by Suttaby et. al., in which case he might also have had access to *The Shepheardes Calender* (1579).
44   'Enclosure elegies' stems from Johanne Clare in *John Clare and the Bounds of Circumstance* (Kingston: McGill-Queen's University Press, 1987). Goodridge is but one scholar who continues to use this collective name for Clare's major poems on enclosure. Goodridge, *John Clare and Community*, p. 127.
45   We find in the communication from Taylor of the interventions made by Lord Milton, a patron of Clare, that in the editing of 'Helpstone' there was an attempt to dilute or even elide the political commentary. See Goodridge, *John Clare and Community*, pp. 105–33.

his introduction to the Carcanet edition outlines the editorial approach to Clare's dialect, and does complicate the simple argument that it was Taylor who simply edited it out. But then, it is evident in reading Clare and Taylor's correspondence that Clare's frustration lead, in some degree, to him relinquishing his control over the language and grammar of his verse.[46] The crucial May Day scene quite literally is 'no more' in the 1827 published version. As I mentioned, the final 'May' contains half the number of lines of Clare's original, and is devoid of this resistance of or reaction to the dominating sight and sound of the Church Clock (save for those schoolboys jumping over gravestones at the beginning). The tensions between Clare and his editors, as well as his patrons, have been illuminated elsewhere, so to consider Clare's response to how this work was contracted, elided and transformed in print, I offer this from *Child Harold*, a poem from the later period, as a means to read the silencing of the bells in the published 'May':

No single hour can stand for nought

No moment hand can move

But calendars an aching thought

Of my first lonely love

[...]

I hide it in the silent shades

Till silence finds a tongue

I make its grave where time invades

Till time becomes a song[.][47]

---

46 In a letter from 1822 in which he likens 'grammer' (sic) to 'Tyranny' Clare also defers to Taylor to 'do your best or let it pass', in *The Letters of John Clare*, p. 231.

47 John Clare, *Child Harold*, *The Later Poems of John Clare, 1837–1864*, ed. by Eric Robinson and David Powell (Oxford: Clarendon Press, 1984), I, p. 58 (lines 493–96, 501–04). On the editing of *The Shepherd's Calendar*, see Eric Robinson and Geoffrey Summerfield, 'John Taylor's Editing of Clare's *The Shepherd's Calendar*', *Review of English Studies*, 14.56 (1963), 359–69. On Clare and his editors and patrons, a non-exhaustive list would include: James C. McKusick, 'John Clare and the Tyranny of Grammar', *Studies in Romanticism*, 33.2 (1994), 255–77; Paul Chirico, *John Clare and the Imagination of the Reader* (Basingstoke: Palgrave Macmillan, 2007) and his chapter in *Authorship, Commerce and the Public* (Basingstoke: Palgrave Macmillan,

Works Cited

Adams, Theresa, 'Representing Rural Leisure: John Clare and the Politics of Popular Culture,' *Studies in Romanticism* 47.3 (Fall, 2008), 371–92.

Bate, Jonathan, *John Clare: A Biography* (London: Picador, 2003).

Benjamin, Walter, 'On the Concept of History', in *Walter Benjamin: Selected Writings*, ed. by Howard Eiland and Michael W. Jennings, trans. by Harry Zohn (Cambridge, MA: Belknap Press, 2006), IV, pp. 389–400.

Bergson, Henri, *Time and Free Will*, trans. by F.L. Pogson (Mineola, NY: Dover Publications, 2001).

Chirico, Paul, 'Authority and Community: John Clare and John Taylor', in *Authorship, Commerce and the Public*, ed. by E. J. Clery, Caroline Franklin and Peter Garside (Basingstoke: Palgrave Macmillan, 2002), pp. 84–99.

——, *John Clare and the Imagination of the Reader* (Basingstoke: Palgrave Macmillan, 2007).

Clare, John, *The Shepherd's Calendar*, ed. by Tim Chilcott (Manchester: Carcanet, 2006).

——, *By Himself*, ed. by Eric Robinson and David Powell (Manchester: Carcanet, 2013).

Clare, Johanne, *John Clare and the Bounds of Circumstance* (Kingston: McGill-Queen's University Press, 1987).

Culler, Jonathan, *Theory of the Lyric* (Cambridge, MA: Harvard University Press, 2015), https://doi.org/10.4159/9780674425781

François, Anne-Lise, 'Ungiving Time', in *Anthropocene Reading*, ed. by Tobias Menely and Jesse Oak Taylor (Pennsylvania, PA: Pennsylvania State University Press, 2017), pp. 239–58.

Goodridge, John, *John Clare and Community* (Cambridge: Cambridge University Press, 2013).

Gorji, Mina, *John Clare and the Place of Poetry* (Liverpool: Liverpool University Press, 2008).

Grainger, Margaret, ed., *Natural History Prose Writings* (Oxford: Clarendon Press, 1983).

Herbert, Ian, 'Poetic justice: villagers defeat phone mast threat by quoting their local bard', *Independent*, 14 December 2004, https://www.independent.co.uk/news/uk/this-britain/poetic-justice-villagers-defeat-phone-mast-threat-by-quoting-their-local-bard-688497.html

---

2002), pp. 84–99; and, Jonathan Bate, *John Clare: A Biography* (London: Picador, 2003), pp. 201–08.

Homer, *The Odyssey*, trans. by Emily Wilson (New York: W. W. Norton & Company, 2017).

Kövesi, Simon, 'John Clare & ... & ... & ... Deleuze and Guattari's Rhizome', in *Ecology and the Literature of the British Left*, ed. by John Rignall (Farnham: Ashgate, 2012), pp. 75–88, https://doi.org/10.4324/9781315578675

Marx, Karl, *The Poverty of Philosophy* in *Marx & Engels Collected Works*, trans. by Frida Knight (Electronic Book: Lawrence & Wishart, 2010), VI, pp. 105–212.

McKusick, James C., 'John Clare and the Tyranny of Grammar', *Studies in Romanticism* 33.2 (Summer, 1994), 255–77.

Milton, John, 'Lycidas', in *Complete Shorter Poems*, ed. by Stella P. Revard (Chichester: Wiley-Blackwell, 2009), pp. 74–80.

Moretti, Franco, *Graphs, Maps, Trees* (London: Verso, 2007).

Postone, Moishe, *Time, Labor and Social Domination: A Reinterpretation of Marx's Critical Theory* (Cambridge: Cambridge University Press, 1993; 2003).

Powell, David, *Catalogue of the John Clare Collection in the Northampton Public Library* (County Borough of Northampton: Public Libraries Museums and Art Galleries Committee, 1964).

Robinson, Eric and Geoffrey Summerfield, 'John Taylor's Editing of Clare's *The Shepherd's Calendar*', *Review of English Studies* 14.56 (1963), 359–69.

Robinson, Eric, Geoffrey Summerfield and David Powell eds, *The Shepherd's Calendar* (Oxford: Oxford University Press, 1964; 2014).

Robinson, Eric and David Powell eds, *Child Harold* in *The Later Poems of John Clare, 1837–1864* (Oxford: Clarendon Press, 1984), I, p. 58.

——, 'The Chiming Bells', in *The Later Poems of John Clare, 1837–1864* (Oxford: Clarendon Press, 1984), II, p. 1036.

Robinson, Eric, David Powell and P.M.S Dawson eds, 'Childhood', in *Poems of the Middle Period* (Oxford: Clarendon Press, 1998), III, pp. 229–52.

——, 'Glinton Spire', in *Poems of the Middle Period, 1822–1837* (Oxford: Clarendon Press, 1998), IV, pp. 252–53.

Sebald, Winfried Georg, *Austerlitz*, trans. by Anthea Bell (London: Penguin, 2011).

Shaw, Matthew, *Time and the French Revolution* (Woodbridge: The Boydell Press, 2011).

Shelley, Mary, *History of a Six Week's Tour* (London: T. Hookham, Jun., 1817).

Storey, Mark, ed., *The Letters of John Clare* (Oxford: Oxford University Press, 1985).

Thompson, Edward Palmer, *Customs in Common* (London: Merlin Press, 1991).

Willis, Eileen M., 'The Invention of Purgatory: Contributions to Abstract Time in Capitalism', *Journal of Sociology of the Australian Sociological Association* 44.3 (2008), 249–64, https://doi.org/10.1177%2F1440783308092883

Vulliamy, B. L., *Some Considerations on the Subject of Public Clocks Particularly Church Clocks: with Hints for their Improvement* (London: McMillan, Bow Street, 1828).

7. Book-Time in Charles Lamb and Washington Irving

Matthew Redmond

This essay considers how two Romantic writers, Charles Lamb and Washington Irving, explore the perception-altering powers of absorbed reading. Both men, with their famously antiquarian tastes, have long been portrayed as enemies of change, retreating from the present moment into the comforting familiarity of old times. Upon our closer examination of their writing, however, that received view breaks down—for Lamb and Irving often use texts within texts to recuperate a fuller range of temporal experience than what the advent of industrialisation in a post-revolutionary world seems to allow. In Lamb's Last Essays of Elia *and Irving's* Sketch-Book of Geoffrey Crayon, Gent., *the image of an ideal reading practice—with all its capacity for surprise, improvisation, and leisurely enjoyment—enables us to conceptualise alternative experiences of modern life. Reading well, in other words, becomes a gateway into book-time, a reprieve (however temporary) from the inhumane workings of clock-time.*

William Hazlitt concludes *The Spirit of the Age* (1825) with a chapter about two essayists who, in his estimation, defy that spirit: Charles Lamb and Washington Irving (or 'Irvine', as he calls the latter). Though Hazlitt sets himself the task of describing 'the beauties and defects of each in treating of somewhat similar subjects', it soon becomes clear that beauties and defects are unevenly portioned out between the two men.[1] He spends the central part of this chapter praising Lamb, who possesses 'the very soul of an antiquarian, as this implies a reflecting humanity;

---

1 William Hazlitt, *The Spirit of the Age* (Oxford: Woodstock Books, 1989), p. 409.

the film of the past hovers for ever before him'.[2] Irving's main attributes, meanwhile, are essentially a caricature of these: his aesthetic represents not antiquarianism, but a mere anachronism that deposits thick scales over his eyes instead of Lamb's hovering film. Seen in this light, the original Knickerbocker becomes a rambling, Quixotic American tourist in England, recording only what his favourite outdated British sources, like *The Spectator*, have taught him to see.

> Instead of tracing the changes that have taken place in society since Addison or Fielding wrote, he transcribes their account in a different hand-writing, and thus keeps us stationary, at least in our most attractive and praise-worthy qualities of simplicity, honesty, hospitality, modesty, and good-nature. This is a very flattering mode of turning fiction into history, or history into fiction; and we should scarcely know ourselves again in the softened and altered likeness, but that it bears the date of 1820, and issues from the press in Albemarle-street.[3]

While Hazlitt's value judgments may startle us with their sharpness, he sets the table for much critical reception of these writers over the last two hundred years. Crucially, he contends that while the differences between Lamb and Irving are significant, so are the similarities. Hazlitt depicts both men retiring to the comforts of history, whether distant or comparatively recent. If Lamb's relationship with the past is more methodical and wider-ranging than Irving's, both are nonetheless living throwbacks, antiques set apart from the crowd by their allegiance to past and passing things. In keeping with this observation, what *The Spirit of the Age* will not attribute to either Lamb or Irving is any coherent sense of the present or the future. Both men, by indulging their old-fashioned tastes, turn away from any sustained contemplation of the changing world around them. Hazlitt brings this point into tight focus with a few pithy phrases directed at Lamb's work: 'He evades the present, he mocks the future. His affections revert to, and settle on the past'.[4] The American 'Irvine' does about the same thing, mostly because he cannot do more.

It is with this patronizing assessment of Irving and Lamb that my analysis begins. Situating itself in a post-revolutionary, rapidly industrializing world full of Thompsonian clock-time, this chapter

---

2   Ibid., p. 411.
3   Ibid., pp. 421–22.
4   Ibid., p. 414.

explores some ways that both men, as figures in their own writing, self-consciously take up valuable time and space with their reading habits, as well as the spatio-temporal stakes of their doing so. In their different national contexts, both writers, repelled by the relentless pace of modern temporalities, strive to imagine environments where time respects the manifold quirks and variations of lived experience, whether at the scale of the individual or that of the modern state. To achieve this labour of imagination, both Lamb's *Last Essays of Elia* and Irving's 'English Writers on America', from *The Sketch-Book of Geoffrey Crayon, Gent.*, build their images of being-in-time around the highly sensitive chronotope of the book. In other words, taking inspiration from the concept of 'heterochrony', or the heterogeneity of modern time, propounded by Laura Bear and Georgiana Born, I submit that Irving and Lamb boldly use fictionalised acts of reading to expand the range— or at least to forestall the narrowing—of available temporal experience in the historical moment of their work.[5]

Charles Lamb: The Volume of the Mind

It would be difficult to overstate how profoundly books and reading shape Lamb's imagination. In a 1796 letter to Coleridge, he frames his recent experience in characteristic fashion: 'My life has been somewhat diversified of late. The six weeks that finished last year and began this, your very humble servant spent very agreeably in a mad house at Hoxton. I am got somewhat rational now, and don't bite any one. But mad I was; and many a vagary my imagination played with me, enough to make a volume if all told'.[6] Notice how Lamb ratifies his return to sanity by bringing out a fictional volume. While at a glance this gesture seems to drive home how numerous the vagaries that plagued Lamb have been, in fact it does the opposite. An ingenious and understated shift occurs in the latter half of the final line: suddenly, what has heretofore sounded

---

[5] Laura Bear, 'Doubt, Conflict, Mediation: The Anthropology of Modern Time', *Journal of the Royal Anthropological Institute*, 30.S1 (2014), 3–30, https://doi.org/10.1111/1467-9655.12091; Georgiana Born, 'Making Time: Temporality, History, and the Cultural Object', *New Literary History*, 46.3 (2015), 361–86, https://doi.org/10.1353/nlh.2015.0025

[6] Charles Lamb, *The Letters of Charles Lamb*, ed. by Alfred Ainger, 2 vols. (London: Macmillan and Co., 1888), I, p. 2.

like a horrible excess of traumatic incidents—and surely one is too many for most of us—becomes almost too few: 'enough to make a volume *if all told*' (my emphasis). Just as Lamb's breezy understatement ('I am got somewhat rational now, and don't bite anyone. But...') threatens to collapse under the strain of remembered hardship, he changes tack and presses that memory firmly between the pages of an imagined volume, in the process making those dark days appear rather mercifully brief. For Lamb, the ability to arrange otherwise unintelligible happenings in book form, even where that book is only imagined, is the truest sign of rationality itself, whereas madness finds all things alike in their illegibility. To such an imagination, tempered by the constant threat of insanity, there can be nothing frivolous about learning to read well.

Granted, Lamb's most famous essays, written under the guise of 'Elia', are not this intense—nor, despite their conspiratorial air, this candid. Whether or not we too recognise him as 'the most lovable figure in English literature', lightness and gentle eccentricity remain the hallmarks of his style.[7] These qualities are perhaps nowhere more quotably expressed than in the opening lines of 'Detached Thoughts on Books and Reading', where Elia explains what role literacy has played in his daily life and worldview.

> At the hazard of losing some credit on this head, I must confess that I dedicate no inconsiderable portion of my time to other people's thoughts. I dream away my life in others' speculations. I love to lose myself in other men's minds. When I am not walking, I am reading; I cannot sit and think. Books think for me.[8]

This benign confession would appear to encourage Hazlitt's view of Charles Lamb as the ultimate retiring antiquarian, as Lamb himself knows full well: the 'hazard' that he accepts at the outset is essentially that of drawing a reaction like what we have seen in *The Spirit of the Age*. Like the perfect antiquarian, Lamb accepts with magnanimity the risk of losing 'credit' in the estimation of nameless, absent critics—that is, to restate Hazlitt's thesis, 'he evades the present, he mocks the future'. Somewhat surprisingly, the upside of losing that credit proves to be

---

[7] Edward Verrall Lucas, *The Life of Charles Lamb* (London: G. P. Putnam's Sons, 1905), p. xvii.

[8] Charles Lamb, *The Last Essays of Elia* (London: Edward Moxon, 1833), p. 44.

more loss: of life, self, and 'no inconsiderable portion' of time. In fact, the lyrical elegance of these lines suggests that Elia, before our very eyes, might even be losing himself in reminiscences about losing himself. In its first few paragraphs, then, 'Detached Thoughts' promises to discover the antiquarian in his most familiar pose, as the ultimate lovable loser.

But does it? The centrifugal force of this opening belies how much later parts of the essay will treat reading as centripetal: a man reading draws people and things toward himself. Indeed, while the ideas that comprise Lamb's text are certainly 'detached' from one another—self-contained little vignettes and reflections that Elia could rearrange without any loss of meaning—each of them represents reading as an exercise that forges *attachment* between things. On the topic of bookbinding, Elia declares that '[t]o be strong-backed and neat-bound is the desideratum of a volume'—but this is only the most literal and simplistic form of binding that emerges from his bookish pursuits.[9] More interesting for my purpose is the binding together of place and time that, for Elia, marks every reading experience.

> I do not remember a more whimsical surprise than having been once detected—by a familiar damsel—reclined at my ease upon the grass, on Primrose Hill (her Cythera), reading—*Pamela*. There was nothing in the book to make a man seriously ashamed at the exposure; but as she seated herself down by me, and seemed determined to read in company, I could have wished it had been—any other book. We read on very sociably for a few pages; and, not finding the author much to her taste, she got up, and—went away. Gentle casuist, I leave it to thee to conjecture, whether the blush (for there was one between us) was the property of the nymph or the swain in this dilemma. From me you shall never get the secret.[10]

The nameless woman's arrival, her proximity to the reclining reader, the grass beneath them, the blush they share, even the shortness of their time together—these details of place and time are what define Elia's 'whimsical' memory. The exercise of reading *Pamela* becomes inextricably linked in Lamb's essay, and in Elia's memory, to a delightful encounter one afternoon on Primrose Hill. As this passage makes clear, even through its rosy tint, getting lost in a good book does not mean losing all sense of one's position in time and space; on the contrary, in

---

9   Ibid., p. 46.
10 Ibid., pp. 52–53.

Lamb's view right reading heightens one's consciousness of physical and temporal setting. His attachment to world and time, far from slipping away, intensifies through exposure to a good book.

In Chapter 1 of his 'Forms of Time and the Chronotope of the Novel', Bakhtin discusses the power of spatial devices in literature to produce chance encounters among characters. The road, Bakhtin's favourite novelistic chronotope of encounter, is a site where 'the unity of time and space markers is exhibited with exceptional precision and clarity', often through the motif of meeting.[11] If we read the Primrose Hill episode through his formalist lens, what spatial marker structures the chance meeting between Elia and his enigmatic fellow reader? The answer is not Primrose Hill itself, but *Pamela*; after all, reading 'sociably' would not be possible without something to read. Whereas the essay's prefatory confession speaks of time 'lost' in reading, this case in point shows us something more elegant: time translated into space. It is worth remarking that Elia measures the duration of this pleasant surprise in 'pages', not minutes. In this detail we observe Lamb's novel keeping time more profoundly than any clock: it fuses itself to the span of several minutes and makes them plastic, like the pages; it enables time to possess meaning, to achieve human plenitude through the infusion of vivid thoughts and sensations. This is not empty and homogeneous clock-time, but vividly human book-time.

Another example shows book-time taking effect in a much less idyllic setting than Primrose Hill, and one more central to Lamb's cosmopolitan aesthetic: the busy companies of London's streets.

> There is a class of street-readers, whom I can never contemplate without affection—the poor gentry, who, not having wherewithal to buy or hire a book, filch a little learning at the open stalls—the owner, with his hard eye, casting envious looks at them all the while, and thinking when they will have done. Venturing tenderly, page after page, expecting every moment when he shall interpose his interdict, and yet unable to deny themselves the gratification, they 'snatch a fearful joy.' Martin B----, in this way, by daily fragments, got through two volumes of Clarissa, when the stall-keeper damped his laudable ambition, by asking him (it was in his younger days) whether he meant to purchase the work.[12]

---

11 Mikhail Bakhtin, 'Forms of Time and the Chronotope of the Novel', in *The Dialogic Imagination: Four Essays* (Austin: University of Texas Press, 1981), p. 98.
12 Lamb, *Last Essays*, pp. 53–54.

Whereas Bakhtin likely would have labelled the novel a 'minor chronotope' embedded within the much larger and more pervasive chronotope of the street, Lamb compels all our attention toward street-*reading*. Elia fuses the passing of 'page after page' to that of 'every moment' before the stall, turning this volume of *Clarissa* into a clock that not only registers, but also deeply inflects, the movement of time in this scene. Both observers, Elia and the bookstall owner, measure time by the turning of these pages: each flip signals that a little more time has passed, heightening the former's amusement and the latter's exasperation. Rather unexpectedly, *Clarissa* grants this seemingly hapless reader a modicum of power over the people around him, whose time-sense throughout the episode depends upon the chronotope (temporarily) in his hands.

But if the novel (or any other text) in Lamb's essay stands revealed as a chronotope, its chronotopicity flows in ways that 'Forms of Time' has not entirely equipped us to recognise. In a sense, Bakhtin's roads mostly run one way, importing chance, contrast, and even chaos into the universe of the text and the life of its hero.

> The road is a particularly good place for random encounters. On the road ("the high road"), the spatial and temporal paths of the most varied people—representatives of all social classes, estates, religions, nationalities, ages—intersect at one spatial and temporal point. People who are normally kept separate by social and spatial distance can accidentally meet; any contrast may crop up, the most varied fates may collide and interweave with one another.[13]

Just one page later, Bakhtin doubles down by calling the road 'especially (but not exclusively) appropriate for portraying events governed by chance'.[14] We have seen a book bring about chance encounters in 'Detached Thoughts' (the Primrose Hill episode), as well as the mixing of different social and economic classes (the street-reading anecdote); but while chance plays a part in Elia's experience as a reader, it is far from the principal ingredient. Lamb will not give himself over to 'randomness' in this extreme way, and therefore the promise of the Elian book-as-chronotope is rather different from anything that Bakhtin imagines. If

---

13 Bakhtin, 'Forms of Time', p. 243.
14 Ibid., p. 244.

we seldom have much say in what roads we must travel and whom we will encounter along the way, there is a simpler, more straightforward agency available to us in the choice of what to read, when to read it, and, perhaps, with whom. Elia unambiguously emphasises the value of that agency: 'Much depends upon when and where you read a book. In the five or six impatient minutes, before the dinner is quite ready, who would think of taking up the Fairy Queen for a stop-gap, or a volume of Bishop Andrewes' sermons?'[15] The correct answer, obviously, is no one, and the point is that impatient minutes before dinner demand speedy reading material—a proper 'stop-gap'. Put another way, the problem that Elia sets before his audience is that of choosing what 'volume' of textual matter may attach itself comfortably to a certain quantity of time. This is chronotopicity raised from an inevitable narrative fact to an art form, and one that characters within the frame of Lamb's essays may practise with complete consciousness of so doing. Suddenly the habit of reading well holds the prospect of mastering space-time itself, with the result that both space and time become not only more pleasant, but more legible as well.

The question of how reading signifies in the Romantic imagination is, of course, not a new one, nor does it show signs of subsiding from view. In a recent *PMLA* article, Jonathan Sachs and Andrew Piper remind us that Wordsworth frames reading—specifically the reading of his poetry—as a corrective against the vicious cycle of landmark historical events and their speedy reportage. An example from lyric poetry is found in Wordsworth's 'Resolution and Independence', where the speaker drops into a state of dreamy perceptiveness that can only be expressed with recourse to literary language.

> At length, himself unsettling, he the Pond
>
> Stirred with his Staff, and fixedly did look
>
> Upon the muddy water, which he conn'd
>
> As if he had been reading in a book.[16]

---

15 Lamb, *Last Essays*, p. 50.
16 *William Wordsworth: The Major Works,* ed. by Stephen Gill (New York: Oxford University Press, 2000), p. 263.

Here, as in *Last Essays*, the author builds a particular relationship to space-time around the image of reading a book. For Wordsworth, 'the slow time of reading becomes a kind of hortatory slowness, one that responds to a perceived excess of speed by engaging and developing formal problems related to the representation of slowness'.[17] While acknowledging this effect of his poetry, Sachs and Piper challenge the received view that Wordsworth and other Romantics reject fast time altogether, exiling themselves to a bee-loud glade. The article, having noted these writers' reliance on advanced publishing methods alongside their fascination with ruins and absorbed contemplation, poses a forceful question: 'What if the oscillation between the craving for rapid communication and the counterforce of slow reading attuned to engagement without eventfulness were reflective of a more holistic sense of time, one that shadows forth the advance of the nineteenth century?'[18] Perhaps even more conspicuously than Wordsworth's meditations on nature, Lamb's book-time, which arises in at least as many forms as there are places to read and varieties of material, accomplishes this elusive shadowing forth. According to his 'holistic sense of time', all forms of reading, ably practised by someone who can tell them apart, are necessary to the life of a fully developed modern subject. In short, I read Lamb's spectacles of reading as another kind of exercise in what Saree Makdisi has called not anti-modernity, but *alter*-modernity, a mode of experience 'where time itself slips, slides, and sticks'.[19] Clock-time is not, perhaps should not be, vanquished—the bookstall owner will have his *Clarissa* back sooner or later; but until then book-time inscribes in modern spaces the opportunity for more heterogeneous experience than the conventional clock would provide.

With all his celebrated sweetness, then, does Lamb merely detach himself from the social and political realities of English life in the 1830s? Are his books a winding escape route that leads away from pressing responsibilities, as Hazlitt, with his obvious admiration of Lamb's style,

---

17 Jonathan Sachs and Andrew Piper, 'Technique and the Time of Reading', *PMLA*, 133.5 (2018), pp. 1259–67 (p. 1261), https://doi.org/10.1632/pmla.2018.133.5.1259
18 Ibid., p. 1261.
19 Saree Makdisi, 'William Blake, Charles Lamb, and Urban Anti-Modernity', *SEL: Studies in English Literary History, 1500–1900*, 56.4 (2016), 737–56 (p. 740), https://doi.org/10.1353/sel.2016.0035

seems nevertheless to imply? I think not. Far from rejecting the present or future, Lamb's bookish lifestyle is concerned with recovering them.

To appreciate the stakes of proper literacy for Lamb, we might contrast 'Detached Thoughts' with the far less harmonious image of texts in time that Lamb develops throughout 'Newspapers Thirty-Five Years Ago', an essay that first appears in an 1831 issue of the *Englishman's Magazine*, and which is subsequently published in *Last Essays of Elia* (1833). Lamb spends this work reflecting on his youthful experience as a writer for two very different periodicals, the *Morning Post* and, later, the *Albion*. The first thing to emerge from these reflections is an unlikely origin story for Hazlitt's detached antiquarian. The *Post* hires Lamb to write joke columns about the whims of contemporary fashion, like pink-coloured hose. It seems that for a while every newspaper employed someone to do this kind of writing, the conventions of which were well established when Lamb came along: 'The chat of the day, scandal, but, above all, *dress*, furnished the material. The length of no paragraph was to exceed seven lines. Shorter they might be, but they must be poignant'.[20]

Besides showing us the education of a younger and less self-assured Charles Lamb, this essay provides a cross-section of the 'magazine revolution' in England that extends from 1800 to around 1830. The revolution is marked by feverish anxieties concerning high and low culture, emergent publishing practices, and the nature of authorship. Enemies of the periodical press find it riddled with so-called Cockneyism, an umbrella term that encompasses every kind of slippage from a rigidly defined 'elite' literacy. More than a disparaging reference to writers' birthplace or background, 'Cockney' in this context strikes at magazines' dangerously metropolitan ethos. 'The fear behind the disputation', Simon Hull explains, 'was that the new magazines, even the more literary ones, mindlessly mirrored the transience and ephemerality of the city that spawned them, by reproducing the city's degrading predilection for spectacle and fashion at the cost of supposedly timeless products of fine art and canonical literature'.[21]

Lamb is a fringe Cockney writer whose idiosyncratic outlook on the movement becomes clear in his 'Newspapers' essay. Taking his

---

20 Lamb, *Last Essays*, p. 155.
21 Simon Hull, *Charles Lamb, Elia, and the London Magazine* (London: Pickering and Chatto, 2010), p. 22, https://doi.org/10.4324/9781315653310

reader inside this storm of anxiety, he shows us quite another kind of degradation: that of the magazine writer himself. He describes in striking detail the pressure that comes with feeding a hungry periodical press. As a joke writer for the *Morning Post*, young Elia is expected to 'furnish a daily quantum of witty paragraphs', an arrangement that his older self cannot deprecate extravagantly enough.

> No fractious operants ever turned out for half the tyranny, which this necessity exercised upon us. Half a dozen jests in a day (bating Sundays too), why, it seems nothing! We make twice the number every day in our lives as a matter of course, and claim no Sabbatical exemptions. But then they come into our head. But when the head has to go out to them—when the mountain must go to Mahomet—
> Reader, try it for once, only for one short twelvemonth.[22]

I am particularly interested in the figure that writing cuts in this periodical piece. For Lamb, the difference between telling jokes 'as a matter of course' and writing them day after day could not be more significant: the first is a natural process that allows the mind to spring forward or recline as it chooses, while the second is a gamut of hard deadlines, unbearably equidistant from each other. According to the elder Elia, jokes simply come into our head; when or why they do so is not, and need not be, specified. Contrasting this serendipitous arrangement with the magazine writer's lot, Lamb twice emphasises that oppressiveness of obligation: 'the head *has to* go out to them [...] the mountain *must* go to Mahomet' (my emphasis). That latter image drives home how totally the natural order of things is reversed during his breathless *Morning Post* days.

Constantly under attack from his own writing schedule, the young Elia has no choice but to cram his daily assignments into so-called 'No Man's Time', the short period during which one waits for breakfast—and a segment of day that his 'Detached Thoughts' essay would consecrate to the sleepy enjoyment of some light reading, if not to actual sleep. (He also takes to drinking heavily in the evening.) All the hours of the day, even those traditionally too nebulous to be claimed by any pursuit, become stuffed with some form of activity. The periodical press forces Elia to endure the worst kind of monotony: life moves at the same

---

22 Lamb, *Last Essays*, p. 159.

blistering speed from morning until night. It is composed exclusively of those 'impatient minutes' that he described in 'Detached Thoughts'—which leave no room to lose oneself in anything. The onerous 'daily quantum' of words, an obligation rooted in time as well as language, changes Elia's relationship to both: instead of combining harmoniously in rich moments of literate experience, they stifle one another and the artist's creative powers. In other words, the problem with writing for magazines is a problem of excessive homogenization—the magazine industry waxing industrial with its 'manufactory of jokes' (90). Carlyle, in 'Signs of the Times', might have treated this routine as one further example of dynamical genius giving way to mechanical process, with the end result that 'nothing follows its spontaneous course, nothing is left to be accomplished by old natural methods'.[23] The *Prelude* offers a similarly stinging rebuke of 'Sages, who in their prescience would control/All accidents, and to the very road/Which they have fashion'd would confine us down'.[24] In the 'Newspapers' essay, daily deadlines and word counts have overrun the young writer's imagination, leaving no space for impractical, unruly things like improvisation and whim. The birth of the magazine writer, it seems, must be ransomed with the death of the reader.

Significantly, if magazines have been the instrument of Elia's imaginative suffocation in the past, he does not permanently fall out with them on that account. At the start of his 'Newspapers' essay, Elia freely grants that articles written in his youth—'the first callow flights in authorship'—however painful they were to produce, make pleasurable reading years later.[25] For Lamb's persona, every kind of reading material is always on the table. As we have seen, Lamb's fictionalised self holds that the art of reading well consists of choosing exactly the right text for the right time of day, month, and year. When such a pairing is successful—when a text fits perfectly into its slot—the result is a heightening of perception wherein time amplifies one's relationship to place and time instead of negating it. More generally, Lamb assures us several times in this collection that periodicals, like other varieties of texts, have their

---

[23] Thomas Carlyle, *Selected Writings*, ed. by Alan Shelston (New York: Penguin, 1986), p. 65.
[24] Gill, *Wordsworth*, p. 444.
[25] Lamb, *Last Essays*, p. 155.

perfect moments in the varied life of a good reader. How lovingly he describes a fortunate encounter with a magazine: 'Coming in to an inn at night—having ordered your supper—what can be more delightful than to find lying in the window-seat, left there time out of mind by the carelessness of some former guest—two or three numbers of the old Town and Country Magazine, with its amusing *tête-à-tête* pictures—'. This, too, is book-time: not an impersonal succession of equally spaced clicks, but a temporality intimately attuned to the unpredictable movements of human subjectivity. Looking around Lamb's corpus, we find a rapturous rhetorical question for almost every kind of reading experience, even the most unlikely. 'In secular occasions, what so pleasant as to be reading a book through a long winter evening, with a friend sitting by—say, a wife—he, or she, too, (if that be probable), reading another, without interruption, or oral communication?' The multiplication of details here tends toward the absurd, an effect that Lamb acknowledges with unrepentant good cheer ('if that be probable'). His point, in these and many similar passages, is how brilliantly the right text fits into the right stretch of time, and vice versa.

All of this is not to say that Charles Lamb preferred reading over writing. The more substantive insight of 'Newspapers Thirty-Five Years Ago', when considered alongside 'Detached Thoughts on Books and Reading', is that reading presents at least as much promise for meaningful engagement with the world outside one's study as does writing, and perhaps much more. It is Elia the magazine writer, not Elia the sociably reading antiquarian, who becomes detached from everything around him, and from his own thoughts. Lines generated mechanically to meet deadlines are themselves dead, whereas lines read in the natural course of life and time deepen the impressions left by that course within the mind of the reader.

American Antiquarian

What about Washington Irving? Is he nothing more than a would-be antiquarian, as *The Spirit of the Age* indicates? His *Sketch-Book of Geoffrey Crayon, Gent.* (1819–20) ridicules overweening antiquarianism itself with spectacle that might have stunned even Hazlitt. In particular, an entry titled 'The Art of Book-Making', set mostly in a reading room of the British Museum, unleashes the wrath of Ben Jonson, John Fletcher, and other reanimated literary giants upon a present generation of book manufacturers who will not stop plundering the past.

> In the height of this literary masquerade, a cry suddenly resounded from every side, of "Thieves! thieves!" I looked, and lo! the portraits about the walls became animated! The old authors thrust out, first a head, then a shoulder, from the canvas, looked down curiously for an instant upon the motley throng, and then descended, with fury in their eyes, to claim their rifled property. The scene of scampering and hubbub that ensued baffles all description. The unhappy culprits endeavored in vain to escape with their plunder. On one side might be seen half a dozen old monks, stripping a modern professor; on another, there was sad devastation carried into the ranks of modern dramatic writers. Beaumont and Fletcher, side by side, raged round the field like Castor and Pollux, and sturdy Ben Jonson enacted more wonders than when a volunteer with the army in Flanders. As to the dapper little compiler of farragos mentioned some time since, he had arrayed himself in as many patches and colors as harlequin, and there was as fierce a contention of claimants about him, as about the dead body of Patroclus.[26]

This sketch uses rampaging Renaissance dramatists and medieval monks to portray the vicelike grip in which nineteenth-century England is held by its own illustrious past. In answer to the stereotype that Americans, with their lack of castles and long history, are incapable of producing art without borrowing from the British, Irving shows us the English borrowing maniacally from themselves. The 'moral' here is that authors of every national affiliation need not, and should not, become mere reproductions of their ancestors.

Still, there is everything to be gained in Irving's world by learning to read properly. Keeping Lamb's literacy and the book-as-chronotope in view, I want to explore a side of Irving different from the meandering tourist that becomes his favourite persona. Another of the less celebrated entries in his *Sketch-Book* is a brief, polemical essay called 'English Writers on America', in which books and reading, with all their perception-altering powers, are put to a practical use. Built on the same logic of discriminating literacy that we find everywhere in Lamb's writing, Irving's essay strives toward an intervention on the globally conscious

---

26 Washington Irving, *The Sketch-Book of Geoffrey Crayon, Gent.*, ed. by Susan Manning (New York: Oxford University Press, 1996), p. 27.

landscape of American culture. What Lamb is satisfied to suggest about the recuperative power of skilful reading, Irving declares boldly and with a patriotic animus.

Appropriately nestled between 'Rip Van Winkle' and the idyllic 'Rural Life in England', 'English Writers on America' pivots continually between the two nations. It is the *Sketch-Book*'s most rigorous and insightful attempt at capturing the transatlantic spirit of the age. In some ways, this offering reads like an outlier, even among the diverse entries in Irving's book. The mask of Geoffrey Crayon, if it is not dropped altogether, seems incidental here as Irving speaks directly and with an un-Crayonesque strain of urgency to his countrymen right from the essay's first line: 'It is with feelings of deep regret that I observe the literary animosity daily growing up between England and America'. In this way, Irving locates himself at a crossroads in American history. He positions himself as the mediator standing between a stubborn father and an unruly child. 'The national character', he continues, 'is yet in a state of fermentation'.[27] Spurred by a strong desire for autonomy, and disgusted by their country's recent state of intellectual 'vassalage' in cultural matters, many American writers and readers have turned away from the lessons that England's past can impart. I say 'many', but the essay implies 'nearly all'. Indeed, Irving's constant denomination of Americans as 'we' belies how much this essay places him against the national zeitgeist—to all appearances, an old-fashioned figure, drifting apart from the main current of American thought.

And yet he soon turns the tables, implying that Americans' single-minded focus on the future keeps *them* in the past. Without pronouncing the actual words, Irving casts current Anglo-American cultural relations as so much fallout of the War of 1812, and even of the Revolutionary War. A growing nation, unprepared for its newfound importance on the world stage, has rushed toward complete autonomy rather than seek wisdom and guidance in past models. 'We are a young people', says the author to his countrymen, the English always implicitly within earshot, 'necessarily an imitative one, and must take our examples and models, in a great degree, from the existing nations of Europe'.[28] As he further

---

27   Ibid., p. 51.
28   Ibid., p. 57.

explains, however, that imitation has its limits, beyond which only cultural servitude awaits.

> Let it be the pride of our writers, therefore, discarding all feelings of irritation, and disdaining to retaliate the illiberality of British authors, to speak of the English nation without prejudice, and with determined candor. While they rebuke the indiscriminating bigotry with which some of our countrymen admire and imitate every thing English, merely because it is English, let them frankly point out what is really worthy of approbation. We may thus place England before us as a perpetual volume of reference, wherein are recorded sound deductions from ages of experience; and while we avoid the errors and absurdities which may have crept into the page, we may draw thence golden maxims of practical wisdom, wherewith to strengthen and to embellish our national character.[29]

Here, in the same breath, Irving rejects the abject imitation of British influence and the indiscriminate dismissal of all British culture. Forging a proper relationship with the mother country will take greater discernment and care than either facile, knee-jerk reaction would reflect. First and foremost, however, it will take time. More offensive to Irving than either of these extremes is the breakneck pace at which American culture has hurtled between them. Wholesale dismissal of English influence is the reckless work of a moment, as is total approbation of that influence in its every detail. In what feels like a typically American manoeuvre, Irving steers us toward the middle ground. Some English attributes are 'attractive and praise-worthy', in Hazlitt's phrase, others less so. Americans must give themselves time to figure out the difference.

This is finally the principal work of Irving's essay: to slow time down, at least intermittently. The chronotopic device of this deceleration comes in the last line, where Irving likens English history to a 'perpetual volume of reference'. One can hardly overstate the importance of 'perpetual' for that phrase, and indeed for the argument of Irving's essay. History is not a magazine that one peruses idly before dinner, but a vast encyclopaedia to be consulted time and again in times of need. Indeed, the 'golden maxims' contained in this volume of reference seem almost beside the point; more significant is the process of searching them out, the structure of gradual development, appropriately guided by exterior influences,

---

29 Ibid.

that careful and repeated consultation of England's history will impress on young nation in a hurry. Put another way: Americans must recognise how valuable a reference work lies within their grasp, and then take all the time necessary to read it well.

Even as 'English Writers on America' confirms his deep regard for history, Irving's bookish prescription also reveals his stake in the future. In almost Bergsonian fashion, Irving asserts that reading the past is work for the present and the future. For America to continue thriving, its people must now cultivate in themselves a more mindful relationship to history, the figure of which in this essay is the reference volume. Repetitive consultations of the national text differ from more impersonal and oppressive varieties of routine, like Lamb's daily quantum of words, because they allow subjectivity to structure chronological time and not the other way around. If American time has accelerated to an excessive rate, the solution lies in treating the world like a book and reading it with Elian levels of discrimination and feeling.

Like Lamb, then, Irving has felt the excessive speed at which events, both great and small, seem to follow upon one another at the present time. If the style of this straight-talking essay seems unusual coming from this author, the worldview undergirding its message is quite familiar. Irving always treats haste as a mistake, whether grave or ridiculous, and his 'English Writers on America' urges patience and bemoans decisions made recklessly by a nation with time to spare. Far be it from Geoffrey Crayon to question the likelihood of unabated progress well into America's future. He does, however, predicate that American success on the antiquarian capabilities of her people—for how can we treat English culture as a volume of reference without first learning how to read an *actual* volume of reference? In a surprise turn of events, the bookworm shall inherit the earth.

Contrary to Hazlitt's claim that Lamb and Irving invariably settle on the past, I would reclaim both men as prophets of a possible future more humane than what came about in England and America through the nineteenth century. If learning to read, according to these essayists, cannot save the world, at least it can make the world habitable from one hour, one day, to the next. An age of monotonous progress and homogeneous time needs literature to restore meaningful difference to the hours that compose an individual human life. As Romantics facing the dawn of full-scale industrialization, both men wish to experience everyday time on a level that is profoundly sensitive to the faltering, inconsistent, endlessly variable movements of human existence.

Works Cited

Ainger, Alfred, ed., *The Letters of Charles Lamb*, vol. I (London: Macmillan and Co., 1888).

Bear, Laura, 'Doubt, Conflict, Mediation: The Anthropology of Modern Time', *Journal of the Royal Anthropological Institute*, 30.S1 (2014), 3–30, https://doi.org/10.1111/1467-9655.12091

Born, Georgina, 'Making Time: Temporality, History, and the Cultural Object', *New Literary History*, 46.3 (2015), 361–86, https://doi.org/10.1353/nlh.2015.0025

Erickson, Lee, 'Charles Lamb on Romantic Reading and Social Decorum', *The Wordsworth Circle*, 39.3 (2008), 79–85, https://doi.org/10.1086/twc24045754

Gill, Stephen ed., *William Wordsworth: The Major Works* (New York: Oxford University Press, 2000).

Hazlitt, William, *The Spirit of the Age* (Oxford: Woodstock Books, 1989).

Holquist, Michael, ed., 'Forms of Time and the Chronotope of the Novel', in *The Dialogic Imagination: Four Essays* by Mikhail Bakhtin, trans. by Caryl Emerson and Michael Holquist (Austin: University of Texas Press, 1981).

Hull, Simon, *Charles Lamb, Elia, and the London Magazine* (London: Pickering and Chatto, 2010), https://doi.org/10.4324/9781315653310

Irving, Washington, *The Sketch-Book of Geoffrey Crayon, Gent.*, ed. by Susan Manning (New York: Oxford University Press, 1996).

Lamb, Charles, *The Last Essays of Elia* (London: Edward Moxon, 1833).

Lucas, Edward Verrall, *The Life of Charles Lamb* (London: G. P. Putnam's Sons, 1905).

Makdisi, Saree, 'William Blake, Charles Lamb, and Urban Anti-Modernity', *SEL: Studies in English Literary History, 1500–1900* 56.4 (2016), 737–56, https://doi.org/10.1353/sel.2016.0035

Manning, Susan, ed., *The Sketch-Book of Geoffrey Crayon, Gent.* by Washington Irving (New York: Oxford University Press, 1996).

Sachs, Jonathan and Andrew Piper, 'Technique and the Time of Reading', *PMLA*, 133.5 (2018), 1259–67, https://doi.org/10.1632/pmla.2018.133.5.1259

Shelston, Alan, ed., *Selected Writings* by Thomas Carlyle (New York: Penguin, 1986).

8. 'A disciple of Albertus Magnus [...] in the eighteenth century': Anachronism and Anachrony in *Frankenstein*

Anne Rouhette

Although Mary Shelley's Frankenstein *is set in the late eighteenth century, its plot depends to a large extent on Victor's alchemical pursuits, making him a living anachronism, a notion which the novel draws attention to at several points. It might more generally be argued that the novel's writing and the effect it produces rest on the superimposition of two or more temporal lines and notably on the blurring of two supposedly antithetical conceptions of time, historical (or linear) time and mythical (or cyclical) time. This blurring and perhaps even co-existence of different timelines is what I explore in this essay by relying on the notion of anachrony, taken in its narratological sense, as a chronological disorder between diegesis and narrative, and in its poetical, creative sense, following Jacques Rancière's definition of the term: "events, notions, significations that are contrary to time, that make meaning circulate in a way that escapes any contemporaneity, any identity of time with itself." I here examine the temporal experience presented by the novel through its complex handling of time before focusing on the anachronistic protagonist, broadening the perspective thanks to other examples taken from Shelley's fiction. Indeed, many of her protagonists are thrust into a time period they do not belong to, either literally, thanks to a process of reanimation, or metaphorically, as they cling to old-fashioned values for instance. From* Frankenstein *onwards, the impact of Shelley's work can be accounted for at least partly by her poetical use of anachrony.*

Fig. 1 Illustration from *Le Monstre et le magicien: mélodrame-féerie en 3 actes* by Antony Béraud and Jean-Toussaint Merle (Paris: Théâtre de la Porte Saint-Martin, 1826). Bibliothèque nationale de France. Public domain.

Le Monstre et le magicien [The Monster and the Magician], a melodrama by Jean-Toussaint Merle and Antony Béraud, opened at Théâtre de la Porte Saint Martin in 1826. A great success, set in sixteenth-century Venice, it tells the story of an alchemist, Zametti, '*livré depuis sa jeunesse aux funestes travaux des Paracelse, des Albert le Grand et des Faustus*' [who from an early age had pursued the dreadful works of the likes of Paracelsus, Albertus Magnus and Faustus].[1] Zametti fashions a hideous monster (see Figure 1) who proceeds to kill his creator's son and blind surrogate father, and finally Zametti himself on board a ship. The monster is then struck down by lightning in godly wrath. These

---

1   Charles Nodier, *Œuvres dramatiques II. Bertram; Le Monstre et le magicien* [by Jean-Toussaint Merle and Antony Béraud]; *Le Songe d'or: fragments*, ed. by Ginette Picat-Guinoiseau (Genève: Droz, 1991), p. 146.

elements, despite time and space differentials, or perhaps precisely because of them, were sufficient for critics and spectators to recognise the play as an adaptation of Mary Shelley's *Frankenstein* (1818), whose plot unfolds in the late eighteenth century. The author herself remarked on the similarities between the two works,[2] reinforced by the presence of T.P. Cooke in the role of the Parisian Monster—the English actor and mime artist had already appeared as Frankenstein's Creature in *Presumption; or, the Fate of Frankenstein*, Richard Brinsley Peake's 1823 stage adaptation of Shelley's novel.

This choice of a Renaissance setting and of a magician as the main protagonist may have been inspired by the first French translation of *Frankenstein* by Jules Saladin, which appeared in 1821 and discreetly but recurrently stresses the supernatural components of Shelley's plot. The translator thus consistently rendered Shelley's 'chemistry' by *'l'alchimie'*, the French term for 'alchemy': 'the more rational theory of chemistry which has resulted from modern discoveries' becomes *'la théorie d'alchimie, la plus raisonnable qui soit résultée des découvertes modernes'* [the theory of alchemy, the most sensible that has resulted from modern discoveries] while M. Waldman teaches an oxymoronic *'alchimie moderne'* instead of 'modern chemistry'.[3] Saladin's use of *'alchimie'* or Zametti's quality as Magician may be considered as adaptations or misinterpretations of *Frankenstein*, but they also arguably identify one very strong element of the novel and relocate Victor in the era, or in one of the eras, to which he belongs in mind, though not in body as he admits: 'it may appear very strange, that a disciple of Albertus Magnus should arise in the eighteenth century'.[4] He is thus a living anachronism, a man at odds with his age. Echoing Victor *verbatim* almost immediately afterwards, M. Krempe also insists on the chronological disorder his young student represents: 'I little expected in this enlightened and scientific age to find a disciple of Albertus Magnus and Paracelsus'.[5] But

---

2 On 11 June 1826, Shelley wrote to John Howard Payne, who was then in Paris: 'How goes Frankenstein of Porte St. Martin?', *The Letters of Mary Wollstonecraft Shelley*, vol. I, ed. by Betty T. Bennett (Baltimore: Johns Hopkins University Press, 1980), p. 52.

3 Mary Shelley, *Frankenstein; or, The Modern Prometheus*, The 1818 Text, ed. by Marilyn Butler (Oxford: Oxford University Press, 2008), pp. 23 and 30 ('Shelley, *Frankenstein*' in the rest of these notes); Mary Shelley, *Frankenstein, ou le Prométhée Moderne*, trans. by Jules Saladin (Paris: Corréard, 1821), pp. 77–78 and 104.

4 Ibid., p. 23.

5 Ibid., p. 29.

what both Saladin's translation and *Le Monstre et le magicien* put forward is that the plot itself should rightfully unfold in the late Middle Ages or in the Renaissance, since its premise, bringing to life the inanimate, or in Victor's words, 'bestow[ing] animation upon lifeless matter',[6] is one of the pursuits of alchemists. The novel's writing, and the effect it produces, depend on the superimposition of two or more temporal lines. Similarly, James Whale's 1931 film *Frankenstein* also attests to the power of the medieval paradigm in Shelley's novel, as Jean-Jacques Lecercle argues, by 'effortlessly mingl[ing] medieval archaism and scientific modernity' with its gleaming laboratory set in a medieval tower.[7] Lecercle focuses on the constant interplay in the novel between seemingly mutually exclusive discourses (religious, scientific, historical and mythical), to whose contradictions *Frankenstein* offers a possible dénouement.

I will here examine this blurring and even co-existence of distinct timelines and their discursive modes with reference to the concept of anachrony. The latter may be understood in its narratological sense of a chronological disorder between diegesis and narrative, defined by Gérard Genette as 'the various forms of discrepancy between the order of the story and the order of the narrative'.[8] This allows for a consideration of the complex handling of time in the novel which engages with the poetical, creative sense of the term in line with Jacques Rancière's definition of 'anachrony', which he prefers over 'anachronism' because it is putatively free of pejorative connotations. By anachronies, Rancière designates 'events, notions, significations that are contrary to time, that make meaning circulate in a way that escapes any contemporaneity, any identity of time with "itself"'. They have the capacity 'to define completely original points of orientation', from which we might see the world, and our temporal experience of it, in unexpected and revealing ways.[9] Even

---

6   Ibid., p. 34. Among the three alchemists mentioned by Victor, Agrippa, Paracelsus, and Albertus, the first two were sixteenth-century natural philosophers, and Albertus was a thirteenth-century thinker, chronologically the most remote from the late eighteenth century; this choice underlines Victor's temporal distance from his own time, but it is also particularly relevant since, more so than Agrippa and Paracelsus, Albertus Magnus was interested in bringing to life the inanimate.
7   Jean-Jacques Lecercle, *Frankenstein, Mythe et Philosophie* (Paris: Presses Universitaires de France, 1988), pp. 7 and 16, my translation.
8   Gérard Genette, *Figures III* (Paris: Seuil, 1971), p. 79, my translation.
9   Jacques Rancière, 'The Concept of Anachronism and the Historian's Truth' [1996], trans. by Noel Fitzpatrick and Tim Stott, *InPrint*, 3.1 (2015), 21–48 (p. 47).

though Rancière here deals with the writing of history, his concept is useful in literary analysis, particularly in a work like *Frankenstein* which builds on a complex and even contradictory temporal experience, if only because its entire plot depends on Victor's anachronistic ambition. In the last part of this essay, I will attempt to broaden this conceptual framework with examples taken from Shelley's fiction in general, with a view to showing how *Frankenstein* and its chronologically displaced protagonist inform the rest of her work.

Frankenstein is set firmly in the eighteenth century, as we know from the dates on Walton's letters which frame the narrative, '17—'.[10] Other details help narrow down the period to the last decade of the century: the Creature thus learns to read from Volney's *Ruins of Empire*, published in French in 1791. Efforts to conclusively establish a clear timeframe, for example Anne K. Mellor's suggestion that Walton's letters encompass nearly a year, from December 1796 to September 1797, have however failed.[11] Thus Leslie S. Klinger identifies Walton's encounter with Victor as taking place in 1799, to account for their quotes from Coleridge's 'The Rime of the Ancient Mariner' and Wordsworth's 'Tintern Abbey', first published in 1798.[12] This though does not explain why both Victor and the Creature quote from Percy Shelley's 'Mutability', published in 1816, or why Victor should refer to the third canto of Byron's *Childe Harold's Pilgrimage* (1816) and to Leigh Hunt's 'Rimini' (1816), or why he quotes from the revised 'Ancient Mariner' of 1800.[13] These literary anachronisms properly constitute forms of paralepsis as defined by Genette, where the reader receives more information than authorised by the narrative code operating within the novel, here a first-person narrator telling a story set in the late eighteenth century.[14] These leaps forward in writing-time disrupt the initially recognised temporal framework of the narrative, substituting the author's timeline for that of the diegesis, and possibly imposing the author's voice in place of that

---

10 Shelley, *Frankenstein*, pp. 5 and 178.
11 Anne Mellor, *Mary Shelley: Her Life, Her Fiction, Her Monsters* (New York: Methuen, 1988), pp. 54–55. On the impossibility of precisely dating the events in *Frankenstein*, see Leonard Wolf, *The Essential Frankenstein* (New York: Plume, 1993), pp. 333–34, https://doi.org/10.4324/9780203435588
12 Mary Shelley, *The New Annotated Frankenstein*, ed. by Leslie S. Klinger (New York: Liveright, 2017).
13 Shelley, *Frankenstein*, pp. 66, 89, 48, 111 and 59.
14 Genette, *Figures III*, p. 211.

of her characters'. The same disruptive effect is apparent when Victor attends an incomprehensible lecture on 'potassium and boron' since as Stuart Peterfreund notes '[b]oron and potassium were first isolated and named by the Shelleys' favorite chemist, Humphrey [sic] Davy, in 1807'.[15] This blurring of temporal markers is exacerbated by the fact that the dates on Walton's letters are incomplete: 'Dec. 11th, 17–' for the first one. If the day and month are specified, the exact year is left blank, or rather, it is erased, replaced by a dash which both 'veils and unveils chronology', as Lecercle remarks.[16] This dash materialises a double movement, a form of affirmation and elision, emphasised by the contrast it creates with the details provided concerning the month and the day.

Both specific and uncertain, accurate and undetermined, this partial date signals a conflict between two conceptions of time. In Mircea Eliade's terms, a distinction may be drawn between the linearity of historical time, or 'profane' time, and the suspension or repetition of mythical or 'sacred' time.[17] Thus historical time, an impression of linearity and ineluctable movement forward through time, is conveyed by the succession of Walton's dated letters and by the other letters in the narrative, Elizabeth's 18 March and 18 May missives, and Alphonse's, dated 12 May, in all of which dashes replace the exact years.[18] This linearity is also apparent in the inherent nature of Victor's and the Creature's autobiographical narratives as they both look back on their lives, Victor beginning with an allusion to his 'ancestors' and the Creature referring to 'the original æra of [his] being'.[19] But Walton's framing narrative functions according to an alternative temporal mode, distinct from these retrospective accounts, recounted in the preterit. He relates for the most part what happens in his very recent past or his present, even writing 'to the moment' in the present tense or in the present perfect: 'I am interrupted [...]. It is midnight [...]. I must arise and examine [...]. Great God! What a scene has just taken place!', for

---

15 Shelley, *Frankenstein*, p. 25; Stuart Peterfreund, 'Composing What May Not Be "Sad Trash": A Reconsideration of Mary Shelley's Use of Paracelsus in *Frankenstein*', *Studies in Romanticism*, 43.1 (2004), n. 6, p. 81.
16 Lecercle, *Frankenstein*, p. 50.
17 Mircea Eliade, *The Sacred and the Profane: The Nature of Religion*, trans. by Willard R. Trask (New York: Harcourt Brace, 1959).
18 Shelley, *Frankenstein*, pp. 48, 159, and 53.
19 Ibid., pp. 18 and 79.

instance.[20] The structure of the novel, which combines the epistolary format and chapters, thus rests on two temporal narrative modes at variance with each other, complicating the experience of chronology.

Nevertheless, all three narrators remark on the passing of time and comment in particular on the change from one season to the next, as the following quotations illustrate:

> [Walton] The winter has been dreadfully severe; but the spring promises well, and it is considered as a remarkably early season [...].
> [...] it is the height of summer [...].
> [Victor] Winter, spring, and summer, passed away during my labours [...].
> Summer passed away in these occupations, and my return to Geneva was fixed for the latter end of autumn; but being delayed by several accidents, winter and snow arrived [...]. The winter, however, was spent cheerfully; and although the spring was uncommonly late, when it came, its beauty compensated for its dilatoriness.
> [The Creature] As the sun became warmer, and the light of day longer, the snow vanished [...].
> The pleasant showers and genial warmth of spring greatly altered the aspect of the earth.
> Autumn passed thus. I saw, with surprise and grief, the leaves decay and fall, and nature again assume the barren and bleak appearance it had worn when I first beheld the woods and the lovely moon.
> The winter advanced, and an entire revolution of the seasons had taken place since I awoke into life.[21]

The natural cycle of the seasons quietly evokes the passing of time, which advances at a relatively regular pace in the novel. Other examples of this type of chronological markers include numerous dates and times of day in addition to those given in letters: the Creature famously opens his eyes 'at one in the morning' 'on a dreary night of November', although the exact day is unspecified; he is seen by Victor at Plainpalais 'at midnight'; William disappears '[l]ast Thursday (May 7th)' and his body is discovered at 'about five in the morning' on the following day. It is also 'about five in the morning' when Victor enters his father's house on his return home; Justine's trial begins at 'eleven o'clock'; 'it was nearly noon when [Victor] arrived at the top of the ascent' and the

---

20 Ibid., p. 186.
21 Ibid., pp. 10, 11, 38, 50, 90, 92, 105–06, and 106.

Creature's 'tale had occupied the whole day' before he returns; Victor leaves London 'on the 27th of March', 'arrive[s] at Havre on the 8th of May', and lands at Evian at 'eight o'clock'.[22]

However, partly because the year on the letters and the day on which the Creature is brought to life are missing, these dates and times are given to some extent in a temporal void, so that the floating character of an unsettled, even suspended or circular timeline conflicts with the linearity of historical time. Instead of progressing in time, the novel doubles back upon itself when the Creature's tale covers the same time span as that of Victor's story and returns to some events already related, namely the murder of William and the framing of Justine. This long analepsis represents an anachrony in Genette's terms, a chronological disorder in the way the elements of the diegesis are presented, whose effect here is to open up fresh perspectives on events previously related. This contributes significantly to the impact of the novel as the Creature's voice is superimposed onto Victor's.

Furthermore, the dates and times given do not seem to operate simply as chronological markers. Some play significant roles as they can have symbolical values: this appears clearly when the first hour of the day, 'one in the morning', signals the beginning of the Creature's life. Their role may remain more elusive, as when Victor arrives home 'at about five in the morning'. The same phrase is used in reference to the discovery of William's body, perhaps hinting that Victor is to blame for the child's murder, perhaps for an altogether different purpose or for no purpose at all; the reader's attention is thus drawn to a coincidence that seems to require interpretation. Other elements further contribute to blur the linearity of the narrative. Events similar in nature take place several times, strikingly so in a relatively short novel (186 pages long in the Oxford World's Classics edition): two characters are wrongfully accused of murder, Victor speaks to an elderly magistrate twice, and he falls very ill three times. Time can even appear to go backwards, a temporal movement that mirrors, as it were, a geographical one, since Walton abandons his voyage of exploration at the end of the novel and returns home. In the space of three pages, Victor gives two different dates for his and Clerval's arrival in Britain: 'It was on a clear morning, in the

---

22 Ibid., pp. 38, 57, 52, 58, 61, 76, 122, 132, 157, and 164.

latter days of December, that I first saw the white cliffs of Britain' thus becomes 'We had arrived in England at the beginning of October' only two pages later.²³ As David Ketterer observes, this mistake 'originated at the Fair Copy, typesetting, or proofing stages' since Shelley's draft indicates 'in the latter days of September', not December.²⁴ Nevertheless it went uncorrected in the 1823 and 1831 editions, which emend other slips, including chronological mistakes,²⁵ and creates for the reader a sense either of reversibility (time going backwards, December turning to October as Victor continues his scientific pursuits of earlier years) or of irrelevance, of arbitrariness. *Frankenstein; Or, The Modern Prometheus* is thus caught between two contrary and yet co-existing conceptions of time, one evolutionary, the linearity of history ('Modern'), and the other circular, the a-temporality of myth ('Prometheus'), to which the paralepses contribute. A telling illustration of this occurs when Shelley has her Creature read Milton's *Paradise Lost* and Plutarch's *Parallel Lives*, referred to as *Plutarch's Lives* in *Frankenstein*, and classify them both as 'histories', a point made even clearer on the following page when he explains having considered *Paradise Lost* 'as a true history'.²⁶ This seemingly impossible fusion between the mythical and historical, emphasised by the shared initials, PL, and of course by the novel's subtitle, is emblematic of Shelley's juxtaposition of contradictory discourses as previously noted. It is fitting that the Creature should operate such a fusion because his creation results precisely from Victor's attempt at aligning myth and history.

Victor describes his scientific career in historical and developmental terms, claiming that he has discarded the alchemy of the '*early* philosophers' and moved on to '*modern* chemistry' (my emphasis) but it is obvious that he never really gives up the initial nature of his interest in science.²⁷ In fact, the 1831 version goes as far as to present

---

23   Ibid., pp. 130–31 and 132.
24   David Ketterer, 'The Corrected *Frankenstein*: Twelve Preferred Readings in the Last Draft', *English Language Notes*, 33.1 (Sept. 1995), 23–35 (p. 32). Shelley's draft of this passage, MS. Abinger c. 57, 46r, is available online on http://shelleygodwinarchive.org/sc/oxford/frankenstein/volume/ii/#/p96.
25   For instance, Victor's departure for England is moved from August to September. A more obvious mistake regarding the date of one of Walton's last letters (September 9th instead of September 19th) was also corrected.
26   Shelley, *Frankenstein*, pp. 103 and 104.
27   Ibid., pp. 24 and 30.

this movement as regressive, inverting the whole history of science, when Victor explains that in his youth, '[he] had retrod the steps of knowledge along the paths of time and exchanged the discoveries of recent inquirers for the dreams of forgotten alchemists'.[28] Although, as will be seen, the shift from 'early' to 'modern' is described in slightly different terms in the 1818 version I am concerned with, this movement backwards in time is evocative of what Victor finds so fascinating about alchemy and underlies the project so dear to his heart, since his creation is described as a by-product of his early interest in the *elixir vitae*, i.e. the search for immortality:

> I entered with the greatest diligence into the search of the philosopher's stone and the elixir of life. But the latter obtained my most undivided attention: wealth was an inferior object; but what glory would attend the discovery, if I could banish disease from the human frame, and render man invulnerable to any but a violent death![29]

Although Victor claims to have rejected the visions of the 'early philosophers' by the time he reaches Ingolstadt, he takes up the same subject a few pages later, after he has made his discovery, thanks to which

> Life and death appeared to me ideal bounds [...] I thought, that if I could bestow animation upon lifeless matter, I might in process of time (although I now found it impossible) renew life where death had apparently devoted the body to corruption.[30]

What Victor desires is not so much to still or abolish time but simply and plainly to bring back the dead, more precisely, to erase his mother's death, as his famous dream after the awakening of the Creature reveals. Jerrold E. Hogle sums up the position of Freudian critics thus: 'Victor's finished product is revealed by his dream at the moment of "birth" to be

---

28 Mary Shelley, *Frankenstein, or, The Modern Prometheus* (1831), ed. by Maurice Hindle (London: Penguin, 1988) p. 91. The variations between the 1818 and the 1831 versions regarding Victor's attitude towards alchemy and modern science are examined in particular by David Ketterer in 'Frankenstein's "Conversion" from Natural Magic to Modern Science—and a *Shifted* (and Converted) Last Draft Insert', *Science-Fiction Studies*, 24.1 (March 1997), 57–78.
29 Shelley, *Frankenstein*, p. 23.
30 Ibid., p. 36.

a cover for his drive to return to his mother'.[31] His ultimate wish is thus to reverse time, escape from the consciousness of man's finitude, from the 'bounds' of 'life and death' and the linearity of human chronological existence, in what can then be defined as a backwards movement.

Although Victor claims that 'the overthrow of Cornelius Agrippa, Albertus Magnus and Paracelsus' was effected when he discovered the power of electricity at the age of fifteen,[32] his move from alchemy to chemistry can best be described in Lecercle's terms as 'repression' more than progress or development:

> Victor's history sums up that of chemistry. He first reads Paracelsus and Cornelius Agrippa, but the sight of a tree destroyed by lightning inspires a passion for electricity and he turns away from those ancient authors. In Ingolstadt, he studies chemistry, and he spends time in charnel-houses not to summon the souls of the dead but to observe the decomposition of tissues. This is however a dubious activity, redolent of magic—for Victor, chemistry springs from alchemy as it represses it. And alchemy returns when Victor discovers the archetypal alchemical secret, that of life. In a strange and contradictory blend, the most archaic dreams and the most modern form of science coexist in Victor's scientific mind.[33]

When Victor describes his reaction after meeting with M. Krempe, a champion of modern science and denigrator of alchemists, his language is fraught with this 'strange and contradictory blend':

> I returned home, not disappointed, for I had long considered those authors useless whom the professor had so strongly reprobated; but I did not feel much inclined to study the books which I procured at his recommendation. M. Krempe was a little squat man, with a gruff voice and repulsive countenance; the teacher, therefore, did not prepossess me in favour of his doctrine. Besides, I had a contempt for the uses of modern natural philosophy. It was very different, when the masters of the science

---

31 Jerrold E. Hogle, 'An Introduction', *Frankenstein's Dream*, A Romantic Circles Praxis Volume, ed. by Jerrold E. Hogle (June 2003), https://romantic-circles.org/praxis/frankenstein/hogle/hogle.html (para. 4 of 18).

32 Shelley, *Frankenstein*, pp. 24–25.

33 Lecercle, *Frankenstein*, p. 42. That Victor's interest in alchemy is not simply to be dismissed as he moves on to more modern and presumably better science is a point also made by several critics, among whom Stuart Peterfreund, 'Composing', pp. 79–81. Science in *Frankenstein* has been the subject of many stimulating analyses in recent years, summed up by Andrew Smith in 'Scientific Contexts', in *The Cambridge Companion to* Frankenstein (Cambridge: Cambridge University Press, 2016), pp. 69–83, https://doi.org/10.1017/CBO9781316091203.007

sought immortality and power; such views, although futile, were grand: but now the scene was changed. The ambition of the inquirer seemed to limit itself to the annihilation of those visions on which my interest in science was chiefly founded. I was required to exchange chimeras of boundless grandeur for realities of little worth.[34]

The reasons that Victor gives for disregarding Krempe's recommendations reveal how little he has progressed since his readings of the now supposedly 'useless' alchemists, if only because Victor's axiology finds itself reversed at the end of this passage where modern realities and not alchemical dreams are deemed to be 'of little worth'. He still clings to the notions expounded by the 'masters of the science' and has not yet given up on 'chimeras of boundless grandeur'. Interestingly, he bases his rejection of Krempe on physiognomy (the teacher is physically repulsive, hence his doctrine is as well), an epistemological system that Albertus Magnus held in high esteem. 'The scene was changed', that is, the time-period has changed, perhaps, but not the visions and ambitions on which Victor's interest in science is based.

Jules Saladin's mistranslation of 'modern chemistry' into *'l'alchimie moderne'* thus turns out to be both oxymoronic and fitting: instead of moving, progressing from 'early science' to 'modern science', Victor operates a fusion, 'attempt[ing] to wed the visions of alchemy to the methodology of science', as Irving H. Buchen argues.[35] Victor's refusal to take historicity into account was already evident when he was as fascinated by the search for the *elixir vitae* as by experiments on an air pump, or when he considered Pliny and Buffon as 'authors [...] of nearly equal interest and utility', showing no awareness of a progression from the former to the latter, or even of a difference between the two.[36] His creation of the monster results from a deep yearning for the co-existence of several temporal planes, aspirations that may be termed a-chronistic rather than anachronistic since they work towards annihilating historical time and replacing it with the timelessness of mythical time. These aspirations lead to the anachrony that is the creation of the Monster,

---

34 Shelley, *Frankenstein*, p. 28.
35 Irving H. Buchen, '*Frankenstein* and the Alchemy of Creation and Evolution', *The Wordsworth Circle*, 8 (Spring 1977), 103–12 (p. 104), https://doi.org/10.1086/twc24039234
36 Shelley, *Frankenstein*, pp. 24 and 25. See also Peterfreund, 'Composing', p. 81.

an event outside of its time and even outside time, thus questioning the finitude of human beings, their beginning and their end. Of course, such transgressive ambition is proved to be destructive in the diegesis of the novel, as instead of restoring the dead to life Victor and his Creature condemn the living to death. But from a literary point of view, the impulse responsible for Victor's creation, this attempt at going backwards, or probably more precisely, at merging history and myth, constitutes the creative drive behind some of Mary Shelley's work. In the last part of this essay, and from this particular perspective, I would like to review the variations her fiction offers on the Frankensteinian motif of the chronologically displaced character.

Victor Frankenstein can be said to be a prototype in Shelley's fiction, which frequently resorts to the device of introducing a character in a time period to which he—for that character is always male—does not belong, usually with dire consequences. This motif occurs in varying guises in terms of content and of form, which reveals its creative potential for Shelley. These chronological displacements or decalages can be conceptual or metaphorical. Such is the case in *Frankenstein*, where Victor's alchemical interests are presented as anachronistic in the eighteenth century in which he lives. Another example would be Richard of York, the doomed hero of *The Fortunes of Perkin Warbeck*, an 1830 historical novel set in the late fifteenth and early sixteenth centuries, who clings to the medieval values of chivalry in the proto-capitalist world of the Renaissance. Richard is portrayed as a quixotic figure, a remnant of a past era who cannot survive the end of the novel.[37] Or again, in the last chapters of *The Last Man* (1826), the narrator, sole relict of the human race annihilated by the plague, wanders in a world to which he very strongly feels that he no longer belongs.[38] These three novels invite contemplation of man's place in time, which is addressed from other perspectives in several of Shelley's short stories.

These depict literal temporal anomalies thanks to the use of supernatural devices and raise more explicitly the metaphysical question

---

37 On this novel and its anachronistic protagonist, see for instance William D. Brewer, 'William Godwin, Chivalry, and Mary Shelley's *The Fortunes of Perkin Warbeck*', *Papers on Language and Literature*, 35.2 (Spring 1999), 187–205.

38 The question of the handling of time in *The Last Man* is addressed in fine detail by Timothy Ruppert in 'Time and the Sybil in Mary Shelley's *The Last Man*', *Studies in the Novel*, 41.2 (Summer 2009), 141–56, https://doi.org/10.1353/sdn.0.0054

of man's existence as a chronological being thanks to the characters' reaction to immortality or resuscitation. What interests me here is the variety of forms this basic premise gives rise to. Like *Frankenstein*, 'The Mortal Immortal', first published in 1833 and frequently anthologised, is a first-person narration. An actual pupil of Cornelius Agrippa, Winzy, the narrator, drinks his master's elixir of life by mistake and watches his wife Bertha grow old and die; aged 323 as he writes his tale, he yearns for death and yet still fears it. The short story draws on several genres: humorous when it describes the disappointment of the elderly alchemist and his difficulty in finding a servant, it becomes sentimental when Winzy relates his courtship of Bertha, and then psychological when he recounts his long years spent in solitude and his ambivalent attitude towards death. Two other short stories offer variations upon the same theme but this time the characters are brought back to life—unlike Winzy's long life, theirs have been discontinued. 'Valerius, Or, The Re-Animated Roman', an unfinished tale probably written in 1819 and first published in Charles E. Robinson's 1976 collection of Mary Shelley's tales and stories, makes use of a rather complex narrative technique, beginning with the intervention of an unidentified first-person narrator followed by two retrospective accounts, the second one covering partly the same grounds as the first, as in *Frankenstein*. As in *Frankenstein* again, the timeline of the story is blurred: 'Valerius' begins with a precise time but imprecise date since the year and the day are missing – it is '[a]bout eleven o'clock in the month of September'.[39] The decalage between the main character, a Roman who lived and died in the first century BC, and the time period, is remarked upon several times, as in the following passage:

> I can compare him to nothing that now exists—his appearance resembled that of the statue of Marcus Aurelius in the Square of the Capitol at Rome. Placid and commanding, his features were Roman; except for his dress you would have imagined him to be a statue of one of the Romans animated with life. He wore the dress now common all over Europe, but it appeared unsuited to him and even as if he were unused to it.[40]

---

39 Mary Shelley, *Collected Tales and Stories*, ed. by Charles E. Robinson (Baltimore and London: The Johns Hopkins University Press, 1990 [1976]), p. 332.
40 Ibid.

The tale also integrates the point of view of Valerius' friend Isabell Harley, who describes him as 'a being cut off from our world' and feels 'that [her] companion was not a being of the earth'.[41] The tone is tragic as the character feels nothing but despair in his second life. Everything that has happened since his first death has been degradation: 'the wretched Italians, who usurp the soil once trod by heroes, fill [him] with bitter disdain' since 'all that is great and good ha[s] departed'.[42] More than Victor's, it is his Creature's voice that Valerius takes up here as he repeatedly stresses his uniqueness and the solitude that it entails.

Inversely, the re-animated character in 'Roger Dodsworth, the Re-Animated Englishman' is described on the whole as full of curiosity and admiration for the nineteenth century in which he awakes. The comic mode predominates in a story written in 1826 but published for the first time in 1863. The tale builds on what Charles E. Robinson calls 'a cryogenic hoax', a story published in *Le Journal du Commerce de Lyon* in June 1826.[43] It is told from the point of view of an author-like persona, an avatar of Shelley herself, and deals with a character 'whose animation had been suspended by the action of the frost [...] as he was returning from Italy, in 1654'.[44] The date becomes '1647' on page 48 and the reader learns that the discovery occurred 'a score or two of years' before 1826, suggesting that, as in *Frankenstein*, the timeline is erratic or even superfluous, although here, instead of destabilizing the reader, the chronological uncertainties highlight the playfulness and fictionality of the tale.[45] Roger Dodsworth is 'dug out from under an avalanche' and 'resuscitated' '[u]pon the application of the usual remedies'.[46] These are unspecified, but they are presumably the same as those used on Victor when found half-frozen by Walton in the Arctic:

> We accordingly brought him back to the deck, and restored him to animation by rubbing him with brandy, and forcing him to swallow a small quantity. As soon as he shewed signs of life, we wrapped him up in blankets, and placed him near the chimney of the kitchen-stove.[47]

---

41 Ibid., pp. 340 and 343.
42 Ibid., pp. 333–34.
43 Ibid., p. 377.
44 Ibid., p. 43.
45 Ibid.
46 Ibid.
47 Shelley, *Frankenstein*, p. 13.

The story alludes to *Frankenstein* elsewhere; Shelley thus imagines her 'youthful antique' dreaming of 'his favourite play-mate, the friend of his later years, his destined and lovely bride', or describes him with 'a *Genevese* watch, which he often consults, as if he were not yet assured that time had made progress in its accustomed manner' (my emphasis).[48] The story also most probably refers to 'Valerius' when the narrator of 'Roger Dodsworth' mentions having 'often made conjectures how such and such heroes of antiquity would act, if they were reborn in these times'.[49] In this most metafictional of Shelley's short stories, the anachronism is explicitly presented as a source of inspiration, as food for imaginative thought; since obviously Roger Dodsworth never returned to England, 'let us be permitted to indulge in conjecture', the narrator writes, which is what Shelley does during the greater part of her story.[50] She makes up dialogues between Dodsworth and his discoverer filled with humorous misunderstandings, and she deals with the character's chronological unfitness here in a comic mode. Comic or tragic, literal or metaphorical, seen from various perspectives and different degrees of narrative complexity, these brief examples draw on one another and on the original text, *Frankenstein*, Shelley's first published work of fiction, which they can be said to resuscitate and adapt to different time periods. In this respect, it is not altogether unreasonable to suggest that the 1831 version represents an attempt at introducing the novel into yet another decade, an attempt perhaps mirrored by the publication of 'Valerius' and 'Roger Dodsworth' long after their author's death, as if the tales themselves had been re-animated. A study of Shelley's fiction from this perspective of anachrony and anachronism thus reveals the power of these concepts as fundamental tropes in *Frankenstein* and beyond.

Works Cited

Bennett, Betty T., ed., *The Letters of Mary Wollstonecraft Shelley*, 3 vols. (Baltimore: Johns Hopkins University Press, 1980).

---

48 Shelley, *Collected Tales*, pp. 44 and 47. Victor refers to Elizabeth as 'my future wife; [...] my playfellow, and, as we grew older, my friend' (Shelley, *Frankenstein*, p. 20).
49 Ibid., p. 48.
50 Ibid., p. 44.

Buchen, Irving H., '*Frankenstein* and the Alchemy of Creation and Evolution', *The Wordsworth Circle*, 8 (Spring 1977), 103–12.

Genette, Gérard, *Figures III* (Paris: Seuil, 1971).

Hogle, Jerrold E., 'An Introduction', in *Frankenstein's Dream*, A Romantic Circles Praxis Volume, ed. by Jerrold E. Hogle (June 2003), http://romantic-circles.org/praxis/frankenstein/hogle/hogle.html

Ketterer, David, 'The Corrected *Frankenstein*: Twelve Preferred Readings in the Last Draft', *English Language Notes*, 33.1 (Sept. 1995), 23–35.

——, 'Frankenstein's "Conversion" from Natural Magic to Modern Science— and a *Shifted* (and Converted) Last Draft Insert', *Science-Fiction Studies*, 24.1 (March 1997), 57–78.

Lecercle, Jean-Jacques, *Frankenstein, Mythe et Philosophie* (Paris: Presses Universitaires de France, 1988).

Peterfreund, Stuart, 'Composing What May Not Be "Sad Trash": A Reconsideration of Mary Shelley's Use of Paracelsus in *Frankenstein*', *Studies in Romanticism*, 43.1 (2004), 79–98, https://doi.org/10.2307/25601660

Rancière, Jacques, 'The Concept of Anachronism and the Historian's Truth' [1996], trans. by Noel Fitzpatrick and Tim Stott, *InPrint*, 3.1 (2015), 21–48.

Shelley, Mary, *Frankenstein, the 1818 Text*, ed. by Marilyn Butler (Oxford: Oxford University Press, 2008).

——, *Frankenstein, or, The Modern Prometheus* (1831), ed. by Maurice Hindle (London: Penguin, 1988).

——, *Frankenstein, ou le Prométhée Moderne*, trans. by Jules Saladin (Paris: Corréard, 1821).

——, *Collected Tales and Stories*, ed. by Charles E. Robinson (Baltimore and London: The Johns Hopkins University Press, 1990 [1976]).

Smith, Andrew, 'Scientific Contexts', in *The Cambridge Companion to* Frankenstein (Cambridge: Cambridge University Press, 2016), 69–83, https://doi.org/10.1017/CBO9781316091203.007

SECTION IV

PERSISTENCE AND AFTERLIVES

9. Heaps of Time in Beckett and Shelley

Laura Quinney

> *Shelley is famous for his "speed"—conceptual precision, figurative economy, and poetics of momentum—and this speed is nowhere more evident or powerful than in his last poem,* The Triumph of Life. *In that poem, speed is also a thematic issue: the rapidity with which the Chariot of Life hurtles forward on its destructive course figures the overwhelming momentum of time, which leaves human agency in the dust. Beckett's rhythms and his treatment of time would seem on the face of it to be inverse. Characters such as Vladimir and Estragon in* Waiting for Godot *seem to have all too much time on their hands. Many characters in Beckett, from Belacqua through the Unnameable, Winnie, and beyond, seem to occupy a purgatorial temporality in which nothing more can take place. These characters find themselves out of synch with time. And yet they are no more immune to time than Shelley's 'great stream / Of people ... hurrying to & fro'. It's because of the nature of time that they are confronted with this cognitive bafflement: they don't know what is happening to them, any more than Winnie or the tramps do. The Augustinian problematic by which the past and future 'had been, and would be not' offers a counter-romantic view of time, not as a theater of absolute loss compensated for by sublime gain (as in* Mont Blanc*) but as a final loss of one's footing, as the difference between speed and vacancy (Shelley and Beckett) becomes undone.*

Shelley is famous for his 'speed'—conceptual precision, figurative economy, and poetics of momentum—and this speed is nowhere more evident or powerful than in his last poem, *The Triumph of Life*.[1] In that

---

1   See the chapter entitled 'Shelley's Speed', in William Keach, *Shelley's Style* (New York: Methuen, 1984), pp. 154–83.

poem, speed also appears as a thematic issue (not for the first time in Shelley): the rapidity with which the Chariot of Life hurtles forward on its destructive course figures the overwhelming momentum of time, which leaves human agency in the dust. Beckett's rhythms and his treatment of time would seem on the face of it to be inverse. Many characters in Beckett, from Belacqua through the Unnameable, Winnie, and beyond, occupy an inertial temporality in which time appears to have slowed to a halt. Nothing more can take place, it appears, though they live on and on. And yet they are no more immune to the effects of time than Shelley's

> great stream
>
> Of people ... hurrying to & fro
>
> Numerous as gnats upon the evening gleam,
>
>
> All hastening onward, yet none seemed to know
>
> Whither he went, or whence he came, or why
>
> He made one of the multitude...[2]

Shelley's anonymous crowds do not know what is happening to them, any more than Winnie or the tramps do. The nature of time has pitched them into this cognitive bafflement, and they dwell in a purgatorial haze. (Not coincidentally, both Beckett and Shelley take Dante's *Purgatorio* as a major source of inspiration.[3]) For *The Triumph of Life* offers a counter-Romantic view of time. Time in this poem is not the theatre of absolute loss compensated by sublime gain, as it is in 'Tintern Abbey' or *Mont Blanc*, but the cause of psychological entropy and self-loss of

---

2 Percy Shelley, 'The Triumph of Life', in *Shelley's Poetry and Prose*, ed. by Donald H. Reiman and Neil Fraistat, 2nd ed. (New York: Norton, 2002), p. 485, lines 44–49.

3 For Shelley, Dante and *The Triumph of Life*, see Anita O'Connell, 'Dante's Linguistic Detail in Shelley's Triumph of Life', *CLCWeb: Comparative Literature and Culture* 13.4 (2011), https://doi.org/10.7771/1481-4374.1683 and Peter Vassalo. 'From Petrarch to Dante: The Discourse of Disenchantment in Shelley's The Triumph of Life.' *Journal of Anglo-Italian Studies* 1 (1991), 102–10. For Beckett and Dante, see Danielle Castelli, *Beckett's Dantes: Intertextuality in the Fiction and Criticism*, 2nd ed. (Manchester: Manchester University Press, 2013), https://doi.org/10.7228/manchester/9780719071560.001.0001

the same kind Beckett obsessively depicts in his plays and novels. Thus the difference between speed and vacancy is undone, revealing an affinity between Beckett and Shelley which might come as a surprise to conventional literary history.

The Grove Companion to Samuel Beckett flatly declares that in Beckett "Shelley" is an 'English poet drawn on when a romantic cliché is needed'.[4] One such 'romantic cliché', evidently, is 'pale for weariness,' as quoted by Estragon and cited in relation to Belacqua, Dante's emblem of laziness, whom Beckett summons a number of times. Beckett draws the line from Shelley's fragment, 'To the Moon':

To the Moon

I

Art thou pale for weariness

Of climbing heaven and gazing on the earth,

Wandering companionless

Among the stars that have a different birth,—

And ever changing, like a joyless eye

That finds no object worth its constancy?[5]

If this fragment exemplifies Romantic cliché, it is not of the prettifying sort. Shelley's anthropomorphised moon is an exile, 'Wandering companionless/Among the stars that have a different birth'. It is alienated and aimless, seeking but unable to find a credible passion, 'like a joyless eye/That finds no object worth its constancy.' It is easy enough to see that Beckett's attitude towards this poem cannot be merely satirical, as the *Grove Companion* suggests. Beckett's relation to lyricism is itself equivocal—he is by no means beyond his own lyrical flights—but it is the thematic bite in this Shelley fragment that, I believe, drew

---

4 C.J. Ackerley and S.E. Gontarski, eds, *The Grove Companion to Samuel Beckett: A Reader's Guide to His Works, Life and Thought* (New York: Grove, 2004), p. 1663.

5 Percy Shelley, *The Major Works*, ed. Zachary Leader and Michael O'Neill (New York: Oxford University Press, 2003), p. 146.

him to it. Estragon amends the quotation to add that the moon is weary specifically 'Of climbing heaven and gazing on the likes of us',[6] but that sentiment of existential disgust is not so far from the spirit of Shelley's poem. 'Weariness' is a temporal effect: the two authors (at times) portray time as performing the same malicious operation, consuming us while we try to discover a suitable employment for it, drawing agency and identity into a losing game of catch-up.

It is necessary to go back into the earlier history of Romanticism in order to understand how Shelley's thought and his temporal figures evolved. The challenge temporality poses to agency and identity had already been broached, in a sophisticated way, by Wordsworth and Coleridge. As developed earlier in the eighteenth century, the 'poem of revisitation' portrays the return of the adult to a place familiar in childhood, and usually explores the melancholy awareness of time passing, and of the dramatic difference between the child and the adult self. Wordsworth and Coleridge adapted this model in poems where the catalyst of self-recognition, the forms of self-division, and the stakes involved, are both more dramatic and more subtle. In 'Tintern Abbey,' 'Frost at Midnight,' 'Dejection', 'the Intimations Ode' and others, the self engages in a fraught dialogue with itself, wherein its perception of its own changes induces larger existential anxieties. Against my will, the speaker implies, time has parted me from myself. (Anyone who has read Proust will recognise this as one of his great themes.) Involuntary changes in the self are symptoms of its passivity, changes wrought upon it by its existence in time, which it resists in vain. The 'I' experiences itself as frustratingly labile and tenuous. It cannot keep up with its own experience, finding itself unable to grasp events or achieve self-knowledge. Yet it cannot dissolve self-consciousness; it remains to wrestle with itself. (The similarity to Beckett's 'brain in a vat' fictions is instantly recognizable.)

Let us take 'Frost at Midnight' as an example: consciousness, when it becomes self-conscious, has no choice but to 'idle', spinning its wheels without engaging the reality from which it stands apart.[7] In

---

6   Samuel Beckett, *The Collected Works of Samuel Beckett: Waiting for Godot: A Tragicomedy in Two Acts* (New York: Grove, 1970), p. 34.
7   Samuel Taylor Coleridge, *Coleridge's Poetry and Prose*, ed. by Nicholas Halmi, Paul Magnuson and Raimonda Modiano (New York: Norton, 2004), p. 120.

the second verse paragraph (as traditionally printed), idling takes the form of reverie, nostalgia, of remembering the dreams of the helpless child. Confinement is the theme, and the speaker does what one does in confinement: he *temporises*. To 'temporise' means 'to let time pass, spend time, 'mark time'' (OED), and then 'to delay' or 'to procrastinate.' The latter terms have a moral nuance; they imply that one ought to be doing something else. However, in Coleridge's poem the thinker has nothing to do but think and dream. Therein lies the important idea behind this sense of the word 'temporise': to idle—to let time pass not inactively, but without effect—is also to 'mark time,' to index the passage of time in the form of one's own passing thoughts or aimless activities. As the imprisoned Richard II laments, 'I have wasted time; and now doth time waste me, for now hath Time made me his numbering clock'.[8] Probably recalling this passage from Shakespeare, Samuel Johnson reworked the metaphor in one of his piquant moral essays on the subject of procrastination (*Idler* #18). Titled 'Disguises of Idleness,' he portrays himself and his strategies of delay in the person of one 'Sober,' whom he encourages to reform. (We are discussing Coleridge and Shelley at this point, but it is worth remarking that Samuel Johnson was a favourite with Beckett, and a passage like the following makes it clear why.)

> His daily amusement is chymistry. He has a small furnace, which he employs in distillation, and which has long been the solace of his life. He draws oils and waters, and essences and spirits, which he knows to be of no use; sits and counts the drops, as they come from his retort, and forgets that, whilst a drop is falling, a moment flies away.[9]

Time moves forward whether or not we 'seize' it. To idle is to tick off the moments blindly, to become oneself a register of the flying moments, without knowing it. Thus one's passivity in relation to time is compounded. For time does not in fact pass emptily. When the mind idles, it feels itself to be outside of time, but with every thought a moment passes in which external and internal changes are taking place, insensibly.

---

8   William Shakespeare, 'Richard II', Act V Scene v, 49–50, in *The Norton Shakespeare*, ed. by Stephen Greenblatt (New York: Norton, 2008).
9   Samuel Johnson, *Essays from the Rambler, Adventurer and Idler*, ed. by Walter Jackson Bate (New Haven: Yale University Press, 1968), p. 293.

Shelley takes up the theme—time's ruination of agency—and gives it an epic treatment in *The Triumph of Life*. The Chariot of Life, a figure for time, moves so rapidly that it sweeps up, or crushes, or outstrips its individual followers. Shelley emphasises its role in defeating human purposes by singling out the eminent benefactors or would-be benefactors of humanity—Aristotle, Plato, Bacon, the Enlightened despots, Napoleon—all compromised, the poems says, in the spirit or in their legacies. There, chained to the Car, like leaders of defeated peoples in a Roman Triumph, languish

> 'The Wise,
>
> 'The great, the unforgotten: they who wore
>
> Mitres and helms and crowns, or wreathes of light,
>
> Signs of thought's empire over thought; their lore
>
> 'Taught them not this—to know themselves; their might
>
> Could not repress the mutiny within,
>
> And for the morn of truth they feigned, deep night
>
> 'Caught them ere evening'.[10]

This passage crackles with subtle thought, challenging the reader to understand how the great ones failed to fulfil the Delphic command, 'know thyself,' how they were undone by a 'mutiny within,' and how they were benighted, doused by an oblivion that mocked their self-conceptions. What we can discern unequivocally is that their failure was both cognitive and moral, that it was consequential and that it is figured in terms of temporal asynchrony: they were belated in relation to themselves.

The poem's most significant representative of defeated purposes is, of course, Rousseau, who has 'fallen by the wayside' in a decayed form

---

10 *Shelley's Poetry and Prose*, p. 489–90, lines 208–15.

the narrator at first mistakes for 'an old root' with grass for hair and holes for eyes. Rousseau says 'I/Am weary' and the narrator observes that he pauses 'wearily,' 'like one who by the weight/Of his own words, is staggered.'[11] When he comes to tell his story, he opens with a declaration of his bafflement:

'Whence I came, partly I seem to know,

'And how and by what paths I have been brought

To this dread pass, methinks even thou mayst guess;

Why this should be my mind can compass not—

'Whither the conqueror hurries me still less.[12]

He reprises this confession of mental haze more dramatically in describing the effect of drinking the Nepenthe proffered by the seductive 'shape all light': 'And suddenly my brain became as sand', on which impressions are scored and erased and scored again in endless succession.[13] These moments contribute to the theme of how time damages or defeats human purposes, specifically, by damaging or defeating human understanding. Time eludes cognition—it resists our understanding—but more importantly, it continually erodes, scrambles and erases knowledge. Agency and identity can hardly be maintained under these circumstances. The medium of time, through which we move, promotes cognitive disruption and hence, discontinuity within the self. (*Contra* Locke, who defined personal identity as present consciousness and its attendant memories). The mind can't keep up. It is always trying and failing to master what time has already brought forth, and is already moving to supersede, or has already superseded. According to Rousseau, the 'spark' within him fights a losing battle with the 'corruption' steadily encroaching upon it.

---

11 Ibid., p. 489, lines 195–96 and 196–97.
12 Ibid., p. 493, lines 300–04.
13 Ibid., p. 496, line 405.

> 'And if the spark with which Heaven lit my spirit
>
> Earth had with purer nutriment supplied
>
> 'Corruption would not now thus much inherit
>
> Of what was once Rousseau—nor this disguise
>
> Stain that within which still disdains to wear it.—[14]

An erosion of this kind, a loss of oneself through and in time, is implicit in the Platonic paradigm of the Intimations Ode. Harold Bloom some time ago noted the ubiquitous presence of Wordsworth in *The Triumph of Life*, though he reads Shelley's 'shape all light' as a 'sublimating metaphor for everything that Wordsworth called nature' while I take it to be a descendent not of nature, but its opposite, the transcendental 'gleam' or 'celestial light' of the Intimations Ode. After its first radiant appearance, it similarly 'fade[s] into the light of common day'.[15] By attributing this disappointing end to the 'shape all light,' Shelley critiques the evasiveness of Wordsworth's accommodation. Wordsworth brings himself to admit that 'Nature,' extended in sense to cover our life on earth, is a 'homely nurse', who 'doth all she can to make her child, her inmate Man, forget the glories he hath known', yet he goes on to claim that memories of childhood 'recollections' of the other world persist and sustain the adult, so that 'our souls' continue to 'have sight of that immortal sea/Can in a moment travel thither,/And see the children sport upon the shore,/And hear the mighty waters rolling evermore'.[16] In Shelley's view, Wordsworth is skirting the implications of his own Platonic paradigm, neglecting the powerful encroachment of 'corruption': in fact, our souls *cannot* keep sight of that immortal sea, memories disintegrate and former selves vanish—the brain becomes as sand. Wordsworth's 'celestial light,' transformed into the 'shape all light,' becomes destructive itself, in Shelley's reckoning, as if to suggest

---

14   Ibid., p. 489, lines 201–05.
15   Harold Bloom, 'Shelley and His Precursors', in *Poetry and Repression* (New Haven: Yale University Press, 1976), p. 107, and William Wordsworth, *Wordsworth's Poetry and Prose*, ed. by Nicholas Halmi (New York: Norton, 2014), p. 436, lines 4 and 77.
16   *Wordsworth's Poetry and Prose*, p. 436, lines 168–72.

that there is no escaping degradation. Even the otherworldly ideal of the intelligible world distracts and damages the imagination:

'And still her feet, no less than the sweet tune

To which they moved, seemed as they moved, to blot

The thoughts of him who gazed on them, and soon

'All that was seemed as if it had been not—

As if the gazer's mind was strewn beneath

Her feet like embers, and she, thought by thought,

'Trampled its fires into the dust of death,

As Day upon the threshold of the east

Treads out the lamps of night [...].[17]

The 'shape all light' works its depredations in a particularly insidious way, entrancing the spectator—worshipper, rather—with a musical motion that erases thought as it goes, emptying memory and so negating history, until 'All that was seemed as if it had been not.' This process of obliteration is likened to an oddly authoritarian sunrise.

The Triumph of Life epitomizes the challenge to agency and cognition in repeated figures of temporal discrepancy. These are instances of what we might call 'non-synchronous temporality', occasions on which two things that should run parallel have become out of sync, that is to say, they have progressed asymmetrically. We saw an example in the fate of the 'Wise, the great, the unforgotten' overtaken in the daytime by 'deep night.' But even progressions that are natural and gradual in nature, such as sunrise—as above—and sunset are represented as violent and untimely usurpations. One kind of time is in the vanguard and another, usually where the human principle is located, has fallen behind it, becoming anachronistic—'backward in time', etymologically, or according to the dictionary definition, 'belonging or appropriate to a

---

17 *Shelley's Poetry and Prose*, p. 495, lines 382–88.

period other than that in which it exists'.[18] The Chariot that outspeeds its followers, leaving them 'farther behind and deeper in the shade', is the chief of these figures, and we have noted others. The Coleridgean theme of death-in-life—survival beyond one's powers or emotional capacity— is common, along with varied images of anachronistic 'lingering', including that of the 'shape all light', which lingers into noon, 'More dimly than a day appearing dream,/The ghost of a forgotten form of sleep'.[19] There is a general failure of temporal economy, economy of the sort implied in the concept of linear time, which underlies ideas of development and maturation, as well as the model of loss and gain, in which one thing arises after the other in a proper order.[20] Shelley's virtuoso treatment of the terza rima form contributes to the effect of momentum and danger, as he splays long sinuous sentences, sustained by dramatic subordinate clauses, across the tercets that drive forward in anticipation of the next interlocking rhyme. The reader finds it hard to keep up with the sense, especially given the pull of the extraordinary music. So skilled and incisive is the verse that we need not actually lose the sense, but the experience of reading the poem is nonetheless likely to be vertiginous.

---

18 *Oxford Pocket Dictionary of Current English,* https://www.encyclopedia.com/literature-and-arts/language-linguistics-and-literary-terms/language-and-linguistics/anachronism
19 *Shelley's Poetry and Prose,* p. 496, lines 427–28.
20 In 'Shelley Disfigured', Paul de Man, who uncovers major elements of this pattern, reads it as an allegory of the destructive effects of figuration, or 'the madness of words', on human cognition. The interpretation offered here is a more traditional thematic one—it is time that works the erosion—though this interpretation is not inconsistent with de Man's view of 'history.' Paul de Man, 'Shelley Disfigured', in *Deconstruction and Criticism* (New York: Continuum, 1979), p. 68. For important reconsiderations of the poem in light of de Man's essay, see (in chronological order), Jerrold Hogle, *Shelley's Process: Radical Transference and the Development of His Major Works* (Oxford: Oxford University Press, 1988); Tilottama Rajan, *The Supplement of Reading: Figures of Understanding in Romantic Theory and Practice* (Cornell: Cornell University Press, 1990), https://doi.org/10.7591/9781501723148; Orrin N. C. Wang, 'Disfiguring Monuments: History in Paul de Man's *Shelley Disfigured* and Percy Bysshe Shelley's *The Triumph of Life*', ELH, vol. 58, 1991,. 633–55, https://doi.org/10.2307/2873459; and Amanda Jo Goldstein, *Sweet Science: Romantic Materialism and the New Logics of Life* (Chicago: University of Chicago Press, 2017), https://doi.org/10.7208/chicago/9780226458588.001.0001. For the very latest, see the issue of *Romantic Circles* devoted to essays on *The Triumph of Life*: 'The Futures of Shelley's Triumph,' ed. by Joel Faflak, *Romantic Circles* Praxis Series, October 2019, https://romantic-circles.org/praxis/triumph.

If Shelley's characteristic figures of temporality involve the swift and overwhelming, Beckett's seem to involve the opposite: a fugal retardation. In the Beckett works that focus on the experience of temporality—*Waiting for Godot*, *Happy Days* and *Krapp's Last Tape*—the characters suffer from tedium and impatience. They feel they have all too much time on their hands. Vladimir and Estragon in *Waiting for Godot* provide the classic example. Impatiently, they 'idle.' They can only 'pass the time' until it finally brings forth whatever it is that, they assume, it is heading toward, though they are haunted, too, by the possibility that time is empty and headed nowhere. Unlike Shelley's 'captives,' they wait for time to catch up with them, rather than the reverse. Yet these works share a number of themes and figurative patterns with Shelley's. *Waiting for Godot* is riddled with temporal discrepancies which prove confusing not only to the audience, but to the characters themselves. Vladimir tries to find his footing in time (and presses Estragon to do so)—unsuccessfully: what do I remember? are my memories accurate? were we here yesterday? how many years have we been together? These questions about temporality are naturally linked to questions of the identity of things, persons, oneself: have we seen Lucky and Pozzo before? Are these the same boots? Is this the same place? Is this the same boy who was here yesterday? Why doesn't he recognise me and confirm my identity? Am I the same person? Temporality is measured by returns, and *Waiting for Godot* courts vertigo by rendering the returns uncertain and/or temporally illogical. Even natural temporality is dislocated, as in *The Triumph of Life*. The tree seems to bloom precipitately, overnight. Pozzo's bizarre claim that night comes 'when you least expect it' is confirmed by the stage direction at the end of Act I: 'The light suddenly fails. In a moment it is night'.[21] This is Shelley's precipitate sunrise in reverse.

The theme of temporal disorientation and passivation by time reaches its climax at the end of Act II, when a devastated Pozzo and an increasingly anxious Vladimir express their disillusionment and weariness in the play's chief figure of temporal discrepancy: birth 'astride a grave'.[22] Pozzo was jauntily mindful of clock time in Act I,

---

21 Samuel Beckett, *Waiting for Godot: A Tragicomedy in Two Acts* (New York: Grove, 1970), pp. 25 and 34.
22 Ibid., pp. 57 and 58.

where he kept taking out his pocket watch and noting the hour, before losing his watch altogether. Now he bursts out:

> Have you not done tormenting me with your accursed time! It's abominable! When! When! One day, is that not enough for you, one day he went dumb, one day I went blind, one day we'll go deaf, one day we were born, one day we shall die, the same day, the same second, is that not enough for you? (Calmer.) They give birth astride of a grave, the light gleams an instant, then it's night once more.[23]

Vladimir echoes him in the last moments of the play, as he allows his despair to surface fully: 'Astride of a grave and a difficult birth. Down in the hole, lingeringly, the grave digger puts on the forceps. We have time to grow old. The air is full of our cries'.[24] The sentiment hearkens back to Hamlet's aphorism: 'A man's life's but to say "one".[25] In objective terms, a human life takes only an instant. But the more important point concerns subjective temporality: even to human beings, who may have found it 'lingeringly' tedious to go through, when it's past, a life snaps shut like a folding fan. This is the chief riddle of *Waiting for Godot*: how the 'waiting' (waiting like Chekhov's characters, for life to begin) seems long and weary in experience, but dream-like and insubstantial in retrospect. As the Kafka parable goes, 'My grandfather used to say: "Life is astoundingly short. To me, looking back over it, life seems so foreshortened that I scarcely understand, for instance, how a young man can decide to ride over to the next village without being afraid that—not to mention accidents—even the span of a normal happy life may fall far short of the time needed for such a journey"'.[26]

Vladimir's complaint against time is paired with his apprehension of loss in agency and knowledge. As he regards Estragon napping, he muses: 'At me too someone is looking, of me too someone is saying, He is sleeping, he knows nothing, let him sleep on'.[27] And of course it is true: we the audience are gazing on him as on a benighted naïf, as someone above might presumably gaze on us. Everyone is asleep in

---

23 Ibid., p. 57.
24 Ibid., p. 58.
25 'Hamlet', Act V Scene, ii, l. 71, in *The Norton Shakespeare*.
26 Franz Kafka, 'The Next Village', in *The Basic Kafka*, ed. by Eric Heller (New York: Simon and Schuster, 1979), p. 148.
27 Beckett, *Waiting for Godot*, p. 58.

time. Everyone is blind in relation to it—as, to borrow W.S. Merwin's words from the poem 'Still Morning,' 'the flying birds know/nothing of the air they are flying through/or of the day that bears them up through themselves'—unable to rise above the medium of time so as to move through it, to 'grasp' it, as a higher being or transcendental audience might.[28] In Lucky's speech, human beings are waiting 'for time to tell', which assuredly it cannot do, being incapable of speech, why we live in it as we do, why 'man in brief in spite of the strides of alimentation and defecation wastes and pines wastes and pines' and 'in spite of the strides of physical culture the practice of sports' etc. 'fades away'.[29]

At the end of the speech I've quoted, Vladimir adds, 'But habit is a great deadener'.[30] Beckett might be thinking here of the lament in the Intimations Ode: 'custom shall lie upon thee with a weight/Heavy as frost, and deep almost as life.' Vladimir's generalization has two meanings: habit 'deadens' existential anxiety, and the awareness of mortality, but also—this is related—habit 'deadens' us to the passage of time. Hence we 'temporise,' or 'mark time', as if we had all the time in the world. The illusion, or contradiction, is captured in this riddling exchange:

Vladimir. Well, that passed the time.

Estragon. It would have passed anyway.[31]

There is our passing time and there is time passing of itself. We exert our agency, we 'pass time'—that is, distract ourselves when we're threatened with boredom, as we wait for time to bring forth what we're waiting for. But it is ticking away. From its point of view, nothing is different and it is elapsing in its usual regular, inexorable increments. The telos, the endpoint we project as the aim of our time, is no affair of time itself.

The framework of the telos—of anticipating a goal—disappears altogether in *Happy Days*. The play could be said to strip down the mise-en-scene of *Waiting for Godot*, subjecting its temporal insights to a more radical treatment. The natural cycles of time no longer occur—there is steady light with no sunrise, no sunset. When Winnie refers to 'days'

---

28 W.S. Merwin, *The Collected Poems: 1996–2011*, ed. by J.D. McClatchy (New York: Library of America, 2013), p. 544.
29 Beckett, *Waiting for Godot*, p. 29.
30 Ibid., p. 58.
31 Ibid., p. 31.

or 'nights', she catches herself and, sighing nostalgically, admits she is speaking in 'the old style'.[32] She has no means of keeping time during the 'day'—no timepiece or natural measures—and therefore doesn't know where she is in the new artificial day, that is, the interval between the bell that summons her to awake and the bell that directs her to sleep. The living of life to some larger and long-term purpose seems to be over. She does not and cannot pursue any such goal, but she does have an aim, the immediate end of 'passing the time'—and perhaps provoking Willie to speak. She imposes various routines upon herself to structure the 'day'—grooming, mainly—but her chief pastime is talking.

And yet in the midst of this emptiness, something is happening: the mound of sand—plainly enough 'the sands of time'—which buries her up to her waist in Act I, rises all the way up to her neck in Act II. Now she is paralyzed and can no longer perform any diverting physical rituals, though she exults in being able to cross her eyes and sight the tip of her nose. Ever-sunny, ever seeking a balm for her terror, she affirms the little things that make these 'happy days'. But her underlying panic becomes harder to subdue and she finally expresses it, though under the camouflage of telling a story, in an insistent scream. For she has been chattering not simply to pass the time—to amuse herself, idly—but to subdue a gnawing anxiety about time. She gives herself odd instructions not to put up the umbrella 'too soon,' and not to sing 'too soon' and not to 'squander all [her] words for the day', as if there were some limit on these activities, in her empty stretch between the bells.[33]

This is one of the modes of temporal discrepancy in *Happy Days*: Winnie's fear of surviving into a time that somehow hangs in its full weight upon consciousness, and cannot *be passed*, her fear, as she puts it 'so great, certain days, of finding oneself...left, with hours still to run, before the bell for sleep, and nothing more to say, nothing more to do.'[34] She speaks of this prospect as the dread moment 'when words must fail', and the mind enter the great silence in which self-consciousness confronts its subordination to time.[35] Winnie is terrified that Willie will

---

32 Samuel Beckett, *Happy Days* (New York: Grove, 1961), p. 22 *et passim*.
33 Ibid., pp. 31 and 41.
34 Ibid., p. 35.
35 Ibid., p. 32.

'go off'—abandon her or die and then she will have no audience.[36] As it is, she says, she is able to reassure herself, 'Something of this is being heard, I am not merely talking to myself, that is in the wilderness, a thing I could never bear to do'.[37] Warding off the psychological peril, Estragon assures Vladimir, 'We always find something, don't we, Didi, to give us the impression we exist?'[38] Like Vladimir, Winnie needs to be recognised, to be heard, by another person in order to confirm her own existence and identity. The silence in which only the passage of time can be heard has the opposite effect, causing the self to question its own substantiality.

It does so, in large part, because of the passage of time, or rather the transmutation and ellipsis of itself in time: its changes, losses and lapses of memory. This process and its consequences are distilled in *Krapp's Last Tape* (1958). Recorded diaries of earlier years force Krapp to recognise the yawning distance between his present and his past selves: 'Hard to believe I was ever that young whelp,' he marvels.[39] The distance enables him to perceive now that he was pompously self-deluded and that he cast love away. Yet, though he mocks it in himself, he feels a secret nostalgia for his youth, with its 'aspirations' and its 'resolutions'[40]: 'Be again, be again...(*Pause.*) All that old misery. (*Pause.*) Once wasn't enough for you.'[41] Time passes differently in the life of an old man: 'What's a year now? The sour cud and the iron stool.'[42] Not only is his sphere of action contracted, but Krapp senses he has been internally residualised: there is very little left of him in his own consciousness – wit, a vital memory, an emotion or two. The spare setting—a table with a light above it, surrounded by darkness—figures this contraction for us. Krapp himself sees it as, paradoxically, an elaboration of his constricting solitude: 'With all this darkness round me I feel less alone. (*Pause.*). In a way. (*Pause.*) I love to get up and move about in it, then back here to... (hesitates)...me.'[43] The hesitation is telling: what is this 'me' he is left with now?

---

36 Ibid., p. 37.
37 Ibid., p. 21.
38 Beckett, *Waiting for Godot*, p. 45.
39 Samuel Beckett, *Collected Shorter Plays* (New York: Grove, 1984), p. 58.
40 Ibid., p. 58.
41 Ibid., p. 63.
42 Ibid., p. 62.
43 Ibid., p. 57.

Like Krapp, Winnie is haunted by signal memories of love, by which she measures the distance between then and now, but she reflects more deliberately on the philosophical problems posed by temporality. One of the chief problems she confronts is how to explain the changes occurring in her seemingly changeless world. Even her possessions, when damaged, are magically replaced. Her parasol explodes into flames, but, Winnie comments, 'Yes, something seems to have occurred, something has seemed to occur, and nothing has occurred, nothing at all…The sunshade will be there again tomorrow, beside me on this mount, to help me through the day'.[44] This assumption is confirmed by the stage directions at the opening of Act II, which stipulate 'Bag and parasol as before.'[45] Winnie takes this persistence of objects as a cause for despair. She comes close to tears in praising it: 'No, one can do nothing. (*Pause.*) That is what I find so wonderful, the way things…(*voice breaks, head down*)…things…so wonderful.'[46]

She experiences frustration with the supernatural identity of objects in her world because she contrasts their indestructability with her own steady deterioration. As the heap of sand rises, as time advances, it diminishes her. Though there are no clocks in her world, the mound of sand makes a living hourglass of her. She cheerfully protests, on occasion, when she is examining her body 'no better, no worse—no change,'[47] but she clearly recognises losses in herself—including her loss of mobility—and she dreads further losses, internal failures of memory and reason: 'I have not lost my reason. (*Pause.*) Not yet. (*Pause.*) Not all. (*Pause.*) Some remains. (*Pause.*) Like little…sunderings, little falls… apart.'[48] In fact, she notes even the perfect mind cannot be trusted to retain the memory, and consequently, the history, of past experience, and to forget it is to expunge it: 'should one day the earth cover my breasts then I shall never have seen my breasts.'[49] As Augustine pointed out, only the present is real, and a memory of the past is only real in the present. If the memory is faulty or is lost, then it is as if what has been had never been, or in Shelley's words, 'All that was seem[s] as if it had

---

44 Beckett, *Happy Days*, p. 39.
45 Ibid., p. 49.
46 Ibid., p. 39.
47 Ibid., p. 9.
48 Ibid., p. 54.
49 Ibid., p. 38.

been not.' The mind as it moves through time is erasing life. When the parasol spontaneously combusts, Winnie remarks, 'I presume this has occurred before, though I cannot recall it.'[50]

The continuity of the self is at stake. The sadder Winnie of Act II observes the challenge that time poses to identity, again *contra* Locke, juxtaposing memory and present consciousness in such a way as to promote a sense not of continuity but its reverse, disjunction: 'Then... now...what difficulties here for the mind. (*Pause.*) To have been always what I am—and so changed from what I was. (*Pause.*) I am the one, I say the one, then the other. (*Pause.*). Now the one, then the other.'[51] (Her sense of alteration becomes so vertiginous that (comically) she thinks 'gravity' and other 'natural laws' are 'not what they were when I was young... and foolish.'[52] She goes farther than Krapp by remarking not only on the great gap between selves, but on the treacherous pace of internal change. The change that seems sudden now has taken place incrementally, and so one failed to perceive it happening. Winnie catches herself having been prey to the illusion: 'I used to say there was no difference between one fraction of a second and the next...I say I used to say, Winnie, you are changeless, there is never any difference between one fraction of a second and the next.'[53] Behind these lines lies an allusion to the sorites paradox, the philosophical problem of the heap: if sand is added to sand one grain at a time, at what point does the group of sands become a heap? When does the qualitative change take place? Not between one grain and the next. The play's mise-en-scene, the enveloping mound, figures not merely the sands of time and their encroachment, but more particularly, the mutation time effects in us, the invisible and stealthy replacement of the self. It is the paradoxical nature of time that it seems to dally while it is, unbeknownst to us, changing us against our will. It paralyses Winnie under a mound of sand, as it had made a grotesque of Rousseau, inwardly 'corrupted' and outwardly reduced to the semblance of an 'old root'. The perception of change brings with it the perception of passivity, and that is what is most destructive.

---

50 Ibid., p. 37.
51 Ibid., p. 51.
52 Ibid., p. 34.
53 Ibid., p. 60.

Winnie tries to keep her spirits up, with an occasional lapse or near-lapse into sob and scream. But her complaint against time—her protest and her lament—escapes in her literary allusions. She is reluctant to say it in her own words, and she only allows it to surface in half-remembered quotations, even if she does say, 'That's what I find so wonderful, a part remains, of one's classics, to help one through the day'.[54] Her allusions serve simultaneously to reveal and distract. Her canon is broadly Romantic (if we include precursors and successors): Shakespeare, Milton, Gray, Keats, Browning, Yeats, and so forth. She brokenly refers to 'Flowers…that smile today'[55], an allusion to Herrick's 'To the Virgins to Make Much of Time':

> Gather ye Rose-buds while ye may.
>
> Old Tyme is still a flying,
>
> and this same flower, that smiles today,
>
> to Morrow will be dying.[56]
>
> (2013: 171)

This allusion to Herrick takes in another to a poem which itself alludes to Herrick: the poem by Shelley that is sometimes entitled 'Mutability':

> The flower that smiles to-day
>
>   To-morrow dies;
>
> All that we wish to stay
>
>   Tempts and then flies.
>
> What is this world's delight?
>
> Lightning that mocks the night[57]

---

54 Ibid., p. 58.
55 Ibid., p. 61.
56 Robert Herrick, *The Complete Poetry of Robert Herrick*, ed. by Tom Cain and Ruth Connolly, 2 vols. (New York: Oxford University Press, 2013), p 171, ll. 1–4, https://doi.org/10.1093/actrade/9780199212842.book.1, https://doi.org/10.1093/actrade/9780199212842.book.2
57 Percy Shelley, *The Major Works*, ed. by Zachary Leader and Michael O'Neill (New York: Oxford University Press, 2003), p. 589, ll. 1–6.

Shelley radically alters the rhetorical frame, converting Herrick's seductive call to action into stark lament. He changes the purchase of the metaphor: the brief life of the flower now serves to illustrate a different point—not that all lives are short and one must seize the day, as in Herrick, but that life 'mocks' us with apparitions of value ('all that we wish to stay') it dangles before us and then dissolves. This is the malice we recognise from *The Triumph of Life*. It portends that, like Shelley's moon or his Rousseau, one may conclude with 'a joyless eye/That finds no object worth its constancy.' Winnie's allusion is clearly much closer in spirit to Shelley's revision of Herrick than to the original, and the allusion, as often, is her form of homage. Neither Winnie's *nor* Beckett's attitude toward the poem dismisses it as 'romantic cliché'. It is fixed in Winnie's mind because it says what she feels.

Satisfying as it may be to end where I began, with Beckett quoting Shelley, I hasten to add that I am not making a genealogical argument. It was not necessary for Beckett to have read Shelley for him to have thought about or represented temporality in the way that he does. The similarity might easily be attributed to their shared background in Cartesian and post-Cartesian psychology. I wish to draw a parallel, and more importantly, to demonstrate the sympathy between bodies of work conventionally held to be antithetical. In *The Triumph of Life*, Shelley was no more sanguine about human agency and identity than Beckett the iconic postmodernist, for the so-called 'Romantic ideology' only came to be by means of undoing itself.

Works Cited

Ackerley, C.J. and S.E. Gontarski, eds, *The Grove Companion to Samuel Beckett: A Reader's Guide to His Works, Life and Thought* (New York: Grove, 2004).

Bate, Walter Jackson, ed., *Samuel Johnson: Essays from the Rambler, Adventurer and Idler* (New Haven: Yale University Press, 1968).

Beckett, Samuel, *Collected Shorter Plays* (New York: Grove, 1984).

——, *Happy Days* (New York: Grove, 1961).

——, *Waiting for Godot: A Tragicomedy in Two Acts* (New York: Grove, 1970).

Bloom, Harold, 'Shelley and His Precursors', in *Poetry and Repression* (New Haven: Yale University Press, 1976), pp. 83–111.

Caselli, Daniela, *Beckett's Dantes: Intertextuality in the Fiction and Criticism*. 2nd ed. (Manchester: Manchester University Press, 2013), https://doi.org/10.7228/manchester/9780719071560.001.0001

Coleridge, Samuel Taylor, *Coleridge's Poetry and Prose*, ed. by Nicholas Halmi, Paul Magnuson and Raimonda Modiano (New York: Norton, 2004).

de Man, Paul, 'Shelley Disfigured', in *The Rhetoric of Romanticism* (New York: Columbia University Press, 1984), pp. 93–124.

Falflak, Joel, ed., 'The Futures of Shelley's *Triumph*,' Romantic Circles Praxis Series, October 2019, https://romantic-circles.org/praxis/triumph

Herrick, Robert, *The Complete Poetry of Robert Herrick*, ed. by Tom Cain and Ruth Connolly, 2 vols. (New York: Oxford University Press, 2013).

Hogle, Jerrold, *Shelley's Process: Radical Transference and the Development of His Major Works* (Oxford: Oxford University Press, 1988).

Goldstein, Amanda Jo, *Sweet Science: Romantic Materialism and the New Logics of Life* (Chicago: University of Chicago Press, 2017), https://doi.org/10.7208/chicago/9780226458588.001.0001

Kafka, Franz, 'The Next Village', in *The Basic Kafka*, ed. by Eric Heller (New York: Simon and Schuster, 1979).

Keach, William, *Shelley's Style* (New York: Methuen, 1984).

Merwin, W.S., *The Collected Poems: 1996–2011*, ed. by J.D. McClatchy (New York: Library of America, 2013).

O'Connell, Anita, 'Dante's Linguistic Detail in Shelley's Triumph of Life', *CLCWeb: Comparative Literature and Culture* 13.4 (2011), https://doi.org/10.7771/1481-4374.1683

Rajan, Tilottama, *The Supplement of Reading: Figures of Understanding in Romantic Theory and Practice* (Cornell: Cornell University Press, 1990).

Shakespeare, William, *The Norton Shakespeare*, ed. by Stephen Greenblatt (New York: Norton, 2008).

Shelley, Percy, *The Major Works*, ed. by Zachary Leader and Michael O'Neill (New York: Oxford University Press, 2003).

——, *Shelley's Poetry and Prose*, ed. by Donald H. Reiman and Neil Fraistat, 2nd ed. (New York: Norton, 2002).

Vassalo, Peter, 'From Petrarch to Dante: The Discourse of Disenchantment in Shelley's The Triumph of Life', *Journal of Anglo-Italian Studies* 1 (1991), 102–10.

Wang, Orrin N.C., 'Disfiguring Monuments: History in Paul de Man's Shelley Disfigured and Percy Bysshe Shelley's The Triumph of Life,' *ELH*, vol. 58, 1991, 633–55, https://doi.org/10.2307/2873459

Wordsworth, William, *Wordsworth's Poetry and Prose*, ed. by Nicholas Halmi (New York: Norton, 2014).

10. 'Thy Wreck a Glory': Venice, Subjectivity, and Temporality in Byron and Shelley and the Post-Romantic Imagination

Mark Sandy

> For the Romantic and Post-Romantic imagination, Venice as both historical place and a-temporal myth, the realised and unrealisable city, is central to a poetics of temporality and selfhood in Byron and Shelley. It is the real and unreal city that commingles its solid architectural structures with watery insubstantiality, myth with history, personal memory with historical monument, and poetic artistry with the writing of history. Byron's poetic reflections on a former self and 'Venice, lost and won' (Childe Harold, IV). Shelley qualifies any Byronic optimistic sense of spiritual or cultural restoration with an abiding infernally nightmarish vision of a corrupted, and corrupting, but not quite fallen Venice. Historically Byron and Shelley acknowledge that Venice is lost, but her presence persists in their a-temporal poetic re-imaginings of her former glory. Venice's self-preserving and self-destructive myth holds an abiding fascination for the Romantic imagination and it poetics of subjectivity: a city at once darkly illuminative that exists as a utopian ideal and a corrupt reality, as a regal yet usurped power, existing within and outside of history. An impossible architectural city of imaginative possibilities that for Byron and Shelley, as well as Nietzsche and Calvino after them, is a perpetually charmed spot and broken spell.

Venice's self-preserving and self-destructive myth holds an abiding fascination for the Romantic and Post-Romantic imagination; a city of shadowy brilliance that exists, within and outside the temporal and historical, as a substantial and insubstantial form created mysteriously from the Adriatic's ebb and flow. An impossible architectural city of imaginative possibilities that, for many writers and artists, is a perpetual enchantment and forgotten incantation. The twentieth-century lyric mastery of Italo Calvino captures the ever-shifting, multifarious nature of the city with his descriptions of multiple fantastical cities, each with their own intrigues, desires, and peculiar spatiality, which are ultimately refractions of a single city: Venice.[1] One of these many cities of Calvino's *Invisible Cities*, Moriana, crystallises the author's sense of Venice's multiplicity as 'From one part to the other, the city seems to continue, in perspective, multiplying its repertory of images'. Yet, in reality, the city 'has no thickness, it consists only of a face and an obverse, like a sheet of paper, with a figure on either side, which can neither be separated nor look at each other'. Like Venice herself, Calvino portrays Moriana as a beguiling and treacherous city of intricate entanglements of light and darkness, of depth and shallowness, of beauty and ugliness, comprised of 'alabaster gates transparent in sunlight' and 'blind walls with fading signs'.[2] For Calvino and others before him, Venice is the endlessly imagined city and the endless city of imagination.

Nietzsche and Venice: Romantic Poetic Legacies and the Art of Aphorism

Friedrich Nietzsche, an inhabitant of the city for a while, equally found a fascination with the phantasmagoria that is Venice. Three years before his move to the Castello quarter of Venice in the spring of 1880, Nietzsche had been an avid reader of a translated volume of Percy Bysshe Shelley's poetry.[3] On his arrival in Venice, Nietzsche requested a trunk of urgently

---

1 Malgorzata Myk, 'The Immortal Waters of Venice: Women as Anodyne in Italo Calvino's *Invisible Cities*', *The Explicator*, 67.3 (2009), 221–24 (p. 221), https://doi.org/10.3200/expl.67.3.221–224
2 Italo Calvino, *Invisible Cities*, trans. by William Weaver (London: Vintage, 1997), p. 95.
3 Nietzsche writes in a letter, dated 28 August 1877, that 'Very recently I spent a veritable day of consecration reading *Prometheus Unbound*. If the poet is not a real genius, I do not know what a genius is...' See *Selected Letters of Friedrich Nietzsche*, trans. by Christopher Middleton (Cambridge: Hackett, 1996), p. 164.

required books, including a hefty volume concerned with Lord Byron.[4] This hasty biographical sketch provides a sense of the extent that the posthumous reception of Byron and Shelley has been influential on what we now think of as Nietzsche's aphoristic poetic style.[5]

James Luchte, the editor of *The Peacock and the Buffalo: The Poetry of Nietzsche* (2010), rightly comments that: 'Nietzsche's practise of writing and composition in itself challenges our strict classifications of poetry, aphorism and prose'.[6] This ability of the aphoristic style to cross over traditional genre boundaries is in keeping with the transgressive form of the lyric from which the aphorism often derives its distilled lyrical conciseness. The impossible possibility of Venice as an imaginary, magical, mythical, and actual city of political ideals and intrigue resonates with those tensions found within the evanescence of the aphoristic style. Venice in her fallen state is an expressive symbol of, and shorthand for, the transgressive nature of the aphoristic style, which gestures towards some larger whole that once was or is ever about to be.

Inspired by Nietzsche's sojourn in Venice, one example of this transgression of the policed borders of poetry, aphorism, and prose, is 'I stand on the bridge'. Nietzsche incorporated this Apollonian-Dionysian moment of poetic reverie into his quasi-autobiography, *Ecce Homo* (1888), as an enigmatic near-aphoristic conclusion to Section Seven. Nietzsche does so by introducing these lines as a means of gesturing towards the tragic joy of not knowing, as he writes in the prose section, 'how to distinguish between tears and music'.[7] The aphoristic poem reads as follows:

> I stood recently upon a bridge in the brown night.

---

[4] The precise title or nature of the volume is unknown. See Curtis Cate, *Friedrich Nietzsche: A Biography* (London: Pimlico, 2003), p. 298.

[5] The following account of Nietzsche's aphoristic style and Venice can be found in my '"A Ruin amidst Ruins": Modernity, Literary Aphorisms, and Romantic Fragments', in *Aphoristic Modernity: 1880 to the Present*, ed. by Kostas Boyiopoulos and Michael Shallcross (Leiden: Brill, 2019), pp. 41–47, https://doi.org/10.1163/9789004400061_004 Reprinted here with the kind permission of the editors.

[6] Friedrich Nietzsche, *The Peacock and the Buffalo: The Poetry of Friedrich Nietzsche*, trans. and ed. by James Luchte (London: Continuum, 2010), p. 30.

[7] Friedrich Nietzsche, *Ecce Homo: How One Becomes What One Is*, trans. and ed. by R.J. Hollingdale (Harmondsworth: Penguin, 1988), [7], p. 62. Subsequent quotations parenthetically given as section number and page number.

From afar came a song;

Golden drops swell

Over the trembling surface.

Gondolas, light, music –

Drunkenly swim into the dawn...

My soul, a stringed game,

Sings to itself, plucks invisibly,

A homely gondola song,

Trembles with colourful happiness.

—Was anyone listening? ([7], p.127)

Here, Nietzsche asks both of the music of the gondolier and his own poetry, 'Was anyone listening?' ('I stand on a bridge') ['Hörte jemand ihr zu?' ('An der Brücke stand')]. His poetry simultaneously gestures towards a potentially contained meaning and a world beyond, as its empty song vaporises meaninglessly into the 'brown night' that the poem conjures into being.

This evanescent sense of the power of language and poetry, for Nietzsche, is anticipated by Shelley's notion that poetic 'words/Are as the air'.[8] For Shelley, the strength of poetic language resides in its weakness, its resilience through its own fragile imaginings, which evaporate as vitally and intangibly 'as the air' we breathe. Words, like the shimmering insubstantial presence of Venice and the city's captivatingly fleeting music, observed by Nietzsche, are as 'Golden drops [which] swell/ Over the trembling surface' ('I stand on the bridge') ['goldener Tropfen quoll's/über die zitternde Fläche weg' ('An der Brücke stand')] of the

---

8   Percy Bysshe Shelley, 'Prometheus Unbound', in *Shelley's Poetry and Prose*, ed. by Donald H. Reiman and Neil Fraistat (New York: Norton, 2002), II, i, l. 109, p. 237. Subsequent quotations from this edition. For a detailed discussion of the poetry of Nietzsche and of Shelley see my '"The Last Great Romantic": Nietzsche's Romanticism Out of the Spirit of Decadence', in *Decadent Romanticism 1780–1914*, ed. by Kostas Boyiopoulos and Mark Sandy (Farnham: Ashgate, 2015), pp. 131–44, https://doi.org/10.4324/9781315576077-10

lagoon. In Nietzsche's 'I stand on the bridge', the outwardly observed unreality of Venice melts into the radical subjectivity of the observer's inward 'soul' ['Seele'] that—recalling the 'gondola song' ['Gondellied dazu']—'Sings to itself' ['sang sich'] in a self-enclosed twilit reverie.

Venice, for Nietzsche, becomes a synonym of—and aphoristic shorthand for—both 'music' and a form of 'happiness' touched by 'a shudder of faintheartedness' ([7], p. 64). By recalling Shelley's own sense that 'words/Are as the air', Nietzsche's 'stringed instrument [Saitenspiel]' of the soul is 'plucked invisibly' and perceptibly by an imagined musician's fingers. Consequently, the soul's internal serenade finds an external correspondent in the gondolier's song, which 'Trembles with colourful happiness' ['zitternd vor bunter Seligkeit'], as outer and inner states blur indeterminately in the Venetian twilight. In 'I stand on the bridge' Nietzsche's sense of, and sensitivity to, sound and colour (and re-colouring) traces a temporal and spatial movement from 'brown night' ['brauner Nacht'] to 'dawn' ['Dämrung hinaus'] but, more importantly, the poem shows the contingent relations between the invisible and visible worlds; between those inward and outward modes of being that impinge upon the world and a world that impinges upon those modes of being. Aphoristic poem and world are not only fashioned out of, but constituted from, their trembling 'colourful' shifts in shade, tone, and feeling that act as a broker between subjective and objective worlds.

Byron, Shelley, Twilight, and Temporality

Byron and Shelley were attracted to the unique quality of light afforded by Venetian twilights and found in them, to varying degrees, an imaginative source of potential transformation at the level of both subjectivity and temporality.[9] Byron re-imagines William Wordsworth's semi-spiritual autobiography of a fall of selfhood from 'celestial light'

---

9   For the significance of twilight to the Romantic imagination see Christopher R. Miller, *The Invention of Evening: Perception and Time in Romantic Poetry* (Cambridge: Cambridge University Press, 2006), https://doi.org/10.1017/cbo9780511720031. For more general reflections on the cultural importance of twilight see Peter Davison, *The Last of the Light: About Twilight* (London: Reakton, 2015).

into the 'light of common day'[10] as the historical decline of political ideals and a fall of nationhood. Canto IV of *Childe Harold's Pilgrimage* meditates on the fortunes and misfortunes of the 'lords of earth and sea'[11] (xxv. 225) of Rome and Venice in particular and, more generally, on the rise and fall of Italian history and culture:

> The commonwealth of kings, the men of Rome!
>
> And even since, and now, fair Italy!
>
> Thou art the garden of the world, the home
>
> Of all Art yields, and Nature can decree;
>
> Even in thy desert, what is like to thee?
>
> Thy very weeds are beautiful, thy waste
>
> More rich than other climes' fertility;
>
> Thy wreck a glory, and thy ruin graced
>
> With an immaculate charm which can not be defaced. (IV. xxvi. 226–34)

Recalling mankind's fall in Eden, Byron finds in Roman and Venetian decline an oxymoronic 'ruined grace' and remnants of a 'glory' in the 'wreck' of this civilisation. That the light of such residual 'glory' still haunts the 'immaculate charm' of present-day Italy captures something of the state, in the 'Ode: Intimations of Immortality', of being 'Not in entire forgetfulness' (62) of former better days, as well as the sense that Italy, as a fallen nation, like the Wordsworthian self dispossessed of heaven, is capable of 'trailing clouds of glory' (64).

Unlike Byron, whose poetic eye turns to an open expanse of 'azure air' (*CH*. IV, 27, 243), Shelley has an eye for the infernal and pestilent quality of Venetian light. Poetically recasting his meeting with Byron and first visit to Venice in August 1818, Shelley's *Julian and Maddalo*,

---

10 William Wordsworth, 'Ode: Intimations of Immortality', in *William Wordsworth: The Major Works*, ed. by Stephen Gill (Oxford: Oxford University Press, 2000), l. 2, l. 76. Subsequent quotations from this edition.

11 George Gordon Byron, 'Childe Harold's Pilgrimage', in *Lord Byron: The Major Works*, ed. and intro. by Jerome J. McGann (Oxford: Oxford University Press, 2000), IV, xxv, l. 225. Unless otherwise stated subsequent quotations are from this edition. Hereafter referred to as *CH*.

written in the same year, portrays a vision of Venice that encompasses these contradictory imaginings about the city and adumbrates the poem's preoccupation with opposed states of mind. Recalling the resplendent myth of Venice and its darker counterpart, the conflicting perspectives on reality, extolled by Julian (reminiscent of Shelley) and Maddalo (modelled after Byron), speak respectively of utopian dream and dystopian reality.

In Shelley's *Julian and Maddalo*, the drawing in of evening suggests a temporal transition as well as shifting perspectives, themes and tones. With the close of day, the reflective musings of Julian and Maddalo readily give themselves over to a more 'serious' and 'darker side' as dusk turns to night. Hinted at in the suggestive detail of Maddalo's 'gay smile [that] had faded in his eye' (119), sources of delight can so easily transmute into darker horrors just as the Maniac attests even 'Love sometimes leads astray to misery' (349).[12]

Before the cool summer evening is entirely extinguished by the darkness of night, Julian and Maddalo, by way of gondola, glimpse the city of Venice itself momentarily enflamed by the setting sun, as 'if the Earth and Sea had been/Dissolved into one lake of fire' (80–81):

–So, o'er the lagune

We glided, and from that funereal bark

I leaned, and saw the city, and could mark

How from their many isles in evening's gleam

Its temples and its palaces did seem

Like fabrics of enchantment piled to Heaven. (88–92)

---

12 For further discussion of the poetic response of Byron and Shelley see my 'Reimagining Venice and Visions of Decay in Wordsworth, the Shelleys, and Thomas Mann', in *Venice and the Cultural Imagination*, ed. by Michael O'Neill, Mark Sandy and Sarah Wootton (London: Pickering & Chatto, 2012), pp. 27–42, https://doi.org/10.4324/9781315655611. This section reprinted with the kind permission of the editors. The following discussion on the effects of light in the poetry of Byron and Shelley appears in my '"Lines of Light": Reading Poetic Variations of Light in Wordsworth, Byron, and Shelley', *Romanticism* 22.3 (2016), special Issue on 'Light' ed. by Sarah Wootton, 260–68, https://doi.org/10.3366/rom.2016.0287. Reprinted with kind permission of the editor.

Transfigured through, and by, the 'rich emblazonry' (70) and 'wondrous hue' (73) of the setting sun, light and shade commingle, culminating in Venice's 'many isles' caught in the magnificent darkling illumination of 'evening's gleam' which, through the reflection and refraction of light, renders the city's manmade structures indistinguishable from the natural elements of sea, earth, fire, and sky. With a Turneresque eye, Shelley's coalescence of Venice's architectural forms ('fabrics') with the elemental collapses any distinction between land and ocean with those 'mountains towering as from waves of flame' (82) and the transformation of the sky and sea into a single, dissolving, fiery mirror of one another. The effect of Shelley's lines is not, as he desires in *Adonais*, to have 'flame transformed to marble' (447) but here the image is reversed to transform marble into flame.

Shelley achieves a comparable effect in *Lines Written Among the Euganean Hills*, when he describes how Venice's skyline at sunrise is 'As within a furnace bright,/A column, tower, and dome, and spire/Shine like obelisks of fire' (105–8). In spite of the visual conflagration of fire and light in *Julian and Maddalo*, what is most strikingly and ominously thrown into contrast, for the reader—like the 'black relief' (106) of the madhouse's 'belfry tower' (107); possibly marking the 'windowless, deformed, and dreary pile' (101) on the isle of San Servolo, which intrudes on the view of the sinking sun—is the doubly dark (both thrown into shadow and painted black) of the 'funereal bark' of the gondola. Transfiguring, enchanting, Apollonian light turns into a Dionysian dark reality just as the transformative 'inmost purple spirit of light' (84) is replaced by the lurid opaqueness of a 'purple sea', and the triumphant, emblazoned, architectural splendour of Venice with nightfall becomes cowering 'churches, ships, and palaces.../Huddled in gloom' (136–37). Elsewhere purple, for Shelley, as in *Lines Written Among the Euganean Hills* or *Epipsychidion*, denotes a peculiar, perceptible, difference in the quality of Venetian and Mediterranean evening light.[13] In *Julian and Maddalo*, celestial 'orange hues of heaven' (138) are consumed by the ghastly 'purple sea' and the fiery splendour of a Venetian sunset (which had fused together both natural and fabricated materials) transmutes into an infernal nightmarish 'strange vision' (128).

---

13 For an insightful discussion of evening as a structural principle in *Lines Written Among the Euganean Hills* see Miller, *The Invention of Evening*, pp. 120–29.

Shelley's eye, like Byron's own, is also drawn to the spectacular 'magical variety diffuse' of the shifting colours of Italianate light, which melts from azure day to 'purple night' ('Lines written in the Bay of Lerici', 12). In 'Lines written in the Bay of Lerici', Shelley holds out imaginatively, against mounting despair, for the remote paradisal prospect of 'some Elysian star' (42). The unfolding tragic celestial drama of this late lyric by Shelley recalls the cosmic drama set in motion by *Epipsychidion*. Abandoned by the 'One'—symbolising here Jane Williams—who could rival the moon as 'Bright wanderer' and 'fair coquette of Heaven' (1), the forlorn speaker of 'Lines written in the Bay of Lerici' is haunted by a series of visual and aural 'echoes' (20) of the one's absented presence.

This scene of a poet-speaker bereft by a once bright visionary female figure is typically Shelleyan and finds ready parallels within the psychodramas of *Epipsychidion* and *Alastor*. In *Epipsychidion*, Shelley both allegorises Emilia Viviani as Emily and spiritualises her materiality by depicting 'the brightness/Of her divinest presence [which] trembles through/Her limbs' to realise a coalescence of incorporeal spirit and physical embodiment. Anticipating the fled presence of the 'One fair' as the 'Bright wanderer' ('Bay of Lerici', 6, 1), Emily's 'divinest presence' is barely traceable 'Amid the splendour winged-stars' and the profundity of her protean form 'too deep/For the brief fathom-line of thought or sense' (*Epipsychidion*, 81, 89–90). Shelley's contradictory sense of Emily's ever-shifting presence as a 'motion which may change but cannot die' (*Epipsychidion*, 114) recollects an earlier account of the poet-figure's visionary 'bright silver dream' (67) and, subsequently, disturbing lost vision of the 'veiled maid' (50) in *Alastor*.

Habitually, 'bright' dreams or visionary presences, for Shelley, quickly give way to the antithesis of an unsettling shade or shadow. Both operating within and reimaging the poetic imagery of *Alastor*, Shelley compares the initial encounter, in *Epipsychidion*, with the elusive, ever-changing, diffuse, and ever-present Emily as an alluring yet potentially treacherous 'shadow of some golden dream' (116). As with the contradictory visionary 'fleeting shade' (206) of *Alastor*, Shelley's enticingly 'bright' visionary female figures remain forever elusive and refuse to be adequately defined in language or fixed in the present.[14]

Similarly, then, it is only by an act of hopeful imaginative projection, in 'Lines written in the Bay of Lerici', that Shelley's paradise of 'some Elysian star' might be regained in a future time. Such a future return to the possibility of a prelapsarian bliss may promise to reunite Shelley's questing poet-speaker with the lost visionary female form, but whether the psychic and imaginative schism that her absence inflicts can be fully healed remains uncertain. The metaphorical voyage towards the improbable 'Elysian star' both acts as a curative—for Shelley's mariner-like thoughts 'sailed for drink to medicine'—and a stinging reminder of the 'sweet and bitter pain' (43, 44) from which relief is sought.

If Shelley's 'Elysian star' serves as a beacon at all, in 'Lines written in the Bay of Lerici', it is one that might either light our way or turn out to be a perilously misleading will-o'-the-wisp. The treachery of this celestial light is implied through Shelley's closing image of those foolish 'fish who came/To worship the delusive flame' of 'the fisher with his lamp/And spear' (53–4; 51–2). Psychic or political utopian states cannot be so easily realised, for Shelley, as a guiding beacon can readily become a treacherous *ignis fatuus*; a bright vision transformed into its own tragic shadowy counterpart; a paradise equally regained as already lost.

When Shelley envisages, towards the close of *Epipsychidion*, a temporally and elementally fragile paradisal 'isle 'twixt Heaven, Air, Earth, and Sea' (456), his lines resonate with Byron's own imaginings of a recoverable utopia 'Buried in air, the deep blue sky of Rome' (*CH.* IV, 111, 991). To such an 'isle under Ionian skies' Shelley entreats Emily to elope even in the full knowledge that this promised utopia is as 'Beautiful as a wreck of Paradise' (422–3). Echoing Byron's sense of a fallen Italy as 'Thy wreck a glory' (*CH.* IV, 26, 233), Shelley's imagery appreciates the tragic and blissful beauty of this 'wreck of Paradise' along with the imaginative, as well as spiritual, possibilities that such a 'Paradise' might afford even as it recognises the inevitable tragedy that would ensue from reclaiming such a utopian isle. In Wordsworth's

---

14 See my 'Quest Poetry: *Alastor* and *Epipsychidion*', in *The Oxford Handbook of Percy Bysshe Shelley*, ed. by Michael O'Neill and Anthony Howe, with the assistance of Madeleine Callaghan (Oxford: Oxford University Press, 2013), pp. 272–88 (pp. 276–77).

terms, to reclaim 'Paradise' in a future moment is only ever to affirm that the 'visionary gleam' is 'fled' ('Ode: Intimations', 56) and a hoped-for Eden as the site of its own past spiritual ruin and wasteland.

Venice as Mindscape: Byron, Subjectivity, and Poetic Mobility

Byronic selfhood is no stranger to the wreck of formerly inhabited selves or modes of being. Byron's treatment of subjectivity marks out an extraordinary imaginative mobility that permits competing and contradictory perspectives on selfhood to coalesce. These contradictory Byronic perspectives (as well as positive and negative external and internal forces that form them) on a mobile series of personae are vital to the imaginatively productive dynamic of Byron's poetics, committed, as it is, to representing the self in all of its extremities, potentialities, and limitations.

History and memory constitute an important part of those forces that contribute to this dynamism of Byron's mobile poetic selfhood. How one is remembered as a historical figure, and more poignantly as a writer, is entirely arbitrary, as Byron reminds us when he observes in *Lara: A Tale* that 'Where History's pen its praise or blame supplies/And lies like Truth, and still most truly lies' (I, 11, 189–90). For Byron, historical record is comprised as much of objective fact as it is subjectively interpretative fiction, as much truth as it is truly a lie, as much illusion as it is reality. Even more playfully, although with a pressing tragic undertow which drags down the lightness of the lines, Byron acknowledges, in *Don Juan*, just how capricious history is and the difficulty of attaining or recovering a posthumous 'Glory': "Tis something, nothing words, illusion, wind—/Depending more upon the historian's style/Than on the name a person leaves behind' (III, 810–12). We glimpse something here of Byron's anticipation of Nietzsche's claim that 'truth is a mobile army of metaphors, metonymies, and anthropomorphisms'.[15] *Childe Harold* derives its poetic power from its ability to energise and dramatise

---

15 Friedrich Nietzsche, 'On Truth and Lie in an Extra-Moral Sense', in *The Portable Nietzsche*, ed. and trans. by Walter Kaufmann (Harmondsworth: Penguin, 1976), p. 46.

a multiplicity of mobile selves and versions of the truth through the figure of the 'Self-exiled' (III, xvi, 146) Childe Harold in which we glimpse fractured aspects of Byron as epic narrator, travelogue writer, observer and participant in the fictional actions and historical events of the poem.

Venice is at once the physical haunt and mindscape of such poetic creation. Venice exists as a mythical and political reality which, for Byron, delights in those blurred boundaries between personal memory and public record, ruin and whole, and nature and cultural artifice. Byron found a corollary for his own predicament in the city of Venice's splendid decay and her captivating ability to hover between those records of the historian's pen and the inspired muse of the poetic imagination, which seeks to preserve Venice as 'a fairy city of the heart' (IV, 28, 2) even as the changing times render her 'proud historic deeds' obsolete (IV, xxvii, 1).[16]

Yet Venice—the city of Byron's sexual promiscuity and creative fecundity—is a place of rich promise and possibilities worthy of preserving for posterity, but it is equally a force already spent, fallen into physical and political ruin. Byron's poetic representation of Venice, in *Childe Harold's Pilgrimage*, the *Ode to Venice*, and *Beppo*, is attuned to the city's permanent state of, as he recognises in Rome's Coliseum in *Manfred*, 'ruinous perfection' (III, iv, 28), floating as an insubstantial conjuring of an 'enchanter's wand' and an idealised—if not immortalised—centre of political and cultural power, whose enfolding 'cloudy wings' miraculously resist, through his own poetic sleight of hand, being reduced to 'marble piles' (IV, i, 8). In his 'Epistle to John Murray', where Byron writes concerning *Beppo*, 'Perhaps some such pen is/Still extant in Venice' (34–5), he hints that his poetic preservation of Venice as a historical and unhistorical phenomenon is partly an exercise in psychodrama and a bid to perpetuate the existence of his own poetic name and 'pen'. This Byronic preoccupation recalls an earlier entreaty from the narrator, in 'To Ianthe', which requests that the reader's own 'name with this my verse be entwined' so that our 'kinder eyes a look

---

16   Jane Stabler offers a perceptive account of how Byron's depictions of Venice suggest a sense of exile from his own past and present environs. Jane Stabler, *The Artistry of Exile: Romantic and Victorian Writers in Italy* (Oxford: Oxford University Press, 2013), pp. 27–30, https://doi.org/10.1093/acprof:oso/9780199590247.001.0001

shall glance/On Harold's page' (37–39). Byron's inextricable binding of imaginative poetic composition with the writing of history permits a mobility of selfhood in which public and private selves spill over into one another as readily as the distinction between historical record and poetic fiction blur.

A famous instance of this occurs in *Beppo*, where we witness satirical procrastination, on the part of the narrator, take a more 'blackly' serious tone to dissolve the Venice of the literary imagination and mythology with the actuality of the immediate present. Before turning to the supposed substance of his story, the narrator unexpectedly breaks off to describe to his audience in painstaking detail the appearance, function, and motion of the Venetian gondola:

Didst ever see a Gondola? For fear

  You should not, I'll describe it you exactly:

'Tis a long covered boat that's common here,

  Carved at the prow, built lightly, but compactly,

Rowed by two rowers, each call'd 'Gondolier,'

  It glides along the water looking blackly,

Just like a coffin clapt in a canoe,

Where none can make out what you say or do.

And up and down the long canals they go,

  And under the Rialto shoot along,

By night and day, all paces, swift or slow,

  And round the theatres, a sable throng,

They wait in their dusk livery of woe,—

  But not to them do woeful things belong,

For sometimes they contain a deal of fun,

Like mourning coaches when the funeral's done. (146–60)

Refracted through the biographical details of Byron's exploits in Venice critics have, unsurprisingly, detected in these lines a certain sexual *frisson*, taking their cue from the narrator's mischievous observation that there 'none can make out what you say or do' and Byron's punning on 'fun' and 'funeral', in the implied strokes of the 'two rowers' and gliding motion of the gondolas that 'under the Rialto shoot along'.

Equally, the 'darkly' graceful gliding to-and-fro movement of the gondolas, driven by strokes of 'all paces, swift and slow' may, as they weave their way through the Grand Canal and its tributaries, put us in mind of the motion of the pen of the poet or historian. A self-awareness of the motion and process of writing evident in Byron's performative, yet casual and arbitrary, declarative flourish that the 'story ends' of *Beppo* because, as we are told, 'My pen is at the bottom of a page' (789). This mobile and agile self-consciousness about the writing of history and poetry is reinforced, elsewhere in his work, when Byron describes the singing of the gondoliers as 'the responsive voices of the choir/Of boatmen answering back with verse for verse' (*Marino Faliero*, 99–100).

There is without doubt a certain sexual tension and release in these lines from *Beppo*, but there is also a further ironic tension between the narrator's endeavour to describe the gondola 'exactly' and his omission that part of the allure—sexual or otherwise—is the secrecy, concealment, and privacy they afford within the public space of the city. The funereal associations of the gondolas, not common until the travelogues of the 1740s, with coffins, 'a livery of woe', and 'mourning coaches' register the contemporary political demise of Venice as much as, in the hands of Byron's narrator, they celebrate the carnivalesque pleasures and imaginative possibilities that the city affords the mercurially mobile Byronic self.[17]

These coffin-like barks gesture towards, on the one hand, a dignified recognition of the historical moment of Venice's demise and, on the other, permits the private space of the self entrance into those monumental moments recorded by, and for, history. Shakespeare's *Othello* and *As You Like It* (from which *Beppo*'s epigraph is derived) is much in Byron's head, but the effect he realises here is closer to the undercutting of

---

17 See Tony Tanner, *Venice Desired* (Oxford: Blackwell, 1992), pp. 48–49. See also Alan M. Weinberg, *Shelley's Italian Experience* (London: Macmillan, 1991), p. 52 and p. 259 n.21.

Enobarbus's sensuous description in the Roman play, *Anthony and Cleopatra*, of Cleopatra as the exotic queen of Egypt seated on her barge 'like a burnished throne' by his account of her 'breathless' hopping through the 'public street'.[18] It is only by virtue of Enobarbus's own imaginative act that he reconciles the image of Cleopatra as the public figure of historical record (witnessed in all her finery and pomp) with her stumbling in the street 'to make defect perfection' (II, ii, 239). As with Shakespeare's Enobarbus, Byron's poeticising or fictionalising of history allows these private pratfalls and indiscretions to comprise (and compromise) historical memory and are a part of posterity as much as those public momentous events. As with Shakespeare's Egypt, Venice, as Byron notes in his *Ode* that meditates on her fate, may not be entirely blameless for the fact that her mellifluous 'throng of gondolas'[19] has been subjugated by tyranny. The enchanting city has fallen under the sway of the 'tyrant's voice' (22) for she had given herself over too long to 'the luxurious and voluptuous flood/Of sweet sensations' (29–30), but these faults are preferable to the 'gloomy error' of other less fair 'nations in their last decay' (32–3).

Still with Venice as his subject, and anticipating charges of plagiarising Otway's drama *Venice Preserved* (1682), Byron remarks, in a footnote, to *Marino Faliero* that 'I need hardly remind the gentlest reader, that such coincidences must be accidental, from the very facility of their detection by reference to so popular a play on the stage'.[20] Paradoxically, Byron's entreaty to the 'gentlest reader' relinquishes and retains authorial control over those apparently 'coincidental' and 'accidental' echoes of Otway's tragedy in Byron's own work. Behind these ever-mobile and shifting frames, lacunae, and rhetorical hoodwinking of his readership, Byron is vitally concerned with how the 'gentlest' of readers *read*, the extent to which their response can or cannot be governed, and whether—left to

---

18 William Shakespeare, *Anthony and Cleopatra*, ed. and intro. by Emrys Jones (Harmondsworth: Penguin, 1977; repr. 1988), II, pp. 2, 195; 236–10. Subsequent references to this edition.
19 George Gordon Byron, 'Ode on Venice', *Byron: Poetical Works*, ed. John Jump and rev. Frederick Page (Oxford: Oxford University Press, 1991), p. 25. Hereafter referred to as *BPW*.
20 'Marino Faliero', in *Byron: Poetical Works*, ed. by Frederick Page and rev. by John Jump (Oxford: Oxford University Press, 1991), fn 2.

their own devices—they can ever read (without misgivings) his poetic works, personality, private biography, or public historical events aright.

Similarly, in 'Substitute For an Epitaph', Byron urges us as 'Kind' readers to decide how to read ('to take your choice to cry or laugh' (*BPW*, 1)) the tragic-comic situation of a deceased 'Harold' bereft of an epitaph, except for the ditty of these Byronic lines that commend the reader to 'try Westminster' where can be found 'Ten thousand [epitaphs] just as fit for him as you' (3–4). On a cursory reading the poem insinuates that no epitaph is worth having, as all epitaphs are equally trite and applicable to all. Yet Byron's parting quip ushers in an uncomfortable realisation of our own, as well as Harold's, mortality that undercuts the playful invitation to interpret these lines and the unlamented demise of Harold with either levity or lightness. 'Fit' in its primary sense of what is deigned appropriate or worthy, loads the dice against the readers' preference for comic lightness, as they are confronted with the weighty question of which of these 'ten thousand' epitaphs would be the most suitable not only for Harold, but for themselves. The full force of this is brought to bear through the secondary meaning of 'fit' in this context, which refers to the manufacture of the 'right size or measure' (*OED*), presumably in this instance, of a coffin, or else the marking out and digging of a grave. Byron's opening gambit of empowered free 'choice' to the reader is checked by the deliberate alignment of the readers' sympathies with Harold's mortality and eventual death. If this Harold, whose fitting epitaph can be found in Westminster (perhaps, within Poets' Corner of the Abbey), gestures towards Byron's many mobile alter egos of *Childe Harold*, then the poem's readers are also hoodwinked into feeling sympathy for a surrogate figure of Byron the poet.

In *Childe Harold,* the lines blur between the actual and the imaginary, between the biographical and the fictional personae, as Byron takes up again the celebration of 'The wandering outlaw of his own dark mind' (III, iii, 20) at the start of Canto III. Childe Harold is, at once, a separate figment of Byron's 'dark mind' and an inextricable embodiment of the madness that Byron hoped, at its best, poetic creation could exorcise. Later in the same Canto, this notion of madness as a contagion of fire that 'once kindled' remains 'quenchless evermore' (III, 43, 375) fully takes hold of Byron's portrait of the troubled figure of Rousseau:

> His love was Passion's essence—as a tree
>
> On fire by lightning; with ethereal flame
>
> Kindled he was, and blasted; for to be
>
> Thus, and enamoured, were in him the same.
>
> But his was not the love of living dame,
>
> Nor of the dead who rise upon our dreams,
>
> But of ideal Beauty, which became
>
> In him existence, and o'erflowing teems
>
> Along his burning page, distempered though it seems.
>
> (*CH*, III, stanza LXXVII)

Byron's deliberate verbal slippage allows a mobility of self that oscillates between observing subject and observed objects (the lone tree and lightning strike) fuses together the interior and exterior worlds in the stanza, which are immersed in, and felt through, those outer and inner spaces of 'ideal Beauty'. This fusion creates an inner or emotional landscape which, pre-empting one of David Caspar Friedrich's emotionally intense pictorial landscapes,[21] conflates the isolated watcher (whether Rousseau, Childe Harold, or Byron himself) of the fire-stricken 'tree' wounded by the 'lightning' strike. Such emotional intensity prepares the reader for a description of the 'burning page' as both subjectively charged ('In him existence') with—and objectively observed as—the creative-destructive energy of the mobile poetic artistry of these selves become mad. Consequently, the 'dark mind[s]' of Byron and Rousseau are both imaginatively 'Kindled' into the life of the 'ethereal flame' and forever tormented ('blasted') by that same destructive fire which can never be quenched.

Elsewhere in Canto III, the anxieties of Byron's poetic persona, Childe Harold, and Byron as poet collide to voice one another's fears that the mobility of poetic selfhood and creation is an act of all-consuming

---

[21] For a detailed account of David Caspar Friedrich's influence on Nietzsche see Caroline Joan Picart, 'Nietzsche as Masked Romantic', *The Journal of Aesthetics and Art Criticism*, 55 (1997), 273–91.

creative madness without any guarantee of artistic success or the assurances that historical or poetical legacies bequeath anything of worth to posterity:

> Could I embody and unbosom now
>
> That which is most within me,—could I wreak
>
> My thoughts upon expression, and thus throw
>
> Soul, heart, mind, passions, feelings, strong or weak,
>
> All that I would have sought, and all I seek,
>
> Bear, know, feel—and yet breathe—into *one* word,
>
> And that one word were Lightning, I would speak;
>
> But as it is, I live and die unheard,
>
> With a most voiceless thought, sheathing it as a sword. (*CH*, III, stanza 97)

This anxiety over a posthumous existence or legacy desires, as Byron's Manfred so often does, to 'embody' (and preserve) its innermost spirit, feeling, and thoughts in a tangible exterior form. For Childe Harold, the fictional travelogue writer, and Byron, the creator of poetic fictions, the fragile evanescence of words is the only medium they have to 'embody' or else destroy upon the 'burning page' their deepest feelings and thoughts.

For all of Byron's immersion in his own and the subjectivity of others, he remained sympathetic yet wary of a negatively capable poetics of subjectivity, and knew the perils of seeking out what Keats understood as the beguiling negative capability of selfhood. When Byron writes, 'But my soul wanders…/To meditate among decay, and stand/A ruin amidst ruins', he realises a self-consciously staged moment, which objectively seeks to rein in an endlessly meandering mobility of selfhood and, subjectively, borders on a solipsistic collapse into a fracturing and fractured self. This splintered, yet unified Byronic self is as much 'absorb'd' (III, 32) in, as it is reflective of, all life's myriad goings-on: 'Even as a broken mirror, which the glass/In every fragment multiplies; and makes/A thousand images as of one that was' (III, 33, 1–3). This moment, like many others in Cantos III and IV, encapsulates the perspectival, contradictory, self-conscious poetic performance of shifting subjectivities that is vital to the dynamism of Byron's mobile poetics of self. Such a myriad shifting images of Romantic selfhood found their counterpart in Venice and anticipate her repertory of innumerable invisible cities in Calvino's Post-Romantic imaginings.

Works Cited

Calvino, Italo, *Invisible Cities*, ed. and trans. by William Weaver (London: Vintage, 1997).

Cate, Curtis, *Friedrich Nietzsche: A Biography* (London: Pimlico, 2003).

Davison, Peter, *The Last of the Light: About Twilight* (London: Reakton, 2015).

Gill, Stephen, ed., *William Wordsworth: The Major Works* (Oxford: Oxford University Press, 2000).

Kaufmann, Walter, ed. and trans., 'On Truth and Lie in an Extra-Moral Sense', in *The Portable Nietzsche* (Harmondsworth: Penguin, 1976), pp. 42–47.

Luchte, James, ed., *The Peacock and the Buffalo: The Poetry of Friedrich Nietzsche* (London: Continuum, 2010).

McGann, Jerome J., ed., *Lord Byron: The Major Works* (Oxford: Oxford University Press, 2000).

Middleton, Christopher, ed. and trans., *Selected Letters of Friedrich Nietzsche* (Cambridge: Hackett, 1996), https://doi.org/10.5840/schoolman197047333

Miller, Christopher R., *The Invention of Evening: Perception and Time in Romantic Poetry* (Cambridge: Cambridge University Press, 2006), https://doi.org/10.1017/cbo9780511720031

Myk, Malgorzata, 'The Immortal Waters of Venice: Women as Anodyne in Italo Calvino's *Invisible Cities*', *The Explicator*, 67.3 (2009), 221–24, https://doi.org/10.3200/expl.67.3.221-224

Page, Frederick and John Jump, eds, *Byron: Poetical Works* (Oxford: Oxford University Press, 1991).

Picart, Caroline Joan, 'Nietzsche as Masked Romantic', *The Journal of Aesthetics and Art Criticism*, 55 (1997), 273–91, https://doi.org/10.2307/431798

Reiman, Donald H. and Neil Fraistat, eds, *Shelley's Poetry and Prose* (New York: Norton, 2002).

Sandy, Mark, '"A Ruin amidst Ruins": Modernity, Literary Aphorisms, and Romantic Fragments', in *Aphoristic Modernity: 1880 to the Present*, ed. by Kostas Boyiopoulos and Michael Shallcross (Leiden: Brill, 2019), pp. 41–47, https://doi.org/10.1163/9789004400061_004

——, '"Lines of Light": Reading Poetic Variations of Light in Wordsworth, Byron, and Shelley', *Romanticism*, 22.3 (2016), special Issue on 'Light', ed. by Sarah Wootton, 260–68, https://doi.org/10.3366/rom.2016.0287

——, '"The Last Great Romantic": Nietzsche's Romanticism Out of the Spirit of Decadence', in *Decadent Romanticism 1780–1914*, ed. by Kostas Boyiopoulos and Mark Sandy (Farnham: Ashgate, 2015), pp. 131–44, https://doi.org/10.4324/9781315576077

——, 'Quest Poetry: *Alastor* and *Epipsychidion*', in *The Oxford Handbook of Percy Bysshe Shelley*, ed. by Michael O'Neill and Anthony Howe, with the assistance of Madeleine Callaghan (Oxford: Oxford University Press, 2013), pp. 276–77, https://doi.org/10.1093/oxfordhb/9780199558360.001.0001

——, 'Reimagining Venice and Visions of Decay in Wordsworth, the Shelleys, and Thomas Mann', in *Venice and the Cultural Imagination*, ed. by Michael O'Neill, Mark Sandy, and Sarah Wootton (London: Pickering & Chatto, 2012), pp. 27–42, https://doi.org/10.4324/9781315655611

Shakespeare, William, *Anthony and Cleopatra*, ed. by Emrys Jones (Harmondsworth: Penguin, 1977; repr. 1988).

Stabler, Jane, *The Artistry of Exile: Romantic and Victorian Writers in Italy* (Oxford: Oxford University Press, 2013), https://doi.org/10.1093/acprof:oso/9780199590247.001.0001

Tanner, Tony, *Venice Desired* (Oxford: Blackwell, 1992).

Weinberg, Alan M., *Shelley's Italian Experience* (London: Macmillan, 1991), https://doi.org/10.1007/978-1-349-21649-9

SECTION V

ROMANTICISM AND PERIODISATION

Romanticism and Periodisation: A Roundtable

David Duff, Nicholas Halmi, Fiona Stafford, Martin Procházka, and Laurent Folliot

Taking the format of a closing roundtable discussion—with prepared statements followed by a formal response (Laurent Folliot) and an open-ended debate between the five contributors—this coda explores the issue of literary periodisation in Romanticism, starting from the Romantics' own efforts at self-periodisation and the emergence of a new critical discourse on the 'spirit of the age' (David Duff, 'Phases of British Romanticism'). It examines the terminology of periodisation, charting the history and shifting meaning of key terms, and the new awareness of historical beginnings and endings prompted by the French Revolution and other world-changing events (Nicholas Halmi, 'Periodisation and the Epochal Event'). The difficulties of periodising a movement so diffuse in its origins and so differentiated in its national and regional manifestations are addressed, as is the impulse to find unifying characteristics amid the unprecedented cultural diversity of the period (Fiona Stafford, 'Romanticism and the "Four Nations": Not Quite in Time'). While the stress is on British Romanticism through its different historical phases and national traditions, the next contribution takes up a more cross-border approach by examining the relationship between British, European, and American Romanticism (Martin Procházka, 'Periodisation as a Problem: The Case of American Romanticism'). In each case, questions of chronology are set alongside other theoretical and methodological problems, the aim being to arrive at tentative conclusions about the usefulness or otherwise of a concept of the 'Romantic period' or of potential subdivisions of it that could reflect the continuities and discontinuities of Romantic literature.

Introduction: Phases of British Romanticism

David Duff

Periodisation is an intellectual process intimately connected with Romantic thought, and the idea of a 'Romantic period' has its roots in the Romantics' own reflections on time. Yet these are highly problematic concepts, which have been vigorously debated since the inception of the Romantic movement and still provoke controversy. Other contributors to this volume have touched on some of the issues we are about to raise but this roundtable discussion confronts them directly, from a range of different perspectives. We start with the Romantics' efforts at self-periodisation and the emergence of a new literary discourse on the 'spirit of the age'. We then examine the terminology of periodisation, charting the history and shifting meanings of key terms such as 'period', 'epoch', 'age', and connecting these semantic shifts with the new awareness of historical beginnings and endings prompted by the French Revolution and other world-changing events. Next, we address the difficulties of periodising a movement so diffuse in its origins and so differentiated in its national and regional manifestations, while also analysing the impulse—as pronounced among Romantic-era writers as among later literary historians—to find unifying characteristics amid the unprecedented cultural diversity of the period. The emphasis of our discussion is on British Romanticism—its different historical phases and national trajectories—but we also consider the relationship between British and European Romanticism, as well as the more problematic case of American Romanticism. At each stage, we set empirical questions of chronology alongside theoretical and methodological problems, the aim of the discussion being to explore the conceptual foundations of periodisation and to assess the usefulness or otherwise of the idea of a 'Romantic period', or potential subdivisions or extensions of it that can register the continuities and discontinuities of Romantic literature. After some introductory remarks, the roundtable will consist of three position statements followed by a prepared response and a final stage of open-ended, ad hoc discussion.

To begin on a personal note, my awareness of the problem of periodisation was heightened by the experience of editing *The Oxford Handbook of British Romanticism*, in which the question took a very practical form: where chronologically to begin and end, what range of forward and backward reference to include, and what sort of diversity and unity to present under the title phrase 'British Romanticism'.[1] I took two key editorial decisions. The first was to foreground the different literary traditions of the 'four nations'—England, Scotland, Ireland and Wales—and to show how they all contributed to the making of 'British' Romanticism. The aim was to trace both the cross-fertilisation and the tensions and rivalries between these traditions, and also to reflect on the significance of the key moment of constitutional change in this period, the Act of Union of 1800, which brought the four nations together to form the United Kingdom of Great Britain and Ireland—but with many of those tensions and rivalries still intact.

The Handbook has a dedicated 'Region and Nation' section with separate chapters on each of the four home nations together with their border regions (Scotland and the North, Wales and the West), but this also was an organising principle throughout the Handbook, so that many other chapters also explore national and regional demarcations and relationships. The book offers, then, a 'discrimination' of British Romanticisms, in Lovejoy's sense, but not one that leads to his negative conclusion, that 'Romanticism' has such a diversity of meanings and applications as to be a largely worthless concept that can tell us nothing definite about the movement or period it supposedly defines.[2] Rather, the premise of the Handbook is that the British Romantic movement is *constituted* by those differences: by the sharpened sense of cultural diversity within the British Isles, and by the opening up of new forms of creative and critical engagement between the various national traditions and scenes of writing.

This internal transnationalism coincides with a broader internationalism, a developing engagement with other countries across Europe and other parts of the world. These exchanges are explored in

---

1   *The Oxford Handbook of British Romanticism*, ed. by David Duff (Oxford: Oxford University Press, 2018), https://doi.org/10.1093/oxfordhb/9780199660896.001.0001

2   Arthur O. Lovejoy, 'On the Discrimination of Romanticisms', *PMLA*, 39 (1924), 229–53, https://doi.org/10.2307/457184

another section of the Handbook, labelled 'Imports and Exports', though again they feature in other chapters too, and I was concerned that the 'four nations' emphasis should not reduce the attention to the broader international connections of British Romanticism, which need asserting equally strongly in face of insular accounts which have sometimes held too much sway.

The second editorial decision was to break down the Romantic period into five sub-periods: pre-1789, the 1790s, the 'new century' to 1815, the post-war years 1815–19, and the 1820s and beyond. These I characterise as different 'historical phases' of the Romantic movement, each with its own set of historical conditions, its own political character, its own cultural and literary preoccupations, and its own mini-zeitgeist, explicitly articulated in some cases. The temporal boundaries—1789, 1800, 1815, 1819/20—were not arbitrary, and the Handbook shows how British literature shaped itself in relation to them, mapping itself onto the chronology produced by the decisive political, military and constitutional events of the period. This new way of conceptualising the period, and understanding its conceptualisation of itself, is linked to the 'four nations' perspective, though two of the turning points are connected with external rather than internal events: the outbreak of the French Revolution and the ending of the Napoleonic Wars.

This self-mapping along the contours of contemporary history was part of the historical consciousness of Romanticism, but there were at least two other kinds of self-periodisation at work. One involved the emergence of a larger sense of period, the idea of an overarching age of literature that linked these historical phases, or micro-periods, and the disparate cultural phenomena they encompassed. When Leigh Hunt, in *The Feast of the Poets* (1815), spoke of Wordsworth as 'being at the head of a new and great age of poetry'; or when Shelley, in *A Defence of Poetry* (1821), spoke of 'the literature of England' as having 'arisen as it were from a new birth', what both writers were voicing was a perception that they were part of a new literary era, radically different from the one that preceded it.[3] The fullest expression of this view, which began to crystallise around 1815, is Hazlitt's *The Spirit of the Age* (1825), a

---

3 Leigh Hunt, *The Feast of the Poets*, 2nd ed. (London, 1815), p. 90; *Shelley's Poetry and Prose*, 2nd ed., ed. by Donald H. Reiman and Neil Fraistat (New York: Norton, 2002), p. 535.

retrospect on the previous forty years focussed on the writers, thinkers, politicians and opinion-formers he saw as having embodied and shaped British culture in this period. But there are many other examples of such reflexive analysis, enough to justify James Chandler's description of the Romantic period as the 'age of the spirit of the age', that is, the age of relentless self-definition and constant preoccupation with the idea that ages have such a thing as a 'spirit'.[4] Another way of putting this is to say that this was the period of periodisation—not the first historical era to periodise, certainly, but the one in which the desire to periodise, to *self-periodise*, became constitutive.

One modification I would propose to Chandler's influential account is suggested by Maike Oergel's recent book about the concept of zeitgeist.[5] Written by a comparative Anglo-German cultural historian, this is the first sustained treatment in English of this topic and it contains much of relevance to our subject. Oergel shows how the concept of zeitgeist has a very long history, and that it first gains currency not in the nineteenth but in the early seventeenth century, in discussion of the *genius saeculi* (the genius of the age, or of the times). In the Romantic period the concept acquires new meaning and force, and the terminology shifts. In the wake of the French Revolution, the concept becomes linked to the idea of public opinion, and the *power* of public opinion: the ability to manipulate and alter the way people think and behave. The idea of zeitgeist is used by contemporary observers to explain the phenomenon of revolutionary change, and the rapid transmission of ideas that was part of the revolutionary dynamic. This explanatory function is a major reason for the concept's remarkable currency in this period. The same applies to the English phrase 'spirit of the age', which becomes common in the 1820s. To understand the history of this term, we therefore need also to trace the related concepts of 'public opinion' and 'public spirit'—to which I would add a third term, 'public mind', another widely used phrase of the time which makes explicit the idea of a collective consciousness (and which gives a psychological, quasi-medical colouring to contemporary cultural commentary). Oergel's work has

---

4   James Chandler, *England in 1819: The Politics of Literary Culture and the Case of Romantic Historicism* (Chicago: University of Chicago Press, 1998), p. 105.
5   Maike Oergel, *Zeitgeist–How Ideas Travel: Politics, Culture and the Public in the Age of Revolution* (Berlin: De Gruyter, 2019), https://doi.org/10.1515/9783110631531

important implications for the way we think about periodisation, and her analysis sheds new light on the central question Chandler asks: *why* was this 'the age of the spirit of the age'? What was it that produced this distinctive kind of historical consciousness?

We have, then, the 'micro-periods' of British Romanticism, and we have the overarching Romantic age whose spirit was being so compulsively invoked and analysed. But there was a third kind of self-periodisation at work at this time, which drew even broader boundaries and sought to connect contemporary literature with the genres and styles of the Middle Ages and Renaissance, which British writers from the 1760s onwards were actively reviving. From this perspective, the literature of the late eighteenth and early nineteenth centuries formed a continuum with these earlier traditions, and this was precisely the sense in which the term 'romantic' was often used, by Continental theorists especially: to denote that continuum, and to contrast it with the classical tradition. Thus defined, Romanticism was a retro movement as well as a revolutionary one, an aesthetic of archaism and innovation, delighting both in the antique (actual or invented) and the thoroughly modern.[6] Moreover, as well as being immersed in the past it was a future-orientated movement, which saw literature, the 'romantic poem', in a state of becoming, progressive and perfectible but never perfected or completed. The Romantics had an acute sense of contemporaneity, of the distinctiveness of their own historical moment, but they were not content to remain in it, instead projecting themselves imaginatively into other periods, past and future, and dissolving temporal boundaries.

This is the synoptic vision of literary history that Mikhail Bakhtin later termed 'great time', and Bakhtin makes the methodological point that we need to study works of literature not only in their 'near' contexts, in the time of their own production and reception, but also in their 'remote' contexts, which lie before and afterwards.[7] Great works of literature, he

---

6   See David Duff, 'Archaism and Innovation', in *Romanticism and the Uses of Genre* (Oxford: Oxford University Press, 2009), pp. 119–59, https://doi.org/10.1093/acpro f:oso/9780199572748.003.0005

7   M.M. Bakhtin, 'Response to a Question from the *Novy Mir* Editorial Staff', in *Speech Genres and Other Late Essays*, ed. by Caryl Emerson and Michael Holquist, trans. by Vern W. McGee (Austin: University of Texas Press, 1986), pp. 4–6; 'Toward a Methodology for the Human Sciences', *Ibid.*, pp. 169–70. For the genealogy of this

says, 'are prepared for by centuries', they 'break through the boundaries of their own time' and come to fulfilment in 'great time', across the course of their posthumous life. Our critical methodologies, he urges, must take account of these longer historical perspectives and liberate authors from the captivity of their own time. This view of literature, so forcefully articulated by Bakhtin in the twentieth century, derives essentially from the Romantic period, from the Schlegels, Novalis, Hegel and other German theorists. An exact analogy to it was Shelley's conception in *A Defence of Poetry* of the 'great poem, which all poets, like the co-operating thoughts of one great mind, have built up since the beginning of the world'.[8] Shelley, like other Romantic poets, saw his own work as a contribution to this 'great poem': as part of the cumulative, collaborative wiki-poem to which all writers, of all periods, knowingly or unknowingly contribute. Rejecting the trajectory of decline posited by Thomas Love Peacock in his *Four Ages of Poetry* (1820), Shelley presents a progressive vision of literature in which chronology is suspended and the 'four ages' become one.

In the temporal consciousness of Romanticism, then, we can discern three levels of periodisation: the micro-period (the different historical phases of the Romantic movement); the macro-period (the Romantic age as a whole); and 'great time' (what might be termed the mega-period, which conceives of all literature, across all time, as part of one seamless, interconnected whole). Understanding how these different constructions of literary time intersect and complicate one another is one of the many challenges we face in addressing the question of periodisation. To elucidate these complexities, and uncover others, I now turn to our other speakers.

---

motif, see David Shepherd, 'A Feeling for History? Bakhtin and "The Problem of Great Time"', *Slavonic and East European Review*, 84.1 (2006), 32–51; and Duff, *Romanticism and the Uses of Genre*, pp. 191–200.

8   *Shelley's Poetry and Prose*, p. 522.

Periodisation and the Epochal Event

Nicholas Halmi

Periodisation is so deeply embedded conceptually and institutionally in our historical understanding and historiographical practice that we do not easily recognise it to be itself the product of historical developments. Semantic history helps illuminate the emergence of periodisation as we are familiar with it, namely as the segmentation of historical time and the identification of the segments with specific events or prevalent conditions. The English word *period* derives from the Greek περίοδος, meaning a circuit or cycle. A synonym of *period* in this etymological sense is *revolution* (from the Old French *revolucion*) in its original sense, as the full course of a recurrent event—expressed, for example, in Lord Bolingbroke's posthumously published 'Reflections upon Exile': 'We shall feel the same revolutions of seasons, and the same sun and moon will guide the course of our year.' Towards the end of the seventeenth century, and particularly in connection with the succession of William and Mary to the British throne, *revolution* acquired the new meaning of a singular, radical change—a turning point from which there is no turning back. Bolingbroke used the word in this sense as well: referring in 1735 to the events of 1688, he declared that 'James's mal-administration rendered a revolution necessary and practicable'.[9]

In the eighteenth century, *period* too, without losing its original sense, acquired a new connotation of temporal singularity as 'any specified portion or division of time' (*OED*). The earliest example attested by the *OED* is once again from Bolingbroke: 'The particular periods into which the whole period should be divided'.[10] The Grimms' dictionary confirms the same semantic development in German from the 1760s, citing for example Lessing's distinction between the first (Shakespearean) and second (Restoration) *Perioden* of the English theatre. A synonym of *period* in its modern historiographical sense is *epoch*, which derives

---

[9] Henry St John, Viscount Bolingbroke, 'Reflections upon Exile' (1726), in *Letters on the Study and Use of History* (London, 1752), vol. 2, pp. 246–47, and 'Of the Study of History' (1735), in *Letters*, vol. 1, p. 44.

[10] Bolingbroke, 'Of the Study of History', *Letters*, vol. 1, p. 236 (proposing to divide 'modern history', from the fifteenth century to the eighteenth, into three periods).

from the Greek ἐποχή via the Latin *epocha* and originally denoted not an expanse of time but the opposite, a fixed point in time from which chronology could be reckoned: the Creation, the Flood, the foundation of Rome, the birth of Christ, the election of a new pope, the accession of a new king. An epoch in the old sense, if perceived to be sufficiently momentous, could be identified as initiating an epoch in the new sense. Thus Helen Maria Williams, recalling in 1795 her reaction to the fall of the Bastille, reports that she viewed 'the revolution with transport, persuaded that it was the epocha of the subversion of despotism'. And Robert Southey, also retaining the Latinate terminal *a*, refers to the 'invention of the steam-engine [as] almost as great an epocha as the invention of printing'.[11]

When history is periodic, it does not require periodisation. Cyclicality ensures predictability and hence exemplarity: the broad patterns discernible in the past can be assumed to apply to the present and the future. It was on this basis that Thucydides recommended the study of history and, over two millennia later, Frederick the Great still did so in the preface to the *Histoire de mon temps* (1746): 'History is the school of princes; it is for them to study the errors of the past centuries in order to avoid them.' But the semantic shifts that occurred during Frederick's lifetime attest to the emergence, in close connection with the concept of indefinite rational progress, of a linear or, as Reinhart Koselleck called it, temporalised conception of history, one that simultaneously enabled and necessitated periodisation.

Necessitated? Periodisation is of course not the only method of organising cultural history—classification by genres, stylistic 'schools', types of artists or audiences, and so on are equally possible—and it can be justified on the strictly pragmatic grounds suggested by the art historian Heinrich Wölfflin: 'Everything is change, and it is difficult to counter someone who considers history an endless flow. For us it is a requirement of intellectual self-preservation to order the infiniteness of events according to a few points of reference [*Zielpunkten*].' Or as, more recently, Marshall Brown has put it, cautioning against reifying periods while conceding their necessity, 'We cannot rest statically in periods,

---

11   Helen Maria Williams, *Letters Containing a Sketch of the Politics of France* (London, 1795), vol. 1, p. 283; Robert Southey, *Letters from England* (London, 1807), vol. 3, p. 74.

but we cannot rest at all without them.'[12] But if periodisation were in practice a purely nominalistic exercise, we would not be discussing it in fora like this. Periodisation is contentious precisely because the temporal segments it distinguishes are supposed to correspond in some way to an empirical historical reality. The issue is analogous to that of taxonomic classification, in which the nomenclature may be arbitrarily chosen, but the characteristics distinguished by means of it are supposed to be genuinely present in the objects of classification. For his part René Wellek defends periodisation as an instrument of literary history by emphasising its realism while trying to dissociate it from taxonomy: 'a period is not a type or a class but a time section defined by a system of norms embedded in the historical process and irremovable from it'.[13] This claim seems to me excessive. But certainly the persistent sense of the empirical justification of periodisation accounts for our inability to dispense with the practice in general and with the concept (which Wellek was defending) of Romanticism in particular, despite the fact that the difficulty of defining it has been lamented since the 1820s and the expedient of abandoning it altogether has been proposed repeatedly.

What distinguishes a period from other kinds of chronological classification? Distinctions between *antiqui* and *moderni* date back to the sixth century, when the word *antiquus* entered the Latin vocabulary. But philological research by E.R. Curtius and Salvatore Settis has established that, until the *Querelle des anciens et des modernes* in the late seventeenth century, the referents of these terms were relative and not historically fixed.[14] In the *Querelle* itself they were only broadly fixed, with all of classical antiquity (Greek and Roman) designated *ancient* and roughly the seventeenth century onwards *modern*. Such broad-brush

---

12   Heinrich Wölfflin, *Kunstgeschlichtliche Grundebegriffe: Das Problem der Stilentwicklung in der neueren Kunst* (Munich: Bruckmann, 1915), p. 238; Marshall Brown, 'Periods and Resistances', *Modern Language Quarterly*, 62 (2001), 309–16 (p. 312), https://doi.org/10.1215/00267929-62-4-309

13   René Wellek and Austin Warren, *Theory of Literature*, 3rd ed. (Harmondsworth: Penguin Books, 1966), pp. 265–66.

14   Ernst Robert Curtius, *European Literature and the Latin Middle Ages*, trans. by Willard Trask (London: Routledge, 1953), pp. 251–55; Salvatore Settis, 'Continuità, distanza, conoscenza: tre usi dell'antico', in *Memoria dell'antico nell'arte italiana*, vol. 3: *Dalla tradizione all'archeologia*, ed. by Settis (Turin: Einaudi, 1996), pp. 375–486 (pp. 465–73).

historicisation also characterises August Wilhelm Schlegel's distinction between *classical* and *romantic* drama, the former referring to the productions of pagan Greece and Rome and the latter to those of post-classical Europe. But a period, apart from being typically shorter in duration than Schlegel's two eras, is supposed to possess a unifying set of dominant characteristics, or what Wellek calls 'a system of norms', which allows it to be distinguished from other periods. In broader historical usage, such a system of norms would constitute what was first conceptualised in the eighteenth century—most explicitly by Johann Gottfried Herder—as a zeitgeist: 'the prevailing views, manners, and customs' of an age.[15]

From the outset of the nineteenth century, two distinct concepts of Romanticism, one typological and the other historical, have co-existed. In his *Histoire du romantisme en France* of 1829—the earliest self-described history of Romanticism—the critic Eugène Ronteix (publishing under an anagrammatic pseudonym) maintained simultaneously that it was a rebellious tendency 'in every century, in every epoch', rejecting conventional ideas and established forms, and that it was a contemporary, primarily French artistic movement inaugurated by René de Chateaubriand in 1801. A sense of the historical specificity of Romanticism as a movement or cultural phenomenon has proved remarkably stable. While defining literary Romanticism in terms of *generic* characteristics—'imagination for the view of poetry, nature for the view of the world, and symbol and myth for poetic style'—Wellek tellingly adhered to the conventional *chronological* designation of Romanticism as extending from the late-eighteenth to the mid-nineteenth century. Wellek's Romantic period thus included a writer whom his normative concept of Romanticism effectively excluded, Lord Byron. For Wellek there was no contradiction between the generic and chronological definitions of Romanticism, because the latter derived from the former: the years in which the aesthetic values identified as Romantic were predominant. To the extent that Byron

---

15 Johann Gottfried Herder, 'Briefe zur Beförderung der Humanität' (1793–97), in *Werke in zehn Bänden*, vol. 7, ed. by H. D. Irmscher (Frankfurt: Deutscher Klassiker Verlag, 1991), p. 103.

did not share those values, then, he was not a Romantic, despite his contemporaneity with Romantic poets like Wordsworth and Novalis.[16]

Wellek cautions that the unity constituting a period 'can be only relative', for if it were absolute 'periods would lie next to each other like blocks of stone, without continuity of development', rather as the classical and modern *épistémès* do in the epistemological 'archaeology' of Foucault's *Les Mots et les choses*. But how do we determine when a system of norms begins or ceases to be dominant? A nominalist objection to periodisation is that the practice is inevitably retrospective, for people experience their lives as a temporal continuum and do not recognise as epochal transitions the events subsequently proclaimed to have been such. Defending the realism (as opposed to the nominalism) of the concept of the historical period, Hans Blumenberg nonetheless concedes, 'There are no witnesses to epochal ruptures [*Epochenumbrüchen*]. The epochal turn [*Epochenwende*] is an imperceptible frontier, bound to no obviously epitomic [*prägnante*] date or event.' He thus illustrates the transition from the medieval to the modern age by contrasting the thought of two philosophers he considers exemplary, Nicholas of Cusa (1401–64) and Giordano Bruno (1548–1600). The specification of a singular event as an epochal threshold can only be, in Blumenberg's view, an act of retrospective self-mythologisation, as in Goethe's purported assurance to the dejected Prussian soldiers at the Battle of Valmy on 19 September 1792 that they were witnesses to the beginning of a 'a new epoch of world history'.[17]

From the perspective of a realist vindication of periodisation, it makes no difference whether the 'inhabitants' of an epoch recognise themselves as such. As Blumenberg observes, one can hardly expect the early Christian philosophers, who sought to minimise the appearance of their differences with pagan philosophy, to have declared an epochal rupture. But if it is true that, as he claims, the concept of the epoch is itself a significant aspect of the modern epoch, then this is more particularly true of Romanticism. For one important source of the sense of Romanticism as a period is the preoccupation of writers towards

---

16   René Wellek, 'Romanticism Re-examined', in *Concepts of Criticism* (New Haven: Yale University Press, 1963), pp. 199–221 (pp. 200–01).
17   Hans Blumenberg, *Die Legitimität der Neuzeit*, 3rd ed. (Frankfurt: Suhrkamp, 1988), pp. 545, 531–34.

the end of the eighteenth century, and especially in connection with the French Revolution, with the historical categorisation of their own time. In his introduction to *The Oxford Handbook of British Romanticism* and again in this volume, David Duff has rightly called attention to the self-periodising statements of Romantic writers, with regard to both literature and broader historical developments. A single example here will stand for many: writing to Byron on 8 September 1816—so after Waterloo and the Congress of Vienna—Percy Shelley declared the French Revolution 'the master theme of the epoch in which we live'. Invested with the status of an epochal boundary, that event (and it is telling that Shelley treats it as a single event) continued to provide the focus for historical self-orientation nearly three decades later.

By allowing the possibility of the appearance of the radically new—a possibility excluded from the older model of exemplary history, which assumes the cyclicality of historical patterns—historicisation fosters not only periodisation as such but the identification of revolutionary turning-points between periods or collective *Weltanschauungen* (the latter a concept that was itself first formulated in the nineteenth century). The crisis or revolution (in the modern sense of the word) is what, by virtue of seeming incommensurable with the historical self-understanding of the existing epoch, terminates that epoch and defines the opposing character of the succeeding one. In its singularity and disruptiveness, the revolution creates the illusion that epochs themselves are self-contained totalities, within which phenomena may be compared synchronically and precisely as representative of an epoch. The epoch-making event in this understanding is more radical and disruptive than the *epocha* of older chronological divisions. Whether, as is likely, Goethe embellished his speech at Valmy when he wrote up the *Campagne in Frankreich* thirty years after the events is beside the point: the plausibility of his account among contemporary readers depended not on their willingness to attribute prophetic powers to him, but on their recognition that he needed no such powers because the French Revolution and its ensuing wars self-evidently constituted an epochal threshold. If he did say in 1792 what he later claimed to have said, it was no more than others were saying at the time, and indeed earlier.

Virginia Woolf's famous declaration, in her essay 'Character in Fiction', that 'on or about December 1910 human character changed' appears jocular only because no event in that month could plausibly have produced such an effect. But we so readily accept that the French Revolution, for example, was an epochal threshold that we do not question the epistemological or empirical bases for that judgement. After all, in France itself many of the Revolutionary reforms (e.g., the Declaration of the Rights of Man, property rights for women, abolition of slavery in the colonies) were reversed under Napoleon, and after Napoleon's defeat the old monarchies re-asserted themselves throughout Europe. To a large extent, however, we remain the children of the first Romantic generation, so to speak, and their historical self-conception. From its beginning the French Revolution was interpreted as an epochal event, historically unprecedented and therefore inexplicable by reference to the past. Within a month of the fall of the Bastille, the British Whig leader Charles James Fox proclaimed it 'much the greatest Event that has ever happened in the world, [which will] in all probability have the most extensive good consequences', and not much later an antipathetic observer, Edmund Burke, declared it 'the most astonishing [thing] that hitherto happened in the world'.[18] How could they know that? The Revolutionaries themselves tried to institutionalise this contemporary perception of permanent historical rupture by instituting a new calendar on the grounds that, in the words of the playwright Philippe Fabre d'Églantine (who devised the calendar's seasonal nomenclature), 'We can no longer count years during which the kings oppressed us as a time in which we lived.'[19] Periodisation demands historical caesurae, so if the French Revolution had not occurred, it would have been necessary for the Romantic generation to invent it.

The theorisation of historical ruptures is a product of exactly what it seeks to account for, the demand for or experience of radical change. Yet

---

18 Fox quoted in L.G. Mitchell, *Charles James Fox* (Oxford: Oxford University Press, 1992), p. 110; Edmund Burke, *Reflections on the Revolution in France*, ed. by L.G. Mitchell (Oxford: Oxford University Press, 1993), p. 10. For further discussion see Nicholas Halmi, 'European Romanticism: Ambivalent Responses to the Sense of a New Epoch', in *The Cambridge History of Modern European Thought*, ed. by Warren Breckman and Peter Gordon (Cambridge: Cambridge University Press, 2019), vol. 1, pp. 40–64 (pp. 44–48), https://doi.org/10.1017/9781316160855.003

19 Quoted in Mona Ozouf, 'Revolutionary Calendar', in *A Critical Dictionary of the French Revolution*, ed. by Ozouf and François Furet, trans. by Arthur Goldhammer (Cambridge, MA: Harvard University Press, 1989), pp. 560–70 (p. 561).

insofar as periods are systems of norms, and hence cannot be separated absolutely from one another, the concept of revolution makes it hard to account for epochal transitions, and indeed is intended to do so, for it allows the present to distinguish itself by its clean break from what it consigns to a definitively overcome past. The challenge for a realist use of periodisation, therefore, is to understand the emergence of norms as a process rather than as an event—to understand an epoch in the new sense without an epoch in the old sense.

Romanticism and the 'Four Nations': Not Quite in Time

Fiona Stafford

English literary history is widely understood as a succession of distinct periods—the demarcations have been variously amended and modified over the years, but the idea of a roughly chronological organisation of texts, authors and prevailing concerns has proved remarkably resilient. David and Nick have already spoken of the beginnings of Romanticism as a recognisable cultural phenomenon, but it is also worth considering the effect of the widening study of English literature in its establishment. In 1843, when Robert Chambers published *A Cyclopedia of English Literature*, aimed at 'the moral advancement of the middle and humbler portions of society', he arranged numerous extracts into a series of 'Periods', with the last, listed rather unimaginatively as 'seventh period', running 'From 1780 to the present Time'.[20] As English continued to develop as a university subject, more elegant labels became standard, with 'Romantic' sandwiched between 'Augustan' and 'Victorian' literature. Romanticism later became the successor to 'the Eighteenth Century', which often ran back to the 1660s as Augustanism refused to be laid entirely to rest. Romanticism is currently being absorbed into both the 'Long Eighteenth Century' and the 'Long Nineteenth Century', though this is unlikely to continue because if all centuries lengthen in this way, they must cease to be 'centuries' at all. If the recent move to revive strictly temporal terms

---

20 *A Cyclopedia of English Literature*, 2 vols, ed. by Robert Chambers (Edinburgh: William and Robert Chambers, 1843), preface.

arose from uneasiness with the perceived connotations of broad, and not very consistent, terms such as Augustan, Romantic and Victorian (each derived from different kinds of identification—classical, aesthetic, regnal), the subsequent tendency to extend centuries demonstrates a conflicting unease about cultural divisions informed entirely by arbitrary units of time. Romanticism seems to attract and resist the idea of being 'in time'.

During the 1980s, resistance to what was then seen as a prevailing emphasis on the 'Big Six' poets—Blake, Wordsworth, Coleridge, Shelley, Keats (and sometimes Byron)—led Jerome McGann, Marilyn Butler and other historicist—and feminist—critics to call for recognition of a 'Romantic Period' rather than 'High Romanticism', which also entailed a redirection of critical attention to writers whose work had been unfairly neglected.[21] Replacement of 'Romanticism' with the 'Romantic period', however, soon brought back many of the problems aired by Lovejoy and Wellek, and already discussed in this forum. A central difficulty relates not so much to time as to the other great co-ordinate, space. Once the idea of the 'Romantic' moves beyond England and literature to Europe and other art forms, it becomes increasingly difficult to define a distinct 'period'. International movements in painting, music or architecture that are widely known as 'Romantic' don't keep quite in time with English literature.

My focus is on the difficulties surrounding literary periodisation within the four nations of England, Ireland, Scotland and Wales—sometimes understood as British Romantic literature, sometimes as quite separate traditions. Romantic writers were often self-consciously dialogical (to invoke Bakhtin again), acutely aware of both predecessors and readers and creating texts fraught with the twin anxieties of influence and reception.[22] Their yearnings for literary immortality were

---

21 See, e.g., Jerome McGann, *The Romantic Ideology* (Chicago: University of Chicago Press, 1983); *The Beauty of Inflections: Literary Investigations in Historical Method and Theory* (Oxford: Clarendon Press, 1985); ed., *The New Oxford Book of Romantic Period Verse* (Oxford: Oxford University Press, 1993). Marilyn Butler, *Romantics, Rebels and Reactionaries: English Literature and Its Background 1760–1830* (Oxford: Oxford University Press, 1980).

22 Bloom's influential work on *The Anxiety of Influence* (New York: Oxford University Press, 1973) has inspired numerous critical analyses not only of Romantic poetry's engagement with 'strong' writers of the past, especially Shakespeare, Milton, Spenser and Dante, but also of their anxious reception by readers: see, e.g., Lucy

piqued by past greats and premised on the recognition that readers of future centuries were inherently unpredictable. Romantic texts might strive to be out of time, but remain dependent on later generations of readers, editors and publishers, whose attitudes are conditioned by their own times—and places. The interpretation of history is conditioned by later events and by the identity of the interpreter.

If literary history is imagined as a long line, it demands stops along the way—if only for the practical purposes of teaching students or providing boundaries for anthologies and critical studies. David has already addressed the issue of how best to divide literary time—by capacious periods or narrower spans of dates—and in either case the timeline needs to begin somewhere. For English Romantic literature, the starting point might be Cowper's *The Task* in 1785, or perhaps Blake's *Songs of Innocence* in 1789, or even *Lyrical Ballads* in 1798 or 1800. There might then be further stops along the way at 1805 (*The Prelude*), 1811 (*Sense and Sensibility*), 1812 (*Childe Harold's Pilgrimage*), 1818 (*Frankenstein*), 1819 (*Don Juan*) and so on and so on (the end point being another tricky matter for debate). These major stops on the English line don't, however, seem quite adequate for twenty-first-century literary travellers—especially if they hail from Ireland, Scotland or Wales. The line of Scottish Romantic period literature might begin a year later in 1786, with Burns's *Poems Chiefly in the Scottish Dialect*, running on to 1802 with the *Edinburgh Review* and *Minstrelsy of the Scottish Border*, to 1805 (*The Lay of the Last Minstrel*), 1810 (*The Lady of the Lake* and *The Scottish Chiefs*), 1814 (*Waverley*) and so on: roughly parallel with the English line, but markedly different. But I would extend the Scottish Romantic period as far back as 1760 and the publication of Macpherson's first *Ossian* poems—which would seem idiosyncratic to many English scholars of the period, but might make sense to Europeans and art historians. When Germaine de Staël, for example, attempted to order European literature in 1800, she opted for a broad geographical division and celebrated Ossian as representative of '*La Littérature du Nord*'.[23]

Newlyn, *Reading, Writing and Romanticism: The Anxiety of Reception* (Oxford: Oxford University Press, 2000); Andrew Bennett, *Romantic Poets and the Culture of Posterity* (Cambridge: Cambridge University Press, 2009), https://doi.org/ 10.1093/acprof: oso/9780198187110.001.0001

23 Germaine de Staël, *De la Littérature, considérée dans ses rapports avec les institutions sociales*, in *Œuvres Complètes*, 8 vols. (Paris, 1820), vol. 4, p. 258.

In addition to the problem of when the Romantic period begins, other issues arise from attempting to disentangle English and Scottish literature. Should the Scottish line include Boswell's *Life of Johnson*—one of the most important publications of the 1790s and yet rarely considered 'Romantic' or 'Scottish'? Separating out national literary lines is not easy—where does Byron sit? His mother was Scottish and he grew up in Aberdeenshire until the age of ten, when he inherited the Byron family estate in England. He was educated at Harrow and Cambridge, spent two years travelling after university and then left the UK at the age of twenty-eight, never to return. Although a single English literary line is inadequate, parallel lines are also problematic. Perhaps what we need are interweavings, intersections and key junctions—a complicated map rather than a timeline. Recent decades have seen increasing demand for distinct national literary histories, along with calls for Scottish political independence, but in terms of literary and cultural history, entirely separate lines may generate as many objections as the absorption of every text into a single narrative. And what about Scottish Gaelic, Irish or Welsh literature? Poems composed in Celtic languages are at once integral parts of the larger nations and yet often very resistant to integration. Are these Romantic literary texts because they were composed in the later eighteenth or early nineteenth centuries? In the case of poems that have survived in the oral tradition, often no one knows when they were written, so placing them in time is much more difficult than locating them geographically, in distinct regional or linguistic traditions.

To see writers historically demands recognition of key events, so Romantic timelines generally include public dates as well as literary births, deaths and publications. 1789 is obviously a key date, irrespective of Blake, and 1815 is better known for Waterloo than Wordsworth. But how many dates and which ones? As Nick has demonstrated, the French Revolution has been a defining aspect of the Romantic period since 1790, but often historical events are brought into focus by modern values. The French Revolution provoked an explosion of contemporary literary responses, but so did Napoleon, and Nelson, and the Battle of the Nile. In the later twentieth century, critical attention focussed heavily on the Revolution debate and the 'radical years' of major poets, while largely ignoring much of the ensuing war. 1805 was the year of

The Prelude, not Trafalgar. In the 1970s and 80s, the price of bread and post-war manifestations of discontent attracted more attention than the war itself from many literary scholars with Marxist and social-historical concerns. There has been far more work on the Revolutionary and Napoleonic Wars in the last two decades and new areas of research continue to emerge from the same rich period: the recent spate of bicentenaries brings home the way we re-read old books according to current concerns. The eruption of Mount Tambora and the ensuing dark summer attracted fresh interest in 2016—whether because of contemporary interest in the Gothic, or the environment, or Europe. In 2009, Scottish celebrations of Robert Burns's 250th birthday were swept along on a wave of devolutionary energy—a very different experience from the low key commemorations of the 1996 bicentenary of his death. Inevitably, we see the past from the present—and this has a major bearing on how we see national literary history—or histories.

In 2008 Murray Pittock's *Scottish and Irish Romanticism*, driven by irritation over the marginalisation of major poets such as Burns from English Romantic literary studies, urged scholars to turn their attention to Scottish and Irish texts and rethink the established paradigms of Romanticism. The impact of his work is still being felt. Although 'Irish Romanticism' is an emerging field, the conjunction of 'Romanticism' and Irish (or Anglo-Irish) texts is far from straightforward, as evident in Jim Kelly's carefully chosen title for his edited collection of 2011, *Ireland and Romanticism*. Claire Connolly's avoidance of the adjective 'Romantic' and choice of dates with special resonance in Ireland for her *A Cultural History of the Irish Novel, 1790–1829* (2012) shows similar sensitivity to the contemporary political dimensions of literary history. Connolly's emphasis on contextualisation and inclusivity is part of the new mainstream, following the widespread rejection of Romantic claims of transcendence by historicists of the 80s and 90s and the concomitant redirection towards regional distinctiveness, politicised language, gender and colonialism. The literature of early nineteenth-century Ireland, which included regional novels, Gothic fiction and non-fictional prose was ripe for critical revisiting. And yet, Ireland remains as much at odds with the 'Romantic period' as with 'Romanticism', because the key dates for English literature have very different resonances. 1798 is the year of the United Irishmen, not *Lyrical Ballads*.

The Irish challenge to traditional English literary history is obvious in *The Field Day Anthology of Irish Writing*, first published in 1991 under the general editorship of the nationalist critic Seamus Deane. Volume One stopped at *c.* 1850 and erased customary literary periodisations by presenting instead 'Drama 1600–1800' and 'Literature in Irish 1600–1800'.[24] Anyone in search of 'Irish Romanticism' has to work hard: Robert Emmet's *Speech from the Dock* of 1803 comes in a section beginning with Oliver Cromwell's *Letters from Ireland* (1649). Key dates and words—'Revolution', 'Republic'—have different connotations in Ireland, while 1800, when the Act of Union was passed, is the great dividing line. For many literary scholars outside Ireland, however, the Act of Union is less likely to appear in a brief timeline of the Romantic period than Waterloo. The question of how helpful it is to separate out the national lines refuses resolution nevertheless—a key text from the key year, Maria Edgeworth's *Castle Rackrent* of 1800, has been widely heralded as foundational, but its pioneering status depends on the critic and the literary heritage being traced. Is Edgeworth's novel more or less significant when seen as an influence on Sydney Owenson, Walter Scott or Jane Austen? This is a small but telling example of the slipperiness of literary history—are texts best understood in a national or international frame? In historical context or a transcendent realm of art?

And what about Wales? The very fact that this question so often appears almost as an afterthought, even in discussions turning on the 'four nations', tells its own tale of prevailing perspectives on the past. Surprisingly few of the numerous analyses of Wordsworth's poetry mention that the climactic ascent of Snowdon took place in North Wales, or that 'the Banks of the Wye' run in sinuous bends along the Welsh/English border, from the river's source in the mountains of Wales. The generic expansion of 'Romanticism' that has begun to transform attitudes to Irish literature of this period is also influencing assumptions about Wales. The *Curious Travellers* project, run by Mary-Ann Constantine and Nigel Leask from the twin points of Aberystwyth and Glasgow, has been tracing the work of Thomas Pennant, a Welsh

---

24 As discussed in Fiona Stafford, 'The Literary Legacies of Irish Romanticism', in *Irish Literature in Transition 1780–1830*, ed. by Claire Connolly (Cambridge: Cambridge University Press, 2020), pp. 402–21, https://doi.org/10.1017/9781108632218.023

antiquarian who travelled widely in Scotland.²⁵ In the past, Pennant and his many followers might have merited only a footnote in a history of Romantic literature, but this exciting new project places travel-writing at its centre. As David's new *Oxford Handbook* makes so clear in its organisation and method, 'Romanticism' is a multi-dimensional phenomenon, whose richness invites approaches through space and place and through literary traditions that are not quite in time.

Periodisation as a Problem: The Case of American Romanticism

Martin Procházka

Periodisation as a problem emerges with the arrival of structuralism and its emphasis on the description of the system, viewed primarily in the synchronic perspective. In order to assume this perspective, structuralists have to shift their focus from history to historicity.

However, historicity is, as Derrida writes, 'difficult to *acknowledge*'.²⁶ In *Speech and Phenomena* he connects it with an 'ideality', which is 'another name for the permanence of the same' given by 'the possibility of repetition'.²⁷ Later, in *The Gift of Death*, he discusses historicity in ethical terms, as the responsibility for the *past*, the *future* or the *other*, which is linked with the self, the nation, the state, etc., by historical events. History, says Derrida commenting on Jan Patočka's *Heretical Essays*, 'can be neither a decidable object nor a totality capable of being mastered, precisely because it is tied to *responsibility*, to *faith*, and to the *gift*'. Despite this, 'historicity must be *admitted to*', which implies that it must remain the 'problem of history', a problem that is never to be resolved.²⁸

---

25   http://curioustravellers.ac.uk
26   Jacques Derrida, *The Gift of Death*, trans. by David Wills (Chicago: University of Chicago Press, 1995), p. 5.
27   Jacques Derrida, 'Speech and Phenomena', in *Speech and Phenomena and Other Essays on Husserl's Theory of Signs*, trans. by David B. Allison (Evanston: Northwestern University Press, 1973), p. 52.
28   Derrida, *The Gift of Death*, p. 5.

Since it resists objectification and closure, history cannot be converted into a system that could be studied by a structuralist method. The effort to get out of this impasse is typical of the new historicist approach, focusing on the links between individual narratives, events and objects and structuring them by simple yet exceedingly versatile patterns: circulation, oscillation, substitution, or exchange.

Although the meaning of period as a portion of time appears, as Nick noted, only in the seventeenth century, or—in the specific literary historical context—in the later eighteenth century, the origins of period as a structural pattern can be traced to the antiquity, and specifically to the third book of Aristotle's *Rhetoric*. Here, time is transformed into empirical sequences (rhythmic patterns), which in turn are formalised by mathematical means. The totality of the Aristotelian period is no longer supported by the supreme authority of myth as in the case of 'ages'. Nor does it stem from what Benedict Anderson called 'simultaneity along time' typical of time perception in traditional religious communities. It is based on *intrinsic balance* controlled by a certain metre called *paian*. This way of structuring can be related to what Anderson calls the 'homogeneous empty time [...] marked [...] by temporal coincidence'.[29]

These features of Aristotle's concept may be said to anticipate some structuralist approaches to systems, whose balance is alternately disrupted and regained in the course of time, such as the notions of the dynamic nature of natural language as a system and of the 'national literature' discussed by the representatives of the Prague School including Jan Mukařovský, and especially Felix Vodička.

It may be objected that this perspective is no longer relevant for the 'world republic of letters'.[30] However, even within this republic, large and influential national literatures may be said to spread 'Eurochronology' or 'ethnocentrism of literary-historical periodisations' and the problem of a structuralist approach to periodisation reappears on a global level.[31]

---

[29] Benedict Anderson, *Imagined Communities* (London: Verso, 1991), p. 24.
[30] Pascale Casanova, *The World Republic of Letters*, trans. by M. B. DeBevoise (Cambridge, MA: Harvard University Press, 2004), pp. 236–37
[31] Arjun Appadurai, *Modernity at Large: Cultural Dimensions of Globalization* (Minneapolis: University of Minnesota Press, 1996), p. 30; Emily S. Apter, *Against World Literature: On the Politics of Untranslatability* (London: Verso, 2013), p. 41;

Vodička's theory of literary historical periods explained in his principal work, *The Structure of Development*, is characterised by a certain ambiguity. On the one hand, a period in literary history should be 'an autonomous field', given by 'dominant elements of literary structures and forms,' that is, chiefly by 'the immanent development' of principal genres. On the other hand, Vodička refers to the extrinsic causes, such as the socio-cultural and political dynamics of 'the community of language users' or 'the morals and morality in literature of a certain period' as determining factors of this development.[32]

The last-mentioned proposition, however, contradicts the previous assumption that literary history must have its own, 'intrinsic' periodisation method. The system ultimately derives its existence from the empirical status of language as a 'community' of its users, which in turn is seen as the origin of its principal unit, the totality of a 'national literature'.[33]

In other words, structuralism can grasp periods only as means of pragmatic systemisation of heterogeneous material, consisting of a number of phenomena which are arbitrary from the point of view of the intrinsic development of literature. Among the responses to this approach, the effort to shift the focus from the totality of the system to the pragmatic nature of its boundaries as *power structures* has to be mentioned, since it plays a great role in a number of attempts at a periodisation of American literature and hence also in American Romanticism.[34]

This term was rarely used by U.S. scholars until recently. The alternative concepts, such as Emerson's 'Transcendentalism' or Matthiessen's 'American Renaissance', are products of ideological assumptions about the exceptionality and world leadership of the U.S. Emerson's 'new idealists', able to look beyond the empirical realities to 'Heaven's own truth' (as Melville put it), are both a construct derived

---

Christopher Prendergast, 'Negotiating World Literature', *New Left Review*, 8 (2001), 100–21 (p. 104).
32 Felix Vodička, *Struktura vývoje* (The Structure of Development, 1969), 2nd enlarged ed. (Prague: Dauphin, 1998), p. 67, my translation.
33 Ibid., pp. 66, 73.
34 Gilles Deleuze and Félix Guattari, *Anti-Oedipus: Capitalism and Schizophrenia*, trans. by Robert Hurley, Mark Seem and Helen Lane (Minneapolis: University of Minnesota Press, 1983), p. 170.

from Kant's transcendental philosophy, modified by the thoughts of Fichte, Coleridge and Carlyle (whose *Sartor Resartus* had a great influence on Emerson), and the sign of a desire to cross the limitations and divisions of U.S. society and its climate in the early 1840s.[35] While the term 'Transcendentalism' can be understood as an expression of the desire for spiritual change, the phrase 'American Renaissance' implies the desire for supremacy in terms of 'Eurochronology': the triumph of art as a form of national consciousness and a privileged representation of a nation as a collective body. In the mid-nineteenth century, this allegedly homogeneous, ethnocentric and male-governed community is, to quote F.O. Matthiessen, 'coming to its maturity and affirming its rightful heritage in the whole expanse of art and culture'.[36] Coining the term 'American Renaissance', Matthiessen does not go beyond numerous assertions of U.S. cultural independence, which were the foundations of all ideological statements of Americanism since the Declaration of Independence. His reduction of the principal canon to Emerson, Thoreau, Hawthorne, Melville and Whitman, and only three rather brief mentions of Emily Dickinson, in *American Renaissance* more than amply demonstrate the arbitrariness of his teleological approach. The power structure of Matthiessen's expanding boundaries of American literature collapses when he discusses the relationship between Emerson and Nietzsche, or Whitman and Hitler, as mere 'apparent harmonies' which were deliberately disrupted by Nietzsche's and Hitler's 'natures less temperate' than Emerson's own.[37]

This rather bizarre conclusion may exemplify numerous reductive statements by earlier historians, which made some later scholars abandon their attempts at using periodisation as a method of defining and integrating objects of literary history. In his 'Introduction' to *The Cambridge History of American Literature*, Sacvan Bercovitch explains

---

35 Herman Melville, *Pierre, or, The Ambiguities*, ed. by Robert S. Forsythe (New York: Knopf, 1930), p. 235. Melville refers to Emerson's essay 'The Transcendentalist' (1842).

36 F.O. Matthiessen, *American Renaissance: Art and Expression in the Age of Emerson and Whitman* (New York: Oxford University Press, 1941), p. vii.

37 George Blaustein, *Nightmare Envy and Other Stories: American Culture and European Reconstruction* (Oxford: Oxford University Press, 2018), p. 178, https://doi.org/10.1093/oso/9780190209209.001.0001. Blaustein quotes *American Renaissance* (pp. 436, 546).

his notion of American literary history as 'a polyphony of large-scale narratives [...] ample enough in [their] scope and detail [...] persuasive by demonstration (rather than by assertion) and hence authoritative in [their] own right'.[38] This 'diversity of perspectives' is complemented by their 'overlap' as 'a strategy of multivocal description' which, among other things, rules out attempts at drawing fixed periodisation boundaries.[39]

Although this experiment may raise serious doubts, it may also suggest a different approach to periodisation. Instead of deriving boundaries from the totality of a system, we may explore them as loci of complexity and sites of transformation. And the research of American Romanticism as a process of transformation and merging of traditional and popular genres (as in the case of Emily Dickinson), novel and essay (in Melville, who both develops and repudiates Emerson's Transcendentalism), novel and romance (in Hawthorne), or even the re-invention of major philosophical and aesthetic categories (as in the case of the 'self' in Whitman's 'Song of Myself') may lead to a *transnational as well as transitional* view of American Romanticism as a core cultural development of modernity, pointing back to the pitfalls of the Enlightenment (as in the Gothic novels of Charles Brockden Brown) and forward to modernist and avant-garde experiments (as in Whitman's and Dickinson's poetry).[40] This approach should not engender a new statement of exceptionalism but lead to a recognition of the limits of 'Eurochronology' and a shift of attention from the European roots of American Romanticism to its transformative powers shaping the new consciousness of literature and the literary public in the post-Civil-War era.

---

38 Sacvan Bercovitch, 'Introduction', in *The Cambridge History of American Literature: Prose Writing 1820–1865*, vol. 2 (Cambridge: Cambridge University Press, 1994), pp. 4–5.
39 Ibid., p. 5.
40 See, e.g., Cristianne Miller, 'Dickinson and the Ballad', *Genre*, 45.1 (2012), 29–45, https://doi.org/10.1215/00166928-1507029; Martin Procházka, 'Walt Whitman', in *Lectures on American Literature*, 2nd ed., ed. by Justin Quinn (Prague: Charles University Press, 2011), p. 111.

Response

Laurent Folliot

It might be best, in view of the wealth and variety of the statements we have just heard, to declare from the outset some theoretical affiliations, or at least inspirations. For my part, I have been very much impressed by the approach outlined by Paul Veyne (later one of Foucault's close associates) in his 1971 *Comment on écrit l'histoire*—a book translated into English as *Writing History*, but whose title might also read as *How They Write History*, such was its polemical thrust against historicist readings of history.[41] Against what would soon become known as grand narratives, Veyne argued for a return to the Aristotelian view of historical events as essentially sublunary—hopelessly particular, singular even—and therefore unamenable to the formality of historical 'laws'; the result was, so to speak, an atomistic view of the historical domain in which the notion of essentially distinct periods appears quite as hopeless as that of a sense or *telos* of history, but in which, at the same time, any particular attempt at periodisation can become relevant, according to the subject considered and the historian's heuristic intentions. Now I wish to suggest that such a conception is not necessarily incompatible with Martin Procházka's, which sees the boundaries of a given system (or period) as 'loci of complexity and sites of transformation'—meaning, as I take it, that a given liminal fact or event may well look backward and/or forward beyond the period it is usually associated with; and it is certainly consistent with the kind of short-term periodisation David has brilliantly put forward as one of several chronological 'scales' on which to consider British Romanticism.

But maybe this was by the way. To (finally) begin with, I would like to come back to what seemed to me the premise of two of the statements we have just read. On the one hand, Nick Halmi has shown us that the need for periodisation could only arise once history had ceased to be periodic in the older sense—i.e., cyclical—and 'a linear [...] temporalised conception of history' had emerged (and here I must say from the outset

---

41 Paul Veyne, *Comment on écrit l'histoire*, 2nd ed. (Paris: Seuil, 1978); *Writing History: Essay on Epistemology*, trans. by M. Moore-Rinvolucri (Manchester: Manchester University Press, 1984).

that I am tempted to understand 'temporalised' as at least suggesting 'secularised'). On the other hand, Martin has suggested that there is an analogy between the Aristotelian period itself—mathematically formalised and wrenched away from mythical temporality—and the 'homogenous, empty time' Benjamin would associate with progress. In both cases, then, the need to periodise seems to stem from a necessity of coming to terms with a secularised understanding of time and history, of history as time. Yet secularisation itself is more of an ongoing, indefinite process than a sudden caesura—it has no clear 'epoch', to take up Nick's first definition of that word—and I want to wonder, with reference both to the French Revolution and to British Romanticism, to what extent older, metaphysical or mythical schemes remained at work in their own historical self-understanding (rather as, in Benjamin's eye, the dwarf theology was to animate the automaton of historical materialism).[42] On the one hand, revolution itself (a quondam synonym for 'period', as Nick has reminded us) was still frequently envisioned, along classical republican lines, as repristination, as a Machiavellian *ritorno ai principii* which was not, ultimately, without relying upon some notion of sanctified origin or *archè*. If Saint-Just said that happiness was a new idea in Europe, he also claimed that the world had been empty since the Romans, and the angel of the Terror, as he has been dubbed, was one who looked backward as well as forward.[43] On the other hand, Romanticism, at least in the case of Wordsworth, Coleridge, and more problematically Blake, was informed by a (very partially) secularised version of the Apocalypse, and the Romantic project might be roughly located, simultaneously, in the repristination of natural man (through a return to natural poetry, for Wordsworth) and in the indefinite unfolding of his higher faculties on a superior level. The question I want to ask, very tentatively, is whether British Romanticism, unlike some of its French and German counterparts, should not be understood as showing some reluctance, some resistance even, not just to the annoying or elusive spirit of the age, but to age-spirits generally, as threatening to trivialise its own endeavours, its own hopes of imminent regeneration?

---

42 Walter Benjamin, 'On the Concept of History', in *Illuminations*, ed. by Hannah Arendt, trans. by Harry Zohn (New York: Schocken Books, 1969).
43 Saint-Just, *Œuvres complètes*, ed. by Michèle Duval (Paris: Gérard Lebovici, 1984), pp. 715, 778.

As an aside, we may remember that modern periodisation could be said to begin with the Italian Humanists who coined the phrase 'Middle Ages' (*media tempestas*) to designate the long period of 'Gothic' darkness between the splendour of Antiquity and the incipient Renaissance of their own time; and we might suggest (a little tongue-in-cheek, perhaps) that there was in Romanticism, insofar as it conceptualised itself as a Renaissance of sorts, a tendency to view all periods between sundry idealised pasts and the present much in the same way as Byron saw the middle age of man, which 'is—I really scarce know what'.[44]

Another related point I wish to make has to do with periodisation in other arts, which tends to re-shuffle temporal units just as much as the four-nation perspective Fiona Stafford has charted. In music, as Charles Rosen and Henri Zerner remind us, Classicism largely overlaps with the Romantic period in literature; Beethoven is the last of the great classical triad, but he also is the fountainhead of Romanticism, which persists up to Wagner and his disciples, and in fact Haydn and Mozart themselves could be seen as Romantics by contemporaries like E.T.A. Hoffmann.[45] Romanticism, therefore, covers most if not all of the nineteenth century, until it is fulfilled and transcended by the Second Viennese School. In architecture, the Neoclassicism that prevailed in countries both revolutionary and counter-revolutionary was soon displaced by eclecticism, a paradoxical consequence of the historicism so often singled out as the defining characteristic of the Romantic era: an ironic consequence of historical awareness in nineteenth-century architects was that, even as they strove to seize and celebrate the spirit of the age, they merely ranged through past centuries, shifting from Venetian to Northern Gothic to Italianate or French Renaissance and back again to neoclassical, as they felt the occasion at hand most specifically required, until the Bauhaus (at least according to teleologically-minded art historians like Nikolaus Pevsner) finally inaugurated the new age that had eluded previous generations for so long. What this might suggest, I think, is that the age of progress may have been somehow averse to self-periodisation, and postponed, as much as possible, the Hegelian dusk in which the owl of Minerva would take its wing and pronounce

---

44 *Don Juan*, Canto XII, line 3.
45 Charles Rosen and Henri Zerner, *Romanticism and Realism: The Mythology of Nineteenth Century Art* (London: Faber, 1984), p. 34.

its closure (perhaps present ages do in general resist seeing themselves as mere periods, and pace Alain Badiou's urgings that we should finally enter the twenty-first century).[46] What it might also suggest is that the epochal character of both the Revolution and Romanticism resulted in the increased difficulty of periodisation, as the present became freer, more atomised, and less amenable to grand syntheses.

Which may bring us, finally, to the apparently simpler question of when British Romanticism begins and ends. Fiona Stafford has reminded us of the inaugural value of Macpherson's *Ossian* for Scotland, and in fact for Britain and Europe more generally: Ossian, as Wordsworth contemptuously noted, was a great favourite with Lucien Bonaparte, and there may well have been a temptation with French commentators (apt as they were to fall into *Franco-chronologies*) to view Romanticism as originally a Scottish/Celtic creation, later fostered and bestowed upon Europe by Gallic taste! The European perspective thus opened, at any rate, might lead us to conjure up the dreaded spectre of 'Pre-Romanticism', and only half-jestingly to ask whether Romanticism was not, somehow, Pre-Romanticism (an 'age of dissatisfaction', as Marshall Brown has called it) made conscious of itself, *für sich*, by the French Revolution.[47] If we consider endpoints, on the other hand, my personal impression is that Romanticism had *la vie dure*, as we say in French (we often view Baudelaire, the Symbolists and even realist and naturalist prose writers as belated offshoots of Romanticism). Although Arnold's 1881 view of Shelley as a 'beautiful ineffectual angel' must have been based in part on the conviction that Arnold's contemporaries had earned whatever convictions they might have the hard way of historical change, it is, I suspect, difficult to understand Tennyson and Browning and Swinburne and Ruskin—or indeed the American Renaissance or American Romanticism, as Martin has reminded us—without reference to the founding/restoring moment that we call Romanticism. 'Romantic' and 'Victorian', for instance, are heterogenous categories; yet the traditional English periodisation through reigns is valid in its cautious empiricism, just as the fuzzy label of 'Romanticism' is valid in its adequacy to the inchoate character of so much nineteenth-century art.

---

46   Alain Badiou, *Le Siècle* (Paris: Seuil, 2005); 'Le XXIe siècle n'a pas encore commencé', interview with Elie During, *Art Press*, 310 (March 2005).
47   Marshall Brown, *Preromanticism* (Stanford: Stanford University Press, 1991), p. 3.

Discussion[48]

DD: Nick, would you like to reply first to Laurent's comments? He has taken up your point about how the French Revolution altered the experience of time and sharpened the distinction between periods—the sense of radical turning points in history, a 'before' and 'after', even if the French Revolutionaries often fantasised about restoring some pristine state of society rather than creating something altogether new.

NH: I would like to address two points raised by Laurent. The first concerns the contemporary interpretation of the French Revolution as an historical caesura. Historians like Stephen Bann and Peter Fritzsche have emphasised the formative role of the Revolution in the modern conception of temporalised history—or what François Hartog calls the modern *régime d'historicité*. By this account the Revolution was perceived as so socially and politically disruptive that the experience of the present and expectations of the future ceased to be interpretable by reference to the past. But as Laurent noted, temporalisation, as the replacement of a cyclical with a linear understanding of historical time, was itself a process, and one result of this process was the possibility of interpreting the fall of the Bastille and its consequences as a uniquely significant event marking a permanent change in European political arrangements. As early as 1762, in Book 3 of *Émile*, Rousseau had forecast an approaching 'state of crisis and century of revolutions', and the early reception of the French Revolution—in contrast, for example, to that of the Seven Years' War—confirms that the expectation of a new epoch preceded any experience that could have justified this expectation. So the Revolution served not to create a temporalised, periodising *régime d'historicité*, but to affirm the one that had already developed in the course of the eighteenth century.

Laurent also mentioned contemporary resistances to the 'spirit of the age', understood as the acceptance of the radically new. This is a very important point, insufficiently acknowledged, I think, by Koselleck and those who accept his basic theories of the temporalisation of history and the experience of temporal acceleration in the so-called *Sattelzeit*

---

[48] With DD standing for David Duff, NH for Nicholas Halmi, MP for Martin Procházka and FS for Fiona Stafford.

('saddle period') of 1750 to 1850. Laurent referred to temporalisation as secularisation, and I would accept the latter term only in the specific sense used by Blumenberg, namely the use of a theological vocabulary to describe secular concepts and events, as in Coleridge's prose 'Argument' to his poem 'Religious Musings' (1794): 'The French Revolution, Millennium. Universal Redemption.' An imminently caused, historically unfolding event is precisely not comparable to the divine intervention prophesied in the Book of Revelation. But the rhetorical identification of the two serves to disguise their conceptual incommensurability, and hence to mitigate the most troubling implication of the admission of epochal ruptures into historical self-understanding—the radical uncertainty of the future. In the aesthetic sphere the eclecticism to which Laurent referred—notably the accurately copied but decontextualised use of multiple historical architecture styles, Doric Greek, Imperial Roman, French Gothic, Florentine Renaissance, etc.—represents an analogous response to the recognition that historicisation, and its consequent demand that art express the contemporary zeitgeist, entailed a severance from artistic traditions and a renunciation of long-established aesthetic norms. The use of historically referential styles fosters the *appearance* of an historical continuity that is recognised not to exist; but exactly because it doesn't exist, all styles are theoretically equivalent and available for use, none having a sustainable claim to normativity. From a philosophical perspective such forms of resistance may be incoherent, but we should not minimise the anxieties underlying them.

DD: Martin, you too invoked classical models of periodicity to set against modern understandings of the term. Do you draw similar conclusions to Nick's from this comparison? Laurent, on the other hand, suggested that your conception of period boundaries as 'loci of complexity and sites of transformation' was compatible with anti-historicist models of history-writing. Do you accept that inference?

MP: I have suggested connecting the term 'period' with the Greek word *peras*, meaning limits, or 'everything that can be expressed by numbers or arithmetical relations'.[49] In Aristotle's *Metaphysics*, reviewing the teaching of the Pythagoreans, *peras* are static and firmly set boundaries of things: 'We call a limit the last point of each thing, i.e., the first point beyond which it is not possible to find any part, and the first point within which every part is'.[50] However, *peras* do not merely determine the 'spatial magnitude' but also 'the end of each thing', its *telos* or purpose ('that towards which the movement and action are [...], that for the sake of which'), and they are also understood epistemologically, as 'the limit of knowledge'.[51]

Commenting on the teaching of the Pythagoreans, Aristotle combines the notions of limit and number: 'the elements of number are the even and the odd, and of these the former is unlimited, and the latter limited', and points out that, according to the Pythagoreans, 'number' is 'forming both [the] modifications and [the] states' of things.[52] As a result, Aristotle's reflections on *numbers as limits* imply that the latter may not only mark the contours of being (as Heidegger put it) but reveal its dynamics, consisting in transitions and transformations.

Aristotle's reflections on numbers read almost as an anticipation of the digital. The dynamic view of *peras* may have a crucial influence on our understanding of period and periodisation. As I have pointed out in my introductory talk, '[i]nstead of deriving boundaries from the totality of a system', 'we may explore them as loci of complexity and sites of transformation'.

Why do I use 'loci' or 'sites', and not 'foci', as Laurent suggests? Because I am aware of the importance of spatial imagination for our understanding of periods as temporal phenomena, evident in our use of terms like 'landmark' but also in more complex approaches to limits and boundaries. An example is the approach of Deleuze and Guattari, who understood a boundary as a specific power structure regulating

---

[49] Vassilis Karasmanis, 'Continuity and Incommensurability in Ancient Greek Philosophy and Mathematics', in *Socratic, Platonic and Aristotelian Studies: Essays in Honor of Gerasimos Santas*, ed. by Georgios Anagnostopoulos (Dordrecht: Springer, 2011), pp. 389–99 (p. 393), https://doi.org/10.1007/978-94-007-1730-5_22

[50] Aristotle, *Metaphysics* 1022a4–5, in *The Complete Works of Aristotle: The Revised Oxford Translation: One Volume Digital Edition*, ed. by Jonathan Barnes, Bollingen Series LXXI.2 (Princeton, NJ: Princeton University Press, 1984), p. 3472. The subsequent quotations follow the text of this edition.

[51] Aristotle, *Metaphysics* 1022a5–11.

[52] Ibid. 986a16–17.

desire by moving it 'in the direction of more intense and more adequate investments of the social field'.⁵³ (Their approach is related to Paul Veyne's 'anti-historicist approach to history writing' mentioned by Laurent and David.) Deleuze and Guattari have illustrated their rather general notion by a metaphor of colonial expansion: Oedipal desire is 'colonization pursued by other means, it is the interior colony, and we shall see that even here at home'.⁵⁴

In other words, the spatiality of boundaries and limits is fundamentally important not only with respect to periodisation, but in the discussion of the history of literatures and cultures, including recent notions as interculturalism or transculturalism, since the understanding of historical development has always been linked to the notions of territoriality or globality, evident even in the recent notions of 'world literature'.⁵⁵ And it has a specific importance in American literature.

DD: Has that got something to do with the frontier mentality?

MP: Definitely. Starting from the American Revolution, the identity of the Americans was being defined in a new way, namely with respect to the polysemic term 'frontier' and its crossing, or rather pushing it westward. In a letter of 12 June 1817, Thomas Jefferson defended the 'natural' right of expatriation as a foundation of 'the pursuit of happiness', which he saw, anticipating Deleuze's and Guattari's view, in the common, 'natural' desire to cross the frontier, specified as a 'geographical line' drawn by 'the whole body of English jurists': if God

> has made the law in the nature of man to pursue his own happiness, he has left him free in the choice of the place as well as mode; and we may safely call on the whole body of English jurists to produce a map on which Nature has traced the geographical line which she forbids him to cross in pursuit of happiness.⁵⁶

---

53   Gilles Deleuze and Félix Guattari, *Anti-Oedipus: Capitalism and Schizophrenia*, trans. by Robert Hurley, Mark Seem and Helen Lane (Minneapolis: University of Minnesota Press, 1983), p. 170.
54   Ibid.
55   See, e.g., the previously cited works by Pascale Casanova, Arjun Appadurai and Christopher Prendergast.
56   Quoted in Charles A. Miller, *Jefferson and Nature: An Interpretation* (Baltimore: Johns Hopkins University Press, 1988), p. 170.

In 1893, Frederick Jackson Turner formulated his Frontier Thesis, representing the U.S. identity as a collective experience of the Frontier and its westward movement that 'molded the distinctive character of Americans, shaping traits such as individualism, hard work, and self-reliance; it was the major determinant of the democratic character of their political institutions'. In doing so, Turner emphasised 'the dominating American character', namely 'perennial rebirth' and 'fluidity of American life' as well as 'its continuous touch with the simplicity of primitive society'.[57] Sadly enough, Turner, following the 'melting-pot theory', imagined this experience as a homogeneous process, in the course of which the myths of the West came to triumph over the 'wild nature' or the 'primitive society' of the Native Americans. Turner ignored the actual history of the settlement of the American West that included the genocide of the Indians and was a product of diverse waves of migration which always had a multi-ethnic and multicultural character.

This takes me back to my original comments on Sacvan Bercovitch's concept of American literary and cultural history. The 'polyphony of large-scale narratives' establishing 'a diversity of perspectives' leads also to the understanding of American literature as a typical frontier phenomenon: 'meanings and possibilities generated by competing ideologies, shifting realities and the confrontation of cultures'.[58] Hence also my approach to the periodisation of American Romanticism.

DD: In his response to your paper, Fiona, Laurent welcomed your nomination of Macpherson's *Ossian* as an inaugural moment for Scottish Romanticism, and perhaps for Irish Romanticism too, since Ossian was also claimed by the Irish and the debate over national ownership was at least as heated as the debate over the authenticity of the Ossian poems. But he was less confident about assigning end points. Do you share his discomfort on that score? A 'four nations' perspective disrupts the chronology of English Romanticism as regards starting points, but does it prove even more disruptive of end points?

FS: I agree that Romanticism's end point is just as elusive as its beginning—not least because a defining characteristic is the emphasis on

---

57 Frederick Jackson Turner, 'The Significance of the Frontier in American History', in *The Frontier in American History* (New York: Henry Holt, 1921), pp. 1–38 (p. 5).
58 Bercovitch, 'Introduction', p. 6.

process rather than perfection, of striving towards rather than arriving. In the light of today's discussion, we might conclude that Romanticism is so various and pervasive that it never really ended, whether we are thinking in terms of the later nineteenth-century poets recalled by Laurent, or of the 'American Renaissance' and 'Transcendentalism' discussed by Martin, or of Bakhtin's notion of 'great time' invoked by David, or of the later legacy of Romantic writers to twentieth- and twenty-first-century literature, or in less specifically literary terms, of the aesthetic appreciation of landscape, ecology and animal rights, the rise of nationalism and the concept of psychology and the modern self. As Nick put it, 'we remain the children of the first Romantic generation'.[59] If we have to think more practically, as editors of literary anthologies and handbooks do when drawing the final lines around their studies, the boundary between 'Romantic' and 'Victorian' (though conveniently erased by the 'long nineteenth century') could be placed at 1824 with the death of Byron, or at 1832 with the death of Walter Scott, the passing of the Great Reform Act and Tennyson's *Poems,* or at 1837, with the accession of Victoria. In Ireland, however, though part of the United Kingdom at this time, the end (in the sense of an achieved purpose) might be 1829 with Catholic Emancipation, or (in the sense of a catastrophe) 1845 when the Famine struck. Romanticism is resistant to ending and yet subject to multiple ends.

One reason why *Ossian* strikes me as an intriguing starting point is that this beginning is inherently elegiac—Ossian, the last of his race, is quintessentially a poet of aftermath, dwelling on the times of old. If, as Nick reminds us, Rousseau was predicting revolution and crisis in the 1760s, James Macpherson and contemporary Scottish Highlanders had already experienced violent upheaval and irreversible social change. The return to antiquity in *Ossian* was therefore a glimpse of the future (and we might extend this future to nineteenth-century America, and the experience of the native peoples, which Martin has already mentioned). At the same time, poems that appealed to later eighteenth-century readers as a glimpse of an earlier, simpler society—of 'natural man'—were also the fragments of an ancient culture, broken almost beyond recognition. And this might resonate with Nick's brilliant point about historically

---

59   Nicholas Halmi in his opening position statement above.

referential styles that offer the appearance of historical continuity, while disguising the underlying anxieties. If decontextualised imitations of the past do signal severance from rather than continuation of living tradition, Macpherson's blend of old and new, translated and created, Celtic and classical is a forerunner of Romantic (and later) eclecticism. In this way, the *Poems of Ossian* could be seen as pre-postmodern as much as pre-romantic.[60]

Macpherson's cultural translation from a predominantly oral culture into print is also worth considering in relation to our thinking about linear time and the sense of history, since legends and traditional tales passed on from generation to generation remain alive and open to remaking, when free from any ideal of the definitive, original, authored text with an established date of composition. The extension of print culture and newspapers was, as Benedict Anderson has argued, a crucial element in the development of the modern imagined communities that began to replace older senses of connection.[61] *The Poems of Ossian* drew on the undated 'times of old' but, in attempting to justify its existence through reference to historical records, exposed its mythic aspect to modern critique.[62]

DD: Laurent also raised a broader question, whether British Romanticism was at some level resistant to 'the annoying or elusive spirit of the age', and to age-spirits generally, insofar as they threatened to trivialise its endeavours and its hopes of regeneration. If he is right, this suggests another modification to Chandler's view of the Romantic period as the 'age of the spirit of the age'. It's also the age of *contestation* of the spirit of the age, of *anti*-periodisation: an era which imagines a future without the need for further radical breaks and period boundaries. That's the French Revolutionary dream in its purest form, a dream which is also, as Laurent says, a secularised version of apocalypse, or what Shelley called the 'far goal of time', the vision of a time beyond time, without the curse of mutability or periodicity. But the Revolutionary dream was

---

[60] For postmodern Ossian, see my essay on 'Romantic Macpherson', in *The Edinburgh Companion to Scottish Romanticism*, ed. by Murray Pittock (Edinburgh: Edinburgh University Press, 2011), pp. 27–38.
[61] Benedict Anderson, *Imagined Communities* (London: Verso, 1991).
[62] James Macpherson, *The Poems of Ossian*, ed. by Howard Gaskill (Edinburgh: Edinburgh University Press, 1996), p. 127.

of course shattered, and the Romantic zeitgeist is characterised as much by the shattering of the dream as the having of it. So we are back to periodicity, periodisation, and back to historical phases, or 'moments', blissful dawns and not-so-blissful afternoons and evenings. Where does this leave us?

FS: If we are thinking about the French Revolutionary, or Shelleyan-Godwinian, secularised version of apocalypse, we might also think about the way in which this finds a dark mirror in the futuristic fiction of a post-human world. Mary Shelley's novel, *The Last Man* (1826) is, by some reckonings, a late Romantic text, which can be read as a rebuke to the ideals her husband expressed in *Prometheus Unbound* and *A Defence of Poetry*. Here we find a secularised apocalypse without any millennial fulfilment—and no possibility of further periodisation, as the human race peters out.

Since *The Last Man* is the work of a woman writer, it is also an opportunity to think about whether our debates over Romanticism and periodisation are affected by gendered traditions. Patterns of patrilineal inheritance have not always been especially beneficial to women, so perhaps linear thinking is less congenial to them as well? It is telling that Helen Maria Williams saw the French Revolution in terms of the 'subversion of despotism'—as a liberation from inherited systems.[63] If the new age depends on the subversion of the old, then literary forms that offer ironic comment on dominant structures are as important as the invention of something new. This may be a reason why the novel, which (again following Bakhtin) is now widely understood as a 'parodic-travestying' genre rather than the agent of a Protestant father figure, appealed to so many women in the Romantic period.[64] Jane Austen's early, unpublished writings are a parodic cornucopia, showing a brilliant young woman rewriting the received, male-authored history of her nation and many of its literary masterpieces. Not that parody,

---

63 As quoted by Nicholas Halmi above.
64 M.M. Bakhtin, *The Dialogic Imagination: Four Essays*, ed. by Michael Holquist, trans. by Caryl Emerson and Michael Holquist (Austin: University of Texas Press, 1982). Bakhtin's argument was a major spur to the numerous critical challenges to Ian Watt's influential case for *Robinson Crusoe*'s foundational status in *The Rise of the Novel* (1957): see, e.g., Michael McKeon, *The Origins of the English Novel, 1600–1740* (Baltimore: Johns Hopkins University Press, 1988).

novels or irony were the exclusive province of women in the period, of course. Percy Bysshe Shelley's vision may have been reflected—or distorted—in his widow's novel, but his own great *Defence* was in itself a response to Thomas Love Peacock's satirical *Four Ages of Poetry*. And yet, if the Romantic yearning towards timelessness seems inseparable from mocking voices asserting the triumph of time, such laughter often had its own redemptive potential. Romanticism is propelled by oppositions, engagements, conversations and reflections, as we seem to be demonstrating among ourselves.

DD: Undoubtedly, though I think we have also demonstrated some agreement about the fundamental issues. I have a final question about René Wellek, whom several of you have cited and whose conceptualisation of 'period' and of 'Romanticism' set the terms for modern discussion of this topic, despite the many challenges it has received. Re-reading some of his work, I was struck by the cogency of the claims he makes about Romantic self-definition, and the wealth the evidence he assembles, in refuting Lovejoy, to show how widely accepted in the Romantic period was the idea that this was a 'new age' of poetry. In my opening remarks, I cited Leigh Hunt, Shelley and Hazlitt as examples, but Wellek cites many other British authors and critics who expressed this view: Southey, Wordsworth, De Quincey, Walter Scott, Nathan Drake, Francis Jeffrey, Thomas Babington Macaulay, James Montgomery, later R.H. Horne in *The New Spirit of the Age* (1844).[65] These are just some of the names. These writers rarely use the term 'Romantic' to describe it but they have a very clear sense of their time as a distinct period, and there is a high measure of agreement about when it began: either in the 1760s, with Percy's *Reliques*, 'the great literary *epocha* of the present reign', as Southey called it (using the term in its old sense, as Nick helpfully explained); or, alternatively, in 1798, with the publication of *Lyrical Ballads*, another epoch-making literary event which radicalised that earlier revivalist aesthetic to produce a true 'revolution in literature', as it was subsequently often called. Wellek's point is that this was a view articulated and widely accepted *at the time*, not a retrospective construction. Contrary to Lovejoy's scepticism, the Romantic movement

---

[65] René Wellek, 'The Concept of Romanticism in Literary History', *Comparative Literature*, 1 (1949), 1–23, 147–72.

was a transformative process that writers and critics observed and commented on *as it was happening*, just as they wrote about the spirit of political transformation that was so palpable a feature of their time. The question of what set that literary transformation in motion, and when, became inescapable. This is how the idea of a 'Romantic period' began, not in the textbooks of later nineteenth-century literary historians, as sceptics allege.

My question, then, is, can we still accept Wellek's argument, in the face of the complications we have explored? And—a more technical question, for Martin especially—given Wellek's roots in Czech structuralism, was he faithful to the methodology of the Prague School? Do we need to understand its tenets to make sense of the debate about periodisation in Romantic studies?

MP: Wellek's methodology developed in a context widely different from that of other members of the Prague School. It was shaped by his early detailed reading of Nietzsche, who inspired him mainly by his perspectivism.[66] Wellek was influenced by the interpretations of Nietzsche by his teacher Otokar Fischer, Professor of German Language and Literature in the Czech section of Charles University. Fischer was isolated in the Czech literary context in his acceptance of the internal contradictions and anti-traditionalism of Nietzsche's doctrine, whose major role he saw in the intuitive diagnostics of the future stages of European culture. For both Wellek and Fischer, one of the most influential of Nietzsche's writings was the second of the *Untimely Meditations*, 'On the Use and Abuse of History for Life' (1874). Fischer also motivated Wellek to study Wilhelm Dilthey, Benedetto Croce, Leo Spitzer and Oskar Walzel. Other scholars recommended to Wellek by Fischer included especially Levin Ludwig Schücking, a Shakespearean and one of the founders of the sociohistorical study of literary taste.

Although Wellek's objectivist notion of the work of art was modified by Wilhelm Dilthey's hermeneutics emphasising the role of intuition, Wellek was still critical of some of Dilthey's concepts, especially that of 'lived experience' (*Erlebnis*). Similarly, he never fully accepted the

---

66 Martin Procházka, 'A Spectre or an Unacknowledged Visionary? Coleridge in Czech Culture', in *The Reception of S.T. Coleridge in Europe*, ed. by Elinor Shaffer and Edoardo Zuccato (London: Continuum, 2007), pp. 254–74 (pp. 268–69).

focus on the close analysis of form, typical of Russian formalism, to the detriment of the study of content and had reservations even as to the methodological orientation of Prague structuralism. Wellek used some formalist terminology (for instance *ostranyenie*, estrangement) but also criticised the formalists for their lack of deeper understanding of Romantic verse theorists. He stressed the principal tension between the formalist approach and German psychologically-oriented theory and maintained that the Prague structuralist theory of verse differed from the Romantic approaches only by a greater degree of formalisation.

This theoretical and critical stance might have led Wellek to express his reservations about the requirement that the members of the Prague Linguistic Circle should use only the structuralist methodology. In his letter to the Committee of the Prague Linguistic Circle, dated 21 September 1934, Wellek claimed that 'the admiration I have for the method of Structuralism does not exclude my use of other, mainly ideographical, methods in literary history, as follows from all my scholarly activities so far'.[67]

Wellek's initially objectivist approach to the work of art was also modified by his emphasis on its fictional nature, influenced by Hans Vaihinger's seminal work *The Philosophy of 'As If'* (1911). Later, Wellek found important inspiration, evident in his and Austin Warren's *Theory of Literature* (1949), in Roman Ingarden's phenomenological structuralism. As Ivo Pospíšil pointed out, 'René Wellek moved [...] on the boundaries of literary methodologies' and the power of this *liminal* approach has not yet been sufficiently appreciated.[68]

DD: That's very helpful, thank you. The theoretical underpinnings of what is sometimes called, reductively, the 'history of ideas' are not well understood, but you've clarified the conceptual basis of modern debates about literary periodisation, just as Nick has explained the history of the terminology the Romantics themselves employed. Perhaps we have begun to embrace some of the possibilities of a 'liminal' methodology by approaching the question of Romantic periodisation in relation to

---

67   Ivo Pospíšil and Miloš Zelenka, *René Wellek a meziválečné Československo (Ke kořenům strukturální estetiky)* (René Wellek and Czechoslovakia between the Two Wars: Towards the Roots of Structural Aesthetics) (Brno: Masarykova Univerzita, 1996), p. 61.
68   Ibid., p. 17.

different national literatures, and from the standpoint of different academic traditions—English, Scottish, French, German, American, Czech. That is part of the value of an international forum of this kind. The conversation we have started will doubtless continue in other times and places, but we need now to bring it to a close. What have we learned? Readers can draw their own conclusions from the arguments put forward, but we have, I think, shown that the question of periodisation in Romanticism is inseparably bound up with questions of secularisation, localisation and institutionalisation. It is the shift away from religious models of time, from Christian teleology and its sequential, providential, symmetrical plot, which throws open the question of how epochs are differentiated from one another, even if 'universal histories' continue to proliferate and the idea of an apocalyptic dénouement retains its hold. The French Revolution crystallises that question by proclaiming a radical break with the past, redefining the measurement of time and imposing its own secular teleology. Although things did not go according to plan, and attention transferred to how, or when, the Revolution ended, that question too became a model for literary historiography. Alongside the search for origins, for a starting point for the 'new age' we now call Romantic, there was an equally intense search for an end point (a search that, in Britain, dominated the critical writing of the 1820s). In trying to determine the first and last Romantics, to demarcate the beginning and ending of the literary revolution on which so many contemporary observers commented, we continue that quest, sharing their obsession and re-enacting the complications of their effort at self-periodisation. Whether, in our institutional practices, we extend the Romantic period (give it its own 'Romantic Century', as the journal *Studies in Romanticism* does, 1750–1850), or assign it a permanent, typological presence (as some analysts of Romanticism propose), or whether we subdivide it into a sequence of micro-periods, each with its own mini-zeitgeist, we are inevitably confronted with the problem of conflicting chronologies as we move from nation to nation, language to language, art form to art form. What seems beyond dispute is that time-consciousness is of the essence in Romanticism, and that part of the adjustment in consciousness that defines the Romantic movement is a desire to constitute itself as a period, however long or short its duration, and however porous and contested its boundaries.

Works Cited

Anderson, Benedict, *Imagined Communities* (London: Verso, 1991).

Appadurai, Arjun, *Modernity at Large: Cultural Dimensions of Globalization* (Minneapolis: University of Minnesota Press, 1996).

Apter, Emily S., *Against World Literature: On the Politics of Untranslatability* (London: Verso, 2013).

Badiou, Alain, *Le Siècle* (Paris: Seuil, 2005).

——, 'Le XXIe siècle n'a pas encore commencé', interview with Elie During, *Art Press*, 310 (March 2005).

Bakhtin, M.M., *The Dialogic Imagination: Four Essays*, ed. by Michael Holquist, trans. by Caryl Emerson and Michael Holquist (Austin: University of Texas Press, 1982).

——, *Speech Genres and Other Late Essays*, ed. by Caryl Emerson and Michael Holquist, trans. by Vern W. McGee (Austin: University of Texas Press, 1986).

Barnes, Jonathan, ed., *The Complete Works of Aristotle: The Revised Oxford Translation: One Volume Digital Edition*, Bollingen Series LXXI.2 (Princeton, NJ: Princeton University Press, 1984).

Benjamin, Walter, 'On the Concept of History', in *Illuminations*, ed. by Hannah Arendt, trans. by Harry Zohn (New York: Schocken Books, 1969).

Bennett, Andrew, *Romantic Poets and the Culture of Posterity* (Cambridge: Cambridge University Press, 2009), https://doi.org/10.1017/CBO9780511484100

Bercovitch, Sacvan, 'Introduction', in *The Cambridge History of American Literature: Prose Writing 1820–1865*, vol. 2 (Cambridge: Cambridge University Press, 1994), pp. 1–8, https://doi.org/10.1017/CHOL9780521301060

Blaustein, George. *Nightmare Envy and Other Stories: American Culture and European Reconstruction* (Oxford: Oxford University Press, 2018), https://doi.org/10.1093/oso/9780190209209.001.0001

Bloom, Harold, *The Anxiety of Influence* (New York: Oxford University Press, 1973).

Blumenberg, Hans, *Die Legitimität der Neuzeit*, 3rd ed. (Frankfurt: Suhrkamp, 1988).

Brown, Marshall, 'Periods and Resistances', *Modern Language Quarterly*, 62 (2001), 309–16.

——, *Preromanticism* (Stanford: Stanford University Press, 1991).

Burke, Edmund, *Reflections on the Revolution in France*, ed. by L.G. Mitchell (Oxford: Oxford University Press, 1993).

Butler, Marilyn, *Romantics, Rebels and Reactionaries: English Literature and Its Background 1760–1830* (Oxford: Oxford University Press, 1980).

Casanova, Pascale, *The World Republic of Letters*, trans. by M. B. DeBevoise (Cambridge, MA: Harvard University Press, 2004).

Chambers, Robert, ed., *A Cyclopedia of English Literature*, 2 vols. (Edinburgh: William and Robert Chambers, 1843).

Chandler, James, *England in 1819: The Politics of Literary Culture and the Case of Romantic Historicism* (Chicago: University of Chicago Press, 1998).

Connolly, Claire, *A Cultural History of the Irish Novel, 1790–1829* (Cambridge: Cambridge University Press, 2012), https://doi.org/10.1017/S0021121400001292

Curtius, Ernst Robert, *European Literature and the Latin Middle Ages*, trans. by Willard Trask (London: Routledge, 1953).

Deane, Seamus, ed., *The Field Day Anthology of Irish Writing* (Derry: Field Day, 1991).

Deleuze, Gilles and Félix Guattari, *Anti-Oedipus: Capitalism and Schizophrenia*, trans. by Robert Hurley, Mark Seem and Helen Lane (Minneapolis: University of Minnesota Press, 1983).

Derrida, Jacques, *The Gift of Death*, trans. by David Wills (Chicago: University of Chicago Press, 1995).

——, 'Speech and Phenomena', in *Speech and Phenomena and Other Essays on Husserl's Theory of Signs*, trans. by David B. Allison (Evanston: Northwestern University Press, 1973).

de Staël, Germaine, *De la Littérature, considérée dans ses rapports avec les institutions sociales*, in *Œuvres Complètes*, 8 vols. (Paris, 1820).

Duff, David, *Romanticism and the Uses of Genre* (Oxford: Oxford University Press, 2009).

——, ed., *The Oxford Handbook of British Romanticism* (Oxford: Oxford University Press, 2018).

Halmi, Nicholas, 'European Romanticism: Ambivalent Responses to the Sense of a New Epoch', in *The Cambridge History of Modern European Thought*, ed. by Warren Breckman and Peter Gordon (Cambridge: Cambridge University Press, 2019), vol. 1, pp. 40–64, https://doi.org/10.1017/9781316160879

Herder, Johann Gottfried, *Briefe zur Beförderung der Humanität* (1793–97), in *Werke in zehn Bänden*, vol. 7, ed. by H. D. Irmscher (Frankfurt: Deutscher Klassiker Verlag, 1991).

Hunt, Leigh, *The Feast of the Poets* (London: James Cawthorn, 1814).

Karasmanis, Vassilis, 'Continuity and Incommensurability in Ancient Greek Philosophy and Mathematics', in *Socratic, Platonic and Aristotelian Studies: Essays in Honor of Gerasimos Santas*, ed. by Georgios Anagnostopoulos (Dordrecht: Springer, 2011), pp. 389–99, https://doi.org/10.1007/978-94-007-1730-5_22

Kelly, Jim, ed., *Ireland and Romanticism: Publics, Nations and Scenes of Cultural Production* (Basingstoke: Palgrave Macmillan, 2011), https://doi.org/10.1057/9780230297623

Lovejoy, Arthur O., 'On the Discrimination of Romanticisms', *PMLA*, 39 (1924), 229–53.

Macpherson, James, *The Poems of Ossian*, ed. by Howard Gaskill (Edinburgh: Edinburgh University Press, 1996).

Matthiessen, F.O., *American Renaissance: Art and Expression in the Age of Emerson and Whitman* (New York: Oxford University Press, 1941).

McGann, Jerome, *The Romantic Ideology* (Chicago: University of Chicago Press, 1983)

——, *The Beauty of Inflections: Literary Investigations in Historical Method and Theory* (Oxford: Clarendon Press, 1985).

——, ed., *The New Oxford Book of Romantic Period Verse* (Oxford: Oxford University Press, 1993).

McKeon, Michael, *The Origins of the English Novel, 1600–1740* (Baltimore: Johns Hopkins University Press, 1988).

Melville, Herman, *Pierre, or, The Ambiguities*, ed. by Robert S. Forsythe (New York: Knopf, 1930).

Miller, Charles A., *Jefferson and Nature: An Interpretation* (Baltimore: Johns Hopkins University Press, 1988).

Miller, Cristianne, 'Dickinson and the Ballad', *Genre*, 45.1 (2012), 29–45, https://doi.org/10.1215/00166928-1507029

Mitchell, L.G., *Charles James Fox* (Oxford: Oxford University Press, 1992).

Newlyn, Lucy, *Reading, Writing and Romanticism: The Anxiety of Reception* (Oxford: Oxford University Press, 2000).

Oergel, Maike, *Zeitgeist–How Ideas Travel: Politics, Culture and the Public in the Age of Revolution* (Berlin: De Gruyter, 2019), https://doi.org/10.1515/9783110631531

Ozouf, Mona, 'Revolutionary Calendar', in *A Critical Dictionary of the French Revolution*, ed. by Ozouf and François Furet, trans. by Arthur Goldhammer (Cambridge, MA: Harvard University Press, 1989), pp. 538–47.

Pittock, Murray, *Scottish and Irish Romanticism* (Oxford: Oxford University Press, 2008), https://doi.org/10.1093/acprof:oso/9780199232796.001.0001

Pospíšil, Ivo and Miloš Zelenka, *René Wellek a meziválečné Československo (Ke kořenům strukturální estetiky)* (René Wellek and Czechoslovakia between the Two Wars: Towards the Roots of Structural Aesthetics) (Brno: Masarykova Univerzita, 1996).

Prendergast, Christopher, 'Negotiating World Literature', *New Left Review*, 8 (2001), 100–21.

Procházka, Martin,'Walt Whitman', *Lectures on American Literature*, 2nd ed., ed. by Justin Quinn (Prague: Charles University Press, 2011).

——, 'A Spectre or an Unacknowledged Visionary? Coleridge in Czech Culture', in *The Reception of S.T. Coleridge in Europe*, ed. by Elinor Shaffer and Edoardo Zuccato (London: Continuum, 2007), pp. 254–74.

Reiman, Donald H. and Neil Fraistat, eds, *Shelley's Poetry and Prose*, 2nd ed. (New York: Norton, 2002).

Rosen, Charles and Henri Zerner, *Romanticism and Realism: The Mythology of Nineteenth Century Art* (London: Faber, 1984).

Saint-Just, *Œuvres complètes*, ed. by Michèle Duval (Paris: Gérard Lebovici, 1984).

Settis, Salvatore, 'Continuità, distanza, conoscenza: tre usi dell'antico', in *Memoria dell'antico nell'arte italiana*, vol. 3: *Dalla tradizione all'archeologia*, ed. by Settis (Turin: Einaudi, 1996), pp. 375–486.

Southey, Robert, *Letters from England* (London, 1807).

Stafford, Fiona, 'The Literary Legacies of Irish Romanticism', in *Irish Literature in Transition 1780–1830*, ed. by Claire Connolly (Cambridge: Cambridge University Press, 2020), pp. 402–21, https://doi.org/10.1017/9781108632218

——, 'Romantic Macpherson', in *The Edinburgh Companion to Scottish Romanticism*, ed. by Murray Pittock (Edinburgh: Edinburgh University Press, 2011), pp. 27–38.

St John, Henry, Lord Viscount Bolingbroke, *Letters on the Study and Use of History* (London: A. Millar, 1752).

Turner, Frederick Jackson, 'The Significance of the Frontier in American History', in *The Frontier in American History* (New York: Henry Holt, 1921), pp. 1–38.

Veyne, Paul, *Comment on écrit l'histoire*, 2nd ed. (Paris: Seuil, 1978).

——, *Writing History: Essay on Epistemology*, trans. by M. Moore-Rinvolucri (Manchester: Manchester University Press, 1984).

Vodička, Felix, *Struktura vývoje* (The Structure of Development, 1969), 2nd enlarged ed. (Prague: Dauphin, 1998).

Wellek, René, 'Romanticism Re-examined', in *Concepts of Criticism* (New Haven: Yale University Press, 1963), pp. 199–221.

——, 'The Concept of Romanticism in Literary History', *Comparative Literature*, 1 (1949), 1–23, 147–72.

—— and Austin Warren, *Theory of Literature*, 3rd ed. (Harmondsworth: Penguin Books, 1966).

Williams, Helen Maria, *Letters Containing a Sketch of the Politics of France* (London: G. G. and J. Robinson, 1795).

Wölfflin, Heinrich, *Kunstgeschlichtliche Grundebegriffe: Das Problem der Stilentwicklung in der neueren Kunst* (Munich: Bruckmann, 1915).

List of Contributors

Gregory Dart is a professor of English at UCL, London (UK). His research is centrally concerned with Romanticism, the City, and the history and development of the essay form from Montaigne to the modern period. His main academic project over the last few years has been a monograph called *Metropolitan Art and Literature 1810-1840: Cockney Adventures* (2012), a study of the development of new kinds of metropolitan art and literature in the years 1815-40. He is currently working on three volumes of a new six-volume *Collected Edition of the Works of Charles and Mary Lamb*, for which he is also General Editor.

Lily Dessau is a doctoral student and teaching assistant in Modern Literature at the Université de Genève. She is working on an ecocritical reading of later Romantic poetics, with a focus on John Clare, through sound and time.

David Duff is Professor of Romanticism at Queen Mary University of London and London Director of the London-Paris Romanticism Seminar. He is the author of *Romance and Revolution: Shelley and the Politics of a Genre* (1994), *Romanticism and the Uses of Genre* (2009), and a number of edited books including *Modern Genre Theory* (2000), *Scotland, Ireland and the Romantic Aesthetic* (with Catherine Jones, 2007) and *The Oxford Handbook of British Romanticism* (2018). He recently co-edited two special issues of *Litteraria Pragensia* on 'Wordsworth and France' (2017) and 'Exiles, Emigrés and Expatriates in Romantic-Era Paris and London' (2019). He is currently writing a book on the Romantic prospectus.

Laurent Folliot is an alumnus of the Ecole Normale Supérieure, where he has also taught, and Associate Professor at Sorbonne-Université. Since completing his Ph.D. on the landscape poetry of Wordsworth and

Coleridge, he has published variously on English Romantic poetry, as well as on essayists and novelists of the period. He is also a translator.

Evan Gottlieb is a Professor of English at Oregon State University (US), where he teaches eighteenth-century and Romantic British literature as well as literary and critical theory. His most recent books are *Engagements with Contemporary Literary and Critical Theory* (2020) and *Romantic Realities: Speculative Realism and British Romanticism* (2016).

Ralf Haekel is Professor of English Literature at Leipzig University. In 2003 he received his Ph.D. from FU Berlin and in 2013 his Habilitation from Göttingen University. His main research interests are Romantic Studies, Early Modern Drama and Theatre, Irish Studies, and Media Theory. He is the author of *The Soul in British Romanticism* (2014) and editor or co-editor of four edited books, including the *Handbook of British Romanticism* (2017).

Nicholas Halmi is Professor of English and Comparative Literature at Oxford University and Margaret Candfield Fellow of University College, Oxford. He is author of *The Genealogy of the Romantic Symbol* (2007) and editor or co-editor of four scholarly editions, including most recently the *Norton Critical Edition of Wordsworth's Poetry and Prose* (2013). He received a Leverhulme Trust Major Research Fellowship for 2015-17 in support of his current project, a book on aesthetics and the sense of the past in western European culture from c. 1650 to c. 1850.

Paul Hamilton is Professor of English at Queen Mary, University of London. His last two books were *Realpoetik: European Romanticism and Literary Politics* (2013) and (ed.) *The Oxford Handbook of European Romanticism* (2016).

Sophie Laniel-Musitelli is Associate Professor at the University of Lille and a Junior Fellow at the Institut Universitaire de France. She is the author of *"The Harmony of Truth": Sciences et poésie dans l'œuvre de P. B. Shelley* (2012), and of several articles and chapters on scientific discourse and literary writing in the works of Erasmus Darwin, William Blake, William Wordsworth, Percy B. Shelley, and Thomas De Quincey. She has edited *Sciences et poésie de Wordsworth à Hopkins* (Etudes Anglaises 2011), co-authored *Muses et ptérodactyles: La poésie de la science de Chénier à*

Rimbaud (2013) and co-edited *Romanticism and the Philosophical Tradition* (2015) and *Romanticism and Philosophy* (2015).

Oriane Monthéard is Senior Lecturer at the University of Rouen-Normandie, where she teaches civilisation, translation, and literature. Her research primarily focuses on Keats's work. She has published articles both on his poetry and his letters and has just published a book entitled *Keats et la rencontre*. She is co-editor of a volume on the translation and adaptation of sonnets in English and European literatures. Her research interests also include graphic novels and intermediality.

Martin Procházka is Professor of English, American and Comparative Literature, and Director of the Ph.D. program Anglophone Literatures and Cultures at Charles University, Prague. He is the author of *Romanticism and Personality* (1996), *Transversals* (2008), and *Ruins in the New World* (2012), a co-author of *Romanticism and Romanticisms* (2005), an editor of 17 collaborative books including *Renaissance Shakespeare: Shakespeare Renaissances* (2014), and the founding editor of an academic journal *Litteraria Pragensia*. He is Trustee of the International Shakespeare Association, member of Advisory Board of the International Association of Byron Societies and was Visiting Professor at the universities of Kent and Porto.

Laura Quinney teaches English and Comparative Literature at Brandeis. She is the author of three books of literary criticism and theory, most recently *William Blake on Self and Soul* (2010), and of two books of poetry, *Corridor* and *New Ghosts* (2008 and 2016).

Matthew Redmond is a Ph.D. candidate in the English Department at Stanford University. His research explores biopolitics, theories of influence, and literary transhistory in nineteenth-century American and British literature. He has published in *The Edgar Allan Poe Review* and *ESQ*.

Anne Rouhette is Senior Lecturer in Eighteenth- and Nineteenth-century British literature at the University of Clermont-Auvergne, France. Her main field of interest is women's fiction from the late eighteenth and the early nineteenth centuries and she has published in particular on Mary

Shelley, Frances Burney and Jane Austen. She also works on the theory and practice of translation.

Céline Sabiron is Associate Professor at the University of Lorraine (Nancy), France. She is the author of *Écrire la frontière: Walter Scott, ou les chemins de l'errance* (2016), and of several articles on Scottish literature and translation. Her latest publications include an edited EJES issue on 'Decentering Commemorations' (2020), and two edited volumes, the first one with Antonella Braida-Laplace and Sophie Laniel-Musitelli, (*Inconstances romantiques: visions et revisions*, 2019), and the second with Catherine Chauvin (*Textuality and Translation*, 2020). She is part of the AHRC-funded 'Prismatic *Jane Eyre*' project headed by Prof. Matthew Reynolds (Oxford University) and Dr. Sowon S. Park (University of California, Santa Barbara).

Mark Sandy is a Professor of English at Durham University, UK. He specializes in Romantic poetics and its legacies. Indeed, his interest extends to the imaginative and cultural legacies that Romanticism confers to the literary and cultural imagination of the late nineteenth century and beyond. His publications include a monograph on *Poetics of Self and Form in Keats and Shelley* (2005) and a second book-length study of *Romanticism, Memory, and Mourning* (2013). He has edited collections on *Romantic Echoes in the Victorian Era* (2008), *Romantic Presences in the Twentieth Century* (2012), and *Venice and the Cultural Imagination* (2012). He is currently editing a volume on *Decadent Romanticism* and researching a book on *Transforming Romanticism: The Legacies of Romantic Poetics in Twentieth-Century American Literature*. He is also a co-director of the Department's 'Romantic Dialogues and Legacies' research group. He is an advisory board member of the inter-disciplinary Centre for Death and Life Studies based in Durham. He is also part of a national network on 'Romanticism and Ageing,' involving Keele University, and the Universities of Lincoln and Nottingham. He is a member of the Executive Committee of the British Association of Romantic Studies (BARS) and the current editor of the Review for BARS.

Fiona Stafford is Professor of English Language and Literature at the University of Oxford. She has wide-ranging interests in Romantic period literature, archipelagic writings, nature writing, environmental humanities, and literature and the visual arts. She is currently working on the Romantic Period Volume of the *Oxford History of English Literature*. Recent books include *Local Attachments* (2010); *Reading Romantic Poetry* (2012); *The Long, Long Life of Trees* (2016); *Jane Austen: A Brief Life* (2017).

List of Figures

Chapter 3

1	Ludwig van Beethoven, Recitative und Duett 'O namenlose Freude', *Leonore* (1805 version) (Leipzig: Breitkopf and Härtel, 1905), p. 221. Public domain.	57
2	Ludwig van Beethoven, 'O Gott, Welch ein Augenblick', *Leonore* (1805 version) (Leipzig: Breitkopf and Härtel, 1905), pp. 246-47. Public domain.	59
3	Ludwig van Beethoven, Melodram (No. 14), *Leonore* (1805 version) (Leipzig: Breitkopf and Härtel, 1905), pp. 188-89. Public domain.	64
4	Ludwig van Beethoven, Duet (No. 14), *Leonore* (1805 version) (Leipzig: Breitkopf and Härtel, 1905), pp. 189-90. Public domain.	68

Chapter 5

1	Francis Towne, *Windermere at Sunset* (1786). Yale Center for British Art, Paul Mellon Collection, B1975.4.1759. Public domain.	101
2	Thomas Hearne, *View from Skiddaw over Derwentwater* (between 1772 and 1782). Yale Center for British Art, Paul Mellon Collection, B1977.14.4685. Public domain.	103
3	Thomas Hearne, *The Ruins of the College of Lincluden, near Dumfries* (ca. 1806). Yale Center for British Art, Paul Mellon Collection, B1975.4.509. Public domain.	107

4	Unknown artist, *Burns's Mausoleum at Dumfries* (with text); page 52 (Volume One), Yale Center for British Art, Paul Mellon Collection, B1974.12.860. Public domain.	109
5	David Octavius Hill, *Burns's Cottage* (1880), The Miriam and Ira D. Wallach Division of Art, Prints and Photographs: Print Collection, The New York Public Library. The New York Public Library Digital Collections. Fair use, https://digitalcollections.nypl.org/items/510d47da-f8f0-a3d9-e040-e00a18064a99	111

Chapter 8

1	Illustration from *Le Monstre et le magicien: mélodrame-féerie en 3 actes* by Antony Béraud and Jean-Toussaint Merle (Paris: Théâtre de la Porte Saint-Martin, 1826). Bibliothèque nationale de France. Public domain.	164

Index

Abrams, M.H. 8
Agamben, Giorgio xiii, xv
agency (historical) x, 73, 152, 183–184, 186, 188, 191, 194–195, 201
Albania 91
alchemy xix, 163, 165, 171–175
Alexander, Czar 6, 8
almanac 123–124, 139
America xi, xii, xix, xxii, 146–147, 157–161, 195, 202, 227–228, 247, 249–251, 255, 259–261, 267–268, 270–271, 275
American Revolution, the 259
anachronism xiii, xix, 80, 146, 163, 165–167, 178
anachrony 163, 166, 170, 174–175
anamnesis, concept of xiii, 85, 87
Anderson, Benedict 77–80, 94, 248, 262
Anthropocene xii, xvii, 25–27, 32, 37, 45, 135
antiquarianism xix, 145–146, 148–149, 154, 157, 161, 247
architecture, historical styles in xx, 242, 254, 257
Aristotle 82, 188, 248, 252–253, 258
Arnold, Matthew 88, 255
Augenblick (the revolutionary moment) 53–54, 58–60, 62, 66
Austria 3, 6, 8, 62

Bakhtin, Mikhail 150–151, 232–233, 242, 261, 263
Balzac, Honoré de 11
Barbauld, Anna 9
Beattie, James 20
Beckett, Samuel xi, xx, 183–187, 193, 195, 199–201

Beethoven, Ludwig van xi, xviii, 49–61, 63–64, 66–71, 254
  Fidelio xi, xviii, 49–51, 53–56, 60–63, 70–73
  Leonore 49–53, 56–57, 59, 62, 64, 68, 70–71
Benjamin, Walter xviii, 14, 40, 77–80, 82, 94–95, 125, 130, 132, 253
  Theses on the Philosophy of History xviii, 77–79, 94–95
Bergson, Henri 4–5, 81, 128, 161
Blake, William ix, x, xiii, xvii, 9, 13–15, 242–244, 253
  Jerusalem 14–15
  Milton 14
  Songs of Innocence and Experience 14, 243
  The Marriage of Heaven and Hell 15
Bloch, Ernst 55
Blumenberg, Hans 238, 257
Bolingbroke, Henry St John, Viscount 234
Bouilly, Jean Nicholas 49, 51–53, 57, 60–61, 71
  Léonore, ou L'Amour Conjugal 49, 51, 53
Britain v, vii, x, xi, xii, xiv, xvii, xviii, xix, xxi, xxii, 6–10, 12, 16, 18–19, 24–25, 27, 29, 32–33, 36–40, 44–47, 82, 88, 92, 95–96, 101, 103, 107, 109, 111, 117, 128, 130, 143, 146, 170, 158, 160, 171, 227–232, 234, 239–240, 242, 252–253, 255, 262, 264, 267, 269, 273–276
Brown, Charles 17, 99, 104, 106, 108, 112, 235–236, 251, 255, 268
Browning, Robert 200, 255
Burke, Edmund 8–10, 240
Burns, Robert 109–111, 113–114, 243, 245

Byron, George Gordon, Lord x, xi, xviii, xx, 7, 9–10, 15, 17–18, 20–23, 43–44, 77, 80, 84, 91–95, 105, 167, 205, 207, 209–211, 213–223, 237, 239, 242, 244, 254, 261
   Beppo 216–218
   Byronic hero 92, 94
   Byronic selfhood 215
   Childe Harold's Pilgrimage xviii, 20–22, 77, 80, 84, 91–92, 94, 167, 210, 215–216, 220, 243
   Don Juan 9, 20–21, 215, 243
   Lara: A Tale 215
   Manfred 216, 222
   Marino Faliero 22, 218–219
   Ode to Venice 216, 219
   'Substitute for an Epitaph' 220
   The Two Foscari 22
   'To Ianthe' 216

Calvino, Italo 205–206, 223
   Invisible Cities 206
Canova, Antonio 21
Castlereagh, Robert Stewart, Viscount 6–7, 15–21
Charles II 13, 18
Chateaubriand, François-René, Vicomte de 6, 8–9, 19, 237
Cherubini, Luigi 51–53, 58, 65–67
Christianity 6, 9, 28, 78–79, 238, 267
chronotope 147, 150–151, 158
church spire 126, 128–129, 131, 134, 212
Clare, John x, xix, 121–141
   The Shepherd's Calendar v, xix, 121–125, 129, 138–141
Clarkson, Thomas 7
classical vs. romantic 232, 237, 262
clock-time 122–123, 126–128, 130, 132, 137, 146, 150, 153, 198
Cobbett, William 19
Coleridge, Samuel Taylor 36, 83–85, 105, 110, 147, 167, 186–187, 192, 242, 250, 253, 257
Comte de Buffon, Georges-Louis Leclerc 27, 174

Congress of Troppau 6–8
Congress of Verona 7, 19
Congress of Vienna 3–4, 6–10, 16, 19, 21, 33, 50, 60, 91, 239
correlationism 25, 29–30, 32–34, 39, 41–42, 45
Croker, John Wilson 15
Cromwell, Oliver 22, 246
Culler, Jonathan 136
Cuvier, Georges 27

Dante Alighieri 10, 184–185, 242
Delacroix, Eugène 11
Deleuze, Gilles 130, 249, 258–259
De Quincey, Thomas xvii, 7, 71, 264
diegesis xix, 133, 163, 166–168, 175

Edgeworth, Maria 246
Egypt 219
elegy 122–123, 136–137, 140, 261
Eliade, Mircea 168
enclosure 121–123, 125, 137, 140
England xi, xvii, xxii, 3, 9, 12–13, 16–17, 19–20, 22, 40–41, 49, 52, 71, 73, 85, 88, 95–96, 98, 100, 117–118, 141, 143, 146–148, 153–154, 158–162, 165, 171, 178–179, 185, 192, 229–231, 234, 241–246, 252, 255, 259–260, 263, 267, 269–270
Enlightenment, the 78, 80, 82, 251
epic xviii, 13, 18, 94–95, 106, 188, 216
epoch, definition of 228, 234–235, 238–239, 241, 253, 256, 267
Europe xi, xvii, xx, xxi, 3–4, 6–10, 12–13, 16–17, 19, 21, 24, 32, 44, 49, 60, 91–92, 94, 100, 127, 159, 176, 227–229, 233, 236–237, 240, 242–243, 245, 250–251, 253, 255–256, 265, 268–269, 271, 274

Fabre d'Églantine, Philippe-François-Nazaire 240
Filmer, Sir Robert 20
Foscolo, Ugo 21–22
Foucault, Michel 238, 252
Fox, Charles James 240
France vii, ix, x, xvii, 3–4, 6–11, 15–19, 27, 32, 39, 49–53, 56, 60–61, 66, 70–74,

124, 143, 165–167, 227–228, 230–231, 234–235, 237, 239–240, 244, 253–257, 262–263, 267–268, 272
Frederick II of Prussia (the Great) 235
Frederick William III of Prussia 6
French Revolution, the 3–4, 7–9, 11, 17, 32, 39, 49, 72–73, 227–228, 230–231, 239–240, 244, 253, 255–256, 262–263, 267

Gaveaux, Pierre 49, 51–53, 57, 60, 71
Genette, Gérard 166–167, 170
Germany xi, xiv, xxi, 8–10, 63, 78–80, 231, 233–234, 253, 265–267
Goethe, Johann Wolfgang 238–239
Gogol, Nikolai 7
Grand Tour 91
Gray, Thomas 136–137, 200
Greece 6, 91–92, 234–237, 257
Gros, Frédéric 104–105, 112
Guattari, Félix 130, 249, 258–259

Harrington, James 16, 22–23
Hartog, François 256
Hazlitt, William x, 17, 19–20, 104, 145–146, 148, 153–154, 157, 160–161, 230, 264
   The Spirit of the Age 145–146, 148, 157, 162, 230
hearing 9, 13–14, 18–19, 33, 55–57, 60, 71, 87, 114–115, 126, 129, 133, 136, 140, 190, 197, 252
Hegel, Georg Wilhelm Friedrich 10, 233, 254
Hemans, Felicia 10
Herder, Johann Gottfried 237
Highlands, the 97, 99, 105
historical materialism 78–79, 95, 253
historicisation. *See* periodisation
historicism 8, 10, 42, 77–79, 94, 242, 245, 248, 252, 254, 257, 259
Historismus 78
Hobhouse, John Cam 20–21
Holy Alliance 6, 8, 20
Horace 9
Hutton, James 27–28, 33, 39

hyper-chaos 42

immediacy 28, 44, 82, 86, 108, 111–114, 116, 196, 217
Industrial Revolution, the 25, 27
Ireland xii, xxii, 12, 15, 17, 19, 23, 229, 242–246, 260–261, 269–271
Irving, Washington xix, 145–147, 157–161
Italy 10–11, 15–17, 21–23, 177, 210, 214, 216, 224

Jarvis, Robin 102, 104, 116

Kant, Immanuel xii, 4, 10, 29, 42, 81, 105, 250
Keats, John x, xviii, 37–39, 44, 97–114, 116, 200, 222, 242
   Keats's letters xviii, 97–102, 104, 106–109, 111–113, 116
   'Ode on a Grecian Urn' 37
Kierkegaard, Søren 5
Koselleck, Reinhart 3, 25–26, 235, 256
Krüdener, Barbara Julienne, Baroness von 6

labour xii, xix, 37, 121–123, 125–127, 129–131, 133, 135, 137–138, 147, 169
Lake District 71, 105
Lamb, Charles x, xix, 145–159, 161
Lamennais, Hugues Félicité Robert de 6
landscape xviii, 81, 98–99, 105–108, 111, 114, 116, 129, 221, 261
Lecercle, Jean-Jacques 166, 168, 173
legitimacy 6, 8, 19, 22
leisure time 103, 123, 125, 129, 131, 137–138, 145
Leopardi, Giacomo 10–12, 21–22
'loom-time' 137
Louis-Philippe I 11
Louis XVIII 18
Lyell, Charles 28, 33, 39
lyric xviii, 21, 130, 133–136, 139, 149, 152, 185, 206–207, 213

magazines 154–157, 160
Marvell, Andrew 16

Marxism 79, 138, 245
Marx, Karl 5, 8, 17, 135
Meillassoux, Quentin 25, 29, 32, 34, 42, 44
melodrama 44, 49, 52, 63–66, 69–70, 72, 164, 280
Metternich, Klemens, Prinz von 8
Milton, John 12–13, 15–16, 19–20, 136–137, 171, 200, 242
  Paradise Lost 12–13, 136, 171
  Paradise Regained 13
  Samson Agonistes 13
modernity 9, 17, 25–26, 32, 78, 153, 166, 251
Moore, Thomas 17–18, 20
  The Fudge Family in Paris 17–18, 20
Morgan (Sydney Owenson), Lady 15–17, 19
Mozart, Wolfgang Amadeus 52, 69–70, 254
Musset, Alfred de 11–12, 14
myth xix, xx, 87, 168, 171, 174–175, 205, 207, 211, 216–217, 237–238, 248, 253, 260, 262

Napoleonic Wars xviii, 32, 91–92, 230, 245
Napoleon I (Napoléon Bonaparte) xviii, 3, 6–10, 12, 17, 19–21, 32, 50, 60, 62, 91–92, 94, 188, 240, 244–245
Neoplatonism 83–84, 88
Nerval, Gérard de 105
Newton, Isaac xii, 81
Nietzsche, Friedrich xi, 5, 10, 105, 205–209, 215, 221, 250, 265
  Ecce Homo 207
  'On Truth and Lie in an Extra-Moral Sense' 215
  The Peacock and the Buffalo 207
nostalgia 21, 123, 125–126, 187, 196–197
Novalis (Georg Philipp Friedrich von Hardenberg) 6, 8–9, 233, 238

Otway, Thomas 219
  Venice Preserved 219
Ovid iv, 9

parish 129
Peacock, Thomas Love 15, 233, 264
perception x, xvii, xviii, 15, 81, 97–102, 104–105, 108, 110–114, 116, 145, 156, 158, 186, 199, 230, 240, 248
period, definition of xx, 227–230, 233–239, 241–243, 248–249, 252–253, 257–258, 262, 264, 267
periodisation xi, xii, xx, 228–236, 238–242, 246–252, 254–255, 258–260, 262–263, 265–267
  and historical ruptures 39, 238, 240, 257
  and norms 236–238, 241
  relation to historicisation 237, 239, 257
Peterloo Massacre 33, 44
Plato 9, 83, 86–87, 188
  Phaedo 83, 87
  Symposium 9
Platonism 80, 83–87, 190
Plotinus 83
  Enneads 83
Poland 6, 52
Pope, Alexander 20
Portugal 7, 92
Post-Romanticism 205, 223
productivity 16, 27–29, 35, 45, 103, 112, 130, 134, 139, 215
Proust, Marcel 3, 186
Prussia 3, 6, 8, 238

Quadruple Alliance 8
Querelle des anciens et des modernes 236

Radcliffe, Ann 105
Rancière, Jacques xiii, 163, 166–167
reading xii, xiv, xix, 15, 40, 43, 79–80, 88–90, 107–108, 116, 122–124, 126, 128–129, 133–134, 137, 139–141, 145, 147–153, 155–159, 161, 173–174, 192, 206, 220, 252, 264–265
régime d'historicité 256
rescue (rescue opera) 49, 51–53, 58
restoration v, xvii, 1, 3–5, 7–14, 17–18, 22–24, 71–72, 205, 234
Revolutionary calendar 4

Risorgimento 11, 17
Rogers, Samuel x, 21
Ronteix, Eugène 237
Rousseau, Jean-Jacques 105, 188–190, 199, 201, 220–221, 256, 261
Russia 3, 6, 266

Sachs, Jonathan 37, 39, 152–153
Saglia, Diego 10
Saladin, Jules 165–166, 174
Sand, George 12
Savigny, Friedrich Karl von 10
Schlegel, August Wilhelm 233, 237
Schlegel, Friedrich 5, 7–8, 21, 233
Scotland xviii, 27, 97–98, 100, 104–105, 110, 113, 117, 229, 242–245, 247, 255, 260–262, 267, 270–271
Scott, Walter 105, 111, 246, 261, 264
Sebald, W. G. 126–127
Shakespeare, William 18, 187, 200, 218–219, 234, 242, 265
   Anthony and Cleopatra 219
   As You Like It 218
   Othello 218
Shelley, Mary x, xix, 33, 35, 163, 165–168, 171, 175–178, 263
   Frankenstein; Or, The Modern Prometheus (1818) xix, 163, 165–167, 171, 173, 175–178, 243
   'Roger Dodsworth, the Re-Animated Englishman' (1826) 177–178
   The Fortunes of Perkin Warbeck (1830) 175
   The Last Man (1826) 175, 263
   'The Mortal Immortal' (1833) 176
   'Valerius, Or, The Re-Animated Roman' (1819 ?) 176, 178
Shelley, Percy Bysshe x, xi, xiii, xvi, xviii, xix, xx, 5, 9, 25, 33, 35–37, 39–42, 45, 82, 105, 167–168, 183–188, 190, 192–193, 198, 200–201, 205–214, 230, 233, 239, 242, 255, 262, 264
   A Defence of Poetry xiv, 5, 9, 45, 230, 233, 263
   Adonais 212
   Alastor 213
   'Darkness' 43–44
   Epipsychidion 212–214
   Julian and Maddalo 210–212
   Lines Written Among the Euganean Hills 212
   'Lines Written in the Bay of Lerici' 213–214
   'Mont Blanc' 35–36
   Prometheus Unbound xv, 17, 42–43, 206, 263
   The Triumph of Life xix, 183–184, 188, 190–193, 201
Sidney, Algernon 16, 20
Smith, Charlotte 25, 34–35, 37
soul, the xviii, 77, 80, 82–88, 90–93, 95, 115, 209
Southey, Robert 235, 264
Spain 7, 51, 92
Spenser, Edmund 121–122, 140, 242
Spenserian stanza 20, 91, 94
Staël, Anne-Louise Germaine de 10–11, 15, 21, 243
   Corinne 15
   De l'Allemagne 15

Talleyrand-Périgord, Charles Maurice de 6
temporalisation 256–257
Terror 8, 49, 51–54, 253
Thoreau, Henry David 105, 250
travel 15, 87, 91, 94, 97, 99, 101, 104, 106, 110–116, 124, 127, 152, 190, 216, 218, 222, 243–244, 247
Turkey 6, 91
twilight 209

Valmy, Battle of 238–239
Vane, Henry 16
Venice xx, 22–23, 92, 164, 205–212, 216–219, 223, 254
Virgil 9, 122, 140
Vulliamy, Benjamin 127–128

walking xviii, xix, 14, 34, 95, 97–100, 102–108, 111–117
   tour xviii, 98–114, 116

Waterloo 6, 17, 39, 44, 92, 239, 244, 246
Wellek, René 236–238, 242, 264–266
West-Pavlov, Russel 81
Wilberforce, William 7
Williams, Helen Maria 235, 263
Wölfflin, Heinrich 235
Wollstonecraft, Mary 7
Wordsworth, Dorothy 110
Wordsworth, William x, xvii, xviii, 4, 12–14, 16, 20, 27–33, 35–36, 45, 71, 77, 80–81, 84–88, 91, 94–95, 103, 107–111, 152–153, 167, 186, 190, 209, 214, 230, 238, 242, 244, 246, 253, 255, 264
  'Home at Grasmere' 13–14
  'Lines written a few miles above Tintern Abbey' 4, 29, 31, 36
  'My heart leaps up' 28–29
  Ode: Intimations of Immortality from Recollections of Early Childhood xviii, 77, 80, 84–88, 90–91, 94, 186, 190, 195, 210
  'spots of time' xviii, 12, 14, 31, 81, 87
  The Excursion 13, 33, 108
  The Prelude 4, 12–13, 31, 71, 87, 156, 243, 245
  'To the Daisy' 30

zeitgeist 159, 230–231, 237, 257, 263, 267

About the Team

Alessandra Tosi was the managing editor for this book.

Lucy Barnes performed the copy-editing and proofreading.

Anna Gatti designed the cover using InDesign. The cover was produced in InDesign using Fontin (titles) and Calibri (text body) fonts.

Melissa Purkiss typeset the book in InDesign and produced the paperback and hardback editions. The text font is Tex Gyre Pagella; the heading font is Californian FB.

Luca Baffa produced the EPUB, MOBI, PDF, HTML, and XML editions—the conversion is performed with open source software freely available on our GitHub page (https://github.com/OpenBookPublishers).

This book need not end here...

Share

All our books — including the one you have just read — are free to access online so that students, researchers and members of the public who can't afford a printed edition will have access to the same ideas. This title will be accessed online by hundreds of readers each month across the globe: why not share the link so that someone you know is one of them?

This book and additional content is available at:

https://doi.org/10.11647/OBP.0232

Customise

Personalise your copy of this book or design new books using OBP and third-party material. Take chapters or whole books from our published list and make a special edition, a new anthology or an illuminating coursepack. Each customised edition will be produced as a paperback and a downloadable PDF.

Find out more at:

https://www.openbookpublishers.com/section/59/1

Like Open Book Publishers

Follow @OpenBookPublish

Read more at the Open Book Publishers BLOG

You may also be interested in:

Tennyson's Poems
New Textual Parallels
R. H. Winnick

https://doi.org/10.11647/OBP.0161

Hyperion, or the Hermit in Greece
Howard Gaskill

https://doi.org/10.11647/OBP.0160

Love and its Critics
From the Song of Songs to Shakespeare and Milton's Eden
Michael Bryson and Arpi Movsesian

https://doi.org/10.11647/OBP.0117

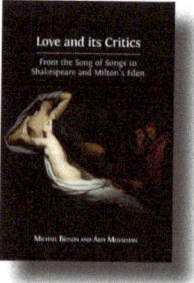

www.ingramcontent.com/pod-product-compliance
Lightning Source LLC
Chambersburg PA
CBHW041731300426
44115CB00022B/2976